EXPOSITORY LECTURES

ON

ST. PAUL'S EPISTLES TO THE CORINTHIANS.

SERMONS

ON

ST. PAUL'S EPISTLES

TO THE

CORINTHIANS:

DELIVERED AT TRINITY CHAPEL, BRIGHTON

BY THE LATE

REV. F. W ROBERTSON, M.A.,

THE INCUMBENT.

BOSTON:

TICKNOR AND FIELDS.

M DCCC LXVIII.

TO

THE CONGREGATION

WORSHIPPING IN

TRINITY CHAPEL, BRIGHTON,

FROM AUGUST 15, 1847, TO AUGUST 15, 1853,

THESE

EXPOSITORY LECTURES,

DELIVERED BY THEIR LATE PASTOR,

ARE DEDICATED.

PREFACE.

A FEW months after Mr. Robertson had entered on his ministry at Trinity Chapel, Brighton, he announced his intention of taking one of the Books of Scripture as the subject of Expository Lectures for the Sunday afternoons. This form of address, he said, gave him greater freedom, both in subject and style, than that of the sermon, with its critical or historical division of some text arbitrarily taken as a prefix. He intended, therefore, to devote each Sunday morning to the sermon; and in the afternoon to go regularly through each chapter of the Book selected, including in his exposition all the topics contained therein.

On this plan he commenced with the First and Second Books of Samuel. In the exposition of these Books many subjects came under review which would not have found a place in an ordinary sermon. He was expounding Hebrew national life, and, incidentally, the experiences of particular individuals of that nation, — in all of which he discerned lessons for the English people, and for the men and women who sat before him. Thus it occurred that topics of national policy, so far as bearing on individuals, — questions of social life — of morals, as they are connected with every-day life, arose naturally, and were treated with unshrinking faithfulness. The period (1848) was one of great political and social excitement, and these Lectures may emphatically be said to have been "preaching tc the times."

Some people were startled at the introduction of what they called "secular subjects" into the pulpit; but the Lecturer, in all his ministrations, refused to recognize the distinction so drawn. He said that the whole life of a Christian was sacred, — that common everyday duties, whether of a trade or a profession, or the minuter details of a woman's household life, were the arenas in which trial and temptation arose; and that, therefore, it became the Christian minister's duty to enter into this familiar working life with his people, and help them to understand its meaning, its trials, and its compensations.

It were, perhaps, out of place here to say how greatly the congregation valued this mode of teaching, although it may be properly observed that it was at this period that his marvellous influence with the working classes commenced.

Subsequently, Mr. Robertson selected the Acts of the Apostles, and the Book of Genesis, for his afternoon expositions; after which he commenced those Lectures on the Epistles to the Corinthians, of which this volume is but a very imperfect transcript. The Epistles to the Corinthians were selected by him, because they afforded the largest scope for the consideration of a great variety of questions in Christian casuistry, which he thought it important to be rightly understood. It will be seen that these Lectures were generally expository of the whole range of Christian principles. They are less a scheme of doctrine than Mr. Robertson's view of St. Paul's ideas on all the subjects included in his Epistles to the Church at Corinth.

They were the fruit of much study and preparation, and, from examination of his papers, it appears that Mr. Robertson prepared very full notes of all the leading divisions in most of these Lectures, while of the minor divisions, a single word was often all that was written down to guide his thought. Occasionally, at the request of some friends, he wrote his lecture out after its delivery; and these, with short-hand notes of others, taken by different people, and which have been carefully collated, with his own manuscript notes, have been the materials from which this volume has been arranged. It is, therefore, necessarily somewhat fragmentary in its character. Mr. Robertson's custom was to preach from forty to fifty minutes, with a clear, unbroken delivery, in which there was no hesitation, or tautology. Hence it will be evident, from the quantity of matter contained in each of these printed Lectures, that a considerable portion of the spoken Lecture has not been given: and this will explain the brevity of some of the discourses, and the apparent incompleteness with which many of the topics are treated.

A few sermons on different texts in the Epistles to the Corinthians have already appeared in the three volumes of Mr. Robertson's Sermons; but it has been considered best to include them in this volume (although they did not form a part of this series), in order that the Lecturer's view of the Epistles might so be rendered more complete. Expositions of two chapters will be found to be omitted altogether; there are no notes of the Lectures on these chapters available for publication.

After concluding these Lectures, Mr. Robertson preached one more Sunday afternoon, on the Parable of the Barren Fig-tree, with a solemnity and an earnestness that now seem to have been prophetic. His voice was never afterwards heard from the pulpit of Trinity Chapel.

Nov. 15 1859.

CONTENTS.

LECTURES

ON THE

EPISTLES TO THE CORINTHIANS.

INTRODUCTORY LECTURE.

June 1, 1851.

Acts, xviii. 1. — "After these things Paul departed from Athens, and came to Corinth."

It has been customary with us for more than three years to devote our Sunday afternoons to the exposition throughout of some one Book of Scripture, and our plan has been to take alternately a Book of the Old and of the New Testament. I have selected for our present exposition the Epistles of the Corinthians, and this for several reasons — amongst others, for variety, our previous work having been entirely historical.* These Epistles are in a different tone altogether; they are eminently practical, rich in Christian casuistry. They contain the answers of an inspired Apostle to many questions which arise in Christian life.

There is, too, another reason for this selection. The state of the Corinthian Church resembles, in a remarkable degree, the state of the Church of this Town, in the present day. There is the same complicated civilization, the religious quarrels and differences of sect are alike, the same questions agitate society, and the same distinctions of class exist now as then. For

* The Book of Genesis.

the heart of Humanity is the same in all times. The principles, therefore, which St. Paul applied to the Corinthian questions will apply to those of this time. The Epistles to the Corinthians are a witness that Religion does not confine itself to the inward being of man alone, nor solely to the examination of orthodox opinions. No! Religion is Life, and right instruction in Religion is not the investigation of obsolete and curious doctrines, but the application of spiritual principles to those questions, and modes of action, which concern present existence, in the Market, the Shop, the Study, and the Street.

Before we can understand these Epistles, it is plain that we must know to whom, and under what circumstances, they were written, how the writer himself was circumstanced, and how he had been prepared for such a work by previous discipline. We make, therefore,

I. Preliminary inquiries respecting Corinth, viewed historically, socially, and morally.

II. Respecting the Apostle Paul.

I. Inquiry respecting Corinth.

We all know that Corinth was a Greek city, but we must not confound the town to which St. Paul wrote with that ancient Corinth which is so celebrated, and with which we are so familiar in Grecian history. That Corinth had been destroyed nearly two centuries before the time of these Epistles, by the Consul Mummius, B. C. 146. This new city, in which the Apostle labored, had been built upon the ruins of the old by Julius Cæsar, not half a century before the Christian Church was formed there. And this rebuilding had taken place under very different circumstances — so different as to constitute a new population.

Greece, in the time of the Roman dictators, had lost her vigor. She had become worn out, corrupt, and depopulated. There were not men enough to supply her armies It was necessary, therefore, if Corinth were to rise again, to people it with fresh inhabitants and to re-invigorate her constitution with new blood.

This was done from Rome. Julius Cæsar sent to his re-elected city freedmen of Rome, who themselves, or their parents, had been slaves. From this importation there arose at once one peculiar characteristic of the new population. It was Roman, not Greek; it was not aristocratic, but democratic; and it held within it all the vices as well as all the advantages of a democracy.

Observe the peculiar bearing of this fact on the Epistles to the Corinthians. It was only in such a city as Corinth that those public meetings could have taken place, in which each one exercised his gifts without order; it was only in such a city that the turbulence, and the interruptions, and the brawls which we read of, and which were so eminently characteristic of a democratic society, could have existed.

It was only in such a community that the *parties* could have been formed which marked the Christian Church there; where private judgment, independence, and general equality existed, out of which parties had to struggle, by dint of force and vehemence, if they were to have any prominence at all. Thus there were in Corinth the advantages of a democracy; for instance, unshackled thought; but also its vices, when men sprang up crying, "I am of Paul, and I of Apollos."

Again, the population was not only democratic, but commercial. This was necessitated by the site of Corinth. The neck of land which connects northern and southern Greece had two ports, Cenchreæ on the east, and Lechæum on the west, and Corinth lay between either seaboard. Thus all merchandise from north to south necessarily passed there, and all commerce from east to west flowed through it also, for the other way round the Capes Malea and Tænarum (Matapan), was both longer and more dangerous for heavily laden ships. Hence it was not by an imperial fiat but by natural circumstances, that Corinth became the emporium of trade. Once rebuilt, the tide of commerce, which had been forced in another direction, surged naturally back again, and streamed, as of old, across the bridge between Europe and Asia.

And from this arose another feature of its society. Its aristocracy was one not of birth, but of wealth. They were merchants not manufacturers. They had not the calm dignity of ancient lineage, nor the intellectual culture of a manufacturing population. For let us remember that manufactories *must* educate. A manufacturer may not be a man of learning, but an educated man he must be, by the very necessity of his position. And his intelligence, contrivance, invention, and skill, which are being drawn out continually every hour, spread their influence through his work among the very lowest of his artizans. But, on the other hand, Trade does not necessarily need more than a clear head, a knowledge of accounts, and a certain clever sagacity. It becomes, too, a life of routine at last, which neither, necessarily, teaches one moral truth, nor, necessarily, enlarges the mind. And the *danger* of a mere trading existence is that it leaves the soul engaged not in producing, but in removing productions from one place to another; it buries the heart in the task of money-getting; and measuring the worthiness of manhood and of all things by what they severally are *worth*, too often worships Mammon instead of God. Such men were the rich merchants of Corinth.

In addition to this adoration of gold, there were also all the demoralizing influences of a trading seaport. Men from all quarters of the globe met in the streets of Corinth, and on the quays of its two harbors. Now, one reason why a population is always demoralized by an influx of strangers continually going and coming is this; a nation shut up in itself may be very narrow, and have its own vices, but it will also have its own growth of native virtues; but when peoples mix, and men see the sanctities of their childhood dispensed with, and other sanctities, which they despise, substituted; when they see the principles of their own country ignored, and all that they have held venerable made profane and common, the natural consequence is that they begin to look upon the manners, religion, and sanctities of their own birth-place as prejudices. They do not get instead those reverences which belong to other countries. They lose their own holy ties and sanctions, and they obtain nothing in their place. And so men, when they mix together, corrupt each other; each contributes his own vices and his irreverence of the other's good, to destroy every standard of goodness, and each in the contact loses his own excellences. Exactly as our young English men and women on their return from foreign countries learn to sneer at the rigidity of English purity, yet never learn instead even that urbanity and hospitality which foreigners have as a kind of equivalent for the laxity of their morals. Retaining our own haughtiness and rudeness, and misanthropy, we graft, upon our natural vices, sins which are against the very grain of our own nature and temperament.

Such as I have described it was the moral state of Corinth. The city was the hot-bed of the world's evil, in which every noxious plant, indigenous or transplanted, rapidly grew and flourished; where luxury and sensuality throve rankly, stimulated by the gambling spirit of commercial life, till Corinth, now in the Apostle's time, as in previous centuries, became a proverbial name for moral corruption.

Another element in the city was the Greek population. To understand the nature of this we must make a distinction. I have already said that Greece was tainted to the core. Her ancient patriotism was gone. Her valor was no more. Her statesmen were no longer pure in policy as in eloquence. Her poets had died with her disgrace. She had but the remembrance of what had been. Foreign conquest had broken her spirit. Despair had settled on her energies. Loss of liberty had ended in loss of manhood. Her children felt the Roman Colossus bestriding their once beloved country. The last and most indispensable element of goodness had perished, for hope was dead. They buried themselves in stagnancy. But remark that amid this universal degeneracy there were two classes. There were, first, the uncultivated and the poor, to whom the ancient glories of their land were yet dear, to whom the old religion was not merely hereditary, but true and living still; whose imagination still saw the solemn conclave of their ancient deities on Mount Olympus, and still heard Pan, and the Fauns, and the wood gods piping in the groves. Such were they who in Lystria came forth to meet Paul and Barnabas, and believed them to be Jupiter and Mercury. With such, paganism was still tenaciously believed, just as in England now, the faith in witchcraft, spells, and the magical virtue of baptismal water, banished from the towns, survives and lingers among our rural population. At this period it was with *that* portion of heathenism alone, that Christianity came in contact, to meet a foe.

Very different, however, was the state of the cultivated and the rich. They had lost their religion. Their civilization and their knowledge of the world had destroyed that; and that being lost, they retained no natural vent for the energies of the restless Greek character. Hence out of that high state of intellectual culture there arose a craving for "Wisdom;" not the wisdom which Solomon spoke of, but wisdom in the sense of intellectual speculation. The energy which had found a safe outlet in War now wasted itself in the Amphitheatre. The enthusiasm which had been stimulated by the noble eloquence of patriotism now preyed on glittering rhetoric. They spent their days in tournaments of speeches, and exulted in gladiatorial oratory. They would not even listen to a sermon from St. Paul, unless it were clothed in dazzling words and full of brilliant thought. They were in a state not uncommon now with fine intellects whose action is cramped. Religion, instead of being solid food for the soul, had become an intellectual banquet. That was another difficulty with which Christianity had to deal.

The next thing we observe as influencing Corinthian society is, that it was the seat of a Roman provincial government. There was there a deputy, that is, a proconsul. "Gallio was deputy of Achaia." Let it surprise no one if I say that this was an influence *favorable* to Christianity. The doctrine of Christ had not as yet come into direct antagonism with Heathenism. It is true that throughout the Acts we read of persecution coming from the Greeks, but at the same time we invariably find that it was the Jews who had "stirred up the Greeks." The persecution always arose first on the part of the Jews; and, indeed, until it became evident that in Christianity there was a Power before which all the principalities of evil, all tyranny and wrong, must perish, the Roman magistrates generally defended it, and interposed their authority between the Christians and their fierce enemies. A signal instance of this is related in this chapter. Gallio, the Roman proconsul, dismisses the charge brought against the Christians. "And when Paul was now about to open his mouth, Gallio said unto the Jews, If it were a matter of wrong or wicked lewdness, O ye Jews, reason would that I should bear with you: But if it be a question of words and names, and of your law, look ye to it; for I will be no judge of such matters."

And his judgment was followed by a similar verdict from the people; for Sosthenes, the ringleader of the accusation, was beaten by the mob before the judgment seat. And "Gallio cared for none of these things," that is, he took no notice of them, he would not interfere; he was, perhaps, even glad that a kind of wild, irregular justice was administered to one who had been foremost in bringing an unjust charge. So that instead of Gallio being, as the commentators make him, a sort of type of religious lukewarmness, he is really a specimen of an upright Roman magistrate. But what principally concerns us in the story now is, that it is an example of the way in which the existence of the Roman Government at Corinth was, on the whole, an advantage for the spread of the Gospel.

The last element in this complex community was the Jews. Every city, Greek or Roman, at this time was rife with them. Then, as now, they had that national peculiarity which scatters them among all nations, while it prevents them from amalgamating with any, which makes them worshippers of Mammon, and yet withal, ready to suffer all things, and even to die for their faith. In their way they were religious; but it was a blind and bigoted adherence to the sensuous side of religion. They had almost ceased to believe in a living God, but they were strenuous believers in the virtue of ordinances. God to them only existed for the benefit of the Jewish nation. To them a Messiah must be a World-Prince. To them a new revelation could only be substantiated by marvels and miracles. To them it could have no self-evident spiritual light; and St. Paul, in the first Epistle to the Corinthians, describes the difficulty which this tendency put in the way of the progress of the Gospel among them thus: "The Jews require a sign."

II. Respecting the Apostle Paul.

To this society, so constituted, so complex, so manifold, St. Paul came, assured that he was in possession of a truth which was adapted and addressed to all, "the power of God unto salvation to every one that believeth, to the Jew first, and also to the Gentile."

Now, for this work he was peculiarly assisted and prepared.

1. By the fellowship of Aquila and Priscilla. We read that when he came to Corinth he found a certain Jew named Aquila, lately come from Italy with his wife Priscilla, because that Claudius had commanded all the Jews to depart from Rome; and that he came to them.

St. Paul had a peculiar gift from God, the power of doing without those solaces which ordinary men require. But we should greatly mistake that noble heart and rare nature, if we conceived of it as hard, stern, and incapable of tender human sympathies. Remember how, when anxious about these very Corinthians, "he felt no rest when he found not Titus his brother, at Troas." Recollect his gentle yearnings after the recovery of Epaphroditus. Such an one thrown alone upon a teeming, busy, commercial population, as he was at Corinth, would have felt crushed. Alone he had been left, for he had sent back his usual companions on several missions. His spirit had been pressed within him at Athens when he saw the city wholly given to idolatry. But that was not so oppressive as the sight of human masses, crowding, hurrying, driving together, all engaged in the mere business of getting rich, or in the more degrading work of seeking mere sensual enjoyment. Nothing so depresses as that. In this crisis, Providential arrangements had prepared for him the assistance of Priscilla and Aquila. In their house he found a home: in their society, companionship. Altogether with them, he gained that refreshment for his spirit, without which it would have been perilous for him to have entered on his work in Corinth.

2. He was sustained by manual work. He wrought with his friends as a tent-maker. That was his "craft." For by the rabbinical law, all Jews were taught a trade. One rabbi had said, that he who did not teach his son a trade, instructed him to steal. Another had declared that the study of theology along with a trade was good for the soul, and without it a temptation from the devil. So, too, it was the custom of the monastic institutions to compel every brother to work, not only for the purpose of supporting the monastery, but also to prevent the entrance of evil thoughts. A wise lesson! For in a life like that of Corinth, in gaiety, or the merely thoughtful existence, in that state of leisure to which so many minds are exposed, woe and trial to the spirit that has nothing *for the hands* to do! Misery to him or her who emancipates himself or herself from the universal law, "In the sweat of thy brow shalt thou eat bread." Evil thoughts, despondency, sensual feelings, sin in every shape is before him, to beset and madden, often to ruin him.

3. By the rich experience he had gained in Athens. There the Apostle had met the philosophers on their own ground. He had shown them that there was a want in Human Nature to which the Gospel was adapted; he had spoken of their cravings after the Unknown; he had declared that he had to preach to them that which they, unconsciously, desired: he had stripped their worship of its anthropomorphism, and had manifested to them that the residuum was the germ of Christianity. And his speech was triumphant as oratory, as logic, and as a specimen of philosophic thought; but in its bearing on conversion, it was unsuccessful. His work at Athens was a failure; Dionysius and a few women are all we read of as converted. There was no church at Athens.

Richly taught by this, he came to Corinth and preached no longer to the wise, the learned, or the rich. "Ye see your calling, brethren," he said, "how that not many wise men after the flesh, not many mighty, not many noble are called." God had chosen the poor of this world to be rich in faith. He no longer confronted the philosopher on his own ground, or tried to accommodate the Gospel to his tastes: and then that memorable resolve is recorded, "I determined to know nothing among you, save Jesus Christ and Him crucified." Not the crucifixion of Christ; but Christ, and that Christ crucified. He preached Christ, though crucified; Christ crucified, though the Greeks might mock and the Jews reject Him with scorn — Christ *as* Christianity; Christ His own evidence. We know the result; the Church of Corinth, the largest and noblest harvest ever given to ministerial toil.

LECTURE II.

JUNE 8, 1851.

1 CORINTHIANS, i. 1–3.—"Paul called to be an Apostle of Jesus Christ through the will of God, and Sosthenes our brother,—Unto the church of God which is at Corinth, to them that are sanctified in Christ Jesus, called to be saints, with all that in every place call upon the name of Jesus Christ our Lord, both theirs and ours:—Grace be unto you, and peace from God our Father, and from the Lord Jesus Christ."

OUR discourse last Sunday put us in possession of the state of Corinth when the Apostle entered it. We know what Corinth was intellectually, politically, morally, and socially. We learned that it contained a democratic population. We found it commercial, rich, and immoral from its being a trading seaport. We spoke of its Roman government, which on the whole acted fairly at that time toward Christianity; of its Greek inhabitants, of whom the richer were sceptics who had lost their religion, and the poorer still full of superstitions, as we discover from the notices of heathen sacrifices which pervade these Epistles. And the last element was the Jewish population, who were devoted to a religion of signs and ordinances.

Our subject for to-day comprises the first three verses of this chapter. From these we take three points for investigation —

I. The designation of the writers.
II. The description of the persons addressed.
III. The benediction.

I. The designation of the writers. Paul "an Apostle"—Sosthenes "our brother." An apostle means "one sent," a missionary to teach the truth committed to him; and the authority of this apostolic mission St. Paul substantiates in the words "called to be an Apostle of Jesus Christ *through the will of God.*" There was a necessity for this vindication of his Apostleship. At the time of writing this Epistle he was at Ephesus, having left Corinth after a stay of eighteen months. There he was informed of the state of the Church in Achaia by those of the house of Chloe, a Christian lady, and by letters from themselves. From this correspondence he learnt that his authority was questioned; — and so St. Paul, unjustly treated and calumniated, opens his Epistle with these words, written partly in self-defence — "Called to be an apostle by the will of God." In the firm conviction of that truth lay all his power. No man felt more strongly than St. Paul his own insignificance. He told his converts again and again that he "was not meet to be called an Apostle;" that he was "the least of all saints," that he was the "chief of sinners." And yet, intensely as he felt all this, more deeply did he feel something above and beyond all this, that he was God's messenger, that his was a true Apostleship, that he had been truly commissioned by the King; and hence he speaks with courage and with freedom. His words were not his own, but His who had sent him. Imagine that conception dawning on his spirit, imagine, if you can, that light suddenly struck out of his own mind in the midst of his despondency, and then you will no longer wonder at the almost joyful boldness with which he stood firm, as on a rock, against the slander of his enemies, and the doubtfulness of his friends. Now, unless this is felt by us, our life and work has lost its impulse. If we think of our profession or line of action, simply as arising from our own independent choice, or from chance, instantly we are paralyzed, and our energies refuse to act vigorously. But what was it which nerved the Apostle's soul to bear reproach and false witness? Was it not this? I have a mission: "I am called to be an Apostle through the will of God." Well, this should be *our* strength. Called to be a Carpenter, a Politician, a Tradesman, a Physician — he is irreverent who believes that? God sent me here to cut wood, to direct justly, to make shoes, to teach children; — Why should not each and all of us feel that? It is one of the greatest truths on which we can rest our life, and by which we can invigorate our work. But we get rid of it by claiming it exclusively for St. Paul. We say that God called the Apostles, but does not speak to us. We say they were inspired and lifted above ordinary Humanity. But observe the modesty of his apostolic claim. He does not say, "I am infallible," but that the Will of God has sent him as It had sent others. He did not wish that his people should receive his truth because he, the Apostle, had said it, but because it *was* truth. He did not seek to bind men, as if they were destitute of reasoning, to any *αὐτὸς ἔφη*, as is set up now by Evangelicalism or Popery, but throughout the whole of this Epistle he uses arguments, he appeals to reason and to sense. He convinces them that he was an Apostle, not by declarations that they *must* believe him, but by appealing to the truth he had taught — "by manifestation of the truth, commending ourselves to every man's conscience in the sight of God." Further, we see in the fact of St. Paul's joining with himself Sosthenes, and calling him his brother, another proof of his desire to avoid erecting himself as the sole guide of the Church. He sends the Epistle from himself and Sosthenes. Is that like one who desired to be Lord alone over God's heritage? "I am an Apostle — sent by the will of God; but Sosthenes is my brother." Of Sosthenes himself, nothing certain is known. He is supposed by some to be the Sosthenes of Acts xvii., the persecutor, the ringleader of the Jews against the Christians, who was beaten before the judgment seat of Gallio. If so, see what a conqueror St. Paul, or rather, Christianity had become. Like the Apostle of the Gentiles, Sosthenes now built up the faith which once he destroyed. But, in truth, we know nothing accurately, except that he was a Corinthian known to the persons addressed, and now with Paul at Ephesus. The proper reflection from the fact of his being joined with the Apostle, is the humility of St. Paul. He never tried to make a Party or form a Sect; he never even thought of placing himself above them as an infallible and autocratic Pope.

II. The persons addressed. "The Church of God which is at Corinth." The Church! What is the Church? That question lies below all the theological differences of the day. The Church, according to the derivation of the word, means the house of God. It is that Body of men in whom the Spirit of God dwells as the Source of their excellence, and who exist on earth for the purpose of exhibiting the Divine Life and the hidden order of Humanity: to destroy evil and to assimilate Humanity to God, to penetrate and purify the world, and as salt, preserve it from corruption. It has an existence continuous throughout the ages; continuous however, not on the principles of hereditary succession or of human election, as in an ordinary corporation, but on the principle of spiritual similarity of character.* The Apostle Paul asserted this spiritual succession when he said that the seed of Abraham were to be reckoned, not on his lineal descendants, but as inheritors of his faith.† And Christ, too, meant the same when he told the Jews that out of the stones before Him God could raise up children unto Abraham. There is, however, a Church visible, and a Church invisible; the latter consists of those spiritual persons who fulfil the notion of the Ideal Church; the former is the Church as it exists in any particular age, embracing within it all who profess Christianity, whether they be proper or improper members of its body. Of the invisible Church, the writer of the Epistle to the Hebrews speaks; ‡ and St. Paul also alludes to this in the description which he gives of the several churches,

* John, i. 13. † Gal. iii. 7. ‡ Heb. xii. 23.

to whom he writes in language which certainly far transcended their *actual* state. As, for instance, in this Epistle, he speaks of them as "called to be saints," as "temples of the Holy Ghost," and then in another place describes them in their actual state, as "carnal, and walking as men." Again, it is of the visible Church he writes, when he reproves their particular errors; and Christ, too, speaks of the same in such parables as that of the net gathering in fishes both good and bad, and the field of wheat which was mingled with tares.

An illustration may make this plain. The abstract conception of a river is that of a stream of pure, unmixed water, but the actual river is the Rhine, or the Rhone, or the Thames, muddy and discolored, and charged with impurity; and the conception of this or that river necessarily contains within it these peculiarities. So of the church of Christ. Abstractedly, and invisibly, it is a kingdom of God in which no evil is; in the concrete, and actually, it is the church of Corinth, of Rome, or of England, tainted with impurity; and yet just as the mudded Rhone is really the Rhone, and not mud and Rhone, so there are not two churches, the church of Corinth and the false church with it, but one visible Church, in which the invisible lies concealed. This principle is taught in the parable, which represents the Church as a Vine. There are not two vines, but one; and the withered branches, which shall be cut off hereafter, are really for the present part and portion of the Vine. So far then, it appears, that in any age, the visible Church is, properly speaking, *the* Church.

But beyond the limits of the Visible, is there no true Church? Are Plato, Socrates, Marcos Antonnius, and such as they, to be reckoned by us as lost? Surely not. The Church exists for the purpose of educating souls for heaven; but it would be a perversion of this purpose were we to think that goodness will not be received by God, because it has not been educated in the Church. Goodness is goodness, find it where we may. A vineyard exists for the purpose of nurturing vines, but he would be a strange vine-dresser who denied the reality of grapes because they had ripened under a less genial soil, and beyond the precincts of the vineyard. The truth is, that the Eternal Word has communicated himself to man in the expressed Thought of God, the Life of Christ. That to whom that Light has been manifested are Christians. But that Word has communicated Himself *silently* to human minds, on which the *manifested* Light has never shone. Such men *lived* with God, and were guided by His Spirit. They entered into the Invisible; they lived by Faith. They were beyond their generation. They were not of the world. The Eternal Word dwelt within them. For the Light that shone forth in a full blaze in Christ, lights also, we are told, "every man that cometh into the world." Instances that lead us to this truth are given in the Scriptures of persons beyond the pale of the Church, who, before their acquaintance with the Jewish nation, had been in the habit of receiving spiritual communications of their own from God: such were Melchisedec, Job, Rahab, and Nebuchadnezzar.

But from this digression, let us return to the visible Church of which the Church of Corinth formed a part. It existed as we have said to exhibit what Humanity should be, to represent the Life Divine on earth, and that chiefly in these particulars: —

1. Self-devotion — "To them that are sanctified in Christ Jesus."

2. Sanctity — "Called to be saints."

3. Universality — "With all that in every place call on the name of Jesus Christ our Lord."

4. Unity — Of Jesus Christ our Lord, both *theirs* and *ours;*" for Christ was their common centre, and every church felt united into one body when they knew that He belonged to *all*, that they all had one Spirit, one Lord, one Faith, one Baptism, one God and Father in Jesus Christ.

First, then, the Church exists to exhibit self-devotion. They were "sanctified in Christ Jesus." Now the true meaning of "to sanctify" is to set apart, and hence to consecrate to any work. Thus spoke Christ, "For their sakes I sanctify, set apart, devote Myself." His life was a voluntary devotion of Himself even to the death, as well to save others as to bear witness to the truth. It is this attribute of the Divine nature in Humanity that the Church exists to exhibit now on earth. And then it is a church most truly when it is most plainly devoted. Thus it was in martyr times, when the death and persecuted existence of the saints of God were at once the life-blood of the Church and a testimony to the truth of its Faith. But then it is not, plainly, the Church, where bishops and priests are striving to aggrandize their own power, and seeking to impress men with the idea of the infallibility of their office. When the ecclesiastical dignity makes godliness a means of gain, or when priestcraft exercises lordship over the heritage of God, then it is falsifying its mission, for it is existing to establish, instead of to destroy, selfishness.

Secondly, It exists to establish *sanctity.*

The Church of Corinth was formed, as we have said, of peculiar elements. It arose out of a democratic, and therefore a factious, community It sprang out of an extremely corrupt society, where pride of wealth abounded, and where superstition and scepticism looked one another in the face. It developed itself in the midst of a Judaism which demanded visible proofs of a divine mission. Ancient vices still infected the Christian converts. They carried into the Church the savor of their old life, for the wine-skin will long retain the flavor with which it has once been imbued. We find from these epistles that gross immorality still existed, and was even considered a thing to boast of. We find their old philosophy still coloring their Christianity, for on the foundation of the oriental idea that the body was the source of all sin, they denied a future resurrection. We find the insolence of wealth at the Lord's Supper. We find spiritual gifts abused by being exhibited for the sake of ostentation. Such was the

Church of Corinth! This is the Early Church so boasted of by some! Yet nowhere do we find, "These are *not* of the Church; these *are* of the Church." Rather *all* are the Church — the profligate brother, the proud rich man, the speculative philosopher, the mere partizan, the superstitious and the seeker after signs, all "are called to be saints." All were temples of the Holy Ghost, though possibly admonished that they might be defiling that temple. "Know ye not that your bodies *are* the temples of the Holy Ghost" — that "Christ is *in you*, except ye be reprobates?" In the face of this the hypothetical view of Baptism is impossible. Publicans and sinners may be in the Church, and yet they are called God's children, His children, redeemed though not sanctified; His people pardoned and reconciled *by right*, though the reconciliation and the pardon are not theirs *in fact*, unless they accept it. For it is possible to open the doors of the prison, and yet for the prisoner to refuse deliverance; it is possible to forgive an injury, and yet for the injurer to retain his anger, and then reconciliation and friendship, which are things of two sides, are incomplete. Nevertheless, all are designed for holiness, all of the professing Church are "called to be saints." Hence the Church of Christ is a visible body of men providentially elected out of the world to exhibit holiness, some of whom really manifest it in this life, while others do not; and the mission of this society is to put down evil.

Thirdly, Its universality. "With all who, in every place, call upon the name of Jesus Christ, both theirs and ours."

The Corinthian Church was, according to these words of the Apostle, not an exclusive *αὐτάρχης* Church, but only a part of the Church universal, as a river is of the sea. He allowed it no proud superiority. He would not permit it to think of itself as more spiritual or as possessing higher dignity than the Church at Jerusalem or Thessalonica. They were called to be saints along with, and on a level with, all who named the Name of Christ.

Is this our idea when we set up Anglicanism against Romanism, and make England the centre of unity instead of Rome? There is no centre of unity but Christ. We go to God with proud notions of our spirituality and our claims. We boast ourselves of our advantages over Dissenters and Romanists. Whereas the same God is "theirs and ours;" the same Christ is "theirs and ours." Oh! only so far as we feel that God is *our* Father not *my* Father, and Christ *our* Saviour not *my* Saviour, do we realize the idea of the Church. "The name of our Lord Jesus Christ, both theirs and ours." What a death blow to Judaism and party spirit in Corinth!

Lastly, *unity*.

Christ was theirs and ours. He was the Saviour of all, and the common Supporter of all. Though individual churches might differ, and though sects might divide even those churches, and though each might have a distinct truth, and manifest distinct gifts, yet Christ existed in all. The same one Spirit, His Spirit, pervaded all, and strengthened all, and bound all together into a living and invisible unity. Each in their several ways contributed to build up the same building on the same Foundation; each in their various ways were distinct members of Christ's Body, performing different offices, yet knit into One under the same Head; and the very variety produced a more perfect and abiding unity.

III. The Benediction. "Grace and peace from God our Father and from the Lord Jesus Christ."

This is, if you will, a formula, but forms like this teach much; they tell of the Spirit from which they originate. The heathen commenced their letters with the salutation, "Health!" There is a life of the Flesh, and there is a life of the Spirit — a truer, more real, and a higher Life, and above and beyond all things the Apostle wished them this. He wished them not "Health" nor "Happiness," but "Grace and Peace" from God our Father. And now comes the question, What is the use of this benediction? How could grace and peace be given as a blessing to those who rejected grace, and not believing felt no peace? Let me try to illustrate this. When the minister in a representative capacity, in the person of Christ, declares absolution to a sinner, his absolution is not lost if the man rejects it, or cannot receive it; for it returns to him again, and he has done what he could to show that in Christ there *is* a full absolution for the sinner, if he will take it. Remember what Christ said to the seventy: "When ye enter into an house, say, Peace be to this house; and if the Son of Peace be there, your peace shall rest upon it, if not, it shall return to you again."

The validity of St. Paul's blessing depended on its reception by the hearts to whom it was addressed. If they received it, they became *in fact* what they had been by right all along, sons of God: they "set to their seal that God was true."

"Grace and peace from God our Father and the Lord Jesus Christ." For the special revelation of Jesus Christ is, that God is our Father, and when we believe that, not merely with our intellects, but with our hearts, and evidence in our lives that we believe it, and that this relationship is the spring of our motives and actions, then will flow in the Peace which passeth all understanding, and we are blessed indeed with the blessing of God.

LECTURE III.

JUNE 15, 1851.

1 CORINTHIANS, i. 4 – 13. — "I thank my God always on your behalf, for the Grace of God which is given you by Jesus Christ; — That in every thing ye are enriched by him, in all utterance, and in all knowledge; — Even as the testimony of Christ was confirmed in you: — So that ye come behind in no gift; waiting for the coming of our Lord Jesus Christ: — Who shall also confirm you unto the end, that ye may be blameless in the day of our Lord Jesus Christ. — God is faithful, by whom ye were called unto the fellowship of his Son Jesus Christ our Lord. — Now I beseech you, brethren, by the name of our Lord Jesus Christ, that ye all speak the same thing, and that there be no divisions among you; but that ye be perfectly joined together in the same mind and in the same judgment. — For it hath been declared unto me of you, my brethren, by them which are of the house of Chloe, that there are contentions among you. — Now this I say, that every one of you saith, I am of Paul; and I of Apollos; and I of Cephas; and I of Christ."

OUR work to-day will be from the commencement of the fourth to the end of the thirteenth verses, in which we find two points; first, the Apostolic congratulations from the fourth to the tenth verse; and, after that, the Apostolic warning and rebuke, from the tenth to the end. First, then, the Apostolic congratulation — "I thank my God always on your behalf," &c. Let us remark here how, in the heart of St. Paul, the unselfishness of Christianity had turned this world into a perpetual feast. He had almost none of the personal enjoyments of existence. If we want to know what his life was, we have only to turn to the eleventh chapter of the second Epistle: "Of the Jews five times received I forty stripes save one, thrice was I beaten with rods, once was I stoned," &c. That was his daily outward life; yet we shall greatly mistake the life of that glorious Apostle if we suppose it to have been an unhappy one. It was filled with blessedness; the blessedness which arises from that high Christian faculty through which a man is able to enjoy the blessings of others as though they were his own. Thus, the Apostle, in all his weariness and persecutions, was, nevertheless, always rejoicing with his Churches; and especially he rejoiced over the gifts and graces given to the Corinthians, of which he here enumerates three: first, Utterance, then Knowledge, and then the grace of that peculiar attitude of Expectation with which they were looking for the coming of the Lord Jesus Christ. He speaks of the gift of Utterance, and we shall understand his reason for calling it a gift rather than a grace, when we remember that, in his conception, Charity was far above Knowledge. To him a blessing was nothing, unless it could be imparted to others. Knowing a truth is one thing; being able to express it, is quite another thing: and then again, to be *able* to express a truth is one thing, but to *dare* to do it is another thing altogether. The Apostle unites both of these in the expression, "utterance:" it is, at the same time, an intellectual gift and a spiritual grace. St. Paul also thanks God for their Knowledge; for utterance without knowledge is worthless. He did not value these things merely for themselves, but only as they were means to an end — channels for conveying truth to others.

The last gift for which the Apostle thanks God in this place was their attitude of Expectation — they were waiting for the coming of the Lord — he says, "So that ye come behind in no gift, waiting for the coming of the Lord;" as though that were the highest gift of all; as if that attitude of expectation were the highest posture that can be attained here by the Christian. It implies a patient, humble spirit, one that is waiting for, one that is looking forward to, something higher and better. The Apostle seems by this to tell us that the highest spirit is shown rather in calm expectation, than in disputing *how* that Kingdom shall come, in believing that it must come, and silently waiting for God's own time for the revealing. St. Paul's congratulation contains a ground of hope for the continuance of those blessings — "God shall confirm you to the end;" and again, "God is faithful." He relies not on any stability of human goodness, he knows that he cannot trust to their inherent firmness or fidelity; his ground of confidence for the future is rather in the character of God. This is *our* only stay, our only hope, the unchanging faithfulness of God. True it is, that doctrine may be abused, we may rest upon it too much, and so become indifferent and supine; but, nevertheless, it is a most precious truth, and without some conviction of this, I cannot understand how any man dares go forth to his work in the morning, or at evening lay his head on his pillow to sleep.

We now pass on, secondly, to consider the Apostle's warning and reproof — Parties had risen in Corinth: let us endeavor briefly to understand what these parties were. You cannot have read the Epistles without perceiving that the Apostles taught very differently — not a different gospel, but each one a different side of the gospel. Contrast the Epistles of St. Paul with those of St. Peter or St. John. These were not contrarieties, but varieties, and so together they made up the unity of the Church of Christ. The first party in Corinth of which we shall speak was that one which called itself by the name of Paul; and the truths which they would chiefly proclaim would doubtless be those of Liberty and Universality. Moreover, St. Paul was not ordained like other teachers, but was called suddenly by special revelation of the Lord. He frequently refers to this, and declares that he was taught — not of man, but of God only. Now, the party calling itself by the name of Paul would doubtless exaggerate this, and teach, instead of liberty, licentiousness; and so with the other peculiarities of his teaching. There was also a party naming itself after Apollos; he had been educated at Alexandria, the university of the world, and we are told that he was mighty in the Scriptures, and remarkable for eloquence. The difference between Apollos and St. Paul seems to be not so much a difference of views as in the mode of stating those views: the eloquence of St. Paul was rough and burning; it stirred men's hearts, kindling in them the living fire of truth: that of Apollos was more refined and polished. There was also the party called by the name of Peter. Christianity in his heart had been regularly and slowly developed; he had known Jesus first as the Son of Man; and afterwards as the Son of God. It was long before he realized God's purpose of love to the Gentiles — in his conception the Messiah was to be chiefly King for the Jews; therefore all the Jewish converts, who still clung to very much that was Jewish, preferred to follow St. Peter. Lastly, there was the party calling itself by the name of Christ Himself. History does not inform us what were the special views of this party; but it is not difficult to imagine that they set themselves up as superior to all others. Doubtless, they prided themselves on their spirituality and inward light, and looked down with contempt on those who professed to follow the opinion of any teacher. Perhaps they ignored the apostolic teaching altogether, and proclaimed the doctrines of direct communion with God without the aid of ministry or ordinances; and these, as well as the others, the Apostle rebuked. The guilt of these partizans did not lie in holding views differing from each other; it was not so much in saying "this is the truth," as it was in saying "this is *not* the truth;" the guilt of schism is when each party, instead of expressing fully his own truth, attacks others, and denies that the others are in the Truth at all.

Avoid, I pray you, the accursed spirit of sectarianism: suffer not yourselves to be called by any party names; One is your Master, even Christ, and all ye are brethren. Let each man strive to work out, bravely and honestly, the truth which God has given to him; and when men oppose us and malign us, let us still, with a love which hopeth all things, strive rather to find good in them — truths special to them — but which as yet they — perhaps unconsciously — falsely represent.

LECTURE IV.

June 22, 1851.

1 Corinthians, i. 13–22. — "Is Christ divided? was Paul crucified for you? or were ye baptized in the name of Paul? — I thank God that I baptized none of you, but Crispus and Gaius; — Lest any should say that I had baptized in my own name. — And I baptized also the household of Stephanas; besides, I know not whether I baptized any other. — For Christ sent me not to baptize, but to preach the Gospel; not with wisdom of words, lest the Cross of Christ should be made of none effect. — For the preaching of the cross is to them that perish foolishness; but unto us which are saved it is the power of God. — For it is written, I will destroy the wisdom of the wise, and will bring to nothing the understanding of the prudent. — Where is the wise? where is the scribe? where is the disputer of this world? — hath not God made foolish the wisdom of this world? — For after that in the wisdom of God the world by wisdom knew not God, it pleased God by the foolishness of preaching to save them that believe. — For the Jews require a sign, and the Greeks seek after wisdom."

Last Sunday we endeavored to arrive at a right understanding respecting the different parties in the Church of Corinth: let us now pass on to consider the argument by which St. Paul met these sectarians. It was an appeal to Baptism, and to understand the force of that appeal, we must endeavor to understand what Christian Baptism is. It contains two things: something on the part of God, and something on the part of man. On God's part it is an authoritative revelation of His Paternity: on man's part it is an acceptance of God's covenant. Now there is a remarkable passage in which we find St. Paul expressing the meaning of Baptism as symbolizing submission, discipleship to any particular teacher: "Moreover, brethren, I would not that ye should be ignorant how that all our fathers were baptized unto Moses in the cloud and in the sea." When the Israelites passed through the Red Sea they cut themselves off for ever from Egypt, so that, figuratively speaking, the Apostle teaches that in that immersion they were baptized unto Moses, for thereby they declared themselves his followers, and left all to go with him. And so, just as the soldier who receives the bounty money is thereby pledged to serve his sovereign, so he who has passed through the Baptismal waters, is pledged to fight under the Redeemer's banner against sin, the world, and the devil. And now the argument of St. Paul becomes plain. He argues thus: To whom were ye then baptized? To whom did you pledge yourselves in discipleship? If to Christ, why do ye name yourselves by the name of Paul? If all were baptized into that One Name, how is it that a few only have adopted it as their own?

Upon this we make two remarks; first, the value and blessedness of the Sacraments. It will be asked, To what purpose are the Sacraments of the Church? if they work no miracle, of what avail are they? Our reply is, Much every way; among others, that they are authoritative signs and symbols. Now there is very much contained in the idea of a recognized authoritative symbol; for instance, in some parts of the country it is the custom to give and receive a ring, in token of betrothal; but that is very different from the marriage-ring, it being not authoritative, and being without the sanction of the Church.

It would have been perfectly possible for man to have invented for himself another symbol of the truth conveyed in Baptism, but then it would not have been authoritative, and consequently it would have been weak and useless. Now, there is another thing, and that is, that these Sacraments are the epitomes of Christian Truth. This is the way in which the Apostle frequently makes use of the Sacraments. From the Epistle to the Romans we find that Antinomianism had crept into the Church, and that there were some who said, that if only they believed, it did not matter that they sinned. How does St. Paul meet this? By an appeal to Baptism? He says, "God forbid, how shall we, who are dead to sin, live any longer therein? Know ye not that so many of us as were baptized into Jesus Christ were baptized into His death?" "Buried with Him by baptism," — in the very form of that Sacrament there was a protest against this Antinomianism. And again, in reference to the Lord's Supper, in the Church of Corinth abuses had crept in; that holy Communion had become a feast of gluttony and a signal of division. This error he endeavors to correct by reference to the institution of the Supper itself, "The bread which we break, is it not the Communion of the Body of Christ?" The single loaf, broken into many fragments, contains within it a truth symbolical, that the Church of Christ is one. Here, in the text, St. Paul makes the same appeal: he appeals to Baptism against sectarianism, and so long as we retain it, it is an everlasting protest against every one who breaks the unity of the Church. The other remark we have to make bears on the peculiar meaning of the Sacrament. We are all aware that there are those in the Church of Christ, whose personal holiness and purity are unquestionable, who yet believe and teach that all children are born into the world children of the devil, and there are those who agree in this belief, though differing as to the remedy; who hold that the special and only instrument for their conversion into God's children is Baptism; and they believe that there is given to the ministers of the Church the power of conveying in that Sacrament the Holy Spirit, which effects this wondrous change. I know not that I have misrepresented this view: I do not think I have, yet I say at least, that if a minister really believes he has this power, then it is only with fear and trembling that he should approach the font in which he is about to baptize a child. But, let us try this view by the passage before us: if this view be true, then the Apostle, in saying that he thanked God he had not baptized, thanked God that he had not regenerated any: he rejoices that he had not conveyed the Spirit of God to any one but Crispus and Gaius, and the household of Stephanas.

And all this merely, lest he should perchance lie under the slander of having made to himself a party! If we reject this hypothesis as impossible, then it is plain that the view we have alluded to rests on no scriptural basis. We pass on, lastly, to consider the compromise which Paul refused to make: he would make none, either with the Jews in their craving after Signs, or with the Greeks in their longing after Wisdom. For fifteen hundred years forms and signs had been the craving of the Jews. St. Peter even had leanings in the same direction. The truth seems to be, that wherever there is life, there will be a form; but wherever a form is, it does not follow that there must be life; St. Paul stood firm — Not Signs, but Christ. Neither would he make any compromise with the craving after an intellectual religion. There was a diametrical contrast between the Jewish and the Grecian spirit: one seemed all body, and the other all mind. The wisdom of which St. Paul speaks, appears to have been of two kinds — speculative philosophy, and wisdom of words — eloquence. Men bow before talent, even if unassociated with goodness, but between these two we must make an everlasting distinction. When once the idolatry of talent enters, then farewell to spirituality; when men ask their teachers, not for that which will make them more humble and God-like, but for the excitement of an intellectual banquet, then farewell to Christian progress. Here also St. Paul again stood firm — Not Wisdom, but Christ crucified. St. Paul might have complied with these requirements of his converts, and then he would have gained admiration, and love — he would have been the leader of a party, but then he would have been false to his Master — he would have been preferring self to Christ.

LECTURE V.

JUNE 29, 1851.

1 CORINTHIANS, i. 23. — "But we preach Christ crucified, unto the Jews a stumbling-block, and unto the Greeks foolishness.

IN the course of our exposition of this Epistle, we have learnt the original constitution of Corinthian society, and have ascertained the state of the religious parties in that city at the time St. Paul wrote. We have seen that the Apostle Paul refused to make a compromise with either of these parties; it remains for us now to consider first the subject which he resolved to dwell upon, and then the results of that teaching on the different classes of his hearers. His subject was — "Christ crucified." The expression, "preaching Christ," is very much misunderstood by many persons. It is, therefore, incumbent on us to endeavor calmly to understand what the Apostle meant by this. We say, then, that to preach Christ is to preach Christianity, that is, the Doctrines which He taught. In Acts, xv. 21, we read, "Moses of old time hath in every city them that preach him." The reading of the Pentateuch was the preaching of Moses. Preaching Christ is setting forth His Doctrines in contra-distinction to those of the World. The World says — Resent an injury; Christ says — Forgive your enemies. If, therefore, we preach Forgiveness, are we not thereby preaching Christ, even though no distinct mention may be made of his Divinity or of the doctrine of the Atonement? In the Sermon on the Mount there is contained no reference to any one special doctrine of Christianity, as we should call it; nor in the Epistle of St. James is there found one word respecting the doctrine of the Atonement; but if we take this Sermon or this Epistle, and simply work out the truths therein contained — tell us, are we not thereby preaching Christ? To preach Goodness, Mercy, Truth, not for the bribe of heaven or from the fear of hell, but in the Name of God the Father, is to preach Christ.

Once more, this expression implies preaching Truth in connection with a *Person:* it is not merely Purity, but the *Pure One;* not merely Goodness, but the *Good One* that we worship. Let us observe the twofold advantage of this mode of preaching: first, because it makes religion practical. The Greek teachers were also teaching Purity, Goodness, Truth; they were striving to lead men's minds to the First Good, the First Fair. The Jewish Rabbis were also endeavoring to do the same, but it is only in Christ that it becomes possible to do this effectually. The second advantage in preaching Christianity in connection with a *Person* is, that it gives us something to adore, for we can adore a *person,* but we cannot adore *principles.* There is implied in this expression, "preaching Christ crucified," the Divine nature of Humility. Paul would not preach Christ as a conqueror, although by that he might please the Jews, or yet as a philosopher, in order that he might satisfy the Greeks; he would only preach Him as the humble, crucified Man of Nazareth.

We are, in the second place, to consider the results of this teaching on the several classes of his hearers. To the Jew it was a stumbling-block, something over which he could not pass; the Jew could not receive the Gospel, unless accompanied by signs and miracles to prove that it was from God. To the Greeks it was foolishness, for the Apostle spoke to them as an uneducated, uncultivated man; and they missed the sophistry, the logic, and the brilliant eloquence of their professional orators. Neither could they see what advantage his teaching could be to them, for it would not show them how to form a statue, build a temple, or make a fortune, which things they looked upon as the chief glories of life. But there was another class on whom his words made a very different impression. They are those whom the Apostle describes as "the Called." To them Christ was the Power and the Wisdom of God. He does not mean to assert here the doctrine of Election or Predestination; on the contrary, he says that this calling was in respect of inward fitness, and not of outward advantages. God prepares the heart of man for the reception of the Gospel — that is God's blessed plan of election.

LECTURE VI.

November 2, 1851.

1 Corinthians, iii. 1–10. — "And I, brethren, could not speak unto you as unto spiritual, but as unto carnal, even as unto babes in Christ. — I have fed you with milk, and not with meat: for hitherto ye were not able to bear it, neither yet now are ye able. — For ye are yet carnal: for whereas there is among you envying, and strife, and divisions, are ye not carnal, and walk as men? — For while one saith, I am of Paul; and another, I am of Apollos; are ye not carnal? — Who then is Paul, and who is Apollos, but ministers by whom ye believed, even as the Lord gave to every man? — I have planted, Apollos watered; but God gave the increase. — So then neither is he that planteth anything, neither he that watereth; but God that giveth the increase. — Now he that planteth and he that watereth are one; and every man shall receive his own reward according to his own labor. — For we are laborers together with God: ye are God's husbandry, ye are God's building. — According to the grace of God which is given unto me, as a wise master-builder, I have laid the foundation, and another buildeth thereon. But let every man take heed how he buildeth thereupon."

The two former chapters of this Epistle refer to St. Paul's ministry while at Corinth, where there existed a church made up of very peculiar elements. The first of these was Roman, and composed of freedmen, through whose influence society became democratic. The second element was Greek, refined, intellectual, inquisitive, and commercial, and this rendered the whole body restless, and apt to divide itself into parties. In addition to these was the Jewish element, which at this time had degenerated into little more than a religion of the senses. From all this there arose, first, a craving for an intellectual religion — appealing merely to taste and philosophical perceptions. But St. Paul refused to preach to them eloquently or philosophically, "lest the Cross of Christ should be made of none effect." St. Paul knew that the human heart often rests in eloquent expression of religious sentiment, instead of carrying it on into religious action. For strong feelings often evaporate in words. Strong expressions about self-sacrifice or self-denial, about a life sustained high above the world, often satisfy the heart and prevent it from rising to the grace talked about; whereas Christianity is not a Creed but a Life, and men who listen to a preacher only to find an intellectual amusement, or pictures of an ideal existence, are not thereby advanced one step nearer to the high life of a Christian.

Secondly. From the Jewish element there arose a craving for a religion of signs; and St. Paul refused to teach by signs. He would not base Christianity upon miracles, or external proofs; because, truth is its own evidence, and the soul alone must be the judge whether a truth is from God or not. Miracles address the senses, and the appetites of hunger and thirst; and it were preposterous to say that the eye, the ear, or the touch can determine accurately of Divine truth while the soul cannot; that the lower part of our nature is an unerring judge, while the soul alone is not infallible in its decisions. For " the natural man (understandeth) receiveth not the things of the Spirit of God: for they are foolishness unto him."

" Howbeit we speak wisdom among them that are perfect, yet not the wisdom of this world, but the wisdom of God, which is hidden in a mystery."

A third consequence of this peculiar constitution of Corinthian society was, its Party spirit. This arose out of its democratic character. Faction does not rend a society in which classes are indisputably divided beyond appeal, as is the case in Hindustan. Where superiority is unquestioned between class and class, rivalry will exist only between individuals. But where all are by social position equal, then there will be a struggle for superiority; for in God's world there is not one monotony of plains without hills, nor a human society on one dead level of equality. There is an *above*, and there is a *below*. There are angels, principalities, powers, there; and here, orders, degrees, and ranks. And the difficulty in social adjudicature is, to determine who ought to be the leaders, and who are to be the led; to abolish false aristocracies, and to establish the true. Now, to say that this is what men aim at, is to say that dispute, faction, party spirit, animosity must exist till that real order is established which is called the Kingdom of God on earth; in which each person is in his right place, and they only rule who are fit to rule. To-day, therefore, our subject will relate to this third consequence; and I shall speak of St. Paul's spiritual treatment of the Corinthian Church, in a state of faction.

I. His economic management of Truth.

II. His depreciation of the Human in the march of progress, by his manifestation of God in it.

I. His economic management of Truth.

I use this word, though it may seem pedantic, because I find no other to answer my purpose so well; it is borrowed from the times of the early Christian Church: "Economic," when used in reference to the management of a household, means a frugal use of provision in opposition to extravagant expenditure. An economist apportions to each department the sum necessary, and no more.

And in the spiritual dispensation of Truth, economy means that prudent distribution which does not squander it uselessly away, when it can do no good, but which apportions to each age, and to each capacity, the amount it can turn to good account. It implies a prudent, wise reserve. Now the principle of this we find stated in the second verse, "I have fed you with milk, and not with meat." And, although in its application some errors might be committed by withholding truths which should be granted, and by failing to distribute them at the required time, still the principle is a simple and a true one. For different ages, different kinds of food. For childhood, or "babes in Christ," milk. For them that are of full age, or who have the power of discerning both good and evil, "strong meat." But reverse this, and the child becomes sick and fevered. And the reason of this is, that what is strength to the man is injury to the child — it cannot bear it.

The doctrine which the Apostle calls "strong meat," if taught at first, would deter from further discipleship; and Christ expresses the same thing. "No man putteth a piece of new cloth unto an old garment, for the rent is made worse. Neither do men put new wine into old bottles, else the bottles break, and the wine runneth out." Now this, remember, was said immediately after the disciples of John had asked, why Jesus had not taught the same severe life (the type of which was fasting) which John had. And so, too, Christ did not preach the Cross to His disciples at first. The first time He did preach it, it shocked them. For it was not until after Peter's memorable acknowledgment of Him in these words, "Thou art the Christ," that He revealed to them His coming death, which, even then, resulted in a kind of revolt against Him, drawing from Peter the exclamation, "This be far from thee, Lord."

Such a case of defection actually did occur in the behavior of the young Ruler, who forced, as it were, from Christ a different method of procedure. At first, Jesus would have given him mere moral duty. "Thou knowest the Commandments, Do not commit adultery, do not kill." But not satisfied with this, he asked for Perfection. "What lack I yet?" And then there was nothing left but to say — "If thou wilt be perfect, go and sell that thou hast and give to the poor, and come and follow Me." For observe, "strong meat" does not mean high doctrine such as Election, Regeneration, Justification by Faith, but "Perfection:" strong demands on Self, a severe, noble Life. St. Paul taught the Corinthians all the Doctrine he had to teach, but not all the conceptions of the Blessed Life which he knew of. He showed them that leaving the principles of doctrine, they were to keep themselves in the Love of Christ, and be strengthened more and more with His Spirit in the inner man, growing up unto Him in all things. But all this by degrees. And so of the weak, we must be content to ask honesty: justice, not generosity, not to sell all, but simple moral teaching. "Thou knowest the Commandments."

With a child, we must ask not sublime forgiveness of injuries: that which would be glorious in a man, in a boy would be pusillanimity; but you must content yourself at first with prohibiting tyranny. There is no greater mistake in education than not attending to this principle. Do not ask of your child to sacrifice all enjoyment for the sake of others, but let him learn first, not to enjoy at the expense of the disadvantage or suffering of another.

Another reason for not neglecting this is, the danger of familiarizing the mind with high spiritual doctrines, and thus engendering hypocrisy; for instance, Self-sacrifice, Self-denial, are large words, which contain much beauty, and are easily got by heart. But the facility of utterance is soon taken for a spiritual state, and while fluently *talking* of these high-sounding words, and of man's or woman's mission and influence, it never occurs to us that as yet we have not power to *live* them out.

Let us avoid such language, and avoid supposing that we have attained such states. It is good to be temperate, but if temperate, do not mistake that for self-denial nor for self-sacrifice. It is good to be honest, to pay one's debts; but when you are simply doing your duty, do not talk of a noble life; be content to say, "we are unprofitable servants — we have done that which was our duty to do."

The danger of extreme demands made on hearts unprepared for such is seen in the case of Ananias. These demands were not, as we see, made by the Apostles, for nothing could be wiser than St. Peter's treatment of the case, representing such sacrifice as purely voluntary, and not compelled. "While it remained, was it not thine own; and after it was sold, was it not in thine own power?" But public opinion, which had made sacrifice *fashionable*, demanded it. And it was a demand, like strong meat to the weak, for Ananias was "unable to bear it."

II. The second remedy in this factious state was to depreciate the part played by man in the great work of progress, and to exhibit the part of God.

"Who, then, is Paul, and who is Apollos, but min isters by whom ye believed?" "Ye are God's husbandry, ye are God's building." In all periods of great social activity, when society becomes conscious of itself, and morbidly observant of its own progress, there is a tendency to exalt the instruments, persons, and means by which it progresses. Hence, in turn, kings, statesmen, parliaments: and then education, science, machinery, and the press, have had their hero-worship. Here, at Corinth, was a new phase, "minister-worship." No marvel, in an age when the mere political progress of the Race was felt to be inferior to the spiritual salvation of the Individual, and to the purification of the Society, that ministers, the particular organs by which this was carried on, should assume in men's eyes peculiar importance, and the special gifts of every such minister, Paul or Apollos, be extravagantly honored. No marvel either, that round the more prominent of these, partizans should gather.

St. Paul's remedy was simply to point out God's part, "Ye are God's husbandry," we are only laborers — different only from wheels and pivots, in that *they* do their work unconsciously, *we* consciously. We execute a plan which we only slightly understand — nay, not at all, till it is completed, like workmen in a tubular bridge, or men employed in Gobelin tapestry, who cannot see the pattern of their work until the whole is executed. Shall the hodman boast? Conceive the laborer saying of some glorious architecture, Behold my work! or some poet, king, or priest, in view of some progress of the race, See what I have done! Who is *Paul*, but a servant of Higher plans than he knows? And thus we come to find that we are but parts in a mighty system, the breadth of which we cannot measure.

And this is the true inspired remedy for all party spirit, "He that planteth, and he that watereth, are one." Each in his way is indispensable. To see the part played by each individual in God's world, which he alone *can* play, to do our own share in the acting, and to feel that each is an integral, essential portion of the whole, not interfering with the rest; to know that each church, each sect, each man, is co-operating best in the work when he expresses his own individuality (as Paul and Cephas, and John and Barnabas did), in truths of word and action which others perhaps cannot grasp, *that* is the only emancipation from partizanship.

Again, observe, St. Paul held this sectarianism, or partizanship, to amount virtually to a denial of their Christianity. For as Christians it was their privilege to have direct access to the Father through Christ; they were made independent of all men but the one Mediator Christ Jesus. Whereas this boast of dependence upon men, instead of *direct* communion with God, was to glory in a forfeiture of their privileges, and to return to the Judaism, or Heathenism, from which they had been freed. He says, "While one saith I am of Paul, and another I am of Apollos, are ye not carnal and walk as men?" So that all sectarianism is slavery and narrowness, for it makes us the followers of such and such a leader. Whereas, says St. Paul, instead of your being that leader's, that leader is yours; your minister, whom you are to use. For "*All* things are yours;" the whole universe is subservient to your moral being and progress. Be free then, and use them: do not be used by them.

Remark, therefore, how the truest spiritual freedom and elevation of soul spring out of Christian humility. All this liberty and noble superiority to Life and Death, all this independence of Men, of Paul, or Apollos, or Cephas, as their masters, arises from this, that "ye are Christ's, and Christ is God's;" that ye, as well as they, are servants only of Christ, who came not to do His own will, but the Will of Him who sent Him.

LECTURE VII.

NOVEMBER 9, 1851.

1 CORINTHIANS, iii. 11–23. — "For other foundation can no man lay than that is laid, which is Jesus Christ. — Now if any man build upon this foundation gold, silver, precious stones, wood, hay, stubble; — Every man's work shall be made manifest: for the day shall declare it, because it shall be revealed by fire; and the fire shall try every man's work of what sort it is. — If any man's work abide which he hath built thereupon, he shall receive a reward. — If any man's work shall be burned, he shall suffer loss: but he himself shall be saved; yet so as by fire. — Know ye not that ye are the temple of God, and that the Spirit of God dwelleth in you? — If any man defile the temple of God, him shall God destroy; for the temple of God is holy, which temple ye are. — Let no man deceive himself. If any man among you seemeth to be wise in this world, let him become a fool, that he may be wise. — For the wisdom of this world is foolishness with God. For it is written, He taketh the wise in their own craftiness. — And again, The Lord knoweth the thoughts of the wise, that they are vain. — Therefore let no man glory in men. For all things are yours; — Whether Paul, or Apollos, or Cephas, or the world, or life, or death, or things present, or things to come; all are yours; — And ye are Christ's; and Christ is God's."

As the last time we treated of the first ten verses of this chapter, to-day we shall go on to the end, merely recapitulating, beforehand, the leading subjects we were then led to enlarge upon; which were, first — Paul's treatment of the Corinthian Church when it was in a state of schism, broken up into parties, one party following Apollos, attracted by his eloquence; another Paul, attracted by his doctrine of Christian liberty; another Peter, whom they looked on as the champion of the Judaistic tendency, while another called themselves by the name of Christ. And the schism which thus prevailed was no light matter, for it was not only a proof of carnal views, but it amounted also to a denial of Christianity. For men emancipated by Christ, and given direct access to God, to return again to allegiance to *men*, and dependence on them, was voluntarily to forfeit all Christian privileges. It is very interesting to observe the difference in St. Paul's treatment of the Corinthian Church from his treatment of other Churches. He says to them, "I have fed you with milk, for hitherto ye were not able to bear meat, neither yet are ye able." There is a remarkable difference between this Epistle to the Corinthians and that to the Ephesians. It is not in the former that we find the Apostle speaking of the breadth and length and depth and height of the love of Christ, which passeth knowledge; nor there do we find him speaking of the beauty and necessity of self-sacrifice. These were subjects too high for them as yet, but instead we find him dealing almost entirely with the hard, stern duties and commandments of every-day life.

St. Paul's twofold method of dealing with the Corinthian Church in their state of faction was, —

1. Through an economic reserve of Truth.

By which we understood, that first principles only were distributed to feeble minds, to men who were incapable of the Higher Life; that they were fed with these, in the same way as children, incapable of receiving meat, are nourished with milk.

2. The depreciation of the Human, through the reduction of ministers to their true position; by pointing out that they were only laborers, servants in God's world, only a part of the curious clockwork of this world of His. Thus each would be a part of one great Whole, each would be called upon to work, as essential to this, but not to exhibit his *own* idea; each would best preserve his own individuality, when most acting as a fellow-worker with God.

Now observe! Here was a true notion of Christian unity as opposed to schism. "He that planteth, and he that watereth, are one." And this is the idea I have so often given you — unity in variety. St. Paul did not say you are wrong, you ought to be all of one way of thinking. No; he said rather, there is one truth, the ritualistic truth, in St. Peter's and St. James's mind ; there is another, the truth of Christian Liberty, which I teach you ; there is another, the truth of grace and beauty in Apollos, and all *together* build up a Church. And he made use of two metaphors, drawn from agriculture and architecture. How foolish it would be to dispute about the respective merits of planting and watering! Could there be a harvest without either? How foolish to talk of the superiority of capital over labor, or labor over capital! Could anything be done without both? And again, who would dream in architecture of a discussion about the comparative importance of the foundation and the superstructure! Are not both necessary to each other's perfection? And so to dispute whether the Gospel according to St. Paul or St. James, is the right Gospel, to call the latter "Straminca Epistola," is to neglect the majestic entireness, and the unity of the truth of God. And observe, St. Paul did not say, as many now would say, you must attain unity by giving up your own views, and each one holding the same. He did not say, Mine are right, and the followers of Apollos and Peter must follow me ; but he said that, whatever became of their particular views, they were to rejoice in this — not that they were Christians of a particular kind, but that they had a common Christianity. There was and could be but One Foundation, and he who worked, whether as builder or architect, on this, was one with all the rest. The chapter concludes with —

I. An address to ministers.
II. To congregations.

I. To ministers. "Let every man take heed, how he buildeth thereupon ; for other foundation can no man lay than that is laid, which is Jesus Christ." First, then, ministers are to preach as the foundation — Christ.

Now, let us protest against all party uses of this expression. The preaching of Christ means simply, the preaching of Christ. Recollect what Paul's own Christianity was. A few facts respecting his Redeemer's life, a few of his Master's precepts, such as, "It is more blessed to give than to receive," out of which he educed all Christian principles, and on which he built that noble superstructure — his Epistles. Remember how he sums all up. "That I might know Him, and the power of His resurrection, and the fellowship of His sufferings, being made conformable unto His death." His Life, Death, and Resurrection, working daily in us, "being made manifest in our body." And again, "Ever bearing about in the body the dying of the Lord Jesus." Settle it in your hearts; Christianity is Christ; understand Him, breathe His Spirit, comprehend His mind: Christianity is a Life, a Spirit. Let self die with Christ, and with Him rise to a life of holiness: and then, whether you are a Minister or ministered to, you need not care what discussions may arise, nor how men may dispute your Christianity, or deny your share in the Gospel. You stand upon a rock.

Next, on this foundation we are to build the superstructure. Christianity is a few living pregnant *principles*, and on these you may construct various buildings. Thus in doctrine you may on this erect Calvinism, or Arminianism; or in ecclesiastical polity, you may build on this a severe, simple worship, or a highly ritual one, or an imaginative one with a splendid cultus. Or, in life, you may live on this devotionally or actively; you may pursue the life of the hermit of the third century, or of the Christian merchant of the nineteenth. For Christianity is capable of endless application to different circumstances, ages, and intellects.

Now, in the words of this twelfth verse, observe that there are not six kinds of superstructure, but two. Gold, silver, and precious stones, which are the materials of the temple; wood, hay, and stubble, with which a cottage is erected; but in these buildings the materials of each are of various degrees of excellence, and in the atter, good, bad, and indifferent. Now, what do these symbolize? As I said before, perhaps doctrines or systems; but more probably they are to make us recollect that the Church is made up of *persons* of different kinds of character built up by different ministers. Some of straw, utterly worthless; some of silver, sound, good, but not brilliant men; some of gold, characters in which there seems nothing of base alloy, true to the very centre; some of precious stones, men in whom gifts are so richly mingled with useful qualities, that they are as jewels in the Redeemer's crown. And such was the author of this Epistle. It does our heart good to know that out of our frail Humanity, anything so good and great has arisen as the Apostle of the Gentiles.

Now there follows from all this, the doctrine of the rewardableness of Work. All were one, on the one foundation, yet St. Paul modifies this: they were not one, in such a sense that all their work was equally valuable, for "every man shall receive his own reward, according to his labor." It is incredible that the mere theologian defending the outworks, writing a book on the Evidences of Christianity, or elaborating a theological system, shall be as blessed as he, who has hungered and thirsted with Christ, and like Christ, suffered. "To sit on the right hand and on the left of the Father," can be given but to them who have drunk of Christ's cup of Self-sacrifice, and been baptized with His Baptism of Suffering. Nevertheless, each in his own way shall gain the exact recompense of what he has done. Therefore, Christian men, work on — your work is not in vain. A cup of cold water, given in the name of a disciple, shall not lose its reward.

There is also here a distinction between the truth of work and its sincerity. In that day nothing shall stand but what is true; but the sincere worker, even of untrue work, shall be saved; "If any man's work shall be burned, he shall suffer loss: but he himself shall be saved; yet so as by fire." Sincerity shall save him in that day, but it cannot accredit his work. But what is this day? When is this day? Generally speaking, we say that it is Time; but more particularly the Trial day, which every advent is, and especially the last: in which nothing will endure but what is real. Nothing gilded or varnished will remain, but only precious stones, gold, silver; and these only so far as they are unmixed; for just as fire burns straw, so must all that is not based on the truth perish. Then the elaborate systems of theology, built by our subtle, restless, over-refined intellects, shall be tried and found worthless. Then many a Church order, elaborately contrived, shall be found something unnecessarily added to the foundation, and overlaying it. And then many a minister, who has prided himself on the number of his listeners, will be stripped of his vain-glory, if the characters, which he has produced, be found wanting; if that which seems to be souls won for God, turns out to be only hearts won for self. Yet here a consolation is given to us, "Yet he himself shall be saved, but so as by fire;" and this is the comfort. Sincerity does not verify doctrine, but it saves the man; his person is accepted, though his work perish. Hence we trust that many a persecutor like Paul shall be received at last; that many a bigot like James and John, desiring to call down fire from heaven, shall obtain mercy, because he did it ignorantly. He shall be saved, while all his work shall be destroyed, just as, to use St. Paul's metaphor, a builder escapes from his house which has been burnt over his head, and stands trembling, yet safe, looking on his work in ruins, "saved, yet so as by fire."

II. An address to congregations.

1. A warning against all Ministers, who should so teach as to split the Church into divisions. "Know ye not that ye are the temple of God, and that the Spirit of God dwelleth in you? If any man defile the temple of God, him shall God destroy; for the temple of God is holy, which temple ye are."

Let us consider in what sense the word "holy" is used. The Bible often speaks of things, not as they are actually in themselves, but as they exist in God's Idea. So it declares of Humanity, that it is "very good;" saying it of *man*, but not of *men*, who are often very bad. And so also the representation of the Church is a thing wholly ideal, "without spot or wrinkle, or any such thing;" whereas, actual churches are infinitely below this ideal. Now observe that St. Paul calls all in the Corinthian Church "holy," and this, though he knew that some were even incestuous — nay, though he says in the very verse where he calls them holy, that some might be defiled, and some destroyed. And hence it follows that we have no right to divide our congregations into regenerate and unregenerate, worldly and unworldly, Christian and un-Christian. Him who doeth this "shall God destroy." Woe, therefore, to that minister, who by arbitrary distinctions respecting worldliness for instance, and unworldliness, so divides the Church of God; making the religious into a party, often making sad hearts which God has not made sad, and nursing a set of Pharisees into a delusion that *they* are a Church of God, because they follow some Paul or some Apollos.

2. A warning against sectarianism, on the ground of Christian liberty. "Therefore let no man glory in men, for all things are yours; whether Paul, or Apollos, or Cephas, or the world, or life, or death, or things present, or things to come; all are yours." Man enters this world, finding himself in the midst of mighty Forces, stronger than himself, of which he seems the sport and prey. But soon Christianity reveals to him God's living, personal Will, which makes these things co-operate for his good. And so he learns his own free-will, and uses them as the sailor does the winds, which *as* he uses them become his enemies or his friends.

Then it is that he is emancipated from the iron bondage to circumstances: then all things are his — this marvellous Life, so full of endless meaning, so pregnant with infinite opportunities. Still more, Death, which *seems* to come like a tyrant, commanding him when it will. Death is his in Christ, his minister to lead him to Higher Life. Paul is his, to teach him freedom. Apollos his, to animate him with his eloquence. Cephas his, to fire him with his courage. Every author his, to impart to him his treasures.

But remark, that St. Paul refers all this to the universal Law of Sacrifice. All things are ours on this condition — that we are Christ's. The Law which made Christ God's has made us Christ's. All things are yours, that is, serve you: but they only discharge the mission and obey the law involuntarily, that you are called on to discharge and obey voluntarily: the great law, which makes obedience Blessedness, the law to which Christ was subject, for Christ "was God's." So that, when the law of the Cross is the law of our being, when we have learnt to surrender ourselves; then, and then only, we are free from all things: they are ours, not we theirs: we use them, instead of being crushed by them. The Christian is "creation's heir." He may say triumphantly, "The world, the world is mine!"

LECTURE VIII.

NOVEMBER 16, 1851.

1 CORINTHIANS, iv. 1-7. — "Let a man so account of us, as of the ministers of Christ, and stewards of the mysteries of God. — Moreover it is required in stewards, that a man be found faithful. — But with me it is a very small thing that I should be judged of you, or of man's judgment; yea, I judge not mine own self. — For I know nothing by myself; yet am I not hereby justified : but he that judgeth me is the Lord. — Therefore judge nothing before the time, until the Lord come, who both will bring to light the hidden things of darkness, and will make manifest the counsel's of the hearts : and then shall every man have praise of God. — And these things, brethren, I have in a figure transferred to myself and to Apollos for your sakes; that ye might learn in us not to think of men above that which is written, that no one of you be puffed up for one against another. — For who maketh thee to differ from another ? and what hast thou that thou didst not receive ? Now if thou didst receive it, why dost thou glory, as if thou hadst not received it ? "

THE fourth chapter, like the third, divides itself into two sections. From the first to the seventh verse, an address is given to a congregation. From the seventh to the end of the chapter, St. Paul addresses ministers. To-day our subject, comprised in the first six verses, is the true estimate of the Christian ministry.

Now the Christian ministry may be either over-glorified or undervalued, and in correction of both these errors, St. Paul says, "Let a man account of us as of the ministers of Christ, and stewards of the mysteries of God."

We consider then,

I. The undue glorification of the Christian ministry.
II. The depreciation of the same.

I. The Christian minister may be glorified or made an idol of in two ways, by party-worship of the *man*, or by attaching a mystical or supernatural power to the *office*.

1st, then, by the worship of the man. This was the particular danger of the Corinthians, as we see distinctly stated in the 6th verse of this chapter. In pronouncing his judgment in this verse, St. Paul, with great delicacy, selects himself and Apollos for his instances, because there could be no suspicion of rivalry between them, for Apollos was of the same school or thought as himself. He speaks of his own party, and that of his friend, as worthy of censure, in order not to blame by name other parties, and the sectarian disciples of other teachers in Corinth. And yet how natural! Let us take these cases as specimens of all. Paul and Apollos each taught a truth, that had taken possession of their souls. St. Paul preached one, as we know, which he called "my Gospel," one peculiarly his own. Such is the case, too, with an inferior minister. Each man, each teacher, now as then, reveals to his hearers that truth which has most filled his own soul, and which is his peculiarly because it most agrees with his character. Well, this truth of his commends itself to kindred spirits in his congregation: it expresses their difficulties, it is a flood of light on many a dark passage of their history; no wonder that they view with gratitude, and an enthusiasm bordering on veneration, the messenger of this blessedness.

And no wonder that the truth thus taught becomes at last the chief, almost the sole, truth proclaimed by him. First, because every man has but one mind, and must, therefore, repeat himself. And, secondly, because that which has won attachment from his congregation, can scarcely be made subordinate in subsequent teaching without losing that attachment; so that, partly for the sake of apparent consistency, partly to avoid offence, and partly from that conservatism of mental habits, which makes it so difficult to break through systems, ministers and congregations often narrow into a party, and hold one truth especially. And so far they do well; but if they shall go on to hold that truth to the exclusion of all other truths, so far as they do that, it is not well; and nothing is more remarkable than the bitter and jealous antagonism with which party-men, who have reached this point, watch all other religious factions but their own. And then the sectarian work is done; the minister is at once the idol and the slave of the party, which he rules by flattering its bigotry, and stimulating its religious antipathies.

Now St. Paul meets this with his usual delicacy: "These things I have in a figure transferred to myself and to Apollos for your sakes, that ye may learn in us not to think of men more highly than it is written, and that no one of you may be puffed up for one against another." And not for Corinth only, but for all who were, or should be, his brethren in Christ, did St. Paul transfer these things to Apollos and himself—for have I not given you a *Home* history?—the exact and likeliest history of many an English party, which began with a truth, and then called it *the* truth; flattering one another, and being "puffed up for one against another," and manifesting that with all their high professions, they were "carnal, and walked as men." But here let us observe the glorious unselfishness of this noble Apostle. Think you, there was no fire of ambition in his heart—that ardent, fiery heart? An Apostle, yes—but not exempt from temptation: with the feelings and passions of a Man! Do you imagine he did not perceive, what is so evident to us, the opportunity within his grasp, of being the great Leader in the Corinthian Church? Think you that he knew nothing of that which is so dear to many a priest and minister in our day—the power of gaining the confidence of his people, the power of having his every word accepted as infallible?

Yet hear this sublime teacher. "I am a minister, a steward only. Who is Paul? I dare not be a party-leader, for I am the servant of Him who came to make all one. He that watereth, and he that planteth, are all one—they, even those Judaizing teachers, who named themselves after Peter, are all servants with me of Christ."

2d. Another mode of undue glorification of the ministry: by attributing supernatural powers and imaginary gifts to the office. Now this mode was quite different, apparently, from the other; so much so, as plainly to mark a party in the opposite extreme; and it was far more necessary to warn some men against this view, for many who would have refused submission to a Man, would have readily yielded it to an Office. Many will refuse obedience to one standing on his personal gifts, or party views; but when one claiming the Power of the Keys, and pretending to the power of miraculous conveyance of the Eternal Spirit in Baptism, or pretending, in shrouded words of mystery, to transform the elements of bread and wine into the very Body and Blood of Christ; or, declaring that he has an *especial* power to receive confession, and a miraculous right to forgive sins, therefore claims homage from the congregation; then, grave men, who turn contemptuously from the tricks of the mere Preacher, are sometimes subdued before those of the Priest. And yet this is but the same thing in another form, against which St. Paul contended in Corinth; for pride and Vanity can assume different forms, and sometimes appear in the very guise of Humility. Power is dear to man, and for the substance, who would not sacrifice the shadow? Who would not depreciate himself, if by magnifying his office he obtained the power he loved?

We have heard of Bernard, who, professing to be unsecular, yet ruled the secular affairs of the world. We have heard of men, who, cut off from human affections, and crushing them relentlessly, have resigned every endearment in life, who nevertheless reigned in their sackcloth with a power which the imperial purple never gave. Affecting to live apart from human policy, and human business, they spread their influence through every department of human thought and life, and government. To appear more than human, to seem a spiritual being, above their fellow-men; for this, men formerly, as well as now, have parted with all that is best in our humanity, its tenderest affections, its most innocent relaxations, and its most sacred and kindliest enjoyments. History affords innumerable examples of this.

II. The depreciation of the Office.

There is a way common enough, but not specially alluded to here, in which the Minister of the Church of Christ is viewed simply in connection with an Establishment as a very useful regulation, on a par with the institutions of the Magistracy and the Police. In this light the minister's chief duty is to lecture the poor, and of all the thousand texts which bear on political existence to preach from only two, "Render unto Cæsar the things which are Cæsar's," and "Let every soul be subject to the higher powers," to be the treasurer and regulator of the different charitable institutions in the town and village, and to bless the rich man's banquet. Thus the office is simply considered a profession, and the common term "living" is the truest exposition of the dignity in which it is held. It is a "living" for the younger branches of noble houses, and an advance for the sons of those of a lower grade who manifest any extraordinary aptness for learning, and who, through the ministry, may rise to a higher position in social life.

In this view a degrading compact is made between the Minister and Society. If he will not interfere with abuses, but leave things as they are: if he will lash only the vices of an age that is *gone by*, and the heresies of *other* churches: if he will teach, not the truth that is welling up in his own soul, but that which the conventionalism of the world pronounces to be the Truth — then shall there be shown to him a certain consideration; not the awful reverence accorded to the Priest, nor the affectionate gratitude yielded to the Christian minister, but the half-respectful, condescending patronage which comes from men, who stand by the Church as they would stand by any other old time-honored Institution; who would think it extremely ill-bred to take God's name in vain in the presence of a clergyman, and extremely unmanly to insult a man whose profession prevents his resenting indignities.

Now it is enough to quote the Apostle's view, "Let a man so account of us as of the ministers of Christ," and at once you are in a different atmosphere of thought.

These things are not essential to the position, for that may cease to be respectable. Society may annihilate a Church Establishment, but yet that which is essential in the office remains: the minister is still a minister of Christ, a steward of the mysteries of God, whose chief glory consists not in that he is respectable, or well-off, or honored, but in that he *serves*, like Him, "Who came not to be ministered unto, but to minister."

Lastly, the office may be depreciated by such a view as these Corinthians were tempted to take.

The Corinthians measured their teachers by their gifts, and in proportion to their acceptability to *them*. So now, men seem to look on the Ministry as an Institution intended for their comfort, for their gratification, nay, even for their pastime. In this way the preaching of the Gospel seems to be something like a lecture, professorial or popular; a thing to be freely found fault with, if it has not given comfort, or shown ability, or been striking or original; a free arena for light discussion and flippant criticism; for, of course, if a man had a right to be an admirer of Paul, he had also to be a blamer of Apollos.

Now see how St. Paul meets this. "With me it is a very small thing that I should be judged of you, or of man's judgment." He simply refuses to submit his authority to any judgment; and this you will say, perchance, was priestly pride, a characteristic haughtiness. Exactly the reverse, it was profound humility. Not because he was above judgment, not because he was infallible, or teaching truths too grand for them, but because he was to be judged before a tribunal far more awful than Corinthian society. Not by man would he be judged, because fidelity is the chief excellence in a steward, and fidelity is precisely that which men cannot judge. They can only judge of gifts, whereas the true dignity of the minister consists not in gifts, nor in popularity, nor in success, but simply in having faithfully used his powers, and boldly spoken the truth which was in him.

St. Paul refuses even to pass judgment on himself. He says, "I know nothing by myself." In the common reading this passage would seem to mean, Whatever I know is not by myself, but by a Higher Power; but what the translator meant, and as it would even now be understood by our north-countrymen, is this, "I know nothing against myself," "I am not conscious of untruth, or lack of fidelity."

"Yet," he goes on to say, "am I not hereby justified: but He that judgeth me is the Lord." Here, then, is what St. Paul appeals to, for another Eye had seen, and He could tell how far the sentence was framed for man's applause; how far the unpleasant truth was softened, not for love's sake, but simply from cowardice. Even the bold unpopularity, that cares not whom it offends, may be, and often is, merely the result of a contentious, warlike spirit, defiant of all around, and proud in a fancied superiority. But God discerns through all this, and sees how far independence is only another name for stubbornness; how even that beautiful avoidance of sectarianism is merely, in many cases, a love of standing alone; a proud resolve not to interfere with any other man's ministry, or to allow any man to interfere with his.

In applying this to our daily life, we must, then,

1. Learn not to judge, for we do not know the heart's secrets. We judge men by gifts, or by a correspondence with our own peculiarities; but God judges by fidelity.

Many a dull sermon is the result of humble powers, honestly cultivated, whilst many a brilliant discourse arises merely from a love of display. Many a diligent and active ministry proceeds from the love of power.

2. Learn to be neither depressed unduly by blame, nor, on the other side, to be too much exalted by praise. Life's experience should teach us this. Even in war, honors fall as by chance, with cruel and ludicrous injustice; often the hero, whom the populace worship, is only made so by accident. Often the coronet falls on brows that least deserve it.

And our own individual experience should teach us how little men know us! How often when we have been most praised and loved, have we been conscious of another motive actuating, than that which the world has given us credit for; and we have been blamed, perhaps disgraced, when, if all the circumstances were known, we should have been covered with honor. Therefore, let us strive, as much as possible, to be tranquil; smile when men sneer; be humble when they praise; patient when they blame. Their judgment will not last; "man's judgment," literally "man's day," is only for a time, but God's is for Eternity. So, would you be secure alike when the world pours its censure or its applause upon you? feel hourly that God will judge. *That* will be your safeguard under both. It will be a small thing to you to be judged of any man's judgment, for your cause will be pleaded before the Judge and the Discerner of all secrets.

LECTURE IX.

NOVEMBER 23, 1851.

1 CORINTHIANS, iv. 7–21. — "For who maketh thee to differ from another? and what hast thou that thou didst not receive? now if thou didst receive it, why dost thou glory, as if thou hadst not received it? — Now ye are full, now ye are rich, ye have reigned as kings without us; and I would to God ye did reign, that we also might reign with you. — For I think that God hath set forth us the Apostles last, as it were appointed to death: for we are made a spectacle unto the world, and to angels, and to men. — We are fools for Christ's sake, but ye are wise in Christ; we are weak, but ye are strong; ye are honorable, but we are despised. — Even unto this present hour we both hunger, and thirst, and are naked, and are buffeted, and have no certain dwelling-place: — And labor, working with our own hands: being reviled, we bless; being persecuted, we suffer it; — Being defamed, we entreat: we are made as the filth of the earth, and are the offscouring of all things unto this day. — I write not these things to shame you, but as my beloved sons I warn you. — For though ye have ten thousand instructors in Christ, yet have ye not many fathers: for in Christ Jesus I have begotten you through the Gospel. — Wherefore I beseech you, be ye followers of me. — For this cause have I sent unto you Timotheus, who is my beloved son, and faithful in the Lord, who shall bring you into remembrance of my ways which be in Christ, as I teach everywhere in every church. — Now some are puffed up, as though I would not come to you. — But I will come to you shortly, if the Lord will, and will know, not the speech of them which are puffed up, but the power. — For the kingdom of God is not in word, but in power. — What will ye? shall I come unto you with a rod, or in love, and in the spirit of meekness?"

THE former part of this chapter is addressed to congregations, in order that a right estimate may be formed by them of the ministerial office, which neither on the one hand ought to be depreciated, nor, on the other, to be unduly valued. We have explained how St. Paul's view was in opposition to all tendencies to worship the man, or to represent the Office as magical or mysterious; and, on the other hand, his view was in direct opposition to all opinions which represent it as a creature and institution of the State, or which value it only as a sphere for the exhibition of gifts and talents. And one definition sufficed the Apostle: "Let a man so account of us as the ministers of Christ, and stewards of the mysteries of God."

And in reference to that right, so liberally assumed, of passing judgment, of awarding praise and blame, of criticizing individual ministers, the Apostle teaches that the same definition excludes this right, because of the impossibility of judgment; for all that a steward can have of merit is fidelity, and fidelity is exactly that which men cannot judge — it is a secret hidden with God.

Now this sin of sectarianism was not imputable to the congregation only. It was also shared by their ministers. There were those who made themselves leaders of parties, those who accepted and gloried in adulation, those who unduly assumed mysterious powers, magnifying their office, that they might personally have that spiritual power which to most men is so grateful.

And here, again, is shown the Apostle's singular delicacy. He names none of those leaders, none of those who were vain of their eloquence or gifts. He only speaks of those who were involuntarily raised to the headship of different factions: Christ, the Lord — Cephas — Apollos — and himself. "These things I have in a figure transferred to myself and to Apollos for your sakes: that ye might learn in us not to think of men above that which is written, that no one of you be puffed up for one against another." That is, these are named for a general, not a specific purpose, that they might learn not to be puffed up for *any* minister. And just because the accusation is not special, therefore should it be universally applied.

We gain nothing from this chapter if we simply learn the historical fact, that in Corinth there were certain parties and sects; and that St. Paul blamed that of Apollos, and that of Cephas, and that likewise which had formed round himself; unless we learn also that there are parties amongst ourselves — one setting up the Church against the Bible, and another the Bible against the Church; one calling itself the "Evangelical" party, *par excellence*, affixing special terms to the names of its reviews and magazines, as if no other publications deserved the name of Christian; another party calling itself "Anglo-Catholic," as though true Catholicity was not rather in spirit than in outward form; every party having its organ, its newspapers and reviews, full of faction and bitterness, and each branding the other with opprobrious names. And unless we learn that St. Paul would have blamed *us*, and taken *our* party spirit as a proof that we are "carnal, and walk as men," we gain nothing from the delicacy of his abstaining from mentioning *names*, that he might teach a *general* principle.

Another lesson, however, we gain. This is an anonymous accusation; but of that rare kind, that not the name of the accuser, but of the accused, is suppressed. If all this were anonymous then, surely it should be so with us now. Our accusations should be personal, that is, directed against ourselves, for the Apostle names himself. There should exist a readiness to see our own faults, and those of our own Party or Church; and not only the faults of other Parties or other Churches.

However, though St. Paul does not name the men, he does not leave them unrebuked. He addresses them in a way that they would understand, and that all would understand for whom comprehension was necessary; for, in verse 7, he turns to those whom he had all along in mind: "Who maketh thee to differ from another? and what hast thou that thou didst not receive? Now if thou didst receive it, why dost thou glory as if thou hadst not received it?" And having thus addressed himself particularly to congregations, St. Paul, in conclusion, speaks especially to ministers.

The first principle that he lays down is —

A warning to those who fostered the personal worship of the ministers — that is, of themselves.

Secondly. To those who unduly magnified the office.

I. To such as fostered a personal worship of the ministers.

The qualities which are requisite for the higher part of the ministry are — great powers of sympathy; a mind masculine in its power, feminine in its tenderness; humbleness; wisdom to direct; that knowledge of the world which the Bible calls the wisdom of the serpent; and a knowledge of evil which comes rather from repulsion from it than from personal contact with it. But those qualifications which adapt a man for the merely showy parts of the Christian ministry are of an inferior order: fluency, self-confidence, tact, a certain histrionic power of conceiving feelings, and expressing them.

Now it was precisely to this class of qualities that Christianity opened a new field in places such as Corinth. Men who had been unknown in their trades, suddenly found an opportunity for public addresses, for activity, and for leadership. They became fluent and ready talkers; and the more shallow and self-sufficient they were, the more likely it was that they would become the leaders of a faction. And how did the Apostle meet this?

He had shown before that Christ was crucified in weakness. Now he shows that the disposition to idolize intellect was directly opposed to this — Christ the crucified was the Power of God. So far, then, as they taught or believed that the power lay in gifts, so far they made the Cross of none effect: "If any man among you seemeth to be wise" (*i. e.* has the reputation), "let him become a fool, that he may be wise."

But he alleges two thoughts in verse 7, to check this tendency. Christian dependence: "Who maketh thee to differ?" Christian responsibility: "What hast thou, that thou didst not receive?"

This tendency, which the Apostle rebukes, besets us ever. Even at school, in the earliest stage of boyhood, we see that brilliancy is admired, whilst plodding industry is almost sure to be sneered at. Yet which of these two characters would St. Paul approve? Which shows fidelity? The dull mediocre talent faithfully used, or the bright talent used only for glitter and display? St. Paul, in the verse quoted, crushes vanity by reminding us of responsibility. His method is the true one, for we cannot meet vanity by denying gifts. If we or our children have beauty of person, have talents and accomplishments, it is in vain we pretend to depreciate, or to shut our eyes to them.

St. Paul did not do this, for he acknowledged their worth. He said, "Covet earnestly the best gifts." He did not sneer at eloquence, nor contemn learning; but he said, These are your responsibilities. You are a steward: you have received. Beware that you be found faithful. Woe unto you if accomplishments have been the bait for admiration, or if beauty has left the mind empty, or even allured others to evil. Woe, if the gifts and manner, that have made you acceptable, have done no more. In truth, this independence of God is man's fall. Adam tried to be a Cause; to make a Right; to be separate from God; to enjoy without God; to be independent, having a will of his own: and just as all things are ours, if we be Christ's, so, if we be not Christ's, if the Giver be ignored in our enjoyments and our work, then all things are not ours: but pleasures are enjoyed, and gifts used in the way of robbery. Stolen pleasures; stolen powers; stolen honors; all is stolen when "we glory as if we had not received."

II. Warning to those who unduly magnified the office.

There were men who prided themselves as being ministers: successors of the Apostles, who exercised lordship, authority, and reigned as kings over the congregations.

The Apostle says, "Now ye are full, now ye are rich." Be it so. How comes then the contrast? "But God hath set forth us the Apostles last, as it were appointed to death; for we are made a spectacle unto the world, and to angels, and to men." Now place these two verses side by side, and think, first of all, of these teachers — admired, flattered, and loaded with presents.

See them first made rich, and then going on to rule as autocrats, so that when a Corinthian entertained his minister, he entertained his oracle, his infallible guide, still more, his very religion.

And then, after having well considered this phrase, turn to contemplate the apostolic life as painted in this last verse. If the one be an Apostle, what is the other? If one be the High life, the Christian life, how can the other be a life to boast of?

Remark here the irony: "Now ye are full, now ye are rich, ye have reigned as kings without us." And again: "We are fools for Christ's sake, but ye are wise in Christ: we are weak, but ye are strong: ye are honorable, but we are despised." It is in vain we deny these words are ironical. People who look upon Christianity as a mere meek, passive, strengthless, effeminate thing, must needs be perplexed with passages such as these, and that other passage, too, in Christ's lips: "Full well ye reject the commandment of God, that ye may keep your own tradition." "Full well!" How terrible the irony to call that *well* which was most *ill!* The truth is, that in Christ, — the perfect Human Nature, — the manlier and more vigorous feelings and emotions did not undergo excision. Resentment, indignation, these are to be guided, controlled, not cut out. True it is, that in *our* practice they are nearly always *evil;* for does not indignation frequently become spite, and resentment turn to malice? Nevertheless, they are both integral parts of human nature. Our character is composed of these elements. In Christ they existed, how strongly! But yet when he used them to rebuke living *men* they are changed at once. He blighted Pharisaism with irony and terrible invective. But to the actual, living Pharisee, how tenderly did he express Himself! "Simon, I have somewhat to say unto thee." Evil is detestable; and the man who mixes himself with it is so far obnoxious to our indignation. But so far as he is a *man*, he is an object of infinite pity and tenderness.

And in St. Paul's irony we remark somewhat of the

same characteristics. It becomes even sarcasm if you will, but there is no shadow of a sneer in it. He who has never experienced the affectionate bitterness of love, who has never known how *earnest* irony, and passionate sarcasm, may be the very language of Love in its deepest, saddest moods, is utterly incapable of even judging this passion. And remark how gracefully it turns with him from loving though angry irony, to loving aspiration: "I would to God ye did reign." They were making this a time for triumph, whereas it was the time for suffering. And St. Paul says, I would the time for reigning were come indeed, for then we should be blessed together. Ye are making a noble time of it with this playing at kings! Be it so. Would to God that it were not an anachronism! Would to God that the time for triumph were come indeed, that these factions might cease, and we be kings together!

See then, here, the true doctrine of the apostolical succession. The apostolical office is one thing; the apostolical character, which includes suffering, is quite another thing; often they are totally opposed.

And just as the true children of Abraham were not his lineal descendants, but the inheritors of his faith, so the true apostolical succession consists not in what these men pride themselves upon — their office, their theological attainments, their ordination, the admiration of their flocks, the costly testimonials of affection, which had made them "rich;" but it consists rather in a life of truth, and in the *suffering* which inevitably comes as the result of being true. Let bishops, let ministers, let *me* ever remember this.

Now, therefore, we can understand the passage with which he ends: "Wherefore, I beseech you, be ye followers of me." Only do not misread it. It might sound as if Paul were inviting them to become his followers, instead of following Cephas or Apollos. But that would be to forget the whole argument. To say that, would have been to have fallen into the very error that he blamed, and to have opposed and contradicted his own depreciation of himself; to have denied every principle he had been establishing. No: you have here no mere partizan trying to outbid and outvie others; it is not the oratory of the platform commending one sect or one society above another.

Paul is not speaking of doctrine, but of life. He says that the *life* he had just described was the one for them to follow. In *this* — "Be ye followers of me," he declares the life of suffering, of hardship in the cause of duty, to be higher than the life of popularity and self-indulgence. He says that the dignity of a minister, and the majesty of a man, consist not in "Most Reverend," or "Most Noble," fixed to his name; not in exempting himself from the common lot, and affecting not to mix with mean occupations and persons; not in affecting that peculiar spirituality which is above human joys, and human pleasures, and human needs. But it lies in this, in being not superhuman, but human; in being through and through a *man*, according to the Divine Idea: a man whose chief privilege it is to be a minister — that is, a servant, a follower of Him who "came not to be ministered unto, but to minister, and to give His Life a ransom for many."

LECTURE X.

THE CHRISTIAN IDEA OF ABSOLUTION.

August 1, 1852.

2 Corinthians, ii. 10–11. — "To whom ye forgive anything, I forgive also: for if I forgave anything, to whom I forgave it, for your sakes forgave I it in the person of Christ. — Lest Satan should get an advantage of us; for we are not ignorant of his devices."

In order that we may more fully understand the meaning of the sentence pronounced upon the Corinthian sinners by St. Paul, I have determined to enter on the question of absolution to-day, and have therefore deviated from the direct line of exposition, and taken a text from the Second Epistle, in which the principle of Christian absolution is fully comprised.

In the first Epistle to the Corinthians St. Paul refers to a crime which had brought great scandal on their Church; and it seems that, instead of being shocked, the Corinthians rather gloried in their laxity, or, as they called it, liberality.

On the offender the Apostle had demanded that a severe punishment should fall. They were to "put away from themselves that wicked person." But in the interval which had elapsed between the two Epistles a great change had taken place. The Corinthians had obeyed, and that in earnest. Their indignation and zeal had been thoroughly roused, and the terrible treatment of society had wrought a deep remorse in the offenders which was threatening to pass into despair.

In this Second Epistle, therefore, he requires forgiveness, he reverses his mode of treatment — ii. 6, 7. In the text he ratifies that forgiveness. Here, then, we are brought face to face with the fact of Christian Absolution. For, let us clearly understand: this forgiveness was not forgiveness of an offence against the Apostle, or against any man. It was not a debt, nor an insult — it was a crime. And yet though a crime against God, Paul says, "I forgive it, you must forgive it." He did not say, "He must confess to God, perhaps God will forgive." Here there is evidently a sin against God forgiven by man. Here, then, is the fact of Absolution.

This is our subject; one which is a battle-ground between Romanists and Protestants. I shall not attempt to steer adroitly a middle course between Romanism and Protestantism, the first asserting an absolving power in the priesthood, the second denying it in every shape and form to any human being. I shall avoid that *via media* which, to timid minds, seems safe and judicious because not going into extremes, but which does yet, like all weak things, manage to embrace the evils of both, and the good of neither. But, as on other occasions, I shall try to seize that deep truth which lies at the root of both views, and which alone can explain the difficulties which beset the question.

First, then — False conceptions respecting Absolution.

Secondly. The Scripture principle on which it rests.

I. The false conceptions.

1. The first would be a denial *in toto* of the existence of such a power in any sense. There are, and were, men who might have objected to St. Paul as the scribes did to his Lord — "Who is this that forgiveth sins also? Who can forgive sins but God only?" And observe there *was* much truth in that objection — Who can forgive sins but God? And if a man may absolve another man, will not sin be committed easily and carelessly? Will not the salutary effect of dread and of uncertainty be done away with? How dangerous to remove the apprehension of punishment! How fearful to send any one to a brother man instead

of to God alone! These are plausible difficulties, and in great part true. But still remember how Christ replied to that objection. He performed a miracle to show that as He could do the difficult thing — as He could say with power — "Arise, and take up thy bed and walk," so He could do the more difficult — "Thy sins be forgiven thee."

Now it is often said that by that miracle He proved His Godhead, that He took them at their word. "No one can forgive sins but God." See, then, I can forgive; therefore I am God. But to read the passage so is utterly to lose the meaning. He did not say that He forgave as God. He expressly said that He forgave as man — "That ye may know that the *Son of Man* hath power on earth to forgive sins." He says nothing about the forgiveness by God in heaven. All He speaks of is respecting the power of forgiveness by man on earth. But whatever we may make of that passage, our text is one which cannot be twisted. We say, Christ forgave as the Messiah, not as Man; He did not speak of a power belonging to *any* son of man, but to *the* Son of Man. Be it so: but here is a passage which cannot be so gotover. His Apostle Paul, *a* son of man, uses words identical with His: "To whom ye forgive anything, I *forgive*." We are driven, then, to the conclusion, that in some sense or other human beings have an absolving power.

2. The second error is, that which would confine this power to the Apostles. "St. Paul absolved — yes: but St. Paul was inspired; he could read hearts, and could absolve because he knew when penitence was real; but you must not extend that to men now." In reply to this observation, take two facts. 1. We have been denying for 300 years that man's forgiveness can be in any sense an assurance of God's. We have fiercely, "like good Protestants," opposed any absolving power in man. What has been our success? Surely it has been failure. We have said, "Go to God, He forgives." But men have not gained rest or peace by this. Out of the very ranks of Protestantism men and women are

crying — "Absolve me from the weight of sin that I cannot bear alone." Shall we then, in rigid dogmatism, cruelly say, "There is nothing for you beyond this — Go to God," which we have said a thousand times? or shall we say, "It is time to pause and ask ourselves what real truth lies at the bottom of this irrepressible desire. However Rome may have caricatured the truth, let us not fear to search it out?"

Again. Whether you will or not, this power is a fact; for thus runs Christ's commission to His Church: "Whosesoever sins ye remit, they are remitted unto them; and whosesoever sins ye retain, they are retained." Say, if you will, that was a peculiar power, limited to the Apostles. Nevertheless, the fact cannot be controverted, that every day and every hour Society — man, exerts this power. For example: There are sins after committing which Society permits a return; there are others in which Society is inexorable. In military life cowardice is branded with irrevocable infamy. Among women, another class of sins admits of no return. You are permitted by the world to defraud your tradesman; debts may be "honorably contracted", which there is no ability of paying: but if a gambler shirks his "debts of honor," he has to fly disgraced. And the results of this are clear. A man may be, in military life, dissipated, which is morally as bad as cowardice; a woman may be selfish or censorious, or kill by bitter words; and yet these are faults not made hopeless by Society: they leave room for other excellences — they do not *blight* character. But for a coward, or a "daughter of shame," once fallen, there is no return. Down, down, and deeper yet to the deeps of infamy, must one sink on whom Society has set its black mark.

Here is a fearful exercise of power. The sins which Society has bound on earth *are* bound; the sins which Society has loosed, are thereby robbed of a portion of their curse. It is a power often wrongly used, but still an incontrovertible, terrific power. Even from unworthy lips these words, "We forgive," have an absolving power, like all our other powers, capable of perversion and misuse. And such a possibility the Apostle intimates here: "lest Satan should get an advantage over us." What he meant by this expression is told in the seventh verse. For he well knew how the sentence of Society crushes. He knew how it drives, first, into despondency, and how despondency seeks a temporary refuge in superstition, and how, that failing, the soul passes into infidelity, desperate and open. That might have been the career of this man. And it would have only proved, that if man will not recognize or allow his power of absolving, he cannot hinder the effects and working of his power of binding sins upon the character.

3. The third error is, that which monopolizes Absolution for the Priesthood. The Romanist claims this most largely. He does not confine it to the Apostles. He asserts it as the privilege of their successors. He says that the power to bind and loose belongs to the Church now; by a special right delegated to the Priesthood only. They cry out for the power of the keys. The descendants of the Apostles have power, and they alone, to bind and loose. "Whosesoever sins ye remit, they are remitted; and whosesoever sins ye retain, they are retained." Well, the question is, In what sense, and by virtue of what power, the Apostles did this? We need no reply beyond the text. If we can find an instance of their doing this, we can understand the nature of the privilege, and to whom it extends. Such an instance we have here. The Apostle Paul, in exercise of the right so delegated, absolves the Corinthian sinner. But observe, in whatever sense he claimed the right for himself, in that sense he also claimed it for the whole Church. He forgave because they did. He asks *them* to forgive. He says, "for your sakes forgave I it." So if the Apostle Paul absolved, then the whole body also of the Corinthian Church absolved.

II. The Principle on which Absolution rests.

It rests on the *mediatorial* character of Humanity.

"For your sakes I forgave *in the person of*" (*i. e.*, in the stead of) "Christ." But understand that the word "mediatorial" is used by us here, not in the theological, but the natural, popular, and simple sense. It means that which is conveyed through a medium. A mediatorial idea is that through the medium of which we apprehend another idea. As, for example, when the inhabitant of the torrid zone is told that ice, which he has never seen, resembles glass, glass is the mediatorial idea through which the other becomes possible to him. A mediatorial dispensation is one which through the medium of things earthly conveys conceptions otherwise unintelligible, as that of the soul's rest in God through the medium of the Sabbath-day. Now, God is knowable by us only through the medium of Humanity. The idea of God is a mediatorial idea. The Love of God would be unintelligible unless we had loving feelings of our own, unless we felt the love of men to us. An orphan who had never seen his parents, nor known any instance of the parental relation, would be shut out from the conception of all those truths which are conveyed in the announcement — God the Father.

Another remark in passing. Only a man can be the express image of God's Person. Only through a man can there be a revelation; only through a perfect man a perfect revelation. Here is the principle of the Incarnation. And God's forgiveness is unintelligible, actually incredible, except through the human forgiveness which we see. And if you were to imagine the case of one to whom human beings had, with no one exception, been unrelenting, then to that one I suppose God's forgiveness would be not only incredible, but also inconceivable. Or, to take a less extreme case. Suppose that this Corinthian offender had been met on every side with horror and detestation, had seen nowhere a pitying eye, in every street had been shunned and shuddered at. Is it not certain, by the laws of our Humanity, that this judgment of Society would have seemed to him a reflection of the judgment of God, an assurance of coming wrath, a knell of a deeper doom?

On the other hand, would not the forgiveness of the Corinthian society have caused the hope of God's forgiveness to dawn upon his heart, made it seem possible, and by degrees probable, actual, certain? And this in exact proportion, just as the men who so forgave were holy men. The more like God they were, the more would their forgiveness be a type and assurance of God's forgiveness. And also this conviction would become stronger in proportion as this declaration was not the isolated act of one individual, which might seem to be personal partiality, but the act of many, of a society, a body, — of the Church.

Let us show this historically. Throughout the ages, God has been declaring Himself, in His character of Absolver, Liberator, Redeemer. For the History of the Past has not been that of Man trying to express his religious instincts in institutions and priesthoods, but of God uttering Himself and His Idea through Humanity.

1. Moses is called a Mediator in the Epistle to the Galatians. How was this? God sent Moses to deliver his people. "*I am* come to deliver them out of the hand of the Egyptians." "I will send *thee* unto Pharaoh." And Moses understood his commission. He slew an Egyptian, and he supposed that they would have understood that he was their liberator, that they would have seen in the human deliverer the Divine Arm. God was revealing Himself through Moses as the Avenger and Redeemer.

2. The Judges. — First of these came Joshua, whose name, originally Oshea, or Saviour, had Jah added to it to make this clear, that he was a deliverer in whom was to be seen the Unseen. A "Divine Deliverer," reminding the people that he was but the representative of One whose prerogative it is to break the rod of the oppressor.

3. The Prophets. They developed another kind of deliverance, founded on no prescriptive authority, but only on the authority of Truth. They stood up against king and priest. They witnessed against kingcraft,

priestcraft, against false social maxims, against superstitions, against all that was enslaving the Jewish soul. And how did they effect this deliverance? They proclaimed God as He is. Their invariable preface was this, "Thus saith the Lord." They fell back on deep first principles. They said, that "to do justice, to love mercy, to walk humbly with God," was better than praying, and fasting, and sacrifice. They revealed and declared the true Character of God, which had become incredible to the people through the false glosses it had received. And so the Prophet also was the deliverer of his people, loosing them from, not slavery, nor political oppression, but a worse bondage, the bondage which comes from ecclesiastical and civil institutions when they have ceased to be *real*. And thus did they once more exhibit to the world the absolving power of Humanity, when it represents accurately the Divine Mind and Character.

One step further. There is a slavery worse than all these; the power by which the soul, through ignorance of God, is bound in sin. Now consider what the Scribes had been doing; they had reduced the teaching about sin to a science; they had defined the nature and degrees of sins; they had priced each sin, named the particular penance and cost at which it could be tolerated. And thus they had represented God as One who, for a certain consideration, might be induced to sell forgiveness, might be bribed to change His will, and forgive those whom He had intended to condemn. Therefore was One manifested who represented the Divine Character without flaw; in whom the mediatorial idea was perfect, in whom Humanity was the exact pattern and type of Deity, in whom God appeared as the Deliverer in the highest sense, where every miracle manifested the Power to loose, and every tender word the Will to forgive; who established the true relation between God and man, as being not that between a judge and a culprit, but as between a Father and a son. For once the Love of Man was identical with the Love of God; for once Human forgiveness was exactly commensurate with the Divine forgiveness: therefore is He the one Absolver of the Race; therefore has He, *because* the Son of Man, "power on earth to forgive sins;" and, therefore, every absolver, so far as he would free consciences and characters from sins, must draw his power out of that same Humanity. He can free only so far as he represents it, or as St. Paul expresses it here, "forgive *in the person of Christ;*" that is, representatively, for "person" means the character sustained on a stage, which represents, or is a medium through which the one represented is conceived.

In conclusion, let us make two applications.

1. From the fact that the whole Corinthian Church absolved, learn that the power of absolution belongs to every man as man — as "made in the image of God." It belongs in the highest degree to the man who most truly reflects that image, who most truly stands in the person of Christ. Are you a rigid Protestant, stiffly content with a miserable negative, sturdily satisfied to reiterate forever, "Who can forgive sins but God only?" Well, remember first, that maxim of which you are so proud was used by the Scribes before you; a superficial half-truth it is, in its depths false. Next remember, that, perhaps every act of yours is proving the case against you. If you will not do by Love the *absolving* work of the Corinthian Church, you may by severity do the terrible, condemning work of the same Church in darkening the light of hope and of God in the souls of the erring. If you represent God as more severe under the Christian than under the Jewish dispensation, or if you represent Him as the Father of a certain section in consideration of their faith, their church-membership, their baptism, or in consideration of *anything*, except His own universal Love; or, if chiming in with the false maxims of society, you pass proudly by the sinful and the wandering; then, so far as you have darkened the hope of any soul, though you may be saying loudly, "None can forgive but God;" yet with a voice louder still, you will have demonstrated

that even if you will disclaim your power to loose, you cannot part with your awful power to bind.

2. Inasmuch as St. Paul absolved, let us learn the true principle of ministerial absolution. Humanity is the representative of Deity. The Church is the representative of Humanity, the ideal of Humanity. The minister is the representative of the Church. When, therefore, the minister reads the absolution, he declares a Fact. It does not depend on his character or his will. It is a true voice of man on earth echoing the Voice of God in heaven. But if the minister forgets his representative character, if he forgets that it is simply in the name of Humanity and God, "in the person of Christ," if by any mysterious language or priestly artifices he fixes men's attention on himself, or his office, as containing in it a supernatural power not shared by other men; then, just so far, he does not absolve or free the soul by declaring God. He binds it again by perplexed and awe-engendering falsehood, and so far, is no priest at all; he has forfeited the priestly power of Christian Humanity, and claimed instead the spurious power of the priesthood of Superstition.

LECTURE XI.

NOVEMBER 30, 1851.

1 CORINTHIANS, v. 1 – 13. — "It is reported commonly that there is fornication among you, and such fornication as is not so much as named among the Gentiles, that one should have his father's wife. — And ye are puffed up, and have not rather mourned, that he that hath done this deed might be taken away from among you. — For I verily, as absent in body, but present in spirit, have judged already, as though I were present, concerning him that hath so done this deed, — In the name of our Lord Jesus Christ, when ye are gathered together, and my spirit, with the power of our Lord Jesus Christ, — To deliver such an one unto Satan for the destruction of the flesh, that the spirit may be saved in the day of the Lord Jesus. — Your glorifying is not good. Know ye not that a little leaven leaveneth the whole lump? — Purge out therefore the old leaven, that ye may be a new lump, as ye are unleavened. For even Christ our passover is sacrificed for us : — Therefore let us keep the feast, not with the old leaven, neither with the leaven of malice and wickedness; but with the unleavened bread of sincerity and truth. — I wrote unto you in an epistle not to company with fornicators : — Yet not altogether with the fornicators of this world, or with the covetous, or extortioners, or with idolaters; for then must ye needs go out of the world. — But now I have written unto you not to keep company, if any man that is called a brother be a fornicator, or covetous, or an idolater, or a railer, or a drunkard, or an extortioner; with such an one no not to eat. — For what have I to do to judge them also that are without? do not ye judge them that are within? — But them that are without God judgeth. Therefore put away from among yourselves that wicked person."

THERE is but one subject in this chapter on which I shall address you to-day — I mean St. Paul's judgment on the scandal which had befallen the Corinthian Church. The same case was treated before you last Sunday. I took the Absolution first, that we might be prepared for a sentence of great severity, and that we should not think that sentence was final. The whole of this chapter is an eloquent, earnest appeal for judgment on the offender.

St. Paul's sentence was excommunication. "I have judged," he says, "to deliver such an one unto Satan." This is the form of words used in excommunication.

The presiding bishop used to say, formally, "I deliver such an one unto Satan." So that, in fact, St. Paul, when he said this, meant — My sentence is, "Let him be excommunicated."

Our subject, then, is Ecclesiastical Excommunication, or rather the grounds upon which human punishment rests. The first ground on which it rests is a representative one. "In the name of our Lord Jesus Christ, when ye are gathered together, and my spirit with the power of our Lord Jesus Christ." There is used here, then, precisely the same formula as that in Absolution. "For your sakes forgave I it, in the person of Christ." In this place, "person" is a dramatic word. It means the character sustained on the stage by one who represents another. So then, absolving "in the person of Christ," excommunicating "in the name of Christ," implied that Paul did both in a representative capacity. Remember, then, man is the image of God, man is the medium through which God's absolution and God's punishment are given and inflicted. Man is the mediator, because he represents God.

If man, then, were a perfect image of God, his forgiveness and his condemnation would be a perfect echo of God's. But in respect of his partaking of a fallen nature, his acts, in this sense, are necessarily imperfect. There is but One, He in whom Humanity was completely restored to the Divine Image, whose forgiveness and condemnation are exactly commensurate with God's. Nevertheless, the Church here is the representative of Humanity, of that ideal man which Christ realized, and hence, in a representative capacity, it condemns and forgives.

Again, as such, that is, as representative, human punishment is expressive of Divine indignation. Strong words are these, "To deliver unto Satan." Strong, too, are those — "Yea, what indignation, yea, what fear, yea, what vehement desire, yea, what zeal, yea, what revenge!" And St. Paul approved that feeling. Now, I cannot explain such words away. I cannot say the wrath of God is a *figurative* expression, nor dare I say the vengeance of the Law is *figurative*, for it is a mistake to suppose that punishment is only to reform and warn. There is, unquestionably, another truth connected with it; it is the expression on earth of God's indignation in Heaven against sin. St. Paul says of the Civil Magistrate, "For he is the Minister of God, a revenger to execute wrath upon him that doeth evil."

Doubtless, our human passions mingle with that word "vengeance." It is hard to use it, and not conceive of something vindictive and passionate. Yet the Bible uses it, and when our hearts are sound and healthy, and our view of moral evil not morbid and sentimental, we feel it too. We feel that the anger of God is a reality, an awful reality, and that we dare not substitute any other expression. There cannot be such a thing as perfect hatred of wrong, and unmixed love of the wrong-doer. He who has done wrong has identified himself with wrong, and *so far* is an object of indignation. This, of course, in infinite degrees.

In our own day we are accustomed to use strange weak words concerning sin and crime: we say, when a man does wrong, that he has mistaken the way to happiness, and that if a correct notion of real happiness could be given to men, crime would cease. We look on sin as residing, not in a guilty will, but in a mistaken understanding. Thus, the Corinthians looked on at this deed of iniquity, and felt no indignation. They had some soft, feeble way of talking about it. They called it "mental disease," "error," "mistake of judgment," "irresistible passion," or I know not what. St. Paul *did* feel indignation; and which was the higher nature, think you? If St. Paul had not been indignant, could he have been the man he was? And this is what we should feel; this it is which, firmly seated in our hearts, would correct our lax ways of viewing injustice, and our lax account of sin.

Observe, the indignation of Society is properly representative of the indignation of God. I tried last

Sunday* to show how the absolution of Society looses a man from the weight of sin, by representing and making credible God's forgiveness — how it opens him to hope and the path to a new life. Now, similarly, see how the anger of Society represents and makes credible God's wrath. So long as the Corinthians petted this sinner, conscience slumbered; but when the voice of men was raised in condemnation, and he felt himself everywhere shunned, conscience began to do its dreadful work, and then their anger became a type of coming doom. Remember, therefore, there is a real power lodged in Humanity to bind as well as to loose; and remember, that Man, God's representative, may exercise this fearful power wrongly, too long, and too severely in venial faults, yet there is still a power, a terrible human power, which may make outcasts, and drive men to infamy and ruin. Whosesoever sins we bind on earth, they are bound.

Only, therefore, so far as man is Christ-like, can he exercise this power in an entirely true and perfect manner. The world's excommunication or banishment is almost always unjust, and that of the nominal Church more or less so.

The second ground on which human punishment rests is the reformation of the offender. "That the spirit may be saved in the day of the Lord Jesus."

Of all the grounds alleged for punishment, that of "an example to others" is the most heartless and the most unchristian. In Scripture I read of two principal objects of punishment: — first, that which has been given already — punishment as an expression of righteous indignation; the other, the amelioration of the sinner, as is expressed in the above verse. And here the peculiarly merciful character of Christianity comes forth: the Church was never to give over the hope of recovering the fallen. Punishment then, here, is remedial. If Paul punished, it was "that the spirit might be saved in the day of the Lord Jesus." And hence

* This subject is also treated of in a Sermon on "Absolution," which is published in the third volume of Mr. Robertson's Sermons.

(putting capital punishment out of the present question) to shut the door of repentance upon any sin, to make outcasts for ever, and thus to produce *despair*, is contrary to the idea of the Church of Christ, and alien from His Spirit. And so far as Society does that now, it is not Christianized, for Christianity never sacrifices, as the world-system does, the individual to the Society. Christianity has brought out strongly the worth of the single soul. Let us not, however, in treating of this subject, overstate the matter, for it would be too much to say that example is never a part of the object of punishment. Perhaps of the highest Christian idea of punishment it is not. Yet in societies, where, as the spirit of the old world still lingers, Christianity can never be fully carried out, it must be tolerated. For example, the army is a society which is incompatible with the existence of Christianity in its perfection. And here, too, we learn to look with an understanding eye at what else we must blame. When we censure the sanguinary laws of the past, we must remember that they did their work. And even now, the severe judgments and animadversions of Society have their use. Christian they are not, worthy of a Society calling itself Christian they are not; but as the system of a Society only half Christian, such as ours, they have their expediency. Individuals are sacrificed, but Society is kept comparatively pure, for many are deterred from wrong-doing by fear, who would be deterred by no other motive.

The third ground is the contagious character of evil. "A little leaven leaveneth the whole lump." Observe, the evil was not a matter of example, but contagion. Scuh an one as this incestuous man — wicked, impenitent, and unpunished — would infect the rest of the Church. Who does not know how the *tone* of evil has communicated itself? Worldly minds, irreverent minds, licentious minds, *leaven* Society. You cannot be long with persons who by innuendo, double meaning, or lax language, show an acquaintance with evil, without feeling in some degree assimilated to them, nor can you easily retain enthusiasm for right amongst those who detract and scoff at goodness. None but Christ could remain with the impenitent and be untainted; and even where repentance has been deeply felt, familiarity with some kinds of vice unfits a man for association with his fellow-men. A penitent man should be forgiven; but unless you can insure the removal of the mental taint, it does not follow that he is fit for safe intimacy. Perhaps, never in this world again; and it may be part of his terrible discipline here, which we would fain hope is remedial, not penal, to retain the stamp of past guilt upon his character, causing him to be avoided, though forgiven.

The fourth ground was, Because to permit this would be to contradict the true idea of the Church of Christ, "Ye are unleavened." This is the idea of the Church of Christ, a body unleavened with evil, and St. Paul uses a metaphor taken from the Paschal Feast. It was eaten with unleavened bread, and every Jewish family scrupulously removed every crumb of leaven from the house before it began. In like manner, as that feast was eaten with no remnant of the old leaven, so is our Christian jubilee to be kept. All the old life has passed away. We may say, as Paul said of the Corinthians, "Ye are unleavened." A new start, as it were, has been given to you in Christ; you may begin afresh for life. Here, then, is the true conception of the Church: regenerated Humanity, new life without the leaven of old evil.

Let us distinguish, however, between the Church visible and invisible. The Church invisible is "the general assembly and Church of the First-born" spoken of in Hebrews, xii. v. 23. It is that Idea of Humanity which exists in the Mind of God: such as Paul described the Church at Ephesus; such as no Church ever really was; such as only Christ of men has ever been; but such as every Church is potentially and conceivably.* But the Church visible is the actual men professing Christ, who exist in this age, or in that: and

* See Mr. Robertson's Sermon on "The Victory of Faith," Vol. III.

the Church visible exists, to represent, and at last to realize, the Church invisible. In the first of these senses, the Apostle describes the Corinthian Church as "unleavened;" *i. e.* he says, *that* is the idea of your existence. In the second sense, he describes them as they are, "puffed up, contentious, carnal, walking as men."

Now, for want of keeping these two things distinct, two grave errors may be committed.

1. Undue severity in the treatment of the lapsed.

2. Wrong purism in the matter of association with the world, its people, its business, and its amusements.

Into the first of these the Corinthians afterwards were tempted to fall, refusing reconciliation with the sinner. Into this the Church did fall, for a period, in the third century, when Novatian, laying down the axiom that the actual state of the Church ought to correspond with its ideal — in fact, declaring that the Idea of the Church was its actual state — very consistently with this false definition, demanded the non-restoration of all who had ever lapsed.

But the attempt to make the Church entirely pure must fail: it is to be left to a higher tribunal. Such an attempt ever has failed. The parable of the wheat and the tares makes it manifest that we cannot eradicate evil from the Church without the danger of destroying good with it. Only, as a Church visible she must separate from her all *visible* evil, she must sever from herself all such foreign elements as bear unmistakable marks of their alien birth. She is not the Church invisible, but she represents it. Her purity must be visible purity, not ideal: representative, not perfect.

The second error was a misconception, into which, from the Apostle's own words, it was easy to fall; an over rigorous purism, or puritanism.

The Corinthians were to separate from the immoral; but in a world where all were immoral, how was this practicable? Should they buy no meat because the seller was a heathen? nor accept an invitation from him, nor transact business with him, because he was an idolater?

Against an extension of this principle he sedulously guards himself, in the ninth and tenth verses. Paul says to them, You are not to go out of the world, only take care that you do not recognize such sinners by associating with them as *brothers*, or as fulfilling, in any degree, the Christian idea. Indeed, afterwards, he tells them they were free to purchase meat which had been used in heathen sacrifices, and he contemplates the possibility of their accepting invitations to heathen entertainments.

Lastly, let us apply the principles we have now gained to practical life as at present existing: let us see the dangerous results of that exclusiveness which affects the society of the religious only.

The first result that follows is the habit of judging. For, if we only associate with those whom we think religious, we must decide who *are* religious, and this becomes a habit. Now, for this judgment, we have absolutely no materials. And the life of Christ, at least, should teach us that the so-called religious party are not always God's religious ones. The publicans and the harlots went into the kingdom of Heaven before the Pharisees.

And the second result is censoriousness; for we must judge who are *not* religious, and then the door is opened for the slander, and the gossip, and the cruel harshness, which make religious cliques worse even than worldly ones.

And the third result is spiritual pride; for we must judge *ourselves*, and so say to others, "I am holier than thou." And then we fall into the very fault of these Corinthians, who were rejoicing, not that they were Christians, but Christians of a peculiar sort, disciples of Paul, or Apollos, or Cephas. Had they been contented to feel that they had a common salvation — that they had been named by the same Name, and redeemed by the same Sacrifice — vanity had been impossible, for we are only vain of that wherein we *differ* from others. So we, too often rejoicing in thin distinctions, "they," — and "we," fall into that sin, almost the most hopeless of all sins, — spiritual pride.

LECTURE XII.

DECEMBER 7, 1851.

1 CORINTHIANS, vi. 1-12.—"Dare any of you, having a matter against another, go to law before the unjust, and not before the saints?—Do ye not know that the saints shall judge the world? and if the world shall be judged by you, are ye unworthy to judge the smallest matters?—Know ye not that we shall judge angels? how much more things that pertain to this life?—If then ye have judgments of things pertaining to this life, set them to judge who are least esteemed in the church.—I speak to your shame. Is it so, that there is not a wise man among you? no, not one that shall be able to judge between his brethren?—But brother goeth to law with brother, and that before the unbelievers.—Now therefore there is utterly a fault among you, because ye go to law one with another. Why do ye not rather take wrong? why do ye not rather suffer yourselves to be defrauded?—Nay, ye do wrong, and defraud, and that your brethren.—Know ye not that the unrighteous shall not inherit the kingdom of God? Be not deceived: neither fornicators, nor idolaters, nor adulterers, nor effeminate, nor abusers of themselves with mankind,—Nor thieves, nor covetous, nor drunkards, nor revilers, nor extortioners, shall inherit the kingdom of God.—And such were some of you: but ye are washed, but ye are sanctified, but ye are justified in the name of the Lord Jesus, and by the Spirit of our God."

THIS Epistle to the Corinthians differs from the other Epistles of St. Paul in this, that instead of being one consecutive argument on connected subjects, it deals with a large variety of isolated questions which the Corinthian Church had put to him on some previous occasion. Hence this Epistle is one of Christian Casuistry, or the application of Christian principles to the various circumstances and cases of conscience which arise continually in the daily life of a highly civilized, and highly artificial community.

This chapter, the sixth, contains the Apostle's judgment on two such questions.

I. The manner of deciding Christian quarrels.

II. The character of Christian liberty, what is meant by it, and how it is limited.

Of the first of these only I shall speak to-day, and the subject ranges from the first to the twelfth verse.

I. The manner of deciding Christian quarrels.

It appears from this account that questions arose among the Corinthian Christians which needed litigation: questions of wrongs done to persons or to property. Of the former of these we have already met one in the fifth chapter. These wrongs they carried to the heathen courts of judicature for redress. For this the Apostle reproves them severely, and he assigns two reasons for his rebuke: —

1. He desired a power in the Church to decide such difficulties for itself. These questions should be tried before "the saints," that is, by Church judicature; and to support this opinion, he reminds them that "the saints shall judge the world." Let us understand this phrase. Putting aside all speculations, we are all agreed on this, and we are drawn to a recollection of it by this Advent time, that this Earth shall be one day a Kingdom of God. We cannot tell *how* it may be consummated, whether, as some think, by a Miraculous and Personal Coming, or, as others hold, by the slow evolving, as ages pass, of Christian principles; by the gradual development of the mustard seed into a tree, and of the leaven throughout the meal. But this, unquestionably, is true, Human society *shall* be thoroughly christianized. "The kingdoms of this world *shall* become the kingdoms of the Lord and of His Christ." Legislation *shall* be Christian legislation. Law shall *not* then be a different thing from equity. And more, a time is coming when statute law shall cease, and self-government and self-control shall supersede all outward or arbitrary law. That will be the reign of the saints.

Let me then pause and examine the principles, as they are declared in Scripture, of this Kingdom which is to be.

"The saints shall judge." The first principle, then, of the kingdom is the Supremacy of Goodness. It is by holiness that the Earth shall be governed hereafter. For the word "judge" in this verse is used in the same sense as it is used of Deborah and Barak, and others who judged or ruled Israel. So here it does not mean that the saints shall be assessors with Christ at the day of Judgment, but that they shall rule the world. Successively have force, hereditary right, talent, wealth, been the aristocracies of the Earth. But then, in *that* Kingdom to come, goodness shall be the only condition of supremacy. That is implied in this expression, "The saints shall judge."

The second principle is, that the best shall rule. "The Apostles shall sit on twelve thrones, judging the twelve tribes of Israel." Now, take that literally, and you have nothing more than a cold barren fact. You lose your time in investigating theories about thrones, and the restoration of the ten tribes, and the future superiority of the Jews. But take it in the spirit of the passage, and it means, and typically expresses, that in *that* Kingdom the best shall rule.

The third principle is, that there each shall have his place according to his capacity. In 1 Cor. xii. 28, this is plainly laid down. Each man took his position in the Church of Christ, not according to his choice, but according to his charism or his gift. A man did not become a prophet, or a teacher, or an apostle, simply because it was his own desire, or because it was convenient for his parents so to bring him up, but because God had placed him there from his capacity for it. Observe here was a new principle. Each man was to do that for which he was most fitted. So in the Kingdom to come we shall not have the anomalies which now prevail. Men are ministers now who are fit only to plough; men are hidden now in professions where there is no scope for their powers; men who might be fit to hold the rod of empire are now weaving cloth. But it shall be altered there. I do not presume to say *how* this is to be brought about. I only say the Bible declares it shall be so; and until it is so the Kingdom of God is only *coming*, and not come. The Advent of the Saviour is yet to be expected.

These are the things that must be hereafter. And it is only in such a belief that human life becomes tolerable. For a time arrives when our own private schemes have failed, and for us there remains little to be either feared or hoped. At that time of life a man begins to cast his eyes on the weltering confusion of this world, its wrongs, its injustices, its cruel anomalies; and if it were not for a firm and deep conviction that there is a better future for the Race, that the Son of God will come to the restitution of all things, who could suffer being here below?

But to return to the case before us. St. Paul argues, this is the future destiny of the Church. Are these principles, then, to be altogether in abeyance now? Is this Advent to be only a sickly dream without any connection with Life, or is it not rather to be the shaping spirit of Life? In the highest spiritual matters the Church shall decide hereafter. Therefore in questions now of earthly matters, such as in petty squabbles about property, the least esteemed Christian among you should be able to decide. "I speak to your shame;" where are your boasted Christian teachers? Can they not judge in a matter of paltry quarrel about property?

Let us not, however, mistake the Apostle. Let us guard against a natural misconception of his meaning. You might think that St. Paul meant to say that the Corinthians should have ecclesiastical instead of civil courts; and for this reason, that churchmen and clergy will decide rightly by a special promise of guidance, and heathen and laymen wrongly. But this has not to do with the case under consideration. It is not a question here between ecclesiastical and civil courts, but between Law and Equity, between Litigation and Arbitration. No stigma is here affixed, or even implied, on the fairness of the heathen magistracy. The Roman Government was most just and most impartial. St. Paul only means to say that Law is one thing, Equity another. The principles of heathen law were not Christian. Here we meet with the difficulty, then, how far Christianity deals with questions of property, politics, or those quarrels of daily life which require legal interference. A man asked Christ, " Master, speak to my brother that he divide the inheritance with me." And the Saviour refused to adjudicate: "Man, who made me a ruler and judge over you?" Yet *here* St. Paul requires the Christian Church to pronounce a judgment. The Redeemer seems to say, Christianity has nothing to do with deciding quarrels: let them be tried before the appointed judge. St. Paul seems to say Christianity has everything to do with it; go not before the magistrate. Contradictory as these two statements appear, there is no real opposition between them. Christ says, not even the Lord of the Church has power as a *Judge* to decide questions about earthly property. St. Paul says, the Church has Principles, according to which all such matters may be set at rest. And the difference between the worldly court of justice and the Christian court of arbitration is a difference then of diametrical opposition. Law says you shall have your rights; the spirit of the true Church says, defraud not your neighbor of *his* rights. Law says you must not be wronged; the Church says, it is better to suffer wrong than to do wrong.

We cannot, then, but understand that the difference is one of utter contrariety; for the spirit in the one case is, I will receive no wrong — in the other, I will scrupulously take care to do none. In application of this principle, the Apostle says: " Now, therefore, there is utterly a fault among you, because ye go to law one with another." As though he had said that state of society is radically wrong in which matters between man and man must be decided by law. In such a state the remedy is, not more elaborate law, nor cheaper law, nor greater facility of law, but more Christianity: less loud cries about "Rights," more earnest anxiety on both and all sides to do no wrong. For this, you will observe, was in fact the Apostle's ground: " Now therefore there is utterly a fault among you, because ye go to law one with another. Why do ye not rather take wrong? — why do ye not rather suffer yourselves to be defrauded? Nay, ye do wrong, and defraud, and that your brethren." He leaves the whole question of arbitration *versus* law, and strikes at the root of the matter. "Why do ye not rather take wrong? why do ye not rather suffer yourselves to be defrauded?" Why so? Because to bear wrong, to endure — that is Christianity. Christ expressed this in proverbial form: "If a man smite thee on the one cheek, turn to him the other." "If any man sue thee at the law, and take away thy coat, let him have thy cloak also." And now consider: Is there, *can* there be any principle but this which shall at last heal the quarrels of the world? For while one party holds out as a matter of principle, the other appeals to law, and both are well assured of their own rights, what then must be the end? "If ye bite and devour one another," says St. Paul, "take heed that ye be not devoured one of another." Whereas, if we were all christianized, if we were all ready to bear and endure injuries, law would be needless — there would be no cry of "my rights, my rights," you will say, perhaps — But if we bear, we shall be wronged. You forget, I say if *all* felt thus, if the spirit of *all* were endurance, there would be no wrong.

And so, at last, Christianity is finality. The world has no remedy for its miseries but the cure of its selfishness. The Cross of Christ, the spirit of that Sacrifice can alone be the regeneration of the world. The coming Revelation can only be a development of the last, as Christianity was of Judaism. There can be no *new* Revelation. "Other foundation can no man lay than that is laid, which is Jesus Christ." Men have attempted to produce a peaceful and just state of society by force, by law, by schemes of socialism; and one after another, all have failed: — all must fail. There remains, then, nothing but the Cross of Christ, the Spirit of the life and death of Him who conquered the world by being the Victim of its sin.

2. The last reason given by the Apostle in rebuking a litigious and quarrelsome disposition in the Corinthian Christians is, that it contradicts the character of the Kingdom of God, of which they were members. A true kingdom of Christ should be altogether free from persons of this character. His argument runs thus: — You ask me how quarrels are to be decided, except by law; how the oppressed are to be freed from gross oppressors, except by an appeal to legal justice; how flagrant crimes — such as that condemned in the fifth chapter — are to be prevented in Christians? I answer, the Church of Christ does not include *such* persons in the Idea of its existence at all. It only contemplates the normal state; and this is the Idea of the Church of Christ: men "washed, sanctified, justified in the name of the Lord Jesus, and by the Spirit of our God." But drunkards, revilers, extortioners, covetous men, gross sensualists, I cannot tell you how to legislate for such, for such ought not to be in your society at all. Regenerate thieves, regenerate libertines, regenerate extortioners! There is a horrible contradiction in the very thought; there is something radically wrong, when such men, remaining in their vices, are imagined as belonging to the true kingdom of God. This is what you *were* as heathens; this is not what you *are* to be as Christians.

And here you observe, as usual, that the Apostle returns again to the great *Idea* of the Church of God, the invisible Church, Humanity as it exists in the Divine Mind; this is the standard he ever puts before them. He says, This you *are*. If you fall from this, you contradict your nature. And now consider how opposite this, St. Paul's way, is to the common way of insisting on man's depravity. He insists on man's dignity: he does not say to a man, You are fallen, you cannot think a good thought, you are half beast, half devil, sin is alone to be expected of you, it is your nature to sin. But he says rather, it is your nature not to sin; you are not the child of the devil, but the child of God.

Brother men — between these two systems you must choose. One is the system of St. Paul and of the Church of England, whose baptismal service tells the child that he *is* a child of God — not that by faith or anything else he can make himself such. The other is a system common enough amongst us, and well known to us, which begins by telling the child he is a child of the devil, to become, *perhaps*, the child of God. You must choose: you cannot take both; will you begin from the foundation Adam or the foundation Christ? The one has in it nothing but what is debasing, discouraging, and resting satisfied with low attainments; the other holds within it all that is invigorating, elevating, and full of hope.

LECTURE XIII.

DECEMBER 14, 1851.

1 CORINTHIANS, vi. 12-20. — "All things are lawful unto me, but all things are not expedient: all things are lawful for me, but I will not be brought under the power of any. — Meats for the belly, and the belly for meats: but God shall destroy both it and them. Now the body is not for fornication, but for the Lord; and the Lord for the body. — And God hath both raised up the Lord, and will also raise up us by his own power. — Know ye not that your bodies are the members of Christ? shall I then take the members of Christ, and make them the members of an harlot? God forbid. — What? know ye not that he which is joined to an harlot is one body? for two, saith he, shall be one flesh. — But he that is joined unto the Lord is one spirit. — Flee fornication. Every sin that a man doeth is without the body; but he that committeth fornication sinneth against his own body. What? know ye not that your body is the temple of the Holy Ghost which is in you, which ye have of God, and ye are not your own? — For ye are bought with a price: therefore glorify God in your body, and in your spirit, which are God's."

WE have divided this chapter into two branches, the first relating to the right method of deciding Christian quarrels. Our subject last Sunday was the sin of a litigious spirit, and this I endeavored to show in a two-fold way: — 1st. As opposed to the power lodged in the Christian Church to settle quarrels by arbitration on the principles of equity and charity, which are principles quite distinct from law; one being the anxiety to get, the other the desire to do right. And in assurance of this power being present with the Church then, St. Paul reminds the Corinthian Christians of the Advent Day when it shall be complete — when "the saints shall judge the world." For the advent of Jesus Christ, — the Kingdom of God, — is but the complete development of powers and principles which are even now at work, changing and moulding the principles of the world. If hereafter the saints shall judge the world, "are ye unworthy now to judge the smallest matters?"

2d. The second point of view from which St. Paul regarded the sinfulness of this litigious spirit was the consideration of the Idea of the Church of Christ. Christian quarrels! Disputes between Christian extortioners! The idea of the Church of God admits of no such thought — "Ye are washed, ye are sanctified, ye are justified in the name of the Lord Jesus, and in the spirit of our God."

I urged this as the apostolic mode of appeal — to men as redeemed, rather than to men as debased, fallen, reprobate. And I said further, that we must make our choice between these systems — the one, that of modern sectarianism; the other, that of St. Paul, and, as I believe, of the Church of England. We must start from the foundation of Adam's fallen nature, or else from the foundation of Jesus Christ: we are either children of the devil, or we are children of God. St. Paul says to all, "Ye are redeemed."

To-day we are to consider another question, What are the limits of Christian rights?

We can scarcely conceive that the Religion of Jesus Christ could ever be thought to sanction sin and self-indulgence. But so it was. Men in the Corinthian Church, having heard the Apostle teach the Law of Liberty, pushed that doctrine so far as to make it mean a right to do whatsoever a man wills to do. Accordingly he found himself called on to oppose a system of self-indulgence and sensuality, a gratification of the appetites and the passions taught systematically as the highest Christianity.

By these teachers self-gratification was maintained on the ground of two rights.

First. The rights of Christian liberty. "All things are lawful for me."

Secondly. The rights of nature. "Meats for the belly, and the belly for meats," and "God shall destroy both it and them."

First. The rights of Christian liberty. They stiffly

stood on these. Their very watchword was, "All things are lawful." It is easy to understand how this exaggeration came about. Men suddenly finding themselves freed from Jewish law, with its thousand restrictions, naturally went very far in their new principles. For the first crude application of a theory either in politics or religion is always wild. They said, We may eat what we will. We are free from the observance of days. All things are lawful. That which is done by a child of God ceases to be sin. St. Paul met this exaggeration by declaring that Christian liberty is limited, first, by Christian expediency — "All things *are* lawful" — yes, "but all things are not expedient;" and secondly, by its own nature — "All things are lawful for me, but I will not be brought under the power of any."

We will consider first the meaning of Christian expediency. It is that which is relatively best — the best attainable. There are two kinds of "best:" — the "best" absolutely, and the "best" under present circumstances. It is absolutely best that war should cease throughout the world. Relatively, it is best, under present circumstances, that a country should be ready to defend itself if attacked. A defensive fleet is expedient, and relatively best, but not the absolutely Christian best.

Now that which limits this liberty is, the profit of others. For example, in the northern part of these islands the observance of the Sabbath is much more rigorous than it is here. The best conceivable would be that all over Christendom the free high views of the Apostle Paul should be spread, the doctrine of the sanctification of all time. But so it is not yet. In the North, on Sunday, men will not sound an instrument of music, nor take a walk except to a place of worship. Now, suppose that an English Christian were to find himself in some Highland village, what would be his duty? "All things are lawful for" him. By the law of Christian liberty he is freed from bondage to meats or drinks, to holidays or Sabbath days; but if his use of this Christian liberty should shock his brother Christians, or should become an excuse for the less conscientious among them to follow his example, against the dictates of their own conscience, then it would be his Christian duty to abridge his own liberty, because the use of it would be inexpedient.

The second limitation to this liberty arises out of its own nature. In that short sentence, "I will not be brought under the power of any," is contained one of the profoundest views of Christian liberty; I will try to elucidate it.

Christian liberty is internal. It resides in the deeps of the soul; a soul freed by faith is safe from superstition. He who fears God will fear nothing else. He who knows moral wrong to be the only evil, will be free from the scrupulosities which torment others. It is that free self-determination which rules all things, which can enjoy or abstain at will. This spirit is expressed in "All things are yours, whether life or death, things present or things to come — all are yours."

Hence is clear what St. Paul so often says in his Epistles. This liberty can manifest itself under outward restrictions; for the spirit, exalted above all outward restrictions, no longer feels them to be restrictions. So if a Christian were in slavery he was Christ's freedman, that is, he has a right to be free; but if by circumstances he is obliged to remain a slave, he is not troubled as if guilty of sin: he can wear a chain or not with equal spiritual freedom.

Now, upon this the Apostle makes this subtle and exquisitely fine remark: — To be *forced* to use liberty is actually a surrender of liberty. If I turn "I may" into "I must," I am in bondage again. "All things are lawful to me." But if I say, Not only lawful, but I *must* use them, I am brought under their power.

For, observe, there are two kinds of bondage. I am not free if I am under sentence of exile, and must leave my country. But also I am not free if I am under arrest, and must not leave it. So, too, if I think I must not touch meat on Friday, or that I must not read any but a religious book on a Sunday, I am in bondage. But again, if I am tormented with a scrupulous feeling that I did wrong in fasting, or if I feel that I must read secular books on Sunday to prove my freedom, then my liberty has become slavery again.

It is a blessed liberation to know that natural inclinations are not necessarily sinful. But if I say all natural and innocent inclinations *must* be obeyed at all times, then I enter into bondage once more. Christ proved to St. Peter that He was free from the necessity of paying tribute, the law being unjust as applied to Him. But had He felt Himself bound by conscience not to pay it, He would not have been free. He paid the tribute, and thereby proved his liberty. For he alone is free who can use outward things with conscientious freedom as circumstances vary; who can take off restrictions from himself, or submit to them for good reasons; who can either do without a form or ritual, or can use it.

See, then, how rare as well as noble a thing is Christian liberty! Free from superstition, but free also from the rude, inconsiderate spirit which thinks there is no liberty where it is not loudly vindicated: free from the observance of rules, of rites, of ceremonies, free also from the popular prejudices which dare not use forms or observe days, and free from the vulgar outcry which is always protesting against the faith or practice of others.

The second plea of the teachers St. Paul is here condemning is, the rights of Nature.

There is some difficulty in the exposition of this chapter, because the Apostle mixes together the pleas of his opponents, with his own answers to those pleas — states them himself, in order that he may reply to them. The first part of the thirteenth verse contains two of these pleas; the second part of this verse, with the fourteenth, contains his reply. 1. "Meats for the belly, and the belly for meats" — a natural correspondency. Here are appetites, and things made on purpose to satisfy appetites. "Therefore," said they, "Nature herself says, 'Enjoy!'" 2. The transitoriness of this enjoyment furnishes an argument for the enjoyment. "God shall bring to an end both it and them." That is, the body will perish, so will the food and the enjoyments — they do not belong to eternity, therefore indulgence is a matter of indifference. It is foolish ignorance to think that these are sins, any more than the appetites of brutes which perish.

Now to these two pleas, St. Paul makes two answers. To the argument about correspondency of appetites with the gratifications provided for them — an argument drawn from our nature to excuse gluttony and sensuality — he replies thus, "The body is not for self-indulgence, but for the Lord, and the Lord for the body." In other words, he tells of a more exact mutual correspondency. He reveals a true and higher nature.

Here, again, we see that St. Paul comes into collision with a common mode of teaching, which says man's nature is utterly vile and corrupt. These Corinthians said that, and St. Paul replied, No! that is a slander upon God. That is not your nature. Your true nature is, the body for the Lord, and the Lord for the body.

There is much confusion and dispute about this word "nature," because it is rather ambiguous. Take an illustration. The nature of a watch is correspondence with the sun, perfect harmony of wheels and balance. But suppose that the regulator was removed, and the mainspring unchecked ran down, throwing all into confusion. Then two things might be said. One might say, It is the nature of that watch to err. But would it not be a higher truth to say, Its nature is to go rightly, and it is just because it has departed from its nature that it errs?

So speaks the Apostle. To be governed by the springs of impulse only — your appetites and passions — this is not your nature. For the nature is the whole man; the passions are but a part of the man. And therefore our redemption from the lower life must consist, not in a perpetual assertion and dinning reiteration of our vileness, but in a reminder of what we are—what our true nature is.

To the other plea, the transitoriness of the body, he replies, You say the body will perish: "God shall bring it to an end." I say the body will not perish. "God hath raised up the Lord, and will also raise up us by his power." It is the outward form of the body alone which is transitory. Itself shall be renewed—a nobler, more glorious form, fitted for a higher and spiritual existence.

Now here, according to St. Paul, was the importance of the doctrine of the resurrection of the body. He taught that the Life which proceeds from faith carries with it the germ of a higher futurity. It will pervade humanity to its full extent until body, soul, and spirit are presented blameless unto the coming of the Lord Jesus.

And hence, too, he drew an awful argument against sin. Some sins are committed without the body; sins of sensuality and animal indulgence are *against* the body. Our bodies, which are "members of Christ," to be ruled by His Spirit, become by such sins unfit for immortality with Christ. This is an awful truth. Sins committed against the body affect that wondrous tissue which we call the nervous system: the source of all our acutest suffering and intensest blessing, is rendered so susceptible by God, as to be at once our punishment or reward. Sin carries with it its own punishment. There is not a sin of indulgence, gluttony, intemperance, or licentiousness of any form, which does not write its terrible retribution on our bodies.

Lax notions repecting self-indulgence are simply false: sinful pleasures are not trifles and indifferent. Irritability, many an hour of isolation, of dark and dreary hopelessness, is the natural result of powers unduly stimulated, unrighteously gratified.

In conclusion, it follows that nothing is really indifferent. In itself, perhaps, it may be; but under special circumstances duty always lies one way or the other, and nothing presents itself to us in our daily life simply in itself, as unconnected with other considerations.

And so Christian love makes all life one great duty.

LECTURE XIV.

DECEMBER 21, 1851.

CORINTHIANS, vii. 1 – 22. — "Now concerning the things whereof ye wrote unto me: It is good for a man not to touch a woman. — Nevertheless, to avoid fornication, let every man have his own wife, and let every woman have her own husband. — Let the husband render unto the wife due benevolence: and likewise also the wife unto the husband. — The wife hath not power of her own body, but the husband: and likewise also the husband hath not power of his own body, but the wife. — Defraud ye not one the other, except it be with consent for a time, that ye may give yourselves to fasting and prayer; and come together again, that Satan tempt you not for your incontinency. — But I speak this by permission, and not of commandment. — For I would that all men were even as I myself. But every man hath his proper gift of God, one after this manner, and another after that. — I say therefore to the unmarried and widows, It is good for them if they abide even as I. — But if they cannot contain, let them marry: for it is better to marry than to burn. — And unto the married, I command, yet not I, but the Lord: Let not the wife depart from her husband. — But and if she depart, let her remain unmarried, or be reconciled to her husband: and let not the husband put away his wife. — But to the rest speak I, not the Lord: If any brother hath a wife that believeth not, and she be pleased to dwell with him, let him not put her away. — And the woman which hath an husband that believeth not, and if he be pleased to dwell with her, let her not leave him. — For the unbelieving husband is sanctified by the wife, and the unbelieving wife is sanctified by the husband: else were your children unclean: but now are they holy. — But if the unbelieving depart, let him depart. A brother or a sister is not under bondage in such cases: but God hath called us to peace. — For what knowest thou, O wife, whether thou shalt save thy husband? or how knowest thou, O man, whether thou shalt save thy wife? — But as God hath distributed to every man, as the Lord hath called every one, so let him walk. And so ordain I in all churches. — Is any man called being circumcised? let him not become uncircumcised. Is any called in uncircumcision? let him not be circumcised. — Circumcision is nothing, and uncircumcision is nothing, but the keeping of the commandments of God. — Let every man abide in the same calling wherein he was called. — Art thou called being a servant? care not for it: but if thou mayest be made free, use it rather. — For he that is called in the Lord, being a servant, is the Lord's freeman: likewise also he that is called, being free, is Christ's servant."

THE whole of this seventh chapter of the First

Epistle of the Apostle Paul to the Corinthians is occupied with some questions of Christian casuistry. In the application of the principles of Christianity to the varying circumstances of life, innumerable difficulties had arisen, and the Corinthians upon these difficulties had put certain questions to the Apostle Paul. We have here the Apostle's answers to many of these questions. There are, however, two great divisions into which these answers generally fall. St. Paul makes a distinction between those things which he speaks by commandment, and those which he speaks only by permission; there is a distinction between what he says as from the Lord, and what only from himself; between that which he speaks to them as being taught of God, and that which he speaks only as a servant, "called of the Lord and faithful." It is manifestly plain that there are many questions in which *right* and *wrong* are not variable, but indissoluble and fixed; while there are questions, on the other hand, where these terms are not fixed, but variable, fluctuating, altering, dependent upon circumstances. As, for instance, those in which the Apostle teaches in the present chapter the several duties and advantages of marriage and celibacy. There may be circumstances in which it is the duty of a Christian man to be married, there are others in which it may be his duty to remain unmarried. For instance, in the case of a missionary it may be right to be married rather than unmarried; on the other hand, in the case of a pauper, not having the wherewithal to bring up and maintain a family, it may be proper to remain unmarried. You will observe, however, that no fixed law can be laid down upon this subject. We cannot say marriage is a Christian duty, nor celibacy is a Christian duty; nor that it is in every case the duty of a missionary to be married, or of a pauper to be unmarried. All these things must vary according to circumstances, and the duty must be stated not universally, but with reference to those circumstances.

These, therefore, are questions of casuistry, which

depend upon the particular *case:* from which word the term "casuistry" is derived. On these points the Apostle speaks, not by commandment, but by permission; not as speaking by God's command, but as having the Spirit of God. A distinction has sometimes been drawn with reference to this chapter between that which the Apostle speaks by inspiration, and what he speaks as a man uninspired. The distinction, however, is an altogether false one, and beside the question. For the real distinction is not between inspired and uninspired, but between a *decision* in matters of Christian duty, and *advice* in matters of Christian prudence. It is abundantly evident that God cannot give advice; He can only issue a command. God cannot say, "It is better to do this;" his perfections demand something absolute: "Thou shalt *do* this; thou shalt *not* do this." Whensoever, therefore, we come to advice there is introduced the human element rather than the divine. In all such cases, therefore, as are dependent upon circumstances, the Apostle speaks not as inspired, but as uninspired; as one whose judgment we have no right to find fault with or to cavil at, who lays down what is a matter of Christian prudence, and not a bounden and universal duty. The matter of the present discourse will take in various verses in this chapter — from the tenth to the twenty-fourth verse — leaving part of the commencement and the conclusion for our consideration, if God permit, next Sunday.

There are three main questions on which the Apostle here gives his inspired decision. The first decision is concerning the sanctity of the marriage-bond between two Christians. His verdict is given in the tenth verse: "Unto the married I command, yet not I, but the Lord, Let not the wife depart from her husband." He lays down this principle, that the union is an indissoluble one. Upon such a subject, Christian brethren, before a mixed congregation, it is manifestly evident that we can only speak in general terms. It will be sufficient to say that marriage is of all earthly unions almost the only one permitting of no change but that of death. It is that engagement in which man exerts his most awful and solemn power — the power of responsibility which belongs to him as one that shall give account — the power of abnegating the right to change — the power of parting with his freedom — the power of doing *that* which in this world can never be reversed. And yet it is perhaps that relationship which is spoken of most frivolously, and entered into most carelessly and most wantonly. It is not an union merely between two creatures, it is an union between two spirits; and the intention of that bond is to perfect the nature of both, by supplementing their deficiencies with the force of contrast, giving to each sex those excellencies in which it is naturally deficient; to the one strength of character and firmness of moral will, to the other sympathy, meekness, tenderness. And just so solemn, and just so glorious as these ends are for which the union was contemplated and intended, just so terrible are the consequences if it be perverted and abused. For there is no earthly relationship which has so much power to ennoble and to exalt. Very strong language does the Apostle use in this chapter respecting it: "What knoweth thou, O wife, whether thou shalt *save* thy husband? or how knowest thou, O man, whether thou shalt save thy wife?" The very power of *saving* belongs to this relationship. And, on the other hand, there is no earthly relationship which has so much power to wreck and ruin the soul. For there are two rocks in this world of ours on which the soul must either anchor or be wrecked. The one is God; the other is the sex opposite to itself. The one is the "Rock of Ages," on which if the human soul anchors it lives the blessed life of faith; against which if the soul be dashed and broken, there ensues the wreck of Atheism — the worst ruin of the soul. The other rock is of another character. Blessed is the man, blessed is the woman, whose life-experience has taught a confiding belief in the excellencies of the sex opposite to their own — a blessedness second only to the blessedness of salvation. And the ruin in the other case is second only to the ruin of everlasting perdition — the same wreck and ruin of the soul. These, then, are the two tremendous alternatives: on the one hand the possibility of securing, in all sympathy and tenderness, the laying of that step on which man rises towards his perfection; on the other hand the blight of all sympathy, to be dragged down to earth, and forced to become frivolous and commonplace; to lose all zest and earnestness in life, to have heart and life degraded by mean and perpetually recurring sources of disagreement; these are the two alternatives: and it is the worst of these alternatives which the young risk when they form an inconsiderate union, excusably indeed — because through inexperience; and it is the worst of these alternatives which parents risk — not excusably, but inexcusably — when they bring up their children with no higher view of what that tie is than the merely prudential one of a rich and honorable marriage.

The second decision which the Apostle makes respecting another of the questions proposed to him by the Corinthians, is as to the sanctity of the marriage bond between a Christian and one who is a heathen. When Christianity first entered into our world, and was little understood, it seemed to threaten the dislocation and alteration of all existing relationships. Many difficulties arose; such, for instance, as the one here started. When of two heathen parties only one was converted to Christianity, the question arose, What in this case is the duty of the Christian? Is not the duty separation? Is not the marriage in itself null and void, as if it were an union between one dead and one living? And that perpetual contact with a heathen, and, therefore, an enemy of God — is not that, in a relation so close and intimate, perpetual defilement? The Apostle decides this with his usual inspired wisdom. He decides that the marriage-bond is sacred still. Diversities of religious opinion, even the farthest and widest diversity, cannot sanction separation. And so he decides, in the 13th verse, "The woman which hath an husband that believeth not, and if he be pleased to dwell with her, let her not leave him." And, "If any brother hath a wife that believeth not, and she be pleased to dwell with him, let him not put her away," verse 12. Now for us, in the present day, the decision on this point is not of so much importance as the reason which is adduced in support of it. The proof which the Apostle gives of the sanctity of the marriage is exceedingly remarkable. Practically it amounts to this: — If this were no marriage, but an unhallowed alliance, it would follow as a necessary consequence that the offspring could not be reckoned in any sense as the children of God; but, on the other hand, it is the instinctive, unwavering conviction of every Christian parent, united though he or she may be to a heathen, "My child is a child of God," or, in the Jewish form of expression, "My child is *clean.*" So the Apostle says, "the unbelieving husband is sanctified by the wife, and the unbelieving wife is sanctified by the husband: else were your children unclean; but now they are holy." For it follows, if the children are holy in the sense of dedicated to God, and are capable of Christian relationship, then the marriage relation was not unhallowed, but sacred and indissoluble. The value of this argument in the present day depends on its relation to baptism. The great question we are deciding in the present day may be reduced to a very few words. This question — the Baptismal question — is this: — Whether we are baptized because we *are* the children of God, or, whether we are the children of God because we are *baptized;* whether, in other words, when the Catechism of the Church of England says that by baptism we are "made the children of God," we are to understand thereby that we are made something which we were not before — magically and mysteriously changed; or, whether we are to understand that we are made the children of God by baptism in the same sense that a sovereign is made a sovereign by coronation?

Here the Apostle's argument is full, decisive, and unanswerable: He does not say that these children were Christian, or clean, because they were *baptized*, but they were the children of God because they were the children of one Christian parent; nay, more than that, such children could scarcely ever have been baptized, because, if the rite met with opposition from one of the parents, it would be an entire and perfect veto to the possibility of baptism. You will observe that the very fundamental idea out of which infant-baptism arises is, that the impression produced upon the mind and character of the child by the Christian parent makes the child one of a Christian community; and, therefore, as Peter argued that Cornelius had received the Holy Ghost, and so was to be baptized, just in the same way, as they are adopted into the Christian family, and receive a Christian impression, the children of Christian parents are also to be baptized.

Observe also the important truth which comes out collaterally from this argument — namely, the sacredness of the impression, which arises from the close connection between parent and child. Stronger far than education — going on before education can commence, possibly from the very first moments of consciousness — is the impression we make on our children. Our character, voice, features, qualities — modified, no doubt, by entering into a new human being, and into a different organization — are impressed upon our children. Not the inculcation of opinions, but much more, the formation of principles, and of the tone of character, the derivation of qualities. Physiologists tell us of the derivation of the mental qualities from the father, and of the moral from the mother. But, be this as it may, there is scarcely one here who cannot trace back his present religious character to some impression, in early life, from one or other of his parents — a tone, a look, a word, a habit, or even, it may be, a bitter, miserable exclamation of remorse.

The third decision which the Apostle gives, the third principle which he lays down, is but the development of the last. Christianity, he says, does not interfere with existing relationships. First, he lays down the principle, and then unfolds the principle in two ways, ecclesiastically and civilly. The principle he lays down in almost every variety of form. In the 17th verse: "As God hath distributed to every man, as the Lord hath called every one, so let him walk." In the 20th verse: "Let every man abide in the same calling wherein he was called." In the 24th verse: "Brethren, let every man wherein he is called therein abide with God." This is the principle. Christianity was not to interfere with existing relationships; Christian men were to remain in those relationships in which they were, and in them to develop the inward spirituality of the Christian life. Then he applies this principle in two ways. First of all, ecclesiastically. With respect to the Church, or ecclesiastical affairs, he says — "Is any man called being circumcised. Let him not become uncircumcised. Is any man in uncircumcision? Let him not be circumcised." In other words, the Jews, after their conversion, were to continue Jews, if they would. Christianity required no change in these outward things, for it was not in *these* that the depth and reality of the kingdom of Christ consisted. So the Apostle Paul took Timothy and circumcised him; so, also, he used all the Jewish customs with which he was familiar, and performed a vow, as related in the Acts of the Apostles, "having shorn his head in Cenchrea; for he had a vow." It was not his opinion that it was the duty of a Christian to overthrow the Jewish system. He knew that the Jewish system could not last, but what he wanted was to vitalize the system — to throw into it not a Jewish, but a Christian feeling; and so doing, he might continue in it so long as it would hold together. And so it was, no doubt, with all the other Apostles. We have no evidence that, before the destruction of the Jewish polity, there was any attempt made by them to overthrow the Jewish external religion. They kept the Jewish Sabbath, and observed the Jewish ritual. One of them, James, the Christian Bishop of Jerusalem, though a Christian, was even among the Jews remarkable and honorable for the regularity with which he observed all his Jewish duties. Now let us apply this to modern duties. The great desire among men now appears to be to alter institutions, to have perfect institutions, as if *they* would make perfect men. Mark the difference between this feeling and that of the Apostle: "Let every man abide in the same calling wherein he was called." We are called to be members of the Church of England—what is our duty now? What would Paul have done? Is this our duty—to put such questions to ourselves as these? "Is there any single, particular sentence in the service of my Church with which I do not entirely agree? Is there any single ceremony with which my whole soul does not go along? If so, then it is my duty to leave it at once?" No, my brethren, all that we have to do is to say, "All our existing institutions are those under which God has placed us, under which we are to mould our lives according to His will." It is our duty to vitalize our forms, to throw into them a holier, deeper meaning. My Christian brethren, surely no man will get true rest, true repose for his soul in these days of controversy, until he has learned the wise significance of these wise words—"Let every man abide in the same calling wherein he was called." He will but gain unrest, he will but disquiet himself, if he says, "I am sinning by continuing in this imperfect system," if he considers it his duty to change his calling if his opinions do not agree in every particular and special point with the system under which God has placed him.

Lastly, the Apostle applies this principle civilly. And you will observe he applies it to that civil relationship which, of all others, was the most difficult to harmonize with Christianity—slavery. "Art thou called," he says, "being a servant? Care not for it." Now, in considering this part of the subject we should carry along with us these two recollections. First, we should recollect that Christianity had made much way among this particular class, the class of slaves. No wonder that men cursed with slavery embraced with joy a religion which was perpetually teaching the worth and dignity of the human soul, and declaring that rich and poor, peer and peasant, master and slave, were equal in the sight of God. And yet, great as this growth was, it contained within it elements of danger. It was to be feared, lest men, hearing for ever of brotherhood and Christian equality, should be tempted and excited to throw off the yoke by *force*, and compel their masters and oppressors to do them right.

The other fact we are to keep in remembrance is this — that all this occurred in an age in which slavery had reached its worst and most fearful form, an age in which the emperors were accustomed, not unfrequently, to feed their fish with living slaves; when captives were led to fight in the amphitheatre with wild beasts or with each other, to glut the Roman appetite for blood upon a Roman holiday. And yet, fearful as it was, the Apostle says, "Care not for it." And, fearful as war was in those days, when the soldiers came to John to be baptized, he did not recommend them to join some "Peace Association," to use the modern term, he simply exhorted them to be content with their wages. And hence we understand the way in which Christianity was to work. It interferes indirectly, and not directly, with existing institutions. No doubt it willat length abolish war and slavery, but there is not one case where we find Christianity interfering with institutions, as such. Even when Onesimus ran away and came to Paul, the Apostle sent him back to his master Philemon, not dissolving the connection between them. And then, as a consolation to the servant, he told him of a higher feeling — a feeling that would make him free, with the chain and shackle upon his arm. And so it was possible for the Christian then, as it is now, to be possessed of the highest liberty even under tyranny. It many times occurred that Christian men found themselves placed under an unjust and tyrannical government, and compelled to pay unjust taxes. The Son of Man showed his freedom, not by refusing, but by paying them. His glorious liberty could do so without any feeling of degradation; obeying the laws, not because they were right, but because institutions are to be upheld with cordiality.

One thing in conclusion we have to observe. It is possible from all this to draw a most inaccurate conclusion. Some men have spoken of Christianity as if it was entirely indifferent about liberty and all public questions — as if with such things as these Christianity did not concern itself at all. This indifference is not to be found in the Apostle Paul. While he asserts that inward liberty is the only true liberty, he still goes on to say, "If thou mayest be free, use it rather." For he well knew that although it was possible for a man to be a high and lofty Christian, even though he were a slave, yet it was not probable that he would be so. Outward institutions are necessary partly to make a perfect Christian character; and thus Christianity works from what is internal to what is external. It gave to the slave the feeling of his dignity as a man, at the same time it gave to the Christian master a new view of his relation to his slave, and taught him to regard him "not now as a servant, but above a servant, a brother beloved." And so by degrees slavery passed into freed servitude, and freed servitude, under God's blessing, may pass into something else. There are two mistakes which are often made upon this subject; one is, the error of supposing that outward institutions are unnecessary for the formation of character, and the other, that of supposing that they are *all* that is required to form the human soul. If we understand rightly the duty of a Christian man, it is this; to make his brethren free inwardly and outwardly: first inwardly, so that they may become masters of themselves, rulers of their passions, having the power of self-rule and self-control; and then outwardly, so that there may be every power and opportunity of developing the inward life; in the language of the prophet, "To break the rod of the oppressor, and let the oppressed go free."

LECTURE XV.

NOVEMBER 16, 1851.

1 CORINTHIANS, vii. 29-31. — "But this I say, brethren, the time is short: it remaineth, that both they that have wives, be as though they had none. — And they that weep, as though they wept not; and they that rejoice, as though they rejoiced not; and they that buy, as though they possessed not. — And they that use this world, as not abusing it: for the fashion of this world passeth away."

THIS was St. Paul's memorable decision, in reply to certain questions proposed to him by the Church of Corinth, on the subject of Unworldliness. Christianity was a new thing in the world, and circumstances daily arose in which it became a question in what way Christianity was to be applied to the circumstances of ordinary daily life.

Christ had said of his disciples, "They are not of the world." It was a question, therefore, — Can a Christian lawfully enter the married state? Can he remain a slave and be a Christian too? — May he make certain worldly compliances? — Should a Christian wife remain with an unchristian husband? Here was the root of the difficult question — What is Worldliness?

Now, observe the large, broad spirit of the Apostle's answer. In effect he says you *may* do all this — you may enter into family relationships, and yet be living in expectation of Christ's coming. If you are a slave, care not for it. If any that believe not invite you to a feast, and you are disposed to go, go without fear. I cannot judge for you, you must judge for yourselves. All that I lay down is, you must *in spirit* live above, and separate from the love of earthly things.

Christianity is a spirit — it is a set of principles, and not a set of rules; it is not a mapping out of the chart of life, with every shoal and rock marked, and the exact line of the ship's course laid down. It does not say, Do not go to this, or, See that you abstain from that. It gives no definite rules for dress, or for the expenditure of time or money. A principle is announced; but the application of that principle is left to each man's own conscience.

Herein Christianity differed essentially from Judaism. Judaism was the education of the spiritual child, Christianity that of the spiritual man. You must teach a child by rules; and, as he does not know the reason of them, his duty consists in implicit and exact obedience. But a man who is governed, not by principles, but by maxims and rules, is a pedant, or a slave; he will never be able to depart from the letter of the rule, not even to preserve the spirit of it. Here is one difference between the Law and Gospel. The Law lays down rules — "Do this, and live." The Gospel lays down principles. Thus Judaism said, Forgive seven times — exactly so much; Christianity said, Forgiveness is a boundless spirit — not three times, nor seven. No rule can be laid down but an infinite one, — seventy times seven. It must be left to the heart.

So, too, the Law said, — "On the Sabbath-day thou shalt do no manner of work." The *spirit* of this was rest for man, and Pharisaism kept literally to the *rule*. It would rather that a man should perish than that any work should be done, or any ground travelled over, on the Sabbath-day, in saving him. Pharisaism regarded the *day* as mysterious and sacred; Christianity proclaimed the *day* to be nothing, — the *spirit*, for which the day was set apart, everything. It said, "The Sabbath was made for man, not man for the Sabbath." It broke the day in the letter, whenever it was necessary in the true spiritual observance of the day to advantage the man.

Unworldliness, then, does not consist in giving up this or that; but in a certain inward principle. Had St. Paul been one of those ministers who love to be the autocrats of their congregations, who make their own limited conceptions the universal rule of right and wrong, he would have hailed this opportunity of deciding the question for them. But he walked in the light and liberty of the Gospel himself, and he desired that his converts should do the same.

This, then, is our subject —

I. The motives for Christian unworldliness.
II. The nature of that unworldliness.

The first motive is, the shortness of time. "This I say, brethren, the time is short." That mysterious word "time," which is a matter of sensation, dependent on the flight of ideas, may be long to one person and short to another. The span of life granted to a summer butterfly is long compared with that granted to the ephemeron, it is short compared with the duration of a cedar of Lebanon. Relative to experience, an hour is long to a child, yet a year is little to a man. Shortness, therefore, is a term entirely relative to something else.

1. It is relative to the way in which we look on time; whether it be regarded from before or after. Time past is a dream, time to come seems immense; the longest night, which seemed as if it would never drag through, is but a speck of memory when it is gone. At sixty-five, a man has on an average five years to live; yet his imagination obstinately attaches solidity and stability to those five coming years, though the sixty-five seem but a moment. To the young such words as these are often perfectly unmeaning; life to them is an inexhaustible treasure. But ask the old man what he thinks of the time he has had; he *feels* what the young can scarcely be brought to believe, — that time future may seem long, but time past is as nothing. Years glide swiftly, though hours and minutes scarcely seem to move.

2. Time is short in relation to opportunities. Literally these words mean — "The opportunity is compressed, — narrowed in," — that is, every season has its own opportunity, which never comes back. A

chance once gone is lost forever. The autumn sun shines as brightly as that of spring, but the seed of spring cannot be sown in autumn. The work of boyhood cannot be done in manhood. Time is short — it is opportunity narrowed in!

The chance will not be given you long. Have you learnt the lesson of yesterday? or the infinite meaning of to-day? It has duties of its own; they cannot be left until to-morrow. To-morrow will bring its own work. There is a solemn feeling in beginning any new work; in the thought, I have begun this to-day, shall I ever complete it? And a voice says, "Work on, for the day of its closing is unknown." The true consciousness of this life is as a tombstone, on which two dates are to be inscribed: the day of birth is engraven at full length, while a blank is left for the day of death. Born on such a day; died ——? The time in which that blank has to be filled up is short. The great idea brought out by Christianity was the eternity of the soul's life. With this idea the Corinthian Church was then struggling. So vast, so absorbing was this idea to them, that there was ground for fear lest it should absorb all considerations of the daily life, and duties, which surrounded these converts. The thought arose, — "Oh! in comparison of that great hereafter, this little life shrivels into nothingness! Is it worth while to attempt to do anything? What does it concern us to marry, to work, to rejoice, or to weep?" All deep minds have felt this at some period or other of their career — all earnest souls have had this temptation presented to them in some form or other. It has come perhaps, when we were watching underneath the quiet, gliding heavens, or perhaps when the ticking of a clock in restless, midnight hours, made us realize the thought that time was speeding on for ever — for this life beating out fast. That strange, awful thing, Time! sliding, gliding, fleeting on — on to the cataract; and then the deep, deep plunge down, bearing with it and swallowing up the world and the ages, until every interest that now seems so great and absorbing is as a straw on the mighty bosom of a flood. Let but a man possess his soul with this idea of Time, and then unworldliness will be the native atmosphere he breathes.

The second motive given is the changefulness of the external world. "The fashion of this world passeth away." It may be needful here to remark, that the word "fashion" has not here the popular meaning which has been generally assigned to it. It does not refer to those customs and conventionalities which vary in different nations and different ages. All these pass away: but the word refers here to all that is external upon earth, all that has form, and shape, and scenery; all that is visible in contradistinction to that which is invisible.

The transitoriness of this world might have been purely a matter of revelation. Instead of gradual and visible decay, God might have arranged his cycles so that change should not have been perceptible within the limits of a lifetime, that dissolution should have come on things suddenly, instead of by slow and gradual steps. Instead of that, He has mercifully chosen that it should not only be a matter of revelation, but of observation also. This visible world is only a form and an appearance. God has written decay on all around us. On the hills, which are everlasting only in poetry; their outlines changing within the memory of man. On the sea-coast, fringed with shingle. Look at it receding from our white cliffs; its boundaries are not what they were. This law is engraven on our own frames. Even in the infant the progress of dissolution has visibly begun. The principle of development is at work, and development is but the necessary step towards decay. There is a force at work in everything — call it what you will — Life or Death: it is reproduction out of decay. The outward form is in a perpetual flux and change.

We stand amidst the ruins of other days, and as they moulder before our eyes they tell us of generations which have mouldered before them, and of nations which have crossed the theatre of life and have dis appeared. We join in the gladness of the baptism, and the years roll on so rapidly that we are almost startled to find ourselves standing at the wedding. But pass on a few years more, and the young heart for which there was so much gladness in the future has had its springs dried up. He belongs to a generation which has passed, and they among whom he lingers feel as if he had lived too long. And then he drops silently into the grave to make way for others. One of our deepest thinkers — a man of profoundest observation, who thought by means of a boundless heart — has told us, in words trite and familiar to us all,

> "All the world's a stage,
> And all the men and women merely players:
> They have their exits and their entrances;
> And one man in his time plays many parts."

Let us look at our own neighborhood. Those with whom we walked in youth are gone, and scattered we know not where, and others have filled their places. We are developing every day new relationships: every day new circumstances are occurring which call upon us to act promptly, manfully, equal to the occasion; for the past is gone.

Therefore strive to be unworldly. Be not buried in the present. To-day becomes yesterday so fast. Mourn not over what will so soon be irreparably gone. There is nothing worth it.

Again, that "fashion of the world" passes away *in us*. Our very minds change — not merely the objects which make the impression on them. The impressions themselves are fleeting. All except the perpetually-repeated sensations of eternity, space, time; all else alters. There is no affliction so sharp, no joy so bright, no shock so severe, — but Time modifies and cures all. The keenest feeling in this world is not eternal. If it remains, it is in an altered form. Our memories are like monumental brasses: the deepest graven inscription becomes at last illegible. Of such a world the Apostle seems to ask, Is this a world for an immortal being to waste itself upon?

II. The nature of Christian unworldliness.

Two points are contained in this last verse. 1st. The spirit or principle of unworldliness; to use this world as not abusing it. 2d. The application of that principle to four cases of life. Domestic relations. — "They that have wives be as though they had none." Joy. — "They that rejoice, as though they rejoiced not." Sorrow. — "They that weep, as though they wept not." The acquisition of Property. — "They that buy, as though they possessed not."

The principle is, to "use this world as not abusing it." Here Christianity stands between the worldly spirit and the narrow religious spirit. The worldly spirit says, "Time is short; take your fill; live while you can." The narrow religious spirit says, "All the pleasure here is a snare and dangerous; keep out of it altogether." In opposition to this narrow spirit, Christianity says, "Use the world," and, in opposition to the worldly spirit, "Do not abuse it. All things are yours. Take them, and use them; but never let them interfere with the higher life which you are called on to lead. 'A man's life consisteth not in the abundance of the things that he possesses.'"

It is therefore a distinct duty to use life, while we are here. We are citizens of the world, we may not shrink from it. We must share its duties, dangers, sorrows, and joys. Time is short; therefore opportunities are so much the more valuable. There is an infinite value stamped upon them. Therefore, use the world. But then it is a duty equally distinct, to live above the world. Unworldliness is the spirit of holding all things as not our own, in the perpetual conviction that they will not last. It is not to put life and God's lovely world aside with self-torturing hand. It is to have the world, and not to let the world have you; to be its master, and not its slave. To have Christ hidden in the heart, calming all, and making all else seem by comparison poor and small.

This principle he applies, first, to domestic life. "They that have wives be as though they had none."

The idea was just then beginning to be discussed, which of the two was in itself the higher state, and more according to God's will, the single or the married. In after ages this question was decided in a very disastrous way; for it was taught that celibacy was the only really pure and angelic life. Marriage was regarded as earthly and sensual, unfit for those who were to serve as priests. Now here observe the apostolic wisdom. He does not say celibacy is the saintly, and marriage the lower and earthlier state. He wisely says, "In whatever state you can most undistractedly serve God, that is the unworldly one to you."

This is a very important principle for consideration in the present day. There is a growing tendency to look on a life of contemplation and retirement, of separation from all earthly ties,—in a word, asceticism,—as the higher life. Let us understand that God has so made man, that ordinarily he who lives alone leaves part of his *heart* uncultivated; for God made man for domestic life. He who would be wiser than his Maker is only wise in appearance. He who cultivates one part of his nature at the expense of the rest, has not produced a perfect man, but an exaggeration. It is easy, in silence and solitude, for the hermit to be abstracted from all human interests and hopes, to be dead to honor, dead to pleasure. But, then, the sympathies which make him a man with men — how shall they grow? He is not the highest Christian who lives alone and single, but he who, whether single or married, lives superior to this earth; he who, in the midst of domestic cares, petty annoyances, or daily vexations, can still be calm, and serene, and sweet. That is real unworldliness; and, in comparison with this, the mere hermit's life is easy indeed.

The second case is unworldliness in sorrow. "They that weep, as though they wept not."

Observe, the Apostle does not here recommend apathy, not merely a reason of prudence. He bids them sorrow; but not as they who have no hope. He does not say, "Weep not;" but "weep, as though they wept not."

This unworldliness consists of two parts: —

1st. The duty and the right of sorrow. "Weep." Christianity does not sear the human heart; it softens it. They who forbid grief should, to be consistent, go further and forbid affection, for grief is only a state of the affections; if joy be felt in the presence of the loved object, grief must be felt in its absence. Christianity destroys selfishness, makes a man quick and sensitive for others, and alive to every call of affection. Moreover, dealing with infinite things, it imparts something of its own infinitude to every feeling. A Christian is a man whose heart is exquisitely attuned to all utterances of grief. Shall *he* not feel nor mourn? His Master wept over the grave of friendship. Tears of patriotism fell from His eyes. There is no unmanliness in shedding tears; it is not unchristian to yield to deep feeling. We may admire the stern old Roman heart; but we must not forget that the Roman stoicism is not of the spirit of Christianity. For Christianity says, "Weep."

2d. Christian unworldliness puts limits to sorrow. "As though they wept not:" that is, as though God had already removed their grief. Else in this world of sorrow and distress, how should we escape despair? Familiarity with eternal things subdues grief, calms and softens it, gives it a true perspective. Christianity does not say to our hearts, when smarting under the bitter pain of disappointment or loss, "It is nothing!" but it says, "It is less than you had supposed it to be; you will, sooner or later, feel that it is easier to bear than you expected." This elasticity of heart receives its only true warrant from Christianity. Have you lost a dear relative? Well, you may weep; but even while weeping, Christ comes to you and says, "Thy brother shall rise again."

The third case is unworldliness in joy. "They that rejoice, as though they rejoiced not." Christ's religion is no grim, ghastly system of gloom. God's world is not like the fabled place of punishment where waters of refreshment rise brimming to the lips, while a stern prohibition sounds forth, "Touch not, taste not, handle not." You will observe, the joy spoken of here is not spiritual, but earthly joy; for, if it had been spiritual joy, the Apostle could not have put any limitation to it. Therefore, Christians *may* have earthly joy. And they that rejoice are emphatically the young. Let the young be happy. Health, spirits, youth, society, accomplishments,—let them enjoy these, and thank God with no misgiving. Let there be no half-remorseful sensations, as though they were stolen joys. Christ had no sympathy with that tone of mind which scowls on human happiness: His first manifestation of power was at a marriage feast. Who would check the swallow's flight, or silence the gush of happy melody which the thrush pours forth in spring? Look round this beautiful world of God's: ocean dimpled into myriad smiles; the sky a trembling, quivering mass of blue, thrilling hearts with ecstasy; every tint, every form replete with beauty. You cannot, except wilfully, misread its meaning. God says, "Be glad!" Do not force young, happy hearts to an unnatural solemnity, as if to be happy were a crime. Let us hear their loud, merry, ringing laugh, even if sterner hearts can be glad no longer; to see innocent mirth and joy does the heart good.

But now, observe, everlasting considerations are to come in, not to sadden joy, but to calm it, to moderate its transports, and make even worldly joy a sublime thing. We are to be calm, cheerful, self-possessed; to sit loose to all these sources of enjoyment, masters of ourselves.

The Apostle lays down no rule respecting worldly amusements. He does not say you must avoid this or that, but he lays down broad principles. People often come to ministers, and ask them to draw a boundary line, within which they may safely walk. There is none. It is at our peril that we attempt to define where God has not defined. We cannot say, "This amusement is right, and that is wrong." And herein is the greater responsibility laid upon all, for we have to live out principles rather than maxims; and the principle here is, Be unworldly.

But, remember, if the enjoyments which you permit yourselves are such, that the thought of passing time, and coming eternity, presents itself as an intrusive thought, which has no business there, which is out of place, and incongruous; if you become secularized, excited, and artificial; if there is left behind a craving for excitement which can only be slaked by more and more intense excitement: then it is at your own peril that you say, All is left open to me, and permitted. Unworldly you *must* become — or die. Dare not to say this is only a matter of opinion; it is *not* a matter of opinion; it is a matter of conscience; and to God you must give account for the way in which you have been dealing with your soul.

The fourth case is unworldliness in the acquisition of property. "They that buy, as though they possessed not."

Unworldliness is not measured by *what* you possess, but by the spirit in which you possess it. It is not said, "Do not buy," but rather "Buy, — possess." You may be a large merchant, an extensive landed proprietor, a thriving tradesman, if only your heart be separate from the *love* of these earthly things, with God's love *paramount* there. The amount of property you possess does not affect the question; it is purely a relative consideration. You go into a regal or ducal palace, and perhaps, unaccustomed to the splendor which you see, you say, "All this is worldliness." But the poor man comes to your house; your dress, simple as it is, seems magnificent to him; your day's expenditure would keep his family for half a year. He sees round him expensively bound books, costly furniture, pictures, silver, and china — a profusion certainly beyond what is absolutely necessary; and to him this seems worldliness too. If the monarch is to live as you live, why should not you live as the laborer lives? If what you call the necessaries of life be the measure of the rich man's worldliness, why should not the poor man's test gauge yours? No! we must take another test than property as the measure of worldliness. Christianity forbids our condemning others; men *may* buy and possess. Christianity prescribes no law for dress, its color, its fashion, or its cost; none for expenditure, none for possessions: it fixes great principles, and requires you to be unaffected, unenslaved by earthly things; to possess them as though you possessed them not. The Christian is one who, if a shipwreck or a fire were to take all luxury away, could descend, without being crushed, into the valleys of existence. He wears all this on the outside, carelessly, and could say, "My *all* was not laid there."

In conclusion, let there be no censoriousness. How others live, and what they permit themselves, may be a matter for Christian charity, but it is no matter for Christian severity. To his own master each must stand or fall. Judge not. It is work enough for any one of us to save his own soul.

Let there be no self-deception. The way in which I have expounded this subject gives large latitude, and any one may abuse it if he will, — any one may take comfort to himself, and say, "Thank God, there are no hard restrictions in Christianity." Remember, however, that Worldliness is a more decisive test of a man's spiritual state than even Sin. Sin may be sudden, the result of temptation, without premeditation, yet afterwards hated — repented of — repudiated — forsaken. But if a man *be at home* in the world's pleasure and pursuits, content that his spirit should have no other heaven but in these things, happy if they could but last for ever, is not his state, genealogy, and character clearly stamped?

Therefore does St. John draw the distinction — "If any man sin, we have an advocate with the Father;" — but "If any man love the world, the love of the Father is not in him."

LECTURE XVI.

THE DIFFERENCE BETWEEN CHRISTIAN AND SECULAR KNOWLEDGE.

NOVEMBER 23, 1851.

1 CORINTHIANS, viii. 1 – 7 — "Now as touching things offered unto idols, we know that we all have knowledge. Knowledge puffeth up, but charity edifieth. — And if any man think that he knoweth anything, he knoweth nothing yet as he ought to know. — But if any man love God, the same is known of him. — As concerning therefore the eating of those things that are offered in sacrifice unto idols, we know that an idol is nothing in the world, and that there is none other God but one. — For though there be that are called gods, whether in heaven or in earth, (as there be gods many and lords many,) — But to us there is but one God, the Father, of whom are all things, and we in him; and one Lord Jesus Christ, by whom are all things, and we by him. — Howbeit there is not in every man that knowledge: for some with conscience of the idol unto this hour eat it as a thing offered unto an idol; and their conscience being weak is defiled."

THE particular occasion of this chapter was a controversy going on in the Church of Corinth respecting a Christian's right to eat meat which had been sacrificed to idols. Now the question was this: — It was customary, when an animal was sacrificed or consecrated to a heathen god, to reserve one portion for the priest, and another for the worshipper. These were either used in the feasts, or sold like common meat in the shambles. Now among the Corinthian converts some had been Jews and some heathens: those who had been Jews would naturally shrink from eating this meat, their previous training being so strongly opposed to idolatry, while those who had been heathen would be still more apt to shrink from the use of this meat than were the Jews; for it is proverbial that none are so bitter against a system as those who have left it, perhaps for the simple reason, that none know so well as they the errors of the system they have left. There was another reason which made the heathen converts shrink from eating this meat, and this was, that they were unable to divest themselves of the idea that the deities they had once adored were living entities; they had ceased to bow before them, but long habit had made them seem living personalities: they looked on them as demons. Hence, the meat of an animal consecrated while living to an idol appeared to them polluted, accursed, contaminated — a thing only fit to be burnt, and utterly unfit for food. This state of feeling may be illustrated by the modern state of belief with reference to apparitions. Science has banished an express faith in their existence, yet we should, probably, be surprised did we know how much credulity on this subject still remains. The statute book is purged from the sentences on witchcraft, and yet a lingering feeling remains that it may still exist in power. Christianity had done the same for the heathen deities. They were dethroned as gods, but they still existed, to the imagination, as beings of a lower order — as demons who were malicious to men and enemies to God. Hence, meat offered to them was regarded as abominable, as unfit for a Christian man to eat; he was said to have compromised his Christianity by doing so. On the other hand, there were men of clearer views who maintained in the language quoted by St. Paul — "An idol is nothing in the world" — a nonentity, a name, a phantom of the imagination: it cannot pollute the meat, since it is nothing, and has no reality. Therefore, they derided the scruple of the weaker brethren and said, "We will eat." Now all this gave rise to the enunciation of a great principle by the Apostle Paul. In laying it down, he draws a sharp distinction between Secular and Christian Knowledge, and also unfolds the Law of Christian Conscience.

It is to the first of these that I shall claim your attention to-day.

A great controversy is going on at the present time in the matter of Education. One party extols the value of instruction, the other insists loudly that secular education without religion is worse than useless. By secular education is meant instruction in such branches as arithmetic, geography, grammar, and history, and by religious education, instruction in the Bible and the catechism. But you will see at once that the Knowledge, of which St. Paul spoke slightingly, was much higher than any, or all of these. He spoke of instruction not merely in history, geography, or grammar, but instruction in the Bible, the catechism, and the articles, as worthless, without training in Humility and Charity. This was the secular knowledge he speaks of, for you will perceive that he treats knowledge of very important religious matters as secular, and rates it very low indeed. He said mere knowledge is worth little; but then by knowledge, he meant not merely knowledge without Christian doctrine, but knowledge without Love. Many a person now zealous on this point of education would be content if only the Bible, without note or comment, were taught. But St. Paul would not have been content, he would have calmly looked on and said, This is also secular knowledge. This, too, is the knowledge which puffeth up; but Christian knowledge is the Charity which alone buildeth up an heavenly spirit.

Let me try to describe more fully this secular knowledge.

It is Knowledge without Humility.—For it is not so much the department of knowledge, as it is the spirit in which it is acquired, which makes the difference between secular and Christian knowledge. It is not so much the thing known, as the way of knowing it. "If any man think that he knoweth anything, he knoweth nothing yet as he ought to know." "*As* he he ought to know." That single word "as" is the point of the sentence; for it is not *what* to know, but *how* to know, which includes all real knowledge. The greatest of modern philosophers, and the greatest of modern historians, Humboldt and Niebuhr, were both eminently humble men. So, too, you will find the *real* talent among mechanics is generally united to great humility. Whereas the persons you would select as puffed up by knowledge are those who have a few religious maxims, and a few shallow religious doctrines. There are two ways, therefore, of knowing all things. One is, that of the man who loves to calculate how far he is advanced beyond others; the other, that of the man who feels how infinite knowledge is, how little he knows, and how deep the darkness of those who know even less than he: who says, not as a cant phrase, but in unaffected sincerity, "I know nothing, and do go into the grave." That knowledge will never puff up.

Again, it is Liberty without Reverence. — These men, to whom the Apostle writes in rebuke, were free from many superstitions. An idol, they said, was nothing in the world. But although freed from the worship of false gods, they had not *therefore* adored the true God. For it is not merely freedom from superstition which is worship of God, but it is loving dependence on Him; the surrender of self. "If any man love God, the same is known of Him." Observe it is not said, "he shall know God," but "shall be known of Him;" that is, God shall acknowledge the likeness and the identity of spirit, and "will come unto him and make His abode with him." There is much of the spirit of these Corinthians existing now. Men throw off what they call the trammels of education, false systems, and superstitions, and then call themselves free: they think it a grand thing to reverence nothing; all seems to them either kingcraft or priestcraft, and to some it is a matter of rejoicing that they have nothing left either to respect or worship. There is a recent work in which the writer has tried to overthrow belief in God, the soul, and immortality, and proclaims this liberty as if it were a gospel for the race! My brother men, this is not high knowledge. It is a great thing to be free from mental slavery, but suppose you are still a slave to your passions? It is a great thing to be emancipated from superstition, but suppose you have no religion? From all these bonds of the spirit Christianity has freed us, says St. Paul, but then it has not left us merely free from these, it has bound us to God. "Though there be gods many, yet to us there is but one God." The true freedom from superstition is free service to religion: the real emancipation from false gods is reverence for the true God. For high knowledge is not negative, but positive; it is to be freed from the fear of the Many, in order to adore and love the One. And not merely is this the only real knowledge, but no other knowledge "buildeth up" the soul. It is all well so long as elasticity of youth and health remain. Then the pride of intellect sustains us strongly; but a time comes when we feel terribly that the Tree of Knowledge is not the Tree of Life. Our souls without God and Christ enter deeper and deeper into the fearful sense of the hollowness and darkness, the coldness, and the death, of a spirit separate from love. "He that increaseth knowledge increaseth sorrow." Separate from love, the more we know, the profounder the mystery of life becomes; the more dreary and the more horrible becomes existence. I can conceive of no dying hour more awful than that of one who has aspired to *know* instead of to *love*, and finds himself at last amidst a world of barren facts and lifeless theories, loving none and adoring nothing.

Again, it is Comprehension without Love to man.— You will observe, these Corinthians had got a most clear conception of what Christianity was. "An idol," said they, is "nothing in the world." There is none other God but One, and there is "but one Lord Jesus Christ, by whom are all things, and we by Him." Well, said the Apostle Paul, and what signifies your profession of that, if you look down with supreme contempt on your ignorant brothers, who cannot reach to these sublime contemplations? What reality is there in your religion, if you look at men struggling in darkness, and are content to congratulate yourselves, that you are in the light? When heathen, they had loved these men; now that they were Christians they despised them! Was their Christianity, then, gain or loss? Did they rise in the scale of manhood or fall?

"Slaves — idolaters — superstitious" — alas! is that all they, or we, have learnt to say? Is that all our Christianity has given us?

Some of us have been taught that knowledge such as *this* is not advance, but retrogression. We have looked on our shelves laden with theology or philosophy, and have enumerated the systems which have been mastered; and we have felt how immeasurably superior in the sight of God is some benighted Romanist, who believes in transubstantiation and purgatory, but who has gone about doing good, or some ignorant, narrow religionist, who has sacrificed time and property to Christ, to the most correct theologian in whose heart there is no love for his fellow-men. For breadth of view is not breadth of heart; and hence the substance of Christianity is love to God and love to man. Hence, too, the last of the Apostles, when too weak to walk to the assemblies of the Church, was borne there, a feeble old man, by his disciples, and addressing the people as he spread abroad his hands, repeated again and again — "Love one another;" and when asked why he said ever the same thing, replied, "Because there is nothing else; attain that, and you have enough." Hence, too, it is a precious fact, that St. Paul, the Apostle of Liberty, whose burning intellect expounded the whole philosophy of Christianity, should have been the one to say that Knowledge is nothing compared to Charity, nay, worse than nothing without it: should have been the one to declare that "Knowledge shall vanish away, but Love never faileth."

LECTURE XVII.

NOVEMBER 30, 1851.

CORINTHIANS, viii. 8-13. — But meat commendeth us not to God: for neither, if we eat, are we the better; neither, if we eat not, are we the worse. — But take heed lest by any means this liberty of yours become a stumbling-block to them that are weak. — For if any man see thee which hast knowledge, sit at meat in the idol's temple, shall not the conscience of him which is weak be emboldened to eat those things which are offered to idols; — And through thy knowledge shall the weak brother perish for whom Christ died? — But when ye sin so against the brethren and wound their weak conscience, ye sin against Christ. — Wherefore if meat make my brother to offend, I will eat no flesh while the world standeth, lest I make my brother to offend."

WE have already divided this chapter into two branches — the former portion of it containing the difference between Christian knowledge and secular knowledge, and the second portion containing the apostolic exposition of the law of Christian conscience. The first of these we endeavored to expound last Sunday, but it may be well briefly to recapitulate the principles of that discourse in a somewhat different form. Corinth, as we all know and remember, was a city built on the sea coast, having a large and free communication with all foreign nations; and there was also within it, and going on amongst its inhabitants, a free interchange of thought, and a vivid power of communicating the philosophy and truths of those days to each other. Now it is plain that to a society in such a state, and to minds so educated, the Gospel of Christ must have presented a peculiar attraction, presenting itself to them as it did, as a law of Christian liberty. And so, in Corinth the gospel had "free course and was glorified," and was received with great joy by almost all men, and by minds of all classes and all sects; and a large number of these attached themselves to the teaching of the Apostle Paul as the most accredited expounder of Christianity — the "royal law of liberty." But it seems, from what we read in this Epistle, that a large number of these men received Christianity as a thing intellectual, and that alone — and not as a thing which touched the conscience, and swayed and purified the affections. And so, this liberty became to them almost *all* — they ran into sin or went to extravagance — they rejoiced in their freedom from the superstitions, the ignorances, and the scruples which bound their weaker brethren; but had no charity — none of that intense charity which characterized the Apostle Paul, for those still struggling in the delusions and darkness from which they themselves were free. More than that, they demanded their right, their Christian liberty of expressing their opinions in the church, merely for the sake of *exhibiting* the Christian graces and spiritual gifts which had been showered upon them so largely; until by degrees those very assemblies became a lamentable exhibition of their own depravity, and led to numerous irregularities, which we find severely rebuked by the Apostle Paul. Their women, rejoicing in the emancipation which had been given to the Christian community, laid aside the old habits of attire which had been consecrated so long by Grecian and Jewish custom, and appeared with their heads uncovered in the Christian community. Still further than that, the Lord's Supper exhibited an absence of all solemnity, and seemed more a meeting for licentious gratification, where "one was hungry, and another was drunken" — a place in which earthly drunkenness, the mere enjoyment of the appetites, had taken the place of Christian charity towards each other. And the same feeling — this love of mere liberty — liberty in itself — manifested itself in many other directions. Holding by this freedom, their philosophy taught that the body, that is, the flesh, was the only cause of sin: that the soul was holy and pure; and that, therefore, to be free from the body would be entire, perfect, Christian emancipation. And so came in that strange wrong doctrine, exhibited in Corinth, where immortality was taught separate from and in opposition to the doctrine of the Resurrection. And afterwards they went on with their conclusions about liberty, to maintain that the body, justified by the sacrifice of Christ, was no longer capable of sin, and that, in the evil which was done by the body, the soul had taken no part. And therefore sin was to them but as a name, from which a Christian conscience was to be freed altogether. So that when one of their number had fallen into grievous sin, and had committed fornication, "such as was not so much as named among the Gentiles," so far from being humbled by it, they were "puffed up," as if they were exhibiting to the world an enlightened, true, perfect Christianity — separate from all prejudices. To such a society and to such a state of mind the Apostle Paul preached, in all their length, breadth, and fulness, the humbling doctrines of the Cross of Christ. He taught that knowledge was one thing — that charity was *another* thing; that "knowledge puffeth up, but charity buildeth up." He reminded them that love was the perfection of knowledge. In other words, his teaching came to this: there are two kinds of knowledge; the one the knowledge of the intellect, the other the knowledge of the heart. Intellectually, God never can be known: He must be known by Love — for, "if any man love God, the same is known of Him." Here, then, we have arrived, in another way, at precisely the same conclusion at which we arrived last Sunday. Here, are two kinds of knowledge, secular knowledge and Christian knowledge; and Christian knowledge is this — to know by Love.

Let us now consider the remainder of the chapter, which treats of the law of Christian conscience. You will observe that it divides itself into two branches — the first containing an exposition of the law itself, and the second, the Christian applications which flow out of this exposition.

1. The way in which the Apostle expounds the law of Christian conscience is this: — Guilt is contracted

by the soul, in so far as it sins against and transgresses the law of God, by doing that which it believes to be wrong: not so much what *is* wrong, as what *appears* to *it* to be wrong. This is the doctrine distinctly laid down in the 7th and 8th verses. The Apostle tells the Corinthians — these strong-minded Corinthians — that the superstitions of their weaker brethren were unquestionably wrong. "Meat," he says, "commendeth us not to God; for neither if we eat, are we the better; neither if we eat not, are we the worse." He then tells them further, that "there is not in every man that knowledge; for some, with conscience of the idol, eat it as a thing offered unto an idol." Here, then, is an ignorant, mistaken, ill-informed conscience; and yet he goes on to tell them that this conscience, so ill-informed, yet binds the possessor of it: "and their conscience being weak, is defiled." For example; there could be no harm in eating the flesh of an animal that had been offered to an idol or false god; for a false god is nothing, and it is impossible for it to have contracted positive defilement by being offered to that which is a positive and absolute negation. And yet if any man thought it wrong to eat such flesh, to him it *was* wrong; for in that act there would be a deliberate act of transgression — a deliberate preference of that which was mere enjoyment, to that which was apparently, though it may be only apparently, sanctioned by the law of God. And so it would carry with it all the disobedience, all the guilt, and all the misery which belongs to the doing of an act altogether wrong; or, as St. Paul expresses it, the conscience would become defiled.

Here, then, we arrive at the first distinction — the distinction between absolute and relative right and wrong. Absolute right and absolute wrong, like absolute truth, can each be but *one* and unalterable in the sight of God. The one absolute *right* — the charity of God and the sacrifice of Christ — this, from eternity to eternity must be the sole measure of eternal right. But human right or human wrong, that is, the merit or demerit of any action done by any particular man, must be measured, not by that absolute standard, but as a matter relative to his particular circumstances, the state of the age in which he lives, and his own knowledge of right and wrong. For we come into this world with a moral sense ; or, to speak more Christianly, with a conscience. And yet that will tell us but very little distinctly. It tells us broadly that which is right and that which is wrong, so that every child can understand this. That charity and self-denial are right — this we see recognized in almost every nation. But the boundaries of these two — when and how far self-denial is right — what are the bounds of charity — this it is for different circumstances yet to bring out and determine. And so, it will be found that there is a different standard among different nations and in different ages. That, for example, which was the standard among the Israelites in the earlier ages, and before their settlement in Canaan, was very different from the higher and truer standard of right and wrong recognized by the later prophets. And the standard in the third and fourth centuries after Christ, was truly and unquestionably an entirely different one from that recognized in the nineteenth century among ourselves. Let me not be mistaken. I do not say that right and wrong are merely conventional, or merely chronological or geographical, or that they vary with latitude and longitude. I do not say that there ever was or ever can be a nation so utterly blinded and perverted in its moral sense as to acknowledge that which is wrong — seen and known to be wrong — as right ; or, on the other hand, to profess that which is seen and understood as right, to be wrong. But what I do say is this : that the form and aspect in which different deeds appear, so vary, that there will be for ever a change and alteration in men's opinions, and that which is really most generous may seem most base, and that which is really most base may appear most generous. So, for example, as I have already said, there are two things universally recognized — recognized as right by every man whose conscience is not absolutely perverted — charity and self-denial. The charity of God, the sacrifice of Christ — these are the two grand, leading principles of the Gospel; and in some form or other you will find these lying at the roots of every profession and state of feeling in almost every age. But the form in which these appear, will vary with all the gradations which are to be found between the lowest savage state and the highest and most enlightened Christianity.

For example: in ancient Israel the law of love was expounded thus: — "Thou shalt love thy neighbor, and hate thine enemy." Among the American Indians and at the Cape, the only homage perchance given to self-denial was the strange admiration given to that prisoner of war who bore with unflinching fortitude the torture of his country's enemies. In ancient India the same principle was exhibited, but in a more strange and perverted manner. The homage there given to self-denial, self-sacrifice, was this — that the highest form of religion was considered to be that exhibited by the devotee who sat in a tree until the birds had built their nests in his hair — until his nails, like those of the King of Babylon, had grown like birds' talons — until they had grown into his hands — and he became absorbed into the Divinity. We will take another instance, and one better known. In ancient Sparta it was the custom to teach children to steal. And here there would seem to be a contradiction to our proposition — here it would seem as if right and wrong were matters merely conventional; for surely stealing can never be anything but wrong. But if we look deeper, we shall see that there is no contradiction here. It was not stealing which was admired; the child was punished if the theft was discovered; but it was the dexterity which was admired, and that because it was a warlike virtue, necessary, it may be, to a people in continual rivalry with their neighbors. It was not that honesty was despised and dishonesty esteemed, but that honesty and dishonesty were made subordinate to that which appeared to them of higher importance, namely, the duty of concealment. And so we come back to the principle which we laid down at first. In every age, among all nations, the same broad principle remains; but the application of it varies. The conscience may be ill-informed, and in this sense only are right and wrong conventional — varying with latitude and longitude, depending upon chronology and geography.

The principle laid down by the Apostle Paul is this: — A man will be judged, not by the abstract law of God, not by the rule of absolute right, but much rather by the relative law of conscience. This he states most distinctly — looking at the question on both sides. That which seems to a man to be right is, in a certain sense, right to him; and that which seems to a man to be wrong, in a certain sense *is* wrong to him. For example: he says, in his Epistle to the Romans (v. 14), that "sin is not imputed when there is no law;" in other words, if a man does not really know a thing to be wrong, there is a sense in which, if not right to him, it ceases to be so wrong as it would otherwise be. With respect to the other of these sides, however, the case is still more distinct and plain. Here, in the judgment which the Apostle delivers in the parallel chapter of the Epistle to the Romans (the 14th), he says, "I know, and am persuaded of the Lord Jesus, that there is nothing unclean of itself; but to him that esteemeth anything to be unclean, to him it is unclean." In other words, whatever may be the abstract merits of the question — however in God's jurisprudence any particular act may stand — to you, thinking it to be wrong, it manifestly *is* wrong, and your conscience will gather round it a stain of guilt if you do it. In order to understand this more fully, let us take a few instances. There is a difference between *truth* and *veracity*. Veracity — mere veracity — is a small, poor thing. Truth is something greater and higher. Veracity is merely the correspondence between some particular statement and facts; truth is the correspondence between a man's whole soul and reality. It is possible for a man to say that which, unknown to him, is false; and yet he may be true; because, if deprived of truth, he is deprived of it unwillingly. It is possible, on the other hand, for a man to utter veracities, and yet at the very time that he is uttering those veracities to be false to himself, to his brother, and to his God. One of the most signal instances of this is to be seen in the Book of Job. Most of what Job's friends said to him were veracious statements. Much of what Job said himself was unveracious and mistaken. And yet those veracities of theirs were so torn from all connection with fact and truth, that they became falsehoods; and they were, as has been said, nothing more than "orthodox liars" in the sight of God. On the other hand, Job, blundering perpetually, and falling into false doctrine, was yet a true man — searching for and striving after the truth; and if deprived of it for a time, deprived of it with all his heart and soul unwillingly. And, therefore, it was that at last the Lord appeared out of the whirlwind, to confound the men of mere veracity, and to stand by and support the honor of the heartily true.

Let us apply the principle further. It is a matter of less importance that a man should state true views, than that he should state views truly. We will put this in its strongest form. Unitarianism is false — Trinitarianism is true. But yet, in the sight of God, and with respect to a man's eternal destinies hereafter, it would surely be better for him earnestly, honestly, truly, to hold the doctrines of Unitarianism, than in a cowardly or indifferent spirit, or influenced by authority, or from considerations of interest, or for the sake of lucre, to hold the doctrines of Trinitarianism. For instance: — Not many years ago, the Church of Scotland was severed into two great divisions, and gave to this age a marvellous proof that there was still amongst us the power of living faith — when five hundred ministers gave up all that earth holds dear — position in the church they had loved; friendships and affections formed, and consecrated by long fellowship, in its communion: and almost their hopes of gaining a livelihood — rather than assert a principle which seemed to them to be a false one. Now, my brethren, surely the question in such a case for us to consider is not this, merely — whether of the two sections held the abstract *right* — held the principle in its integrity — but surely far rather, this: who on either side was true to the light within, true to God, true to the truth as God had revealed it to his soul.

Now, it is precisely upon this principle that we are enabled to indulge a Christian hope that many of those who in ancient times were persecutors, for example, may yet be absolved at the bar of Christ. Nothing can make persecution right — it is wrong, essentially, eternally wrong in the sight of God. And yet, if a man sincerely and assuredly thinks that Christ has laid upon him a command to persecute with fire and sword, it is surely better that he should, in spite of all feelings of tenderness and compassion, cast aside the dearest affections at the supposed command of his Redeemer, than that he should, in mere laxity and tenderness, turn aside from what seems to him to be his duty. At least, this appears to be the opinion of the Apostle Paul. He tells us, that he was "a blasphemer and a persecutor and injurious," that "he did many things contrary to the name of Jesus of Nazareth," that "being exceedingly mad against the disciples, he persecuted them even unto strange cities." But he tells us further, that "for this cause he obtained mercy, because he did it ignorantly in unbelief." Now, take a case precisely opposite. In ancient times the Jews did that by which it appeared to them that they would contract defilement and guilt — they spared the lives of the enemies which they had taken in battle. Brethren, the eternal law is, that charity is right, and that law is eternally right which says, "Thou shalt love thine enemy." And had the Jews acted upon this principle, they would have done well to spare their enemies: but they did it thinking it to be wrong, transgressing that law which commanded them to slay their idolatrous enemies, not from generosity, but in cupidity — not from charity, but from lax zeal. And doing thus, the act was altogether wrong.

2. Such is the Apostle's exposition of the law of Christian conscience. Let us now, in the second place, consider the applications, both of a personal and of a public nature, which arise out of it.

The first application is a personal one. It is this:— Do what seems to *you* to be right: it is only so that you will at last learn by the grace of God to see clearly what *is* right. A man thinks within himself that it is God's law and God's will that he should act thus and thus. There is nothing possible for us to say—there is no advice for us to give,—but this, "You *must* so act." He is responsible for the opinions he holds, and still more for the way in which he arrived at them—whether in a slothful and selfish, or in an honest and truth-seeking manner; but being now his soul's convictions, you can give no other law than this—"You must obey your conscience." For no man's conscience gets so seared by doing what is wrong unknowingly, as by doing that which appears to be wrong to his conscience. The Jews' consciences did not get seared by their slaying the Canaanites, but they did become seared by their failing to do what appeared to them to be right. Therefore, woe to you if you do what others think right, instead of obeying the dictates of your own conscience; woe to you if you allow authority, or prescription, or fashion, or influence, or any other human thing, to interfere with that awful and sacred thing—your own responsibility. "Every man," said the Apostle, "must give an account of himself to God."

The second application of this principle has reference to others. No doubt, to the large, free, enlightened mind of the Apostle Paul, all these scruples and superstitions must have seemed mean, trivial, and small indeed. It was a matter to him of far less importance that truth should be *established*, than that it should be arrived at truly—a matter of far less importance, even, that right should be done, than that right should be done *rightly*. Conscience was far more sacred to him than even Liberty—it was to him a prerogative far more precious to assert the rights of Christian conscience, than to magnify the privileges of Christian liberty. The scruple may be small and foolish, but it may be impossible to uproot the scruple without tearing up the feeling of the sanctity of conscience, and of reverence for the law of God, associated with this scruple. And therefore the Apostle Paul counsels these men to abridge their Christian liberty, and not to eat of those things which had been sacrificed to idols, but to have compassion upon the scruples of their weaker brethren. And this, for two reasons: — The first of these is a mere reason of Christian feeling. It might cause exquisite pain to sensitive minds to see those things which appeared to them to be wrong, done by Christian brethren. Now you may take a parallel case. It may be, if you will, mere superstition to bow at the name of Jesus. It may be, and no doubt is, founded upon a mistaken interpretation of that passage in the Epistle to the Philippians (ii. 10), which says, that "at the name of Jesus every knee shall bow." But there are many congregations in which this has been the long-established rule, and there are many Christians who would feel pained to see such a practice discontinued — as if it implied a declension from the reverence due to "that name which is above every name." Now, what in this case is the Christian duty? Is it this — to stand upon our Christian liberty? Or is it not rather this — to comply with a prejudice which is manifestly a harmless one, rather than give pain to a Christian brother? Take another case. It may be a mistaken scruple, but there is no doubt that it causes much pain to many Christians to see a carriage used on the Lord's day. But you, with higher views of the spirit of Christianity, who know that "the Sabbath was made for man, and not man for the Sabbath" — who can enter more deeply into the truth taught by our blessed Lord, that every day is to be dedicated to Him and consecrated to His service — upon the high principle of Christian liberty, you can use your carriage — you can exercise your liberty. But if there are Christian brethren to whom this would give pain — then I humbly, but most earnestly, ask you — What is the duty here? Is it not this — to abridge your Christian liberty — and to go through rain, and mud, and snow, rather than give pain to one Christian conscience? I will give one more instance. The words, and garb, and customs of that sect of Christians called Quakers, may be formal enough; founded no doubt, as in the former case, upon a mistaken interpretation of a passage in the Bible. But they are at least harmless; and have long been associated with the simplicity, and benevolence, and devout humbleness of this body of Christians — the followers of one who, three hundred years ago, set out upon the glorious enterprise of making all men friends. Now, would it be Christian, or would it not rather be something more than un-Christian — would it not also be gross rudeness and coarse unfeelingness to treat such words, and habits, and customs, with anything but respect and reverence?

Further: the Apostle enjoined this duty of abridging their Christian liberty upon the Corinthian converts, not merely because to indulge it might give pain to others, but also because it might even lead their brethren into sin. For, if any man should eat of the flesh offered to an idol, feeling himself justified by his conscience, it were well: but if any man, overborne by authority or interest, were to do this, not according to conscience, but against it, there would be a distinct and direct act of disobedience — a conflict between his sense of right, and the gratification of his appetites or the power of influence; and then his compliance would as much damage his conscience and moral sense as if the act had been wrong in itself.

Now, in the personal application of these remarks, there are three things which I have to say. The first is this: — Distinguish, I pray you, between this tenderness for a brother's conscience and mere time-serving. This same Apostle, whom we here see so gracefully giving way upon the ground of expediency when Christian principles were left entire, was the same who stood firm and strong as a rock, when anything was demandea which trenched upon Christian principle. When some required, as a matter of necessity for salvation, that these converts should be circumcised, the Apostle says — "To whom we gave place by subjection, no, not for an hour!" It was not indifference — it was not cowardice — it was not the mere love of peace, purchased by the sacrifice of principle, that prompted this counsel — but it was Christian love — that delicate and Christian love which dreads to tamper with the sanctities of a brother's conscience.

The second thing we have to say is this — that this abridgment of their liberty is a duty more especially incumbent upon all who are possessed of influence. There are some men, happily for themselves we may say, who are so insignificant that they can take their course quietly in the valleys of life, and who can exercise the fullest Christian liberty without giving pain to others. But it is the price which all, who are possessed of influence, must pay — that their acts must be measured, not in themselves, but according to their influence on others. So, my Christian brethren, to bring this matter home to every-day experience and common life, if the landlord uses his authority and influence to induce his tenant to vote against his conscience, it may be he has secured one voice to the principle which is right, or, at all events, to that which seemed to him to be right: but he has gained that single voice at the sacrifice and expense of a brother's soul. Or, again — if for the sake of ensuring personal politeness and attention, the rich man puts a gratuity into the hand of a servant of some company which has forbidden him to receive it, he gains the attention, he ensures the politeness, but he gains it at the sacrifice and expense of a man and a Christian brother.

The last remark which we have to make is this: — How possible is it to mix together the vigor of a masculine and manly intellect with the tenderness and charity which is taught by the gospel of Christ! No man ever breathed so freely, when on earth, the air and atmosphere of heaven as the Apostle Paul — no man ever soared so high above all prejudices, narrowness, littlenesses, scruples, as he: and yet no man ever bound himself as Paul bound himself to the ignorance, the scruples, the prejudices of his brethren. So that, what in other cases was infirmity, imbecility, and superstition, gathered round it in his case the pure, high spirit of Christian charity and Christian delicacy. And now, out of the writings, and sayings, and deeds of those who loudly proclaim "the rights of man" and the "rights of liberty," match us if you can with one sentence so sublime, so noble, — one that will so stand at the bar of God hereafter, — as this single glorious sentence of his, in which he asserts the rights of Christian conscience above the claims of Christian liberty — "Wherefore if meat make my brother to offend, I will eat no flesh while the world standeth, lest I make my brother to offend."

LECTURE XVIII.

DECEMBER 7, 1851.

1 CORINTHIANS, ix. — "Am I not an apostle? am I not free? have I not seen Jesus Christ our Lord? are not ye my work in the Lord? — If I be not an apostle unto others, yet doubtless I am to you: for the seal of mine apostleship are ye in the Lord. — Mine answer to them that do examine me is this, — Have we not power to eat and to drink? — Have we not power to lead about a sister, a wife, as well as other apostles, and as the brethren of the Lord, and Cephas? — Or I only and Barnabas, have not we power to forbearworking? — Who goeth a warfare any time at his own charges? who planteth a vineyard, and eateth not of the fruit thereof? or who feedeth a flock, and eateth not of the milk of the flock? — Say I these things as a man? or saith not the law the same also? — For it is written in the law of Moses, Thou shalt not muzzle the mouth of the ox that treadeth out the corn. Doth God take care for oxen? — Or saith he it altogether for our sakes? For our sakes, no doubt, this is written: that he that ploweth should plow in hope; and that he that thresheth in hope should be partaker of his hope. — If we have sown unto you spiritual things, is it a great thing if we shall reap your carnal things? — If others be partakers of this power over you, are not we rather? Nevertheless we have not used this power; but suffer all things, lest we should hinder the gospel of Christ. — Do ye not know that they which minister about holy things live of the things of the temple? and they which wait at the altar are partakers with the altar? — Even so hath the Lord ordained that they which preach the gospel should live of the gospel. — But I have used none of these things: neither have I written these things, that it should be so done unto me: for it were better for me to die, than that any man should make my glorying void. — For though I preach the gospel, I have nothing to glory of: for necessity is laid upon me; yea, woe is unto me, if I preach not the gospel! For if I do this thing willingly, I have a reward: but if against my will, a dispensation of the gospel is committed unto me. — What is my reward then? Verily that, when I preach the gospel, I may make the gospel of Christ without charge, that I abuse not my power in the gospel. — For though I be free from all men, yet have I made myself servant unto all, that I might gain the more. — And unto the Jews I became as a Jew, that I might gain the Jews; to them that are under the law, as under the law, that I might gain them that are under the law; — To them that are without law, as without law, (being not without law to God, but under the law to Christ,) that I might gain them that are without law. — To the weak became I as weak, that I might gain the weak: I am

made all things to all men, that I might by all means save some. — And this I do for the gospel's sake, that I might be partaker thereof with you. — Know ye not that they which run in a race run all, but one receiveth the prize? So run, that ye may obtain. — And every man that striveth for the mastery is temperate in all things. Now they do it to obtain a corruptible crown; but we an incorruptible. — I therefore so run, not as uncertainly; so fight I, not as one that beateth the air: — But I keep under my body, and bring it into subjection: lest that by any means, when I have preached to others, I myself should be a castaway."

THIS last verse is unintelligible, except taken in connection with the preceding part of the chapter. It is commonly quoted in the Calvinistic Controversy, to prove or disprove the possibility of the believer's final fall. It is contended by some that St. Paul was not certain of salvation, and that it was possible, after all his labor in the cause of Christ, he might be a castaway. In reality, the passage has nothing whatever to do with this. The word here translated "castaway," is literally "reprobate," — that which being tested fails. "Reprobate silver shall men call them:" St. Paul says, "Lest after, when I have preached to others, I myself, when tried by the same standard, should fail." We shall find that this will become more intelligible by the exposition of this chapter.

In the last chapter St. Paul had laid down the principle that it was good to avoid all injuries to the scruples and conscientious superstitions of weaker brethren. When Christian liberty permits indulgence — very often Christian love says, "Abstain." As in the sentence, "Wherefore if meat make my brother to offend, I will eat no flesh while the world standeth, lest I make my brother to offend."

Let us, however, understand the Apostle's principle, so as not to misrepresent or exaggerate it. Distinguish this principle of avoiding offence to conscientious scruples, from yielding to *all* scruples. You are not, in order to avoid hurting another's conscience, to act against your own. Nor are you to yield or concede in a case where his conscience or scruples recommend something wrong. In this case conscience required the Corinthians to do what was evidently harmless; abstaining from eating meats was an act of reverence to God, and was accepted by Him because done in faith. So in the instances alleged in the last lecture — the dress of the Quakers — bowing at the name of Jesus — the abstinence from a cavil in these matters is accepted just as the sacrifices were. For you would be pleased if an ignorant person were to present you with something you did not value, but on which, because he thought you did value it, he had spent time and pains. To you it is worthless intrinsically, but as an evidence of affection it is invaluable.

So in the case of fasting — abstinence on certain days is well pleasing to God, if done in faith. And it would be rude and coarse, harsh and unloving, to sneer at such acts, or to tempt men who believe them to be sacred duties, by ridicule or example, to give them up.

But if something were done which is not only not commanded, but forbidden, it is no Christian duty to connive. You would bow at the name of Jesus because, where it was universally the custom, you might hurt the feelings of your brethren by refusing to do so: but you would not bow at the passing of the host, because that would imply a belief in a downright falsehood; and, therefore, as you could not avoid insulting a Romish prejudice, you would hold it to be your duty to absent yourself from the most magnificent ceremony, or from the sublimest music that ever thrilled through St. Peter's.

Again, let us note another exception. Practices which in themselves are harmless may be withstood, because of their consequences at peculiar times. Thus St. Paul was gentle about trifles, whereas the Reformers were stiff. He yielded to Jewish prejudices about sacrifices, because they implied reverence to a truth. They were unyielding in the matter of Romish rites and forms — trifling enough in themselves — because they implied adherence to false and dangerous errors. And so, too, St. Paul at one time circumcised Timothy because it implied symbolic holiness. At another he refused to circumcise Titus, because it was then and there reckoned essential to salvation, and for that reason insisted on.

This, then, was St. Paul's principle. But to this teaching an objection might be raised. Some may say, It is easy enough to advise: fine doctrine this of conscience and tenderness to weaker brethren — conscientious prejudices. Does the Apostle practise what he preaches? Or is it merely a fine sentiment? Does he preach to others — himself being a castaway — that is, one who being tested is found wanting?

The whole of the ninth chapter bears on this question. It is an assertion of his own consistency. He proves that he submitted himself for love's sake to restriction, to which he was not in absolute duty bound.

I. The first part of this chapter is occupied in proving his right to certain privileges.

II. His salutary abstinence from many of them.

I. The privileges to which he had a right were domestic solaces and ministerial maintenance. Have we not power to lead about a sister-wife, that is, a wife who was one of the Christian sisterhood? Have we not, Barnabas and I, power to forbear working? The right to the first of these privileges he proves by the position of the other Apostles. Cephas and others were married men. His right to the second, that of maintenance, he proves by his Apostleship. "Am I not an Apostle? Am I not free?" that is, not compelled to labor.

The apostolic or ministerial right, he bases on four arguments. 1. By a principle universally recognized in human practice. A king warring on behalf of a people, wars at their charge — a planter of a vineyard expects to eat of the fruit — a shepherd is entitled to eat of the milk of the flock. All who toil for the good of others derive an equivalent from them. Gratuitous devotion of life is nowhere considered obligatory. 2. By a principle implied in a scriptural particular exact-ment, "Thou shalt not muzzle the ox that treadeth out the corn." Did God, in this, take special care for oxen? or was it a great general principle, — human, not confined to a single isolated case, but capable of extension to the plougher and the sower. The ox was provided for, not because it was an ox, but because it was a laborer. 3. By a principle of fairness and reciprocity, as taught in the second verse, great services establish a claim. One who has saved another's life has a right to recompense. It is not merely a matter of option. If they owed to the Apostle their souls, his time had a claim on their gold. 4. By the law of the Temple Service, the priests were supported by a special provision: animals sacrificed to God belonged partly to them. The whole Jewish ritual — the institution of Levites and priests, — implied the principle that there are two kinds of labor — of hand and of brain: and that the toilers with the brain, though not producers, have a claim on the community. They are essential to its well-being, and are not mere drones. By all these arguments he proves his right.

Now it is our business at this time to insist on the right. True, the Apostle waived it for himself; but he did this under special circumstances. He felt peculiarly bound, as specially and wonderfully saved. He had a peculiar gift qualifying him for celibacy. He lived in peculiar times, when it was necessary to have unmistakably *clean hands*, to be above all suspicion of mercenary motives.

But what was a duty in his case might be contrary to duty in another; for example, when a family is to be maintained, the forfeiture of the stipend would be distinctly wrong. There is, therefore, no shame in receiving hire: there is no disgrace in toil, no dishonor in receiving wages. It is a false shame and false delicacy to feel that the fee with hire is a stain, or the receiving of it a mercenary act.

II. We consider, secondly, his own valiant abstinence from these privileges and indulgences (verses

12, 15). And, first, his reasons. In order to do his work in a free, princely, and not a slavish spirit, he was *forced* to preach the gospel, and for the preaching of it no thanks were due. If he did it against his will, a dispensation of the gospel was committed to him, and "woe is unto me, if I preach not the gospel!" He was *bound* to do it. But he turned his necessity to glorious gain. That was his "reward," that is, made him rewardable — by forfeiting pay he got reward: and in doing *freely* what he must do, he became free. When "I must" is changed into "I will," you are free. And so in a profession you dislike — an alliance which is distasteful — a duty that must be done — acquiescence in Christian liberty. It is deliverance from the Law.

His second reason was to gain others. "For though I be free from all men, yet have I made myself servant unto all, that I might gain the more." For this was only one instance out of many; his whole life was one great illustration of the principle: free from all, he became the servant of all. He condescended to the mode of looking at life that was peculiar to the Gentiles with respect to their education and associations: to the Jews also, when form was expressive of a true and reverential spirit. Nor less to the weak and superstitious; he sympathized with their weakness, tried to understand them, and to feel as they felt.

Lastly, consider the general principles of our human life. The conditions of this existence are not that you can run as you will — but they are as the conditions of a race: "Know ye not that they which run in a race run all, but one receiveth the prize? So run, that ye may obtain." You cannot go on saying, I have a right to do this, therefore I will do it. You must think how it will *appear*, not for the sake of mere respectability, or merely to obtain a character for consistency, but for the sake of others. And its conditions are as those of a wrestling match — you must be *temperate* in all things — that is, abstain from even *lawful* indulgences. For he who trained for the amphitheatre abridged himself of indulgences which, under other circumstances, he might and would have used. Then the Apostle closes his triumphant argument: "I therefore so run, not as uncertainly; so fight I, not as one that beateth the air;" — not at hazard, but taking it coolly, as if sure of victory.

Remember, no man liveth to himself. The cry, "Am I my brother's keeper?" is met by St. Paul's clear, steadfast answer, "You are." Herein is opened out to us the exceeding love of the Christian Life. Heathenism, in its highest efforts, contented itself with doing right: Christianity demands that your right shall not lead others wrong: that it shall do no violence to that most sacred and delicate thing, a Human Conscience.

There is another inference from this chapter, which is entirely incidental. In the first part of the chapter Paul introduces the name of Barnabas as associated with himself as his fellow worker. Now, in earlier life, these two men had quarrelled about Mark, the nephew of Barnabas; and from that time to this, outwardly there had been an estrangement, but now there comes forth this most touching recollection of their past friendship. Let us learn from this what it is that binds men truly together. It is not union in pleasures, for the companions of our pleasures are separated from us, and we look back to them only with pain and shame. That which separated these two men was in one a sterner sense of duty; in the other, a tenderness of love; but that which bound them one for ever was self-sacrifice. If there were too much tenderness in Barnabas, there was no love of gold, for he, like Paul, preached the Gospel without charge. Union in God through the sacrifice of self — this is alone the indissoluble union; all others are for time.

LECTURE XIX.

DECEMBER 14, 1851.

1 CORINTHIANS, x. — "Moreover, brethren, I would not that ye should be ignorant, how that all our fathers were under the cloud, and all passed through the sea; — And were all baptized unto Moses in the cloud and in the sea; — And did all eat the same spiritual meat; — And did all drink the same spiritual drink: for they drank of that spiritual Rock that followed them: and that Rock was Christ. — But with many of them God was not well pleased: for they were overthrown in the wilderness. — Now these things were our examples, to the intent we should not lust after evil things, as they also lusted. — Neither be ye idolaters, as were some of them; as it is written, The people sat down to eat and drink, and rose up to play. — Neither let us commit fornication, as some of them committed, and fell in one day three and twenty thousand. — Neither let us tempt Christ, as some of them also tempted, and were destroyed of serpents. — Neither murmur ye, as some of them also murmured, and were destroyed of the destroyer. — Now all these things happened unto them for ensamples: and they are written for our admonition, upon whom the ends of the world are come. — Wherefore let him that thinketh he standeth take heed lest he fall. — There hath no temptation taken you but such as is common to man: but God is faithful, who will not suffer you to be tempted above that ye are able; but will with the temptation also make a way to escape, that ye may be able to bear it. — Wherefore, my dearly beloved, flee from idolatry. — I speak as to wise men; judge ye what I say. — The cup of blessing which we bless, is it not the communion of the blood of Christ? The bread which we break, is it not the communion of the body of Christ? — For we being many are one bread, and one body: for we are all partakers of that one bread. — Behold Israel after the flesh: are not they which eat of the sacrifices partakers of the altar? — What say I then? that the idol is any thing, or that which is offered in sacrifice to idols is any thing? — But I say, that the things which the Gentiles sacrifice, they sacrifice to devils, and not to God: and I would not that ye should have fellowship with devils. — Ye cannot drink the cup of the Lord, and the cup of devils: ye cannot be partakers of the Lord's table, and of the table of devils. — Do we provoke the Lord to jealousy? are we stronger than he? — All things are lawful for me, but all things are not expedient: all things are lawful for me, but all things edify not. — Let no man seek his own, but every man another's wealth. — Whatsoever is sold in the shambles, that eat, asking no questions for conscience sake: — For the earth is the Lord's, and the fulness thereof. — If any of them that believe not bid you to a feast, and

ye be disposed to go; whatsoever is set before you, eat, asking no question for conscience sake. — But if any man say unto you, This is offered in sacrifice unto idols, eat not for his sake that shewed it, and for conscience sake: for the earth is the Lord's, and the fulness thereof: — Conscience, I say, not thine own, but of the other: for why is my liberty judged of another man's conscience?— For if I by grace be a partaker, why am I evil spoken of for that for which I give thanks? — Whether therefore ye eat, or drink, or whatsoever ye do, do all to the glory of God. — Give none offence neither to the Jews, nor to the Gentiles, nor to the church of God. — Even as I please all men in all things, not seeking mine own profit, but the profit of many, that they may be saved."

THIS chapter closes with a return to the subject which had been already discussed in the eighth and ninth chapters. Obviously, the intermediate argument is connected with it, although this connection is not clear at first sight. St. Paul had laid down a principle that Christian liberty is limited by Christian charity: "All things are lawful to me, but all things are not expedient." Then he had shown that he himself obeyed the same law which he imposed on his converts. He had abridged his own liberty: he had foregone his right to domestic solaces and ministerial support: he had not preached to others, and been himself a castaway. But then this very word "castaway" brought the subject into a more serious light, and the idea contained in it is the hinge on which this chapter turns.

There was much "light and liberty" in Corinth. Large words were there, and a large comprehension of the Gospel scheme. But it was light without warmth or life, and liberty without charity. There were large words without large action, and a faith which worked not by love. And all this gave rise to serious misgivings in the Apostle's mind. This boasted Church of Corinth, with its sharp and restless intellect, would it stand? Were the symptoms it exhibited those of bursting health, or only of active disease? So thought St. Paul, and therefore the key-note of the whole chapter is the twelfth verse: "Let him that thinketh he standeth take heed lest he fall."

Consider, then, I. The danger of the Corinthian Church.

Their peril lay in their false security: they were tempted to think that all things were safe to do, because all things were lawful. They were ready to rest satisfied with the knowledge that they were God's people, and God's Church. Now the Apostle shakes this sense of their safety by reminding them that the ancient Church of Israel fell, although they had the same privileges: therefore he infers that spiritual privileges are not perfect security. Now the argument by which he proves that the privileges of ancient Israel were similar to theirs, is remarkable. That people had a baptism as well as they, and a spiritual food and drink: "They were all baptized unto Moses in the cloud and in the sea; and did all eat the same spiritual meat; and did all drink the same spiritual drink." Baptism is the solemn profession of our Christianity: and the passing through the Red Sea was the Israelites' profession of discipleship to Moses: then they passed the Rubicon, the die was cast, and thenceforward there was no return for them. One solemn step had severed them for ever from Egypt: and the cloud, guidance which then began, kept the memory of this act before them by a constant witness in all their journeyings. So far, then, this is equivalent to baptism, which is discipleship: a sacrament or oath of obedience, the force of which is kept up and recalled by an outward sign. They had another sacrament in the "rock which followed them." The rock did not literally follow them, as the Rabbins have with dulness dreamed; but go where they would, the wondrous waters from the rock flowed by their path and camp. Figuratively, therefore, it followed, the life of it streamed after them: they were never without its life-giving influence; and, therefore, never destitute of a sacrament: "that rock was Christ." And here observe the Apostle's view of the "sacramental principle." As Christ said of the Bread, "this is my body," so St. Paul declares, "that rock was Christ;" not that the bread was literally transformed into His body, or that the rock was changed into Christ; nor, again, merely that bread represented the body of Christ, or that the rock represented Christ; but this — that which is wondrous in the bread and rock, the life-giving power in both, is Christ. The symbol as a material is nothing, the spirit in it — Christ — is everything.

Now the mystic and formalist say these signs, and these only, convey grace: sacraments are miraculous. But St. Paul says to the Corinthians, the Jews had symbols as living as yours. Bread, Wine, Water, Cloud; it matters nought what the material is. God's Presence is everything; God's Power, God's Life — wherever these exist, *there* there is a sacrament. What is the lesson, then, which we learn? Is it that God's Life, and Love, and Grace are limited to certain materials, such as the Rock, the Bread, or the Wine? is it that we are doing an awful act only when we baptize? or is it not much rather, that all here is sacramental, that we live in a fearful and a Divine world; that every simple meal, that every gushing stream, every rolling river, and every drifting cloud, is the Symbol of God, and a sacrament to every *open* heart? And the power of recognizing and feeling this, makes all the difference between the religious and the irreligious spirit. There were those, doubtless, in the wilderness, who saw nothing mysterious or wonderful in the following water. They rationalized upon its origin: it quenched their thirst, and that was all it meant to *them*. But there were others to whom it was the very Love and Power of God.

Having, then, established this parallel, the Apostle draws his conclusion. The Jews had as full privileges as you Corinthians have, and yet they fell; you have your privileges, but you may see in these examples that privileges are no cause for security, but only for greater heed. "Let him that thinketh he standeth take heed lest he fall." But according to a common view of the Christian state, it is one of easier requirement than the Jewish, more merciful and more lax in its commandments and their sanctions. The Jews, it is urged, were severely punished if they sinned, but Christians may sin, and be more mercifully dealt with. You cannot read this Epistle, or that to the Hebrews, and think so. "All these things happened unto them for ensamples, and were written for *our* admonition, upon whom the ends of the world are come." And the punishments which their offences met with are specimens of those which we may expect. Four special sins of the Israelites are mentioned by St. Paul as corresponding to the circumstances in which he found the Corinthian Church; idolatry, impurity, doubt, and discontent. "Is God among us, or not?" said the people in the wilderness, tempting Jehovah. Think you we shall be less punished than they, if we similarly tempt our God? This chapter gives the answer. Here, then, we meet a very solemn truth: the sacrifice of Christ does not alter God's Will: it does not make sin a trifle: it does not make it safer to commit offences. It does not abrogate, but declares God's law. "He that despised Moses' law died without mercy under two or three witnesses; of how much sorer punishment shall he be thought worthy, who hath trodden under foot the Son of God, and put Him to an open shame!" And these Corinthians were boasting of their privileges, vaunting their liberties, talking of rights instead of doing duties, speaking of Freedom, Brotherhood, and Reason, and all the time the same God who judged the people in the wilderness was ruling *them* by the same unalterable laws.

II. The second thing contained in this chapter is the resumption of the argument on the difficulty about eating meat offered to idols, with further advice respecting it.

Let me recall briefly what the difficulty was. If they eat the meat they seemed to sanctify idolatry: if they abstained, they seemed to say that an idol was a real being, and so they gave a sanction to superstition. It was one of those circumstances where a true decision on a duty lay in great obscurity. Now the Apostle admits it to be a difficulty, but he will not allow them to think it an inextricable one. There is no excuse here for acting wrong: "there has no temptation taken you which is not common to man:" there is a way of escape, and by it they may rescue themselves without either guilt or hypocrisy. He had already counselled them to abstain for the sake of Love, lest their example might lead their weaker brethren to sin by violating their conscience: now he takes higher ground: and this is his argument. Every sacrificial feast in all religions is a kind of worship: in the Christian religion there was the Lord's Supper, and all they who participated in that rite were Christians. They communicated with Christ, they declared His character was their standard of life: "the Cup of Blessing which we bless, is it not the Communion of the Blood of Christ?" And, further, in the Jewish religion all who ate of the Jewish offerings were Jews; they professed themselves to be such by sharing in the act. Thus, in the same way as all who partook of Christian sacrifices were Christians, and all who took part in Jewish were Jews, so all who sat at meat in idolatrous feasts communicated with idols, and formed one society with idolatrous worshippers. Such acts as these brought confusion into opinion, and the Church: "Ye cannot drink the cup of devils."

Here, however, a difficulty arose. Could the Apostle mean this literally? Partaking of Jewish altars, they shared, he said, with God; of Christian, with Christ; of heathen, with idols! Then the idol was a real thing after all? But in answer to this St. Paul explains himself: "What say I then? that the idol is anything, or that which is offered in sacrifice to idols anything?" No: but the Gentiles sacrifice their offerings *as to* a demon. The heathen thought it a sacrifice to a real god, and would reckon any one who ate of it as a fellow-worshipper with them of a demon: hence the Corinthian Church could not do it without conveying a false impression: their presence would be taken as a sanction of heathenism. Thus these religious banquets being not only an injurv to the Church, but also to the heathen, the Apostle, indignant at this wrong, breaks out into forcible language, "Do we provoke the Lord to jealousy? are we stronger than He?"

With St. Paul we infer, in conclusion, two practical truths.

1. The law by which the Lord's Supper binds us to God. "Ye cannot drink the cup of the Lord and the cup of devils." The term Sacrament has been already discussed: that Feast is now called "Communion:" in it we have fellowship with God and His Church: it is the witness to the communion of saints. To some who attend it the Lord's Supper is a mere form; with others it is a means of some good, they know not what. But, except so far as it keeps us from evil, it is only a fresh cause of guilt: for to go to that table, meaning to sin, to be selfish and worldly, — well, then, you are a traitor to God and His Church.

2. The duty of attending to appearances.

Nothing can be more plain than the wise Christian casuistry by which St. Paul taught the Corinthians how to avoid hypocrisy on the one side, and a sanction of idolatry on the other. They were not to torment themselves with unnecessary scruples, else life would be a haunted thing. Live on freely and trustfully, said the Apostle; all things are yours. Enjoy all: but if any man be likely to mistake the act, if he observe on it, or call it inconsistent, eat not. Now we may think this time-serving; but the motive made all the difference: "Conscience, I say, not thine own, but of the other." Study appearances, therefore, so far as they are likely to be injurious to others. Here, then, is the principle and the rule; we cannot live in this world indifferent to appearances. Year by year we are more and more taught this truth. It is irksome, no doubt, to be under restraint, to have to ask not only, "Does God permit this?" but, "Will it not be misconstrued by others?" and to a free, open, fiery spirit, such as the Apostle of the Gentiles, doubly irksome, and almost intolerable. Nevertheless, it was to him a most solemn consideration:

Why should I make my goodness and my right the occasion of blasphemy? Truly, then, and boldly, and not carelessly, he determined to give no offence to Jews or Gentiles, or to the Church of God, but to please all men. And the measure or restraint of this resolution was, that in carrying it into practice he would seek not his own profit, but the profit of many, that they might be saved.

LECTURE XX.

DECEMBER 21, 1851.

1 CORINTHIANS, xi. 1 – 17. — "Be ye followers of me, even as I also am of Christ. — Now I praise you, brethren, that ye remember me in all things, and keep the ordinances, as I delivered them to you. — But I would have you know, that the head of every man is Christ; and the head of the woman is the man; and the head of Christ is God. — Every man praying or prophesying, having his head covered, dishonoreth his head. — But every woman that prayeth or prophesieth with her head uncovered, dishonoreth her head: for that is even all one as if she were shaven. — For if the woman be not covered, let her also be shorn: but if it be a shame for a woman to be shorn or shaven, let her be covered. — For a man indeed ought not to cover his head, forasmuch as he is the image and glory of God: but the woman is the glory of the man. — For the man is not of the woman; but the woman of the man. — Neither was the man created for the woman; but the woman for the man. — For this cause ought the woman to have power on her head because of the angels. — Nevertheless, neither is the man without the woman, neither the woman without the man, in the Lord. — For as the woman is of the man, even so is the man also by the woman, but all things of God. — Judge in yourselves: is it comely that a woman pray unto God uncovered? — Doth not even nature itself teach you, that, if a man have long hair, it is a shame unto him? — But if a woman have long hair, it is a glory to her: for her hair is given her for a covering. — But if any man seem to be contentious, we have no such custom, neither the churches of God. — Now, in this that I declare unto you I praise you not, that ye come together not for the better, but for the worse."

As the Gospels declare the principles of Christianity, so the Epistles exhibit those principles in their application to actual life. Specially valuable in this respect is this Epistle to the Corinthians, which might be defined as Christianity applied to the details of ordinary life. Now large principles, when taken up by ardent and enthusiastic minds, without the modifications learnt by experience, are almost sure to run into extravagances, and hence the spirit of law is by degrees reduced to rules, and guarded by customs. Of this danger Christianity, which is a set of great principles, partook, a fact well proved by the existent state of the Corinthian Church: and for this reason in actual life it is expressed in rules and customs, such as we find laid down by the Apostle Paul in this Epistle. In this chapter we meet two of those extravagant abuses of Christian truth which arose from its too enthusiastic reception.

I. Respecting the conduct and deportment of Christian women.

II. Respecting the administration of the Lord's Supper.

Of the first I will speak to-day.

A broad principle laid down by Christianity was human equality: "One is your Master, even Christ;" and again, "There is neither Jew nor Greek, there is neither bond nor free, there is neither male nor female, but ye are all one in Christ Jesus." Observe, not only is the distinction between Jew and Gentile abolished, but also the equality of man and woman is declared. We all know how fruitful a cause of popular commotion the teaching of equality has been in every age. Yet it *is* Scripture doctrine. Now similarly, in the Corinthian Church, this doctrine of the abolition of distinctions between the sexes threatened to lead to much social confusion. A claim was made for a right and power in woman to do all that men should do. They demanded that they should teach, preach, and pray in public, and have political privileges of exact equality. Strange, too, as it may seem, a Christian right was claimed to appear unveiled in the public assemblies.

Now respecting the first of these claims, the Apostle's rule was that laid down in 1 Tim. ii. 12: "But I suffer not a woman to teach, nor to usurp authority over the man, but to be in silence." Respecting the second, St. Paul in this chapter commands the woman not to affect an attire that was unbecoming to her sex. Let us first take the verses in order which have reference to attire.

It is one advantage attending on this our habit of exposition, that in turn every part of the Word of God must be expounded. Many passages that are rarely treated force themselves thus upon us; and in honesty we are bound to pass nothing. And this I hold to be true reverence for God's Word, true proof of belief in its inspiration. For many who are vehement upon the doctrine of inspiration never read large portions of the Scriptures all their lives, and confine their attention to certain passages and certain parts of the Bible. Now here are some verses which, left to ourselves, we should certainly have left untouched, because they are difficult to treat in such a way as shall afford no pretext for flippant listeners to smile. And really, if they only concerned a transient fashion of attire, such as then existed in Corinth, they might be omitted, for the Eternal Spirit surely does not condescend to fix unalterable rules of dress. But let us see what principles lie below St. Paul's decision.

The first reason of his prohibition is, that it was a rash defiance of those established rules of decorum that were rooted in the feelings of the country. The veiled head in the text is a symbol of dependence, and a token also of modesty; for to pray unveiled was to insult all the conventional feelings of Jew and Gentile. Here let us distinguish between rules and principles: of course there is no eternal rule in this: it cannot be a law for ever that man should appear habited in one way, and woman in another, and it is valuable to us only so far as a principle is involved.

Though in eastern countries reverence was exhibited by taking off the sandal, yet the Holy Ghost has not caused this mode of showing reverence to be imposed on the Church, nor yet this fashion of a veil; but the principle contained in these observances is not temporary, but eternal. If it be true, as it most unquestionably is true, that we know not how much of our English liberty we owe to our attachment to the past, so also is it almost impossible to decide how much of our public morality and private purity is owing to that same spirit which refuses to overstep the smallest bound of ordinary decorum.

Once more, the use of the veil was a representation and symbol of dependence. It is the doctrine of St. Paul, that as Christ is dependent on God, and man is dependent on Christ, so is woman dependent on man. St. Paul perceived that the law of Christian equality was quite consistent with the vast system of subordination running through the universe: "But I would have you know, that the head of every man is Christ; and the head of the woman is the man; and the head of Christ is God;" which two things we see he distinctly unites in verses eleven and twelve when he says, "Nevertheless, neither is the man without the woman, neither the woman without the man, in the Lord; for as the woman is of the man, even so is the man also by the woman; but all things of God." He asserts subordination in one sense, and denies it in another; and therefore bids the foolish question of 'Which is the greater?' to cease for ever: for he distinguishes between inferiority and subordination, that each sex exists in a certain order, not one as greater than the other, but both great and right in being what God intended them to be.

The second reason assigned for the Apostle's prohibition is an appeal to natural instincts and perceptions, to natural propriety. "Doth not even nature itself teach you, that, if a man have long hair, it is a shame unto him? But if a woman have long hair, it is a glory to her: for her hair is given to her as a veil." And this he extends still further in Tim. ii. 12, so far as to forbid public expositions by women altogether; for, inspired with strong feeling, such as accompanied the outpouring of the Spirit in the early ages, the Christian women broke out at the church-gatherings into prophesyings.

Observe how the Apostle Paul falls back on Nature. In nothing is the difference greater between fanaticism and Christianity, than in their treatment of natural instincts and affections. Fanaticism defies nature.

Christianity refines it, and respects it. Christianity does not denaturalize, but only sanctifies and refines according to the laws of nature. Christianity does not destroy our natural instincts, but gives them a higher and a nobler direction: — for instance, natural resentment becomes elevated into holy indignation. Christianity does not dry up tears, forbidding their flow; but rather infuses into them a heavenly hope. It does not make Scythian, Barbarian, and "Israelites indeed" all alike; — but retains their peculiar differences. It does not make Peter, Paul, and John mere repetitions of one aspect of human character; but draws out into distinctive prominence the courage of one, the self-denying zeal of another, and the tender love of a third. And just as the white light of heaven does not make all things white, but the intenser it is, so much more intense becomes the green, the blue, or the red; and just as the rain of heaven falling on tree and plant develops the vigor of each — every tree and herb "yielding seed after his kind;" and just as leaven does not change the mass into something new, but makes elastic, and firm, and springy, that which was dull and heavy before: so the Spirit of Christ develops each nation, sex, and individual, according to their own nature, and not the nature of another — making man more manly, and woman more womanly. And thus, in all those questions which belong to equality, the ultimate decision is not by theoretical abstractions, but by an appeal to nature and to fact. But let us not forget that here, too, there are exceptions. Beware of a dead, hard rule. Let each develop himself, according to his own nature. Whatever contradicts feelings which are universally received is questionable, to say the least.

Observe, however, there are modifications about this doctrine of liberty. Theoretically all men are equal, and all have equal rights; but when we apply this to daily life, we are clouded in uncertainty. Therefore, the only remedy is that given by St. Paul in this chapter — that the abstract principle shall be modified by common sense, human nature, and holy Christian experience.

There is also the modification of the right of private judgment. It is a well-known rule, that that which has been held everywhere, and at all times, is to be received as true; this modifies, though it does not destroy the right of private judgment. There have been many instances in which one man standing against the world has been right, and the world wrong — as Elijah, Athanasius, Luther, and others. Therefore these two things must modify each other. But in questions of morality, propriety, decency, when we find ourselves — our own individual desires and private judgment — contradicted by the general experience, habit, and belief of all the purest and the best around us, then most assuredly Christian modesty and the doctrine of this chapter command us to believe that the many are right, and that we are wrong.

LECTURE XXI.

DECEMBER 28, 1851.

1 CORINTHIANS, xi. 18-34. — "For first of all, when ye come together in the church, I hear that there be divisions among you; and I partly believe it. — For there must be also heresies among you, that they which are approved may be made manifest among you. — When ye come together therefore into one place, this is not to eat the Lord's supper. — For in eating every one taketh before other his own supper: and one is hungry and another is drunken. — What? have ye not houses to eat and to drink in? or despise ye the church of God, and shame them that have not? What shall I say to you? shall I praise you in this? I praise you not. — For I have received of the Lord that which also I delivered unto you, that the Lord Jesus the same night in which he was betrayed took bread: — And when he had given thanks, he brake it, and said, Take, eat: this is my body, which is broken for you: this do in remembrance of me. — After the same manner also he took the cup, when he had supped, saying, This cup is the new testament in my blood: this do ye, as oft as ye drink it, in remembrance of me. — For as often as ye eat this bread, and drink this cup, ye do shew the Lord's death till he come. — Wherefore whosoever shall eat this bread, and drink this cup of the Lord, unworthily, shall be guilty of the body and blood of the Lord. — But let a man examine himself, and so let him eat of that bread, and drink of that cup. — For he that eateth and drinketh unworthily, eateth and drinketh damnation to himself, not discerning the Lord's body. — For this cause many are weak and sickly among you, and many sleep. — For if we would judge ourselves, we should not be judged. — But when we are judged, we are chastened of the Lord, that we should not be condemned with the world. — Wherefore, my brethren, when ye come together to eat, tarry one for another. — And if any man hunger, let him eat at home; that ye come not together unto condemnation. And the rest will I set in order when I come."

THE remainder of this chapter treats ot an abuse in the administration of the Lord's Supper, as practised in the Church of Corinth. It may be necessary here to go a little into historical investigation.

Every Church has a right to introduce new forms and ordinances; and the Church of Corinth, taking advantage of this right, introduced what was called a love-feast, in which the Churches met together previons to the reception of the Lord's Supper, to partake of a common meal — rich and poor bringing their own provisions. This idea seemed in strict accordance with the original institution of the Lord's Supper, as that certainly was preceded by a common meal. There was a great beauty in this arrangement, because it showed the conviction of the Church of Corinth that differences of birth and rank are not eternal but temporary, and are intended to join by reciprocal bonds the different classes together. Still, beautiful as the idea was, it was liable to great abuse. Thus there arises a perpetual lesson for the Church of Christ; it is never good to mix things religious with things worldly. In the highest conceivable form of the Church of Christ, the two will be identified, for the kingdoms of the world are to become the kingdoms of God and of His Christ. In order to make these two one, the Christian plan has been to set apart certain days as holy, that through these all other days may be sanctified: to set apart a certain class of men, through them to sanctify all other men: to set apart one particular meal, that all meals through that one may be dedicated to God.

The World's way is rather this: to identify things religious and worldly by throwing the spirit of the week-day into the Sabbath; to make Christian Ministers like other men, by throwing into them its own secular spirit; and to eat and drink of the Lord's Supper in the spirit of a common meal.

In order to rectify the abuses which had grown out of these love-feasts, the Apostle recalls to their remembrance the reasons for the original institution of the Lord's Supper, and from them deduces the guilt and responsibility of their desecration of that ordinance. He says that it was meant as a memorial of the Redeemer's sacrifice.

There may appear to us something superfluous in this; we should be inclined probably to say, "We need no memorial of that; it is graven on our hearts as on the rock for ever." The Son of Man knew our nature far too well to trust such a pledge even if it could have been given. He knew that the remembrance of it would fade without perpetual repetition, and also an appeal to the senses; therefore by touch, by taste, by sight, an appeal is made to the senses, reminding us perpetually that Christianity is not a thing of mere feeling, but a real historical actuality. It sets Jesus Christ forth evidently crucified among us.

Let us draw something practical from this. Memory depends on two things — on repetition, and on the impression being a sensible one, that is, one of which the senses take cognizance.

Does any man wish to forget God? Does any man wish to live in sin without being disturbed by the painful thought of Judgment? We can tell him how he may insure that — for a time at least. Let him attempt to be wiser than his Maker: let him say, "I can read my Bible at home, and worship God in the open beauties of Nature, as well as in a church;" let him give up private prayer, and never attend the Lord's table, giving up all that is symbolical in religion. Let him do this, and we will insure him most terrible success; for *so* "judgment to come" will be to him only a hypothesis, and God's own existence merely a *perhaps*.

The second reason for the institution of the Lord's Supper was to keep in mind Christ's second Advent: "Till He come." When Christ left this world, it was with a promise that he would return again. Ever since that time have the souls of the faithful been preparing and watching for that coming. So, then, there are two feelings which belong to this Supper — abasement and triumph; abasement, because everything that tells of Christ's sacrifice reminds us of human guilt; and triumph, because the idea of His coming again, "without sin unto salvation," is full of highest rapture. These two feelings are intended to go hand in hand through life, for that sadness is not Christian but morbid, which has not in it a sense of triumph, neither is joy Christian which is without some sense of sorrow. We dearly love the way in which the Church of England celebrates the Supper of the Lord, with a solemn stillness so well befitting the feelings and the occasion.

The next reason for the institution of the Lord's Supper is to teach the communion of saints. The symbolic elements themselves are intended to teach the Church's unity. The feeling of unity in the Church is that which belongs to fellow-countrymen meeting in a foreign land, or to ancient warriors who have fought side by side in the same battle, and meet in recollection of dangers shared together. So is it with us; we are fellow soldiers and fellow pilgrims. This relationship can alone be perpetual: the relation between father and child changes even in this short existence to friendship; even the marriage relationship is only for this life, for in heaven they neither marry nor are given in marriage. While all other ties shall be dissolved, God stamps on *this* alone something of His own Eternity united in Christ, you are united for ever.

LECTURE XXII.

JANUARY 5, 1852.

I CORINTHIANS, xii. 1 – 31. — "Now concerning spiritual gifts, brethren, I would not have you ignorant. — Ye know that ye were Gentiles, carried away unto these dumb idols, even as ye were led. — Wherefore I give you to understand, that no man speaking by the spirit of God calleth Jesus accursed : and that no man can say that Jesus is the Lord, but by the Holy Ghost. — Now there are diversities of gifts, but the same Spirit. — And there are differences of administrations, but the same Lord. — And there are diversities of operations, but it is the same God which worketh all in all. — But the manifestation of the Spirit is given to every man to profit withal, — For to one is given by the Spirit the word of wisdom; to another the word of knowledge by the same Spirit; — To another faith by the same Spirit ; to another the gifts of healing by the same Spirit; — To another the working of miracles; to another prophecy; to another discerning of spirits; to another divers kinds of tongues; to another the interpretation of tongues : — But all these worketh that one and the selfsame Spirit, dividing to every man severally as he will. — For as the body is one, and hath many members, and all the members of that one body, being many, are one body : so also is Christ. — For by one Spirit are we all baptized into one body, whether we be Jews or Gentiles, whether we be bond or free ; and have been all made to drink into one Spirit. — For the body is not one member, but many. — If the foot shall say, Because I am not the hand, I am not of the body; is it therefore not of the body? — And if the ear shall say, Because I am not the eye, I am not of the body; is it therefore not of the body? — If the whole body were an eye, where were the hearing? — If the whole were hearing, where were the smelling? — But now hath God set the members every one of them in the body, as it hath pleased Him. — And if they were all one member, where were the body? — But now are they many members, yet but one body. — And the eye cannot say unto the hand, I have no need of thee : nor again the head to the feet, I have no need of you. — Nay, much more those members of the body, which seem to be more feeble, are necessary : — And those members of the body, which we think to be less honorable, upon these we bestow more abundant honor; and our uncomely parts have more abundant comeliness. — For our comely parts have no need : but God hath tempered the body together, having given more abundant honor to that part which lacked : — That there should be no schism in the body; but that the members should have the same care one for another. — And whether one member suffer, all the members suffer with it; or one member be honored, all the members rejoice with it. — Now ye are the body of Christ, and members in particular. — And God hath set some in the church, first Apostles, secondarily prophets, thirdly teachers, after that miracles, then gifts of healings, helps, governments, diversities of tongues. — Are all apostles? are all prophets? are all teachers? are all workers of miracles? — Have all the gifts of healing? do all speak with tongues? do all interpret? — But covet earnestly the best gifts: and yet shew I unto you a more excellent way."

In the course of this exposition, we have often had to remind ourselves that this Epistle was addressed to a Church in a state of faction. One cause of rivalry was respecting the merits of their respective teachers; another cause of rivalry was the endowments of various kinds given to the members of the Church. Instead of occupying and spending themselves in the blessed work of using these endowments to the edification of the Church, they spent their time in quarrelling about the precedence which should be given to these different gifts. This was the natural result of great spiritual activity: it is so in politics: whenever there is freedom and earnestness in debate, there will assuredly arise dissensions. Well did St. Paul know that there must be heresies and factions among them; but he would not say that schism was a trifle: it might be that earnestness could not exist without it, but yet he refused to say that schism was right. This chapter teaches two things: In it St. Paul sets himself to discuss spiritual gifts and inspiration. First, the Apostle lays down a broad general principle respecting spiritual inspiration; secondly, he determines the place and value of different degrees of spiritual inspiration.

First he lays down the general principle respecting inspiration in the third verse. "No man can say that Jesus is the Lord, but by the Holy Ghost!" This made the broad separation between the Christian Church and the Gentile world. This, the great bond of Christians, St. Paul tells us, is far above all distinctions as to the degree of spiritual gifts or inspiration. It is of far more importance to ascertain that a man is a Christian than to find out what sort of Christian he is. This he tells us in the fourth, fifth, and sixth verses.

In other words, our Christianity is a fact far above our special and particular endowments. Not that in which we differ from other Christians, but that in which we differ from the world lying in wickedness; in *that* consists our distinction in the sight of God. In the thirteenth verse he appeals to the sacraments: does baptism teach of a difference between Christians? does it not rather teach that all the baptized are baptized into one body? There are varieties, differences — yes, says the Apostle, but they are all of "the selfsame Spirit."

And now, brethren, let us bring this home personally to ourselves: for the teaching of the pulpit loses its force if mere abstract truths are stated without applying them to ourselves, for human nature is the same throughout all ages. What was it that waked up the energies of these Corinthians most? Was it that which stimulated the sublime spirit of the Apostle at Athens when he saw the city wholly given over to idolatry? — or was it not rather the difference between sect and sect, party and party? My Christian brethren, what is it that wakes up, in all their force, the polemical energies of this day? Is it opposition to sensuality, to pride, to vice, to evil generally? — or is it opposition to some doctrine held by this or that section of the Christian world? Against whom are all the energies of Christian teachers directed? Is it against the oppressor, the tyrant, the seducer? — or is it against some poor erring Christian, who, it may be, is wrong in doctrine, but is trying with all his heart to live the *Life* of Christ? Let me bring this more closely home to you, and earnestly entreat the members of this congregation to sever themselves from that bitter spirit of controversy which is tearing asunder Christian society in this town. My Christian brethren, if Christ be your Master, what in this world is your foe? Not Tractarianism nor Dissent, neither Popery nor Evangelism: these may be more or less forms of error; but they who hold them are your brethren, battling against the same evil as you are. Your foe in this world is vice, the devil nature, in you and in me; it is in ourselves that our foe is; conquer *that*, spend half the energy in trampling *that* down which is spent in religious controversy with Christians, and the Kingdom of God will soon be established in this world: and if you will not, then the Word of God gives this solemn warning, "If ye bite and devour one another, take heed that ye be not consumed one of another."

We pass on, secondly, to consider the place and value assigned by St. Paul to these differences of spiritual gifts. He states the fact of that difference from the eighth to the tenth verses, and the principle of diversities in the seventeeth and eighteenth verses. He begins by stating these as the very conditions of Christian unity. God has given to one man eloquence, to another business-like habits, to some exquisitely fine feelings, to others a more blunted feeling; for even that is a gift, without which some duties could not be suitably performed. The anatomist tells us that precisely as we ascend in the scale of being, so do we find greater diversity in our complexity. Thus is it that we have the distinction between a society and an association; artificial association binds man to man on the principle of similarity, natural society binds men together in diversity. The idea of the Church presented in the Bible is that of a family, which certainly is not a union of similarity, for the father differs from the mother, the child from the parent, brother from sister, servant from child, and yet together they form a most blessed type of unity. St. Paul carries on this beautiful principle, and draws out of it special personal duties; he says that gifts are granted to individuals for the sake of the whole Church. As he expresses it in another part: "No man liveth to himself, and no man dieth to himself." After this, he carries on the application further, and shows that the principle branches out into a twofold duty: first, the duty of those gifted with the inferior gifts; and after that, the duty of those gifted with the higher powers. The duties of those possessed of inferior gifts he states to be two; not to envy, and not to despond. First, not to envy:—Observe here the difference be tween the Christian doctrine of unity and equality, and the world's doctrine by levelling all to one standard, The intention of God with respect to the body is not that the rude hand should have the delicacy of the eye, or the foot have the power of the brain. The intention of God is to proclaim the real equality of each in mutual sympathy and love. The second duty of those with inferior gifts is not to despond. There are few temptations more common to ardent spirits than that which leads them to repine at the lot in which they are cast, believing that in some other situation they could serve God better; and therefore to every such man St. Paul speaks, telling him that it is his duty to try to be himself: simply to try to do his own duty; for here in this world we are nothing apart from the strange and curious clockwork of the world; and if each man had the spirit of Self-surrender, the Spirit of the Cross, it would not matter to him whether he were doing the work of the mainspring, or of one of the inferior parts. Lastly, St. Paul applies this principle to the duty of those gifted with higher powers; this is also a twofold duty, that of humility and sympathy. They were not to despise those who were inferior. As with the natural body, the rudest parts are the most useful, and the delicate parts require most care, so is it with the body politic; the meanest trades are those with which we can least dispense; a nation may exist without an astronomer or philosopher, but the day-laborer is essential to the existence of man. The second duty of the more highly gifted is taught in the twenty-sixth verse. The spirit and the law of the Life of Christ is to be that of every member of the Church, and the law of the Life of Christ is that of sympathy. Until we have learnt something of this spirit, we cannot have a Church at all. How little, during eighteen hundred years, have the hearts of men been got to beat together! Nor can we say that this is the fault of the capitalists and the masters only; it is the fault of the servants and dependents also.

LECTURE XXIII.

NOVEMBER 16, 1851.

1 CORINTHIANS, xii. 31; xiii. 1-3.—"But covet earnestly the best gifts: and yet show I unto you a more excellent way.—Though I speak with the tongues of men and of angels, and have not charity, I am become as sounding brass, or a tinkling cymbal.—And though I have the gift of prophecy, and understand all mysteries, and all knowledge; and though I have all faith, so that I could remove mountains, and have not charity, I am nothing.—And though I bestow all my goods to feed the poor, and though I give my body to be burned, and have not charity, it profiteth me nothing."

THE twelfth chapter of this epistle discusses the gifts of the Spirit, the thirteenth contrasts them with the grace of Charity or Love, but the connection between the two is unintelligible unless the last verse of the former be joined to the first of the latter: It is the link between both chapters: "Covet earnestly the best gifts: and yet shew I unto you a more excellent way." Now the more excellent way is Charity.

We will consider, then, the Christian estimate of gifts.

I. In themselves.
II. In reference to graces.

I. The way in which a Christian should esteem gifts.

Let me first show that this rule applies to ourselves; for it might be doubted, since the Corinthian gifts were in part what we call miraculous, while ours are natural. But you will find that in all essential particulars the resemblance is complete. The gifts of the Church of Corinth were bestowed according to God's pleasure: they were "divided to every man severally as *He* willed." They were profitable to others: "The manifestation of the Spirit is given to every man to profit withal." They were not the highest perfection of human nature, for a man might have them and yet perish. So is it with ours: we have gifts freely granted, capable of profiting others, and yet capable of being separated from personal or saving holiness. Therefore, to all such gifts essentially coinciding with the nature of the Corinthian gifts, the Apostle's rule must apply; and his rule is this: "Covet earnestly the best gifts."

First, then, consider what a gift is. It is that in which our main strength lies. One man is remarkable for intellectual, and another for moral qualifications. One is highly sensitive, and another firm and unimpressionable. One has exquisite taste, and another capacity for business. One nation is inventive, and another, like the English, persevering and able to improve inventions. It is well for us to dwell on this, because in our unchristian way of viewing things, we are apt to forget they are gifts, because they seem so simple. But all God's gifts are not sublime. You would all acknowledge prophecy to be a gift, but St Paul says the humblest faculties are also gifts. The eye is precious, but the foot, in its way, is no less so.

Next, observe that all these *are* gifts, but sometimes we fancy they are not, because sad and melancholy moralists remind us that these things are vain. Beauty is fleeting, such men cry; strength is soon but labor and sorrow. Sound sense does not save: "Life is thorny, and youth is vain. The path of glory leads but to the grave." A noble name, an honored position, an existence of fame, what are these but dreams? True, all these *are* transient; and because so, we are forbidden to set our hearts upon them: "the world passeth away, and the lust thereof." But still, in spite of moralizing, men covet them. And the Apostle says it is right: God gave them: do you honor Him by despising them? They *are* good, but not the higher good. Good so long as they are desired in subservience to the greater good, but evil if they are put in the place of this.

Thirdly, remark that they are to be earnestly cultivated.

There is a mistake into which religious people are apt to fall, but which the Apostle avoids: and this is one of the negative marks of his inspiration. The Apostles were never fanatical; but ordinary men, when strongly influenced, exaggerate. Now the world makes very little of charity; and religious men, perceiving the transcendent excellence of this grace, make very little of talents: nay, some depreciate them as almost worthless. They talk contemptuously of the "*mere* moral man." They speak of cleverness and gifts of intellect, as in themselves bad and dangerous. They weed the finest works of human genius from their libraries. And hence the religious character has a tendency to become feeble, to lose all breadth of view, and all manly grasp of realities. Now, on the contrary, St. Paul prays that the whole soul, ψυχή, the natural man as well as the spirit, may "be preserved blameless till the coming of Christ."

And again he allows a distinction — "the *best* gifts." The same Apostle who so earnestly urged contentment with the gifts we have, and forbade contemptuous scorn of others with feeble gifts, bids us yet to aspire. And just as St. Peter said, "Add to your faith, virtue; and to virtue, knowledge; and to knowledge, temperance;" so would St. Paul have said, "Add to your nobility of rank, nobleness of mind; to your naturally-strong constitution, health by exercise; to your memory, judgment; to your power of imitating, invention." He permits no dream of fantastic equality, no pretence that all gifts are equal, or all alike precious. He never would have said that the builder who executed was equal to the architect who planned.

Be contented, yet aspire: that should be the faith of all, and the two are quite compatible. And there arises from such a belief the possibility of generous admiration: all the miserable shutting-up of ourselves in superciliousness is done away. Desirous of reaching something higher, we recognize and love what is above ourselves; and this is the condition of excellence, for we become that which we admire.

II. The estimate of gifts in comparison with graces.

They are less excellent than charity. They are not the perfection of our nature. He who treads the brilliant road of the highest accomplishments is, as a man, inferior to him who treads the path of Love. For in the spiritual world a man is measured not by his genius, but by his likeness to God. Intellect is not divine; Love is the most essential of all the attributes of God. God does not reason, nor remember, but He loves. Thus, to the Apostle's mind, there was emptiness in eloquence, nothingness in knowledge and even in faith, uselessness in liberality and sacrifice, where Love was not. And none could be better qualified than he to speak. In all these gifts he was pre-eminent; none taught like him the philosophy of Christianity. None had so strong a faith, nor so deep a spirit of self-sacrifice. In no other writings are we so refined and exalted by "the thoughts which breathe and words that burn." And yet, in solitary pre-eminence above all these gifts, he puts the grace of Love.

LECTURE XXIV.

APRIL 25, 1852.

1 CORINTHIANS, xiii. 4–13. — "Charity suffereth long, and is kind charity envieth not; charity vaunteth not itself, is not puffed up, — Doth not behave itself unseemly, seeketh not her own, is not easily provoked, thinketh no evil; — Rejoiceth not in iniquity, but rejoiceth in the truth; — Beareth all things, believeth all things, hopeth all things, endureth all things. — Charity never faileth: but whether there be prophecies, they shall fail; whether there be tongues, they shall cease; whether there be knowledge, it shall vanish away. — For we know in part, and we prophesy in part. — But when that which is perfect is come, then that which is in part shall be done away. — When I was a child, I spake as a child, I understood as a child, I thought as a child: but when I became a man, I put away childish things. — For now we see through a glass, darkly; but then face to face: now I know in part; but then shall I know even as also I am known. — And now abideth faith, hope, charity, these three; but the greatest of these is charity."

It is a notable circumstance that the most elaborate description given in Scripture of the grace of Charity is from the pen, not of St. John, who was preeminently the man of Love, but of the Apostle Paul, whose great characteristic was his soaring Faith.

To each of the Apostles was given a peculiar work; each had one feature in his character predominant over the rest. If we had been asked what this was in St. Paul, we should have said Faith; for he has assigned to faith that high position which makes it the efficacious instrument in justifying the soul. St. John, on the contrary, was the Apostle of Love. To him we owe the pregnant expressions, "God is love;" "Little children, love one another;" "He that loveth dwelleth in God, and God in him." And yet it was not to him that the office was assigned of illustrating and expounding his own especial grace, but to one of a very different character — one in whom the man-like predominated over the woman-like; a man daring, impetuous, intellectual; one in whom all the qualities of the man strongly flourished, and who yet emphatically declares all those — faith, great strength, intellect, gifts, manliness — to be inferior to Love. There are some very intelligible reasons for this arrangement in God's providential dealings. If the Apostle Paul had exalted the grace of Faith only, and St. John that of Love only, we might have conceived that each magnified especially his own gift, and that his judgment was guided by his peculiarities of temperament. But when the gifted Apostle, at the same time that he acknowledges the worth of talents, counts them as nothing in comparison of Love, no doubt remains. It is as if he would show that the graces of the Christian character may be mixed in different proportions, but must *all* be found in every one who lives the life of Christ. For no man can conquer the world, except by Faith; no man can resemble God, except by Love. It was by Faith that St. Paul removed mountains of impossibility; it was by Love that he became like God.

Our subject, then, is Charity: we will consider two points.

I. Its description.

II. The reason of its superiority to Gifts.

I. The description of this grace is contained in the fourth to the seventh verses.

This description is needed, because no single word in any language will express the fulness of the Christian grace here spoken of. Charity is by conventional usage appropriated to one particular form of St. Paul's charity, almsgiving, and we cannot use the term without thinking of this. Love is appropriated to another human feeling, given by God as one of the means whereby we are freed from self, but which, in its highest forms, is too personal and too exclusive to be the Christian grace; in its lowest forms, too earthly. To the Greeks the world was saturated with this earthly idea of love, and it needed this elaborate description to purge from their minds the thoughts connected with it

Benevolence or Philanthropy is somewhat nearer, but still insufficient to be what St. Paul meant. Benevolence is too often merely passive, too often merely instinctive: a sentiment, and nothing more. Besides, many a man is actively benevolent, charitable among the poor, full of schemes and plans for the benefit of others, and yet utterly deficient in that religious sense which accompanies the Christian grace of Love. Therefore, St. Paul gives this exquisite description of what he means by the word, distinguishing it from almsgiving, passion, sentiment, and philanthropy, while something of them all is contained within it.

Upon this description I make two remarks.

1. Observe that many of those qualities which the Apostle names as characteristic of charity are what we should assign to other graces; for example, patience, "she suffereth long, and is kind;" generosity, "she envieth not;" humility, "she vaunteth not herself;" dignified demeanor, "doth not behave itself unseemly;" peaceableness, "she seeketh not her own;" good temper, "she is not easily provoked;" innocence and unsuspiciousness, "she thinketh no evil;" love of realities, "she rejoiceth in the truth." For St. Paul saw down to the root; he saw that it was perfectly possible for any one of these to exist alone, but it was in the co-existence of them all that the real life of the under-root of Love was shown.

For example, you may find a man rejoicing in the truth, and generous — nay, good-tempered too; but there is in his deportment a certain restlessness, a want of ease, and a desire to eclipse others: the Apostle would describe him as behaving himself unseemly. Well, then, he *is* good tempered, he *is* generous, but he lacks charity, which pervades every grace, coloring them all, as our life gives hues to the hair, the lips and the eyes. For real love would have made him shrink from giving pain by showing superiority. In his desire to appear better than others, self is uppermost, whereas Love is the abnegation and forgetfulness of self.

2. I make another remark: for you will observe only general remarks can be made: complete exposition is out of the question; every one of these sentences might furnish matter for a sermon. Besides, to illustrate or improve this description would be "to gild refined gold;" gold thrice refined in the eloquence and heart of St. Paul.

The second remark I make is, that the Apostle here describes a Christian gentleman. There is a thing which we call high-breeding or courtesy: its name proclaims that it is the manners of the Court, and it is supposed to belong exclusively to persons highly born. There is another thing which we call Christian courtesy; the difference between the two is, that high-breeding gracefully insists upon its own rights; Christian courtesy gracefully remembers the rights of others. In the narrow, limited sense of the word, "gentleman" can only be applicable to persons born in a certain class, and "gentle" is only the old English word, "genteel," but in the larger, higher meaning, it belongs to those who are gentle in character rather than in blood; and just as "gentle" has been corrupted into "genteel," so the words "gentleman," "courtesy," "politeness," have come to be considered the exclusive property of one class.

The Spirit of Christ does *really* what high-breeding only does outwardly. A high-bred man never forgets himself, controls his temper, does nothing in excess, is urbane, dignified, and that even to persons whom he is inwardly cursing in his heart, or wishing far away. But a Christian *is* what the world *seems* to be. Love gives him a delicate tact which never offends, because it is full of sympathy. It discerns far off what would hurt fastidious feelings, feels with others, and is ever on the watch to anticipate their thoughts. And hence the only true deep refinement — that which lies not on the surface, but goes deep down into the character — comes from Christian love.

And hence, too, we understand what is meant by elevating and refining the poorer classes. My brethren,

Christianity desires to make them all gentlemen. Do not be alarmed! for it is not in the world's sense of the word, nor in the socialistic, but only in the Christian meaning, that we would see them all refined. And assuredly, if Christian charity were universal, if every man were his brother's teacher, a rude clown, or unmannered peasant, or coarse-minded workman, could not be met with. But these, you say, are only dreams, and that it is absurd to expect or aim at the refinement of the working classes. Tell me, then, is it equally absurd to expect that they may become Christian? And if they are Christian, can they be so far unrefined? Only read this description of Christian charity, and conceive it existing in a peasant's breast. Could he be uncourteous, rude, selfish, and inconsiderate of the feelings, opinions, and thoughts of those around him? "If he did not behave himself unseemly, if he suffered long and was kind, or was not easily provoked, but bore all things quietly," would he not be a gentleman in heart?

II. We come to the reasons for the superiority of Christian love to the gifts spoken of in the last chapter.

1. Its permanence. "Charity never faileth."

In contrast with this, Paul shows the temporary character of those marvellous gifts, which we find mentioned in the eighth verse: Charity endures, but prophecy, tongues, and knowledge "fail." But let us take them in the modern, and not in the miraculous sense: for what the Corinthians got by miracle we now obtain by the persevering use of our natural faculties. Prophecy means the power of interpreting Scripture. This, doubtless, is a precious gift, but only valuable as means to an end; and when that is attained, the preciousness of the gift immediately ceases. "A time will come when they shall not teach every man his neighbor, saying, Know the Lord, but all shall know Him, from the least to the greatest." All those qualifications which go to make up the character of the expounder of Scripture, such as eloquence, critical knowledge, biblical lore, what are they? They are only designed for Time, and soon they shall be obsolete. Tongues also, of which the Apostle here speaks, shall "fail" — that is, pass away.

They were then miraculous. What they were we shall explain in the approaching lecture: now, however, they are naturally acquired. It is remarked that this faculty gives more cause for vanity than any other. He who knows two languages, is able to express his thoughts to two persons: this is very valuable, but it is not necessarily a double means of thought. And yet we see that the expert linguist is generally found more proud of his gifts, and more vain, than the deep thinker and knower: so with the Corinthians, this gift produced more vanity than the more useful ones of prophecy and teaching.

And yet suppose a man had known fifty languages in the days of St. Paul, how many — or rather how few — would be of use now? The dialects of "Parthia, Media, of the Elamite, of Mesopotamia, Judæa, and Cappadocia," they are now all obsolete: "Whether there be tongues, they shall cease." And knowledge also "shall vanish away," for it is but a temporary state of the human mind. For instance, that of the Physician, which arises out of the existence of disease: were there no disease, his knowledge would disappear. And it is the same with "gifts of healing:" when the time comes in which "they shall hunger no more, and thirst no more," when sickness and death shall cease, this power shall be needless. And so also with the knowledge of the lawyer, which depends on human crime: were there no wrongs done to persons or property, the necessity of legal knowledge would be at an end. All the knowledge hived in centuries by the barrister and the judge will vanish when Christianity reigns upon earth.

Again, we see the same with science, which is ever shifting and becoming obsolete. The science of St. Paul's day, the deep philosophy of the Greek, is only curious now; for a brighter light has shone, and the geography, the astronomy, and the physics of that age have vanished. And this is surely reason enough to make a man humble; for if time so deals with the man of profoundest science, if in a few years his knowledge cannot suffice the schoolboy, what must be the humbleness due from us, who know so little? Therefore, the next time you are inclined to be vain of a few facts, or a little reading, or a smattering of science, pause and think, that all the knowledge of the great and wise men of the Apostle Paul's day, except the knowledge of Christ crucified, is worthless now. All they knew has vanished, all has failed but this, that they "washed their robes, and made them white in the blood of the Lamb."

2. The second reason is the completeness of Christian love. Gifts, knowledge, tongues are only means towards an end. Love remains the completion and perfection of our human being, just as stem, flower, bud, and leaf in the tree are all subservient to the fruit.

St. Paul uses two illustrations to make this plain. "When I was a child, I spake as a child, I understood as a child, I thought as a child; but when I became a man, I put away childish things." "Now we see through a glass darkly; but then face to face: now I know in part; but then shall I know even as also I am known."

In the first, the Apostle evidently considers our human existence as progressive; and just what childhood is to manhood, the most advanced manhood is to our heavenly being. We put away childish things in manhood; we shall put away even manly or human things entirely in the spiritual state. In childhood, there is ignorance which fancies itself knowledge, there is a selfishness which does not own the wants of others, there is a slavery to present impulses: but when age has taught us how little we know, has taught us that if society is to exist at all, we must give up some of our selfishness, and has taught us prudence, then manhood puts away the things of a child.

And so similarly, there are many things now which subserve a high purpose, but do not belong to the highest state. For instance, ambition, the last infirmity of noble minds; what a spur it is to exertion! how deadening to sloth! And if you were to quench it altogether, how few of the present noble works would be done! Again, patriotism is a virtue, but not the highest; you could not dispense with it: our Master felt it when on earth; He was a Jew, and felt deeply for His country. But when we enter into that clime, where there is neither Jew nor Greek, bond nor free, then patriotism shall pass away.

Consider also friendship, and other particular attachments. But these are no substitutes for the charity which contemplates likeness to Christ, rather than personal affinities. While on earth, Christ had personal attachments: a strong human affection for St. John, from their mutual similarities of character. But observe His Divine charity: "Who is my mother, and who are my brethren?" He said. And then pointing to His disciples — Behold them: "For, whosoever shall do the will of my Father which is in Heaven, the same is my brother, and sister, and mother." These things are manly and human now, but will have to be put away then; patriotism, ambition, exclusive friendship will then disappear, and be succeeded by higher impulses. And the last comparison is to imperfect vision as contrasted with perfect: "now we see through a glass darkly." Glass in this place more properly means window, for the ancient windows were made of horn, or talc, or thin metal, through which things were seen, but in a dim, confused, and colorless manner. So, now we see Divine things "darkly." We see God through the colored glass, as it were, of our own limited human impressions. "The Father" has scarcely even all the poor conceptions we have gained from the earthly relationship from which the name is borrowed. And God, as "Love," is seen by us only as one who loves as we love, — weakly, partially, selfishly. Heaven, also, is but a place erected by our earthly imagination. To the Indian, a hunting-ground; to the old Norseman, a battle banquet; to the Mahometan, a place of earthly rapture; to the man of science, a place where Nature shall yield up all her secrets. "We see through a glass darkly: we know but in part." But just what the going out of a room lighted through horn windows into the clear daylight would be to us now, will be the entrance of the purified spirit into God's realities out of this world of shadows — of things half seen — of restless dreams. "It doth not yet appear," says St. John, "what we shall be: but we know that when He shall appear, we shall be like Him, for we shall see Him as He is." "And every man that hath this hope in Him purifieth himself, even as He is pure."

Here, therefore, we bring the subject to a conclusion. All gifts are to be cultivated; let no Christian despise them. Every accomplishment, every intellectual faculty that can adorn and grace human nature, should be cultivated and polished to its highest capability. Yet these are not the things that bring us nearer God. "Blessed are the pure in heart, for they shall see God." "If we love one another, God dwelleth in us, and His love is perfected in us."

You may have strong, eagle-eyed Faith: well — you will probably be enabled to do great things in life, to work wonders, to trample on impossibilities. You may have sanguine Hope: well — your life will pass brightly, not gloomily. But the vision of God as He is, to see the King in His beauty, is vouchsafed not to science, nor to talent, but only to Purity and Love.

LECTURE XXV.

MAY 2, 1852.

1 CORINTHIANS, xiv. 1. — "Follow after charity, and desire spiritual gifts, but rather that ye may prophesy."

THE first verse of this chapter contains a *résumé* of all that has been said in the thirteenth and fourteenth chapters, and serves as a point from whence the fourteenth chapter begins. And we observe that charity holds the first place, and then spiritual gifts follow in the second. And of spiritual gifts, some for certain reasons, as for instance, prophecy, are preferable to others. And this is exactly the subject of these three last chapters. He says, graces, like charity, are superior to gifts: "Follow after charity, and desire spiritual gifts, but rather that ye may prophesy." We will consider why is prophecy preferable?

It will be necessary, in order to explain this, to define what we mean, and to show the difference between a grace and a gift. A grace does not differ from a gift in this, that the former is from God, and the latter from nature: as a creative power, there is no such thing as nature: all is God's. A grace is that which has in it some moral quality; whereas a gift does not necessarily share in this. Charity implies a certain character; but a gift, as for instance that of tongues, does not. A man may be fluent, learned, skilful, and be a good man likewise, another may have the same powers, and yet be a bad man — proud, mean, or obstinate. Now this distinction explains at once why graces are preferable.

Graces are what the man *is;* but enumerate his gifts, and you will only know what he *has.* He *is* loving: he *has* eloquence, or medical skill, or legal knowledge, or the gift of acquiring languages, or that of healing. You only have to cut out his tongue, or to impair his memory, and the gift is gone. But on the contrary, you must destroy his very being, change him into another man, and obliterate his identity, before he ceases to be a loving man. Therefore you may contemplate the gift separate from the man; and whilst you admire it, you may despise him: as many a gifted man is contemptible through being a slave to low vices or to his own high gifts. But you cannot contemplate the grace separate from the man: *he* is loveable or admirable, according as he has charity, faith, or self-control.

And, hence, the Apostle bids the Corinthians undervalue gifts in comparison with graces. "Follow after charity." But as to gifts, they are not ourselves, but our accidents, like property, ancestors, birth, or position in the world.

But hence also, on the other hand, arises the reason for our due admiration of gifts: "desire spiritual gifts."

Many religious persons go into the contrary extreme: they call gifts dangerous, ignore them, sneer at them, and say they are "of the world." No, says the Apostle, "desire" them: look them in the face, as goods: not the highest goods, but still desirable, like wealth or health. Only remember, you are not worthy or good because of them. And remember other people are not bound to honor you for them. Admire a Napoleon's genius: do not despise it: but do not let your admiration of that induce you to give honor to the man. Let there be no mere "hero-worship" — that false modern spirit which recognizes the "force that is in a man" as the only thing worthy of homage. The subject of this fourteenth chapter is — not the principle on which graces are preferable to gifts, but the principle on which one gift is preferable to another. "Rather that ye may prophesy." Now the principle of this preference is very briefly stated. Of gifts, St. Paul prefers those which are useful to those that are showy. The gift of prophecy was useful to others, whilst that of tongues was only a luxury for self. Now the principle of this preference is stated generally in the twelfth verse; "Even so ye, forasmuch as ye are zealous of spiritual gifts, seek that ye may excel to the edifying of the Church."

We come, therefore, to-day, to the exposition of a chapter confessedly of extreme difficulty, a chapter on Prophecy and the gift of Tongues. It was from a strange and wild misinterpretation of this chapter, untenable on any sound grounds of interpretation, that the great and gifted Irving fell into such fatal error.

For some reasons it might be well to omit this chapter altogether; in simple modesty for one, since I cannot but feel diffident of entering upon ground where so many have slipped and fallen. But this would be contrary to the principle I have laid down, of endeavoring with straightforwardness and simplicity to expound the whole counsel of God.

I must ask you to bear with me while endeavoring to expound this extremely difficult question. There is no minister of the Church of England who can pretend to a power of infallible interpretation. I give you the result of patient study and much thought. Let those who are tempted to despise flippantly, first qualify themselves for an opinion by similar prayerful study.

To-day we shall exclusively direct our attention to acquiring a clear view of what the prophecy was which the Apostle preferred to Tongues, as this will of course be necessary, before we can proceed to apply his principle of preference to our own day.

I. What was prophecy?

In these days, when we use the word prophet, we mean it almost always to signify a predictor of future events. But in the Old Testament it has this meaning only *sometimes*, whilst in the New Testament *generally* it has not this interpretation. A prophet was one commissioned to declare the will of God — a revealer of truth; it might be of facts future, or the far higher truth of the meaning of facts present.

Hence, in the third verse, "He that prophesieth, speaketh unto men to edification, and exhortation, and comfort." Here, then, is the essence of the prophet's office, but there is not one word spoken here of prediction. We can imagine that it might have been necessary, in order fully to expound a spiritual principle, or a principle of divine politics, to foretell the result of transgression against it; as when the captivity, or the fate of Babylon and Nineveh was predicted; but this was not the essence of the prophet's duty: the essence of his duty was to reveal truth.

Again, in the twenty-fourth verse, the exercise of this gift is spoken of as one specially instrumental in the conversion of unbelievers. "If all prophesy, and there come in one that believeth not, or one unlearned, he is convinced of all, he is judged of all." Observe here, prediction has nothing to do with the matter; for before a prediction *could* be fulfilled, the unbeliever "falls down, acknowledges God," and reports that "God is in you of a truth." Moreover, the prophecy was something which touched his conscience, read his very soul, interpreted the secrets of his heart: "he is convinced of all."

And this surely makes the question sufficiently plain for all practical purposes. Prophecy was a gift eminently useful: it was the power of expounding the Will and the Word of God. And for us to embrace the essence of the matter, it does not signify whether it is, as it was then, a gift miraculous, or, as it is now, a gift slowly improved. The deep insight into truth, the happy faculty of imparting truth; these two endowments together made up that which was essential to the prophet of the early Church.

II. We pass on now to a subject much more difficult: what is meant by the gift of tongues.

From the account given in the second chapter of Acts, in which "Parthians, Medes, the dwellers in Mesopotamia," and various others, said of those who had the gift of tongues that they spoke so that the multitude "heard, every man in his own tongue wherein he was born, the wonderful works of God;" it is generally taken for granted that it was a miraculous gift of speaking foreign languages, and that the object of such a gift was the conversion of the heathen world. After a long and patient examination of the subject, I humbly doubt this altogether, and I do not think that it seems tenable for ten minutes of fair discussion. I believe that the gift was a far higher one than that of the linguist.

And first, for this reason amongst others, that St. Paul prefers prophecy to the gift of "tongues" because of its being more useful, since prophecy edified others, and tongues did not. Now could he have said this, had the gift been the power of speaking foreign languages? Was there no tendency to edification — no profitableness in a gift which would have so marvellously facilitated preaching to the nations of the world? We will proceed to collect the hints given of the effects of the gift, and of the gift itself, which are to be found in this chapter. We gather, first, that the "tongues" were inarticulate or incoherent: in the second verse it is said, "No man understandeth him." And lest you should say this is just what would be true of foreign languages, observe that the tongues spoken of were rather of the nature of an impassioned utterance of devotional feeling, than of preaching intended to be understood. The man spoke with tongues — "not unto men, but unto God." And what is this but that rapt, ecstatic outpouring of unutterable feeling, for which language is insufficient and poor, in which a man is not trying to make himself logically clear to men, but pouring out his soul to God?

Again in the fourth verse: "He that speaketh in an unknown tongue edifieth himself." Here we find another characteristic point given: this gift was something internal, a kind of inspired and impassionate soliloquy, or it may be meditation uttered aloud. There was an unconscious need of expressing audibly the feelings arising within; but when so uttered, they merely ended, as the Apostle says, in "edifying" the person who uttered them. May I, without profaneness, compare these utterances, by way of illustration, to the broken murmur with which a poet full of deep thought might be supposed, in solitude, or in unconsciousness of the presence of others, to put his feelings into incoherent muttered words? What would this be but an exercise of feeling irrepressible, bursting into utterance for relief, and so edifying itself!

Once again; in the seventh and eighth verses: "And even things without life, giving sound, whether pipe or harp, except they give a distinction in the sounds, how shall it be known what is piped or harped? For if the trumpet give an uncertain sound, who shall prepare himself to the battle?" — where the Apostle proceeds to compare the gift of "tongues" with the unworded and inarticulate sounds of musical instruments. These *have* a meaning. St. Paul does not say they have none, but he says that not being definite, they are unintelligible except to a person in sympathy with the same mood of feeling as that of him who plays the pipe or trumpet. And although they *have* a meaning, it is one which is *felt* rather than measured by the intellect. To the mere understanding musical sounds signify nothing. The mathematician would ask, "What does that prove?" the historian would say, "Tell us what information or fact does it communicate." So also we see that one speaking with "tongues" would leave on most people a vague, indefinite impression, as of a wild, rude melody — the utterance of feelings felt to be infinite, and incapable of being put into words.

Have you ever heard the low moanings of hopelessness? or those airs which to us are harsh and unmelodious, but which to the Swiss mountaineer tell of home, bringing him back to the scenes of his childhood; speaking to him in a language clearer than the tongue? or have you ever listened to the merry, unmeaning shouts of boyhood, getting rid of exuberance of life, uttering in sound a joy which boyhood only knows, and for which manhood has no words? Well, in all these you have dim illustrations of the way in which new feelings, deep feelings, irrepressible feelings, found for themselves utterance, in sounds which were called "Tongues."

Again, they are spoken of in another way in the twenty-third verse: "If, therefore, the whole Church be come together into one place, and all speak with tongues, and others come in there that are unlearned and unbelievers, they will not say that ye are mad?" Thus the sound of these utterances of strong feeling when unrepressed, and *weakly* allowed full vent, was like the ravings of insanity. So indeed men did imagine on the day of Pentecost: "Others mocking, said, These men are full of new wine." Remember it was a great part of the Apostle's object in this chapter to remind the Corinthians that they were bound to *control* this power; else it would degenerate into mere imbecility, or Fanaticism. Feeling is a precious gift; but when men parade it, exhibit it, and give way to it, it is weakness instead of strength.

Lastly, let us consider the eleventh verse. "Therefore, if I know not the meaning of the voice, I shall be unto him that speaketh a barbarian, and he that speaketh shall be a barbarian unto me." Here the gift is compared to a barbarian tongue, to a man speaking what the hearer knew not. Therefore we see that it is *not a barbarian tongue* itself which is here intended, but merely that the indefinable language uttered is *likened* to one.

Here, however, we arrive at a most important peculiarity in this gift. From the thirteenth verse we learn that it could be interpreted. And without this interpretation the "tongues" were obviously useless. The gift might be a personal indulgence and luxury, but to the world it was valueless: as in the fourteenth verse, "My spirit prayeth, but my understanding remaineth unfruitful." Now, if it had been a foreign language, it would have been simply necessary that the interpreter should be a native of the country where the language was spoken. But here the power of interpretation is reckoned a spiritual gift from God as much as the power of tongues: a gift granted in answer to prayer. "Wherefore let him that speaketh in an unknown tongue pray that he may interpret."

Now this we shall best understand by analogies. It is a great principle that all the deeper feelings can only be comprehended by one who is in the same state of feeling as the person who utters, or attempts to utter them. Sympathy is the only condition for interpretation of feeling. Take the Apostle's own illustration: he compares the gift of tongues to music. Now music needs an interpreter, and the interpretation must be given, not in words, but in corresponding feelings. There must be "music in the soul" as the condition of understanding harmony: to him who has not this, the *language* of music is simply unintelligible. None but one of kindred spirit with the sweet singer of Israel could interpret the melodies of David: others who felt not with him, said, as of the prophet of old, "Doth he not speak parables?"

Take another instance where the feelings need interpretation. A child is often the subject of feelings which he does not understand: observe how he is affected by the reading of a tale or a moving hymn: he will not say, How touching, how well imagined! but he will hide his face, or he hums, or laughs, or becomes peevish because he does not know what is the matter with him. He is ashamed of sensations which he does not understand. He has no words like a man to express his new feelings. One not understanding him would say it was caprice and ill-behavior. But the grown man can interpret them; and, sympathizing with the child, he says, "The child cannot contain his feelings."

Or take the instance of a physician finding words for physical feelings, because he understands them better than the patient who is unable to express them. In the same way the early Christians, being the subjects of new, deep, and spiritual feeling, declared their joy, their aspiration, their ecstatic devotion, in inarticulate utterances. They felt truths, which were just as true and deep to them as when articulately expressed. But the drawing out of these emotions into words, the explaining what they felt, and what their hurried, huddled words unconsciously meant, that was the office of the interpreter. For example, a stranger might have been at a loss to know what was really meant. "Are you happy or miserable, O Christian, by those wild utterances? Is it madness, or new wine, or inspiration?" And none but a person in the same mood of mind, or one who had passed through that mood and understood it by the unerring tact of sympathy, could say to the stranger, "This is the overflow of gratefulness: he is blessing in the Spirit: it is a hymn of joy that his heart is singing to itself;" or, "It is a burst of prayer." And therefore St. Paul writes the fifteenth, sixteenth, and seventeenth verses, which contain the very points I have mentioned, "praying," "singing," "blessing," and "giving of thanks." It seems to me that the early Christians were the subjects of feelings too deep to be put into words.

LECTURE XXVI.

May 9, 1851.

1 Corinthians xiv. 2–40. — "For he that speaketh in an unknown tongue speaketh not unto men, but unto God: for no man understandeth him; howbeit in the spirit he speaketh mysteries. — But he that prophesieth speaketh unto men to edification, and exhortation, and comfort. — He that speaketh in an unknown tongue edifieth himself; but he that prophesieth edifieth the church. — I would that ye all spake with tongues, but rather that ye prophesied: for greater is he that prophesieth than he that speaketh with tongues, except he interpret, that the church may receive edifying. — Now, brethren, if I come unto you speaking with tongues, what shall I profit you, except I shall speak to you either by revelation, or by knowledge, or by prophesying, or by doctrine? — And even things without life giving sound, whether pipe or harp, except they give a distinction in the sounds, how shall it be known what is piped or harped? — For if the trumpet give an uncertain sound, who shall prepare himself to the battle? — So likewise ye, except ye utter by the tongue words easy to be understood, how shall it be known what is spoken? for ye shall speak into the air. — There are, it may be, so many kinds of voices in the world, and none of them is without signification. — Therefore if I know not the meaning of the voice, I shall be unto him that speaketh a barbarian, and he that speaketh shall be a barbarian unto me. — Even so ye, forasmuch as ye are zealous of spiritual gifts, seek that ye may excel to the edifying of the church. — Wherefore let him that speaketh in an unknown tongue pray that he may interpret. — For if I pray in an unknown tongue, my spirit prayeth, but my understanding is unfruitful. — What is it then? — I will pray with the spirit, and I will pray with the understanding also: I will sing with the spirit, and I will sing with the understanding also. — Else when thou shalt bless with the spirit, how shall he that occupieth the room of the unlearned say Amen at thy giving of thanks, seeing he understandeth not what thou sayest? — For thou verily givest thanks well, but the other is not edified. — I thank my God, I speak with tongues more than ye all: — Yet in the church I had rather speak five words with my understanding, that by my voice I might teach others also, than ten thousand words in an unknown tongue. — Brethren, be not children in understanding: howbeit in malice be ye children, but in understanding be men. — In the law it is written, With men of other tongues and other lips will I speak unto this people; and yet for all that will they not hear me, saith the Lord. — Wherefore tongues are for a sign, not to them that believe, but to them that believe not: but prophesying serveth not for them that

believe not, but for them which believe. If therefore the whole church be come together into one place, and all speak with tongues, and there come in those that are unlearned, or unbelievers, will they not say that ye are mad? — But if all prophesy, and there come in one that believeth not, or one unlearned, he is convinced of all, he is judged of all: — And thus are the secrets of his heart made manifest; and so falling down on his face he will worship God, and report that God is in you of a truth. — How is it then, brethren? when ye come together, every one of you hath a psalm, hath a doctrine, hath a tongue, hath a revelation, hath an interpretation. Let all things be done unto edifying. — If any man speak in an unknown tongue, let it be by two, or at the most by three, and that by course; and let one interpret. — But if there be no interpreter, let him keep silence in the church; and let him speak to himself, and to God. — Let the prophets speak two or three, and let the other judge. — If anything be revealed to another that sitteth by, let the first hold his peace. — For ye may all prophesy one by one, that all may learn, and all may be comforted. — And the spirits of the prophets are subject to the prophets. — For God is not the author of confusion, but of peace, as in all churches of the saints. — Let your women keep silence in the churches: for it is not permitted unto them to speak; but they are commanded to be under obedience, as also saith the law. — And if they will learn anything, let them ask their husbands at home: for it is a shame for women to speak in the church. — What? came the word of God out from you? or came it unto you only? — If any man think himself to be a prophet, or spiritual, let him acknowledge that the things that I write unto you are the commandments of the Lord. — But if any man be ignorant, let him be ignorant. — Wherefore, brethren, covet to prophesy, and forbid not to speak with tongues. — Let all things be done decently and in order."

We were occupied last Sunday in endeavoring to ascertain merely what the gifts of prophecy and tongues were.

Prophecy we found to be in its essence the faculty of comforting, exhorting, &c., by spiritual truths addressed to the understanding. The prophet had the gift of insight, and also the power of explaining the meaning of truth. Collecting the information scattered through the chapter respecting "Tongues," we found that while under their influence men spoke incoherently and unintelligibly, — ver. 2; in a soliloquy edifying self, — ver. 4; they are compared with the sound of inarticulate musical instruments, — ver. 7; to barbarian tongues, — ver. 11; to ravings of insanity, — ver. 23; as capable of interpretation by persons spiritually gifted, in spite of their incoherency and inarticulateness, — ver. 13.

Putting all this together, we concluded that new intense feelings from the Holy Spirit were uttered incoherently, not in some foreign language, but in each man's own language, in broken sentences, which were unintelligible to all, except to those who, by sympathy and a corresponding spiritual state, were able to interpret, and say whether they expressed unutterable joy or blessing, or giving thanks, or devotion.

In like manner we saw that the sound of the Alpine horn, the awkward attempts of a child, when affected by a moving anecdote, to conceal his feelings, boyish joy intoxicated with happiness, though they may appear to be meaningless, yet have deep significance for those who are in sympathy with them. Or again, thanks uttered by any one overpowered by feeling — how incoherent! yet how much better than wordy, fluent sententiousness! Abraham's laugh, for example — it was a strange tongue in which to express happiness: who could fairly interpret that, and say it was intense joy? It was not irreverence or unbelief in David dancing before the Ark. What was it but the human utterance of Divine joy? Consider, again, Elisha's silent sorrow. "Knowest thou," said the sons of the prophets, unable to interpret the apparent apathy of his silence, "that the Lord will take away the light of Israel?" Observe how a sympathetic spirit was needed: silence had been better in them. "Yea, I know it; hold ye your peace." His silence had a language of its own; it was a tongue of grief, which needed interpretation from the heart.

We will now consider the nature of spiritual gifts, and also some directions for their use.

The New Testament speaks much of spiritual gifts. Thus St. Paul says, in his Epistle to the Romans, "I long to see you, that I may impart unto you some spiritual gift, to the end ye may be established." Let us distinctly understand what a "spiritual gift" is. It means the faculty in each man in which the Holy Spirit reveals Himself. Every man has some such, in which his chief force lies: this is a gift. Well, this, either then exhibited for the first time in a visible, perceptible effect, or some old power sanctified and elevated, was called a spiritual gift. For it did not matter that it was a natural gift or power; provided only that the spiritual life in the man raised it and ennobled it, it then became a spiritual gift.

There are certain epochs in the world's history which may be called creative epochs, when intense feelings elevate all the powers preternaturally. Such, for example, was the close of the last century, when the revolutionary spirit of the age manifested itself in the creation of almost preternatural abundance of military talent.

The first age of Christianity was emphatically such an epoch. The Holy Spirit was poured out largely, and under Its influence mind and body were transfigured — whatever It touched, It vivified: as when a person was healed, and "his ankle-bones received strength.' Thus we learn that the Holy Ghost may mingle with man in three ways — with his body, and then you have what is called a miracle; with his spirit, and then you have that exalted feeling which finds vent in what is called "Tongues;" or with his intellect, and then you have prophecy. In the case of tongues, men *felt*, and could not logically express feeling, as "groanings which cannot be uttered," or especial illumination of the uneducated.

In the case of prophecy, cultivated minds were themselves able to develop in consecutive words, by the understanding to the understanding, what the Spirit meant. But the essential in all this was the Divine element of Life. The gift was not independent of life: just as when a flood of rain falls on dry and thirsty ground, and the result is greenness and vigor in the plants — greenness and vigor not being gifts, but simply the outward manifestation of invisible life — so the new life penetrated the whole man, and gave force to every faculty.

Consider what this gift of prophecy must have done in developing the Christian Church! Men came into

Christian assemblies for once, and were astonished by the flood of luminous and irresistible truth which passed from the prophetic lips: it became an instrument of conversion: but in the "Tongues" the clear understanding vanished into ecstasy: the utterer, unless he controlled them, was carried away by his feelings.

For this was not an address, nor an exhortation, nor exactly a prayer: utterly indifferent to the presence of others, the man was occupied only with God and his own soul. Consider St. Paul's ecstasy when he was caught up into the third heaven; yet even this he deprecates as comparatively worthless. That state, if not under control, would have produced "tongues." Hence "tongues" is the plural, for there were different kinds of utterance by different feelings, innumerable phases of feeling, innumerable modes of utterance.

In the twenty-ninth verse, St. Paul gives a direction concerning prophecy, from which we learn that private inspiration was always to be judged by the general inspiration — *i. e.*, it was not to be taken for granted because spoken: — had this simple rule been attended to, how much fanaticism would have been prevented! We must remember that inspiration is one thing, infallibility is another. God the Holy Ghost, as a Sanctifying Spirit, dwells in human beings with partial sin; is it inconceivable that God, the Inspiring Spirit, should dwell with partial error? Did he not do so, He could not dwell with man at all. Therefore, St. Paul says that the spirits of the prophets are to be subject to the prophets. Neglect of this has been a fruitful cause of fanaticism. From the thirty-second verse, we learn the responsibility attaching to every possessor of gifts; it is a duty to rule — that is, to control — his gift. For inspiration might be abused: this is the great lessen of the passage; the afflatus was not irresistible: a man was not to be borne away by his gift, but to be master of it, and responsible for it. The prophets were not mere trumpets, *forced* to utter rightly what God said.

The first direction respecting "tongues" was repression of feeling in public. It is plain that what the

Apostle dreaded was self-deception and enthusiasm. This state of ecstasy was so pleasurable, and the admiration awarded to it so easy to be procured, that it became the object of anxious pursuit to numbers, who, instead of steady well-doing, spent life in exhibiting intense feeling or "showing off." Now this, in its essence, is not confined to Christian souls. "Enthusiasm" means "possessed by the god"—a heathen word used of the Pythonesses or frantic devotees; for there is a bad as well as a fine frenzy. And the camp meetings in America, and the convulsions of the Ranters, all bear testimony to the same truth; how uncontrolled religious feeling may overpower reason and sense—mere natural and animal feeling mingling itself with the movements of Divine life.

There is great danger in ungoverned feeling. There are persons more highly gifted with fine delicate sensibilities than others: they are not moved to action like others, by convictions of the intellect or by a strong sense of duty: they can do nothing, except through their affections. All this is very precious, no doubt, if well used: but just in proportion as feelings are strong do they require discipline. The temptation is great to indulge from mere pleasure of indulgence, and from the admiration given to feeling. It is easier to gain credit for goodness by a glistening eye, while listening to some story of self-sacrifice, than by patient usefulness. It is easier to get credit for spirituality by thrilling at some impassioned speech on the platform, or sermon from the pulpit, than by living a life of justice, mercy, and truth. And hence, religious life degenerates into mere indulgence of feeling, the excitement of religious meetings, or the *utterance* of strong feeling. In this sickly strife, life wastes away, and the man or woman becomes weak instead of strong; for invariably utterance weakens feeling.

What a lesson! These divine high feelings, in the Church of Corinth—to what had they degenerated! Loud, tumultuous, disorderly cries; such, that a stranger coming in would pronounce of the speakers that they were mad!

The second direction respecting tongues is, "Forbid not to speak with tongues." See the inspired wisdom of the Apostle's teaching! A common man would have said, "All this is wild fanaticism: away with it!" St. Paul said, "It is not *all* fanaticism: part is true, part is error." The true is God's Spirit, the false is the admixture of human emotion, vanity, and turbid excitement. A similar wise distinction we find in that expression, "Be not drunk with wine,. but be ye filled with the Spirit. He implies there are two kinds of excitement — one pure, one impure; one proceeding from a higher state of being, the other from one lower; which yet resemble each other — intoxication with wine or with spiritual joy; and both are capable of abuse. They are alike in this, that in both the senses and the conscious will may be mastered.

The lesson, therefore, from this second requirement, is to learn to sympathize with deep feeling: believe that it *has* a meaning, though you may not have experienced it. Sympathy is needful in order rightly to understand the higher feelings. There are cold, intellectual men, afraid of enthusiasm, who frown on and forbid every manifestation of feeling: they will talk of the elocution of Isaiah, or the logic of St. Paul, and they think to fathom the meaning of Spiriture by grammatical criticism; whereas only the Spirit can interpret the Spirit. You must get into the same region of feeling in which prophets breathe, and then only can you understand them.

The third Apostolic direction is to prefer gifts which are useful to others, rather than those which are brilliant and draw admiration to ourselves. And yet *we* pique and pride ourselves on gifts which make us unapproachable, and raise us above the crowd of men in solitary superiority. For example: it is a great thing to be an astronomer, reading the laws of the universe; yet an astronomer might be cold, heartless, atheistical, looking down with profound scorn on the vulgar herd.

Still, I suppose few would not rather be the astronomer with whose name Europe now rings, than an obscure country surgeon, attending to and soothing the sufferings of peasants; there are few who would not rather be the gifted singer, at whose strains breathless multitudes melt into tears, than some nurse of an hospital soothing pain, or a Dorcas making garments for the poor. Tell me, which would he have preferred, who, gifted above all other men with inspired wisdom and sublime feelings, yet said, "I thank my God, I speak with tongues more than ye all; yet in the Church I had rather speak five words with my understanding, that by my voice I might teach others also, than ten thousand words in an unknown tongue?"

It is better to be useful than brilliant. You do not think so? Well, then, your heart does not beat to the same music which regulated the pulses of the Apostle Paul.

Lastly, I infer the real union of the human race lies in oneness of heart. Consider what this gift was: it was not a gift of foreign languages; a Corinthian Greek might be speaking in the Spirit in the Church, and another Greek might not understand him; but a Roman, or a Mesopotamian, might understand him, though he spoke the Greek language: and this not by a gift of language, but by a gift of sympathy. Had it been a gift of foreign tongues, it would have only perpetuated the Babel confusion; but being a gift of the Spirit, it neutralized that confusion. The world is craving for unity; this is the distinct conscious longing of our age. It may be that centuries shall pass before this unity comes. Still, it is something to be on the right track; it is something to know *what* we are to cultivate in order to make it come, and what we are to avoid.

Now some expect this by uniformity of customs, ecclesiastical rites and dress: let us, they say, have the same services, the same hours, the same liturgies, and we shall be one. Others expect it through oneness of language. Philosophers speculate on the probability of one language, perhaps the English, predominating.

They see the vast American and Australian continents — the New Worlds — speaking this, while other languages are only learnt as pcnte accomplishments. Hence they hope that a time is coming when nations shall understand each other perfectly, and be one.

Christianity casts aside all these plans and speculations as utterly insufficient. It does not look to political economy, to ecclesiastical drill, nor to the absorption of all languages into one; but it looks to the eternal Spirit of God, which proceeds from the eternal Son, the Man Christ Jesus. One heart, and then many languages will be no barrier. One spirit, and man will understand man.

As an application, at this time, we will consider one thing only. There are gifts which draw admiration to a man's self, others which solace and soothe him personally, and a third class which benefit others. The World and the Bible are at issue on the comparative worth of these. A gifted singer soon makes a fortune, and men give their guinea and their ten guineas ungrudgingly for a morning's enjoyment. An humble teacher in a school, or a missionary, can often but only just live. Gifts that are showy, and gifts that please — before these the world yields her homage, while the lowly teachers of the poor and the ignorant are forgotten and unnoticed. Only remember that, in the sight of the Everlasting Eye, the one is creating sounds which perish with the hour that gave them birth, the other is doing a Work that is For Ever — building and forming for the Eternal World an immortal human spirit.

LECTURE XXVII.

DECEMBER 7, 1851.

1 CORINTHIANS, xv. 1–12. — "Moreover, brethren, I declare unto you the gospel which I preached unto you, which also ye have received, and wherein ye stand; — By which also ye are saved, if ye keep in memory what I preached unto you, unless ye have believed in vain. — For I delivered unto you first of all that which I also received, how that Christ died for our sins according to the scriptures; — And that he was buried, and that he rose again the third day according to the scriptures: — And that he was seen of Cephas, then of the twelve: — After that, he was seen of above five hundred brethren at once; of whom the greater part remain unto this present, but some are fallen asleep. — After that, he was seen of James; then of all the apostles. — And last of all he was seen of me also, as of one born out of due time. — For I am the least of the apostles, that am not meet to be called an apostle, because I persecuted the Church of God. — But by the grace of God I am what I am: and his grace which was bestowed upon me was not in vain; but I labored more abundantly than they all: yet not I, but the grace of God which was with me. — Therefore whether it were I or they, so we preach, and so ye believed. — Now if Christ be preached that he rose from the dead, how say some among you that there is no resurrection of the dead?"

IN the regular course of our Sunday afternoon Expositions, we are now arrived at the 15th chapter of St Paul's First Epistle to the Corinthians. We are all aware that this is the chapter selected by our Church to be read at the Funeral Service, and to almost all of us every syllable stands associated in our memory with some sad and mournful moment in our lives; when every word, as it fell from the lips of the minister, seemed like the knell of death to our hearts. This is one reason why the exposition of this chapter is attended with some difficulty. For we have been so little accustomed to look upon it as consisting of Argument and Doctrine, and it has been, by long and solemn associations, so hallowed in our memories, that it sounds more like stately music heard in the stillness of night, than like an argument; and to separate it into parts, to break it up into fragments, appears to us to be almost a profanation, even though it be for the purpose of exposition.

The whole of this chapter is occupied with the proof of the doctrine of the Resurrection. On the present occasion, however, we confine ourselves to the first twelve verses. This subject, like almost all the others treated of in this Epistle, had been forced upon the Apostle in consequence of certain errors and heresies which had crept into the Corinthian Church. That Church presented a singular spectacle — that of a Christian body, large numbers of which denied the doctrine of the Resurrection, who, notwithstanding, were still reckoned by St. Paul as not having forfeited their Christianity. The first thing we learn from this is, the great difference made by the Apostle between moral wrong-doing and intellectual error. For we have found in an earlier chapter, when in this same Church, the crime of incest had been committed by one of its members, the Apostle at once commanded that they should separate the guilty person from their communion; but here, although some had fallen into error upon a doctrine which was one of the cardinal doctrines of the Church, the Apostle does not excommunicate them, nor does he hold that they have forfeited their Christian profession. They are wrong, greatly wrong, but still he expostulates with them, and endeavors to set them right.

Let us examine this a little further. In the present day disbelief of the doctrine of the Resurrection is almost equivalent to the deepest infidelity. A man who doubts, or openly denies the doctrine of a life to come, is a man we can in no case call a Christian. But there is a vast difference between this doubt as expressed in the time of the Apostle, and as in the present day. In the present day this denial arises out of materialism. That is, there are men who believe that Life and Soul and Spirit are merely the results and phenomena of the juxtaposition of certain particles of matter. Place these particles in a certain position, they say, and the result will be Motion, or Electricity —call it what you will; place them in another position, and there will result those phenomena which we call Life, or those which we call Spirit; and then separate those particles, and all the phenomena will cease, and this is the condition which we term Death. Now the unbelief of those distant ages was something very different from this. It was not materialism, but an ultra-spiritualism which led the Corinthians into error. They denied the resurrection of the body, because they believed that the materials of which that body was composed were the cause of all evil; and they hailed the Gospel as the brightest boon ever given to man, chiefly because it gave them the hope of being liberated from the flesh with its corrupt desires. They looked upon the resurrection taught by the Apostle as if it were merely a figurative expression. They said, "Just as out of the depth of winter, spring rises into glory, so, figuratively speaking, you may say there is a resurrection of the soul when it rises above the flesh and the carnal desires of nature. *That* is the resurrection; beyond it there is none." On examining the Epistles of St. Paul, we find many traces of the prevalence of such doctrine. So, for instance, in one place we find the Apostle speaking in condemnation of some "who concerning the truth have erred, saying that the resurrection was passed already." That is, as we have already said, they thought that the only resurrection was the regeneration of society. And again, in the beginning of his Second Epistle to this same Church we read: "We that are in this tabernacle do groan, being burdened; not for that we would be unclothed, but clothed upon, that mortality might be swallowed up of life." That is, in opposition to this erroneous doctrine, the Apostle taught that that which the Christian doctrine desires is not merely to be separated from the body, or, in their language, to be "unclothed," but something higher far, to be "clothed upon;" not the destruction or transition merely of our desires and appetites, but the enlarging and ennobling these into a higher and better life. In this chapter, the Apostle sets himself to controvert this erroneous notion. And he does it by a twofold line of argument; first, by historical proofs of the resurrection of Jesus Christ, and after that he proves the truth of the resurrection by the demonstration of the absurdity of all opposite views.

I. In the first place, by historical proofs of the resurrection of Jesus Christ. These are contained manifestly in the earlier verses, from the fourth to the end of the eighth verse, where he shows that Christ was seen, after His resurrection, by Cephas, then by the twelve; after that, by above five hundred brethren at once; and, last of all, by himself also, "as of one born out of due time." The first thing here which the Apostle has to do, is to set at rest at once and for ever the question of *what* was the apostolic doctrine. For these men did not set themselves up against the Apostle's teaching, but they misunderstood what that teaching actually was. For example, there are instances where St. Paul himself applies the term *resurrection* to the spiritual life, and these passages were taken up by these Corinthians, as if they referred to the *only* Resurrection. In the eleventh verse, therefore, he tells them, "Whether it were I or they"—*i. e.* the other Apostles—"*so* we preached, and *so* ye believed:" and then he tells them that the Christian doctrine was not merely that there should be an Immortality, but rather *this*, that there should be a resurrection; not that there should be a mere formless existence, but that there should be an existence in a Form. And he tells them further, that the resurrection was not merely *a* resurrection, but *the* resurrection; *the* historical fact of the resurrection of Jesus Christ being the substantial pledge of *our* immortality and *our* resurrection. By all his earnestness in saying this, the Apostle Paul testifies to the immense value and importance of historical Christianity.

Now, brethren, let us understand this matter. There are two forms in which it is conceivable that Chris tianity may exist: the one is essential Christianity; the other, historical Christianity. By the first we mean the essentials of the Christian doctrine. If we may suppose, for the sake of argument, that without the aid of Christ, without the intervention of His mediatorial intercession, a man could arrive at all the chief Christian doctrines; for instance, that God is the Father of all the human race, and not of a mere section of it; that all men are His children; that it is a Divine Spirit which is the source of all goodness in man; that the righteousness acceptable in His sight is not ceremonial, but moral, goodness; that the only *principle* which reconciles the soul to God, making it at one with God, is Self-sacrifice — he would have arrived at the essence of Christianity. And this is not a mere supposition, a simple hypothesis. For history tells us that before the Redeemer's advent there were a few who, by the aid of the Spirit of God, had reached to a knowledge which is marvellous and astonishing to us. And, indeed, the ancient fathers loved to teach of such men, that they, even although heathen, by the Eternal Word within them had been led to the reception of those truths which Christ came to teach: so that as amongst the Gentiles, "they, without the law, did by nature the things contained in the law," so likewise those men, without the *knowledge* of the actual historical Jesus Christ, had gained the knowledge of truths which came from his Spirit.

By historical Christianity, however, we mean not those truths abstractedly considered, but as actually existing in the life of Jesus Christ; not merely the truth that God is our Father, but the belief that though "no man hath seen God at any time," yet "the only-begotten Son in the bosom of the Father, He hath declared Him;" not merely the truth of the sonship of our Humanity, but that there is One above all others who, in the highest and truest sense, is the only-begotten Son of God; not merely that goodness and spiritual excellence is the righteousness which is acceptable in God's sight, but that these are not mere dreams and aspirations of our Humanity, but that they are actual realities, and have truly existed here below in the life of One — "the man Christ Jesus:" not merely the abstract *law* of self-sacrifice, but the *real* Self-sacrifice — the one atoning Sacrifice which has redeemed the whole world. Now, to this historical Christianity the Apostle bears the strongest testimony when he comes to these facts, that Jesus Christ had been seen by Cephas, and the other Apostles, and by the five hundred brethren, and by himself.

Brethren, let us understand this fully. The principle we lay down is this: Reverence in persons precedes the belief in truths. We will grant that there have been a few remarkable exceptions in the human race, who, by God's Spirit within them, have reached truth without knowing Him who is the Way, the Truth, and the Life; but this is not the rule. One in ten thousand may have so attained it, but for the remaining nine thousand nine hundred and ninety-nine the rule is rather, that it is not by our desires or aspirations, or our intellect, that we reach the truth, but it is by believing first in persons who have held the truth. And so, those truths which you hold deepest you have reached, not by the illumination of your own intellect, but you have reached them first by trusting in some great or good *one*, and then, through him, by obtaining credible evidence of those truths.

Take, for instance, the doctrine of the resurrection: sometimes it appears distinct and credible, at others it appears almost incredible. And if we look into ourselves we shall find that the times when it appeared almost incredible were those in which we began to despair of human nature — when some great crime or meanness had taken place which made us almost disgusted with our humanity, and set us wondering *why* such things should be permitted to live hereafter. And the moments when we believed most strongly and mightily in our resurrection and immortality, were the moments when we felt assured that human perfectibility was no dream, since we saw the evidence of a goodness most like God's, which could not be limited by death. Carry on this principle, and then you have the very spirit of historical Christianity. For, brethren, we do not believe that there shall be a Life to come, merely because there is something within us which craves for it, but because we have believed in the life, and death, and resurrection of the Man of Nazareth; because that glorious life has kindled our lives, and because Humanity through Him has become a noble thing; and all the littleness which we meet with in ourselves and in our fellow-men is but as nothing when balanced against that great, that perfect Humanity. Hence it is that the language often used in our own day about an absolute Christianity, separate from the personality of Jesus Christ, is after all but a dream. Our Christianity is not merely the abstract truths which Christ taught, but Christ Himself, who lived, and died, and rose again for us, our Redeemer and our God.

II. We pass on now to consider the second line of argument by which the Apostle substantiated the truth of the Life to come, and of a Resurrection in Form, which is one of a totally different description. The argument is well known among logicians by the name of the *reductio ad absurdum*, when a man can show, not so much that his own opinions are true, as that all others which contradict them are false, and end in a monstrous absurdity. This is precisely the line taken by the Apostle Paul in these first twenty verses. And the first monstrous absurdity to which he drives the opponents of the doctrine of the Resurrection is this — "If there be no resurrection of the dead, then is Christ not risen." Now, let us endeavor to understand the absurdity implied here. You will observe the Apostle waives, at once, all those arguments which might arise out of the eternal nature of Jesus Christ, and contemplates Him for a moment simply as a mortal man; and he says it is an absurdity to believe that *that* Man perished. Here, when on this earth, the Son of Man grounded His pretensions on this, that He should rise again from the dead. If, then, He did rise from the dead, His testimony was true; if He did not, He was an impostor. On this point He joined issue both with the Pharisees and the Sadducees while he was yet in the world. The Sadducees denied the possibility of *a* resurrection; the Pharisees denied the possibility of *His* resurrection; and the High Priest laid a seal on His grave, that His disciples might not hold out to the world that He *had* risen from the dead. Now, if Christ be not risen, argued the Apostle, you are driven to this monstrous supposition, that the Pharisees and Sadducees were right, and that the Son of Man was wrong; you are driven to this supposition, that a pure and just and holy life is not a whit more certain of attaining to God's truth than a false, and selfish, and hypocritical one. Nay, more: you are driven to this supposition, that when the Son of Man hung upon the cross, and there came across his mind one moment of agonizing doubt, followed by a bright moment of joyful and confiding trust — you are driven to the supposition that the doubt was right, and that the trust was wrong; that when He said, "Father, into thy hands I commend my spirit," God's reply to that prayer was "Annihilation!" that He, who had made His life one perpetual act of consecration to His Father's service, received for His reward the same fate as attended the blaspheming malefactor. Brethren, there may be some who can entertain such belief, but the credulity which receives the most monstrous superstitious is infinitely less than theirs. The mind, which can on such supposition disbelieve the Resurrection, is such a marvellous mixture of credulity and incredulity, as must be almost unparalleled in the history of the human species.

2. Once more: the Apostle drives his opponents to this absurdity — If there be no Resurrection of the dead, the Christian faith is vain; ye are yet in your sins. "If Christ be not risen, then is our preaching vain, and your faith is also vain." Now, what he here implies is, that the Christian faith, in such a case, must have failed in redeeming man from sin. Because he

assumes that, except in the belief of the Resurrection, the quitting of sin, and the rising in mastery over the flesh and its desires, is utterly impossible to man. "Let us eat and drink, for to-morrow we die," is an inevitable conclusion. And you are driven also to this conclusion — that, just as all other religions have failed in redeeming man from sin, the Christian religion has also failed. It has become the fashion in these days to hold that, just in proportion as a belief in the resurrection enters into our motives for right-doing, that right-doing loses its value; and in a very remarkable but very sophistical work, published not many months ago, it is argued, that he alone can be enabled to do any really good spiritual work who disbelieves in a life hereafter, and, for this reason, that he alone does good for its own sake, and not from the hope of reward. It is not for a future life that such a one works, but for posterity: he loves the men around him, knowing all the while that he himself must perish. Brethren, let us examine the depths of this sophistry. In the first place, you will observe that, in removing the hope of the Life to come, you have taken away all value from the *present* life — all that makes life worth possessing, or mankind worth living for. Why should we live and labor for such a posterity, for beings scarcely higher than the "half-reasoning elephant." And thus, in endeavoring to give worth to human goodness, you have taken away the dignity and value of human existence. Besides, you will observe the sophistry of the argument in this respect, that to do right christianly is not doing so for the sake of *happiness* in the world to come, but for *Life*. This it is which is the deep, irrepressible craving of the human soul. "More life and fuller 'tis we want." So that the Apostle forces us to the conclusion, that if there be no resurrection from the dead, there is nothing whatever that can save man from sin: and the Gospel, sanctioned as it is by the Cross of Christ itself, turns out to be one fatal, tremendous, awful failure.

3. Again: an absurdity arises from such a supposition as this, that the Apostles would be found false

witnesses. Yea, and we are found false witnesses of God; because we have testified of God that He raised up Christ: whom He raised not up, if so be that the dead rise not." There is something very touching, Christian brethren, in the manner in which the Apostle writes this monstrous supposition. That *he* should be a false witness! — a thing to him incredible and monstrous. You will observe, he does not leave room one moment for supposing the possibility of a mistake. There was no mistake. It was either true, or it was a falsehood. The resurrection of Christ was a matter of fact; James, Cephas, the twelve, the five hundred, either had, or had not, seen the Lord Jesus; Thomas either had, or had not, put his finger into the print of the nails: either the resurrection was a fact, or else it followed with the certainty of demonstration that the Apostles were intentional false witnesses before God. There may be some, however, to whom this would not seem so monstrous a supposition as it did to the Apostle Paul. Well, let us examine it a little more closely. There is a certain instinct within us generally which enables us to detect when a man is speaking the truth. When you are listening to an advocate, you can generally tell whether he really believes what he says. You may generally see whether he is earnest merely to gain his cause, or because he believes that his client's cause is right. Truth, so to speak, has a certain *ring* by which it may be known. Now, this chapter *rings* with truth; every word is, as it were, alive with it; and before you can believe that there is no resurrection of the dead, you must believe that this glorious chapter, with all its earnestness of argument, and all its richness of metaphor and force of illustration, was written by one who was speaking what was false, and who, moreover, *knew* at his heart that he was speaking what was false.

Another witness to this fact was the Apostle Peter. Brethren, there are two things which rarely go together, courage and falsehood: a brave man is almost always an honest man, and St. Peter was by nature a brave man. But let us qualify this assertion. There are circumstances in which a brave and honest man may be betrayed by the sudden force of temptation into a dereliction from the truth, and such a thing had occurred in the life of St. Peter. In the moment of Christ's apprehension he said that which was not true, and afterwards, as we should have expected from his character, "he went out and wept bitterly." Now, it was after this bitter repentance, when his whole demeanor was changed, and his trembling hesitation had given way to certainty, that he went forth and stood, as upon a rock, before the kings and councils of the world, protesting that he *knew* that the Lord was risen. Brethren, there must be a cause given for this. Can we believe that the man who laid his hand on the axe's sharp edge; or he who asked that he might be crucified with his head downwards, as unworthy to die as his Redeemer died — can we believe that *he* went through all his life falsely? that his life was not only a falsehood, but a systematic and continued falsehood, kept up to the very last; and that the brave-hearted, true man, with his dying lips gave utterance to a lie?

4. Once more: the opponents of this doctrine of the resurrection are driven to the conclusion, that those who have fallen asleep in Christ have perished. Brethren, let us examine *that* absurdity. And, in the first place, distinguish that monstrous supposition from one which somewhat resembles it. The Apostle does not say that it is impossible that *man* should perish. It is a favorite argument with many to point to the lofty attainments and the irrepressible aspirations of the human soul as a proof of its immortality. I am free to confess, that arguments such as these, founded upon the excellence of human nature, have no power with me. For human life, taken in itself and viewed in its common aspects, is a mean and paltry thing, and there are days and hours when it seems to us almost incredible that such things as we are should live again at all. There is nothing which makes annihilation impossible. God, in the superabundance of His power, creates *seeds* merely to cast them again into annihilation. We do not see why

He cannot create souls, and cast them again into nothingness, as easily as He does seeds. They have lived — they have had their twenty, or forty, or sixty years oι existence — why should they ask for more? This is not St. Paul's argument. He does not speak of the excellence of human nature: it is not from this, that he draws his inference and proof of immortality. It is this, that if there be no resurrection of the dead, then they "who have fallen asleep in Christ" have perished: in other words, the best, the purest, the noblest of the human race. For even our adversaries will grant us this, that since the days of Christ there have been exhibited to the world a purity, a self-sacrifice, a humility, such as the world never saw before: earth in all its ages has nothing which can be compared with "the noble army of martyrs." Now, you are called upon to believe that all these have perished everlastingly: that they served God, loved Him, did His will, and that He sent *them* down, like the Son of God, into annihilation! You are required to believe, moreover, that as they attained to this goodness, purity, and excellence by believing what was false, namely, the Resurrection, so it is only by believing what is true, that they could arrive at the opposite, that is, the selfish and base character. So that we are driven to this strange paradox — that by believing that which is false, we become pure and noble; and by believing that which is true, we become base and selfish! Believe this who can?

These are the difficulties of infidelity, — we put them before the infidel triumphantly. And if you are unable to believe his argument, if you cannot come to his conclusion, then there remains the other and the plain conclusion of the Apostle: "Now *is* Christ risen from the dead, and become the first-fruits of them that slept."

LECTURE XXVIII.

1 CORINTHIANS, XV. 13–20. — "But if there be no resurrection of the dead, then is Christ not risen: — And if Christ be not risen, then is our preaching vain, and your faith is also vain. — Yea, and we are found false witnesses of God; because we have testified of God that he raised up Christ: whom he raised not up, if so be that the dead rise not. — For if the dead rise not, then is not Christ raised: — And if Christ be not raised, your faith is vain; ye are yet in your sins. — Then they also which are fallen asleep in Christ are perished. — If in this life only we have hope in Christ, we are of all men most miserable. — But now is Christ risen from the dead, and become the first-fruits of them that slept."

THE Church of Corinth exhibited in the time of the Apostle Paul the remarkable spectacle of a Christianity existing together with a disbelief in immortality. The history of the anomaly was this, that when Christianity first came into contact with the then existing philosophy and religion of the world, it partly superseded them, and partly engrafted itself upon them. The result of that engraftation was, that the fruit which arose from the admixture savored partly of the new graft, and partly of the old stock. Among the philosophies of the world then existing, there was an opinion which regarded all evil as belonging to the body — not that which the Apostle speaks of as "the body of sin and death" — but the real material body. It was held, that the cause of sin in the world was the admixture of pure spirit with an inherently corrupt materialism. The result of this opinion was a twofold heresy, which branched into directions totally divergent. According to the first, men believing in the depravity of matter, held that materialism was all evil, that the spirit was itself innocent, and that to the body alone was guilt to be referred. The result of this conception of Christianity was the belief, that the spirit was permitted to act as it chose, for to the body was all the sin imputed. This was the origin of that Antinomianism which St. James so forcibly contradicts. The other heresy was in a totally different direction: men believing that the body was the cause of all evil, endeavored to crush and entirely subdue it; and this was the origin of that ascetic system, against which St. Paul sets himself in so many of his Epistles.

These opinions then existing in the world, it was to be expected that when Christianity was preached to such men, the expressions of Christianity should be misunderstood and misinterpreted. For every expression used by the Apostles had already been used by those philosophers; so that when the Apostles spake of Regeneration, "Yes," said these men, "this is the religion we want; we desire the regeneration of society." When they spake of the resurrection of Christ, and told men to rise above the lusts of the flesh: "Yes," they replied, "this is the resurrection we need; a spiritual not a literal one: the resurrection is past already, the only grave from which we are to be delivered is the grave of sin." And when, again, the Apostle told of the redemption of the body, "Yes," said they, "we will cleave to this, for it is the redemption of the body that we want." So that, in the Church of Corinth, the resurrection, plainly as it was preached by the Apostles, had become diluted into a question of the temporal regeneration of society.

Now what was remarkable in this form of infidelity was, that it was to some extent spiritual, sublime, and unselfish. Sublime, for it commanded to dispense with all enjoyments of the senses; spiritual and unselfish, because it demanded virtue quite separate from the hope of immortality. And what makes this interesting to us now is, that ours somewhat resembles that old infidelity; there are sounds heard which, widely as they may differ from those Corinthian views in some respects, agree in this, that there is much in them spiritual and sublime. We are told that men die, and that an end then comes upon them; that the hope of immortality is merely a remnant of our selfishness, and that the only immortality for man is to enter by faith into the kingdom of goodness. Now the way in which the Apostle Paul met these views was with that line of argument which consists in demonstrating the impossibility of such a supposition, by deducing from it all the absurdities in which it clothes itself. For one moment he grants it; there is then no resurrection, no immortality! Let us, therefore, see the consequences: they are so awful and incredible, that no sane mind can possibly receive them. In other words, the Apostle demonstrates that, great as may be the difficulty in believing in immortality, the difficulty in disbelieving it is tenfold greater.

We will then endeavor, to-day, to elaborate and draw out the four incredibilities of which the Apostle speaks. The first absurdity of which he speaks, resulting from a denial of the resurrection of Jesus, is, "we are found false witnesses before God." *False* witnesses, not *mistaken* witnesses. He allows no loophole of escape: the resurrection is a fact, or else a falsehood. And now consider the results of that supposition, — Who are they that are the false witnesses of the resurrection? Among them we find prominently two; with these two the Book of the Acts of the Apostles is chiefly occupied. The first is St. Peter, the other St. Paul. St. Peter goes forth into the world strong in his conviction that Jesus Christ is risen from the dead; for in the early ages of Christianity the doctrine most preached was not the Cross, but the Resurrection. From a mistaken view of the writings of the Apostle Paul, as when he said, "I preach Christ crucified," it has been inferred, that the chief doctrine of his life was the Crucifixion; but it was the crucified and risen Saviour that he preached, rather than the mere fact of the Crucifixion. In the early ages it was almost unnecessary to speak of the Cross, for the crucifixion of the Redeemer was a thing not done in a corner: no one thought of denying *that*. But instead of this, the Apostles went forth, preaching that from which the world recoiled, that Christ had risen. If the Apostle Peter went forth to proclaim the

Gospel to the Jews, even before the Sanhedrim and before all the people, this was his doctrine, "Jesus and the Resurrection." Thus taught the Apostle Peter. His character was well known to be this, brave — fearless, impetuous — exactly that character to which falsehood is impossible. The brave man never is habitually a liar; in moments of fearfulness, as when Peter denied his Lord, he may be untrue; but he will not be so when he has courage in his soul.

Another remark respecting these men being false witnesses is, that St. Paul must have been a false declarer of the truth, and the incredibility of this we are content to rest on the single chapter now before us, namely, the fifteenth chapter of the first Epistle to the Corinthians. In common life we judge of a witness by his look and actions; so let us judge this chapter. You will observe, that it is not the eloquence of a hired writer, neither is it the eloquence of a priest, concealing and mystifying the doctrine: the denial of the Resurrection had kindled the earnest, glorious nature of the Apostle into one burning, glowing fire; every word is full of life. We defy you to read the chapter and believe that Paul was doubtful of the truths he there asserted. This is one of the impossibilities; if there be no resurrection of the dead, then these two glorious Apostles were false witnesses!

The second incredible thing is this: if there be no resurrection, Christ is not risen. Remark the severe, rigorous logic of St. Paul: he refuses to place the Human race in one category, and Jesus Christ in another. If Jesus rose, then the Human race shall also rise; but if there be no resurrection for man, then the Apostle, holding to his logic, says, Jesus Christ, the Son of God, is not risen.

Now let us endeavor to understand the results of this conclusion, and what was its bearing. Last Friday we tried to meditate on that death which all men, with varied meanings in their expressions, have agreed to call Divine. We endeavored to meditate on the darkness of that Human Soul, struggling in weakness and perplexity with the mystery of death. We tried to think on that Love, mightier than death, which even in the hour of insult could calmly excuse the circumstances of that insult, and forgive it. We tried to think of that sentence, as the sentence of God, which promised forgiveness and a place in Paradise to the dying penitent. We meditated on that infinite tenderness of human affection, which, in the dying hour, provided for a mother a son, and for a friend a brother; seeming to assure us that these domestic affections shall last beyond the grave. We tried to think, too, of His trust in commending His soul into His Father's hands. And, lastly, we considered that marvellous expression — in the original, one single word — which declared that the Duty and the Life of Christ were only closed together. Now if there be no resurrection of the dead, then that Life was cast aside by God as worthless. It was, and is not: and that pardon which He besought, and which seemed so worthy of God to grant, was not ratified above: and that earthly darkness was but the prelude to that eternal night into which the Soul of the Redeemer was entering; that sublime trust was not accepted by the Father, but sternly and cruelly rejected; Judas forsook Him, and God, like Judas, forsook Him too! The Pharisees conquered, and God stood by and ratified their triumph! And then the disbeliever in immortality asks us to believe in, to trust, and to love that God who treated Jesus so. This is the impossibility, the incredibility, founded on the moral character of God, which we are compelled to receive, if we deny the Resurrection!

The third absurdity is, that the Christian faith is then unable to free from sin. The ground upon which the Apostle stood was this, that no faith can save from sin without the belief in immortality. We are then driven to this conclusion, that since every other faith has failed hitherto, the Christian faith has failed also, since the immortality it professes is vain. Now one objection by which this argument has been met is this: "That goodness," say the objectors, "which rests only on the belief of immortality, is but a form of selfishness after all." And I do believe that there are men who reject the doctrine of the Resurrection chiefly on this ground, because they think that only by denying it can they deliver man from selfishness. And, because this view is plausible, and because it contains in it some germ of truth, let us look at it for a moment. If a man does good for the sake of reward, or if he avoids evil on account of the punishment due to it, so far his goodness is but a form of selfishness; and observe, that the introduction of the element of eternity does not alter the *quality* of it. But when we come to look at the effect produced upon us in liberating us from sin by the belief in immortality, we shall see that it is not the thought of reward that enters into that conception; when you have got to the lowest depth of your heart, you will find that it is not the mere desire of happiness, but a craving as natural to us as the desire for food — the craving for nobler, higher life. To be with God, to see God, and to understand Him — this is meant by the desire of everlasting life. This is the language of Christianity: "Ye are the children of light." Ye are stated in the Bible in words, and symbolically in baptism, to be the children of God; ye are the heirs of Immortality; do not live as if ye were only the heirs of Time. Narrow this conception, limit that infinite existence to seventy years, and all is inevitably contracted, every hope stunted, high aims become simply impossible.

And now, my Christian brethren, we ask, what is the single motive that can be brought forward to liberate a man from selfishness, when you have taken away this belief in immortality? Will you tell him to live for posterity? — what is posterity to him? or for the human race in ages hereafter? — but what is the human race to him, especially when its eternity is taken from it, and you have declared it to be only mortal? The sentence of the Apostle is plain: "Your faith is vain, ye are yet in your sins." Infidelity must be selfish: if to-morrow we die, then to-day let us eat and drink; it is but a matter of taste how we live. If man is to die the death of the swine, why may he not live the life of the swine? If there be no immortality, why am I to be the declarer and defender of injured rights? Why am I not to execute vengeance, knowing that if it be not executed now, it never can be? Tell us why, when every passion is craving for gratification, a man is to deny himself the satisfaction, if he is no exalted thing, no heir of immortality, but only a mere sensitive worm, endowed with the questionable good of a consciousness of his own misery? These are the questions which infidelity has to answer.

The last incredibility from which the Apostle argues is, that, if there be no resurrection, then they that have fallen asleep in Christ have perished. When the Apostle speaks of those fallen asleep in Christ, he does not necessarily mean only those who have borne the Christian name, but those who have lived with the mind of Christ and died with His Spirit. Those who in the elder dispensation only dimly descried the coming of that purer day, scarcely knowing what it was; who still in that faith lived the high and noble life of the ancient Jew; also those, neither Jew nor Christian, who lived in heathen days, but were yet not disobedient to the Eternal Voice speaking in their hearts; and who by means of that lived above their generations, penetrating into the invisible, and so became heirs of the righteousness which is by faith; all those, therefore, have perished! Now see what these skeptics require us to believe: that all those who have shed a sunshine upon earth, and whose affections were so pure and good that they seemed to tell you of an Eternity, perished utterly, as the selfish and impure! You are required to believe that those who died in the field of battle, bravely giving up their lives for others, died even as the false and the coward dies. You are required to believe that, when there arose a great cry at midnight, and the Wreck went down, they who passed out of the world with the oath of blasphemy, or the shriek of despair, shared the same fate with those who calmly resigned their departing spirits into their Father's hand, with nothing but an awful silence to greet them, like that which greeted the priests of Baal on Mount Carmel! You are required to believe that the pure and wise of this world have all been wrong, and the selfish and sensual all right. If from this you shrink as from a thing derogatory to God, then there remains but that conclusion to which St. Paul conducts us: "Now is Christ risen from the dead." The spiritual resurrection is but the mere foretaste and pledge of the literal. Let us, brethren, seek to rise with Christ above this world and our own selves, for every act tells on that Eternity, every thought and every word reap an everlasting harvest.

"Therefore," says the Apostle, in the conclusion of this chapter, "be ye steadfast, unmovable, always abounding in the work of the Lord, forasmuch as ye know that your labor is not in vain in the Lord."

LECTURE XXIX.

1 Corinthians, xv. 21–34. — "For since by man came death, by man came also the resurrection of the dead. — For as in Adam all die, even so in Christ shall all be made alive. — But every man in his own order: Christ the first-fruits; afterward they that are Christ's at his coming. — Then cometh the end, when he shall have delivered up the kingdom to God, even the Father; when he shall have put down all rule and all authority and power. — For he must reign, till he hath put all enemies under his feet. — The last enemy that shall be destroyed is death. — For he hath put all things under his feet. But when he saith, All things are put under him, it is manifest that he is excepted, which did put all things under him. — And when all things shall be subdued unto him, then shall the Son also himself be subject unto him that put all things under him, that God may be all in all. — Else what shall they do which are baptized for the dead, if the dead rise not at all? why are they then baptized for the dead? — And why stand we in jeopardy every hour? — I protest by your rejoicing which I have in Christ Jesus our Lord, I die daily.—If after the manner of men I have fought with beasts at Ephesus, what advantageth it me, if the dead rise not? let us eat and drink; for to-morrow we die. — Be not deceived: evil communications corrupt good manners.—Awake to righteousness, and sin not; for some have not the knowledge of God: I speak this to your shame."

In following the train of argument contained in this chapter, it must be clearly kept in remembrance that the error combated by St. Paul was not the denial of immortality, but the denial of a resurrection. The ultra-spiritualizers in Corinth did not say, "Man perishes for ever in the grave," but, "The form in which the spirit lived shall never be restored. From the moment death touches earthly life, Man becomes for ever a bodiless spirit." No doubt in this chapter there are passages in which the Apostle speaks of Immortality, but they are only incidental to the general argument, as for example, "Let us eat and drink, for to-morrow we die." The chief thing, therefore, to lay stress on is, that in the early Church there was not so much a denial of an Immortality, as of a Resurrection.

In the earlier part of this chapter St. Paul proved the Resurrection by the fact of the resurrection of Christ, which he treats neither as a doctrine, nor a hope, nor an aspiration of the soul, but as a historical reality which, duly recorded and witnessed, took place actually and visibly upon this earth. Eye-witnesses tell us, said the Apostle, that on numerous occasions openly, and after death, they saw, felt, heard, and talked with Christ. On that fact Christianity rests, and if there is anything in the universe that can be substantiated it is that fact. With this he triumphantly concludes that *reductio ad absurdum*, which is contained in verses 13–20. "Now *is* Christ risen from the dead."

To-day we consider—

I. The results of Christ's resurrection to us.
II. Corroborative proofs.

I. The first result is thus expressed: "He is become the first-fruits of them that sleep." The expression is Jewish; and to discover what it implies, we must remember the ancient custom. The first-fruits of the harvest were dedicated to God, whereby He put in His claim for the whole, just as shutting up a road once a year puts in a claim of proprietorship to the right of way for ever. It was thus St. Paul understood the ceremony: "for if the first-fruits be holy, the lump is also holy." Thus when the Apostle says that "Christ is the first-fruits of them that slept," he implies that part of the harvest has been claimed for God, and, therefore, that the rest is His too. The resurrection of Christ is a pledge of the resurrection of all who share in His Humanity.

Now two questions arise on this. 1. Why does this result take place? 2. When will it take place?

1. The ground on which it rests:—"For as in Adam all die, even so in Christ shall all be made alive."—ver. 22. Two doctrines are given to us in this text

— original sin, and original righteousness; the doctrine of the natural corruption and fault of our nature, and the doctrine of the Divine life which belongs to our higher nature.

And first: "In Adam all die."

Do not understand this as if the Apostle merely said, "If you sin as Adam sinned, you will die as Adam died." This were mere Pelagianism, and is expressly condemned in the article of our Church on Original Sin. According to the Scriptures we inherit the first man's nature, and that nature has in it the mortal, not the immortal. And yet there are in all of us two natures, that of the animal and that of the spirit, an Adam and a Christ.

Let us see what St. Paul meant by being "in Adam." He explains himself: "The first man was of the earth, earthy; and again, "The first man Adam was made a living soul." But here we must recollect that the term "a living soul" means a mere natural man. The soul, as used by St. Paul, is distinguished from the body and the spirit, as that part of our complex humanity which embraces all our natural powers. "A living soul" is, then, the term used by the Apostle to express the natural man endowed with intellectual powers, with passions, and with those appetites which belong to us in common with the animals. In this our immortality does not reside; and it is from fixing our attention on the decay of these that doubt of our immortality begins. It is a dismal and appalling thing to witness the slow failure of living powers: as life goes on to watch the eye losing its lustre, and the cheek its roundness; to see the limbs it was once such a pure delight to gaze on, becoming feeble and worn; to perceive the memory wander, and the features no longer bright with the light of expression; to mark the mind relax its grasp; and to ask the dreary question — Are these things immortal? You cannot but disbelieve, if you rest your hope of immortality on their endurance. When you have identified these things with *the man*, no wonder if a cold and faithless feeling steals over the heart —

no wonder if the gloomy thought be yours. The end is coming, the long night on which no dawn shall ever break!

Now the simple reply to all this is, that the extinction of these powers is no proof against immortality, because they are not the seat of the immortal. They belong to the animal — to the organs of our intercourse with the visible world. And though it may be proved that that eye shall never open again, those limbs never again thrill with life, yet such proof does not touch the truth that the man — the spirit — shall live for evermore. Therefore, it is not in what we inherit from Adam the man, but in what we hold from Christ the Spirit, that our immortality resides.

Nay, more: It is in the order of God's providence that the growth of the Christ within us shall be in exact proportion to the decay of the Adam. "Though our outward man perish, yet the inward man is renewed day by day." And this evidence of our immortality, blessed be God! is perpetually and not uncommonly before us. It is no strange or unknown thing to see the spirit ripening in exact proportion to the decay of the body. Many a sufferer in protracted illness feels each day more deeply the powers of the world to come. Many an aged one there is, who loses one by one all his physical powers, and yet the spiritual in him is mightiest at the last. Who can read that ancient legend of the Apostle John carried into the Christian Church, able only to articulate, "Little children, love one another," without feeling that age and death touch not the Immortal Love?

2. The next question which we proposed was, When will this result take place? This is answered by St. Paul in the twenty-third and following verses: "every man in his own order: Christ the first-fruits; afterward they that are Christ's at His coming; then cometh the end."

Confessedly this is a mysterious passage; nevertheless, let us see how much is clear. First, that the resurrection cannot be till the Kingdom is complete

Paul does not say that the consciousness of the departed shall not begin till then, but that *the Resurrection* — that finished condition when Humanity shall be fulfilled — is not to commence till the second coming of Christ.

Secondly, that certain hindrances at present prevent the perfect operation of God in our souls. Evil in a thousand forms surrounds us. We are the victims of physical and moral evil, and till this is put down for ever, the completeness of the individual cannot be; for we are bound up with the universe. Talk of the perfect happiness of any unit man while the race still mourns! Why, the evils of the race fall on him every day. Talk of the perfect bliss of any spirit while the spiritual kingdom is incomplete! No, the golden close is yet to come, and the blessing of the individual parts can only be with the blessing of the whole. And so the Apostle speaks of the whole creation groaning and travailing in pain together until now, "waiting for the adoption, to wit, the redemption of our body."

Thirdly, that the mediatorial Kingdom of Christ shall be superseded by an immediate one; therefore, the present form in which God has revealed Himself is only temporary. When the object of the present Kingdom of Christ has been attained in the conquest of evil, there will be no longer need of a mediator. Then God will be known immediately. We shall know Him, when the mediatorial has merged in the immediatorial, in a way more high, more intimate, more sublime, than even through Christ. Then, when the last hindrance, the last enemy, is removed, which prevents the entire entrance of God into the soul, we shall see Him face to face, know Him even as we are known, awake up satisfied in His likeness, and be transformed into pure recipients of the Divine Glory. That will be the Resurrection.

II. Corroborative proofs.

These are two in number, and both are *argumenta ad hominem*. They are not proofs valid to all men, but cogent only to Christians, as these Corinthians were. They assume Christian grounds which would be admitted by all who believed in Christ. They only go to prove, not that a resurrection must be, but that it is the doctrine of Christianity, although a party in the Corinthian Church denied it.

The first of these proofs is given in the twenty-ninth verse. It is well known that it is a disputed passage; and, after many years' study of it, I am compelled to come to this conclusion, that no interpretation that has been offered is entirely free from objection. All that I can do is, to put before you the chief interpretations. By some it is supposed to refer to vicarious baptism, a custom which certainly prevailed in later ages of the Church, when a living Christian was baptized in the place of a catechumen who had died before this sacrament could be administered. According to this idea, the Christian work was not so much to convert the living as to baptize for the dead. There is an immense improbability that Paul could have sustained a superstition so abject, even by an allusion. He could not have even spoken of it without anger. It is more probable that the custom arose from an erroneous interpretation of this passage. There is another opinion worth mentioning, namely, that the passage is an elliptical one. When baptized, Christians made a profession of a belief in a resurrection, and St. Paul asks them here, "What, then, was the meaning of their profession? Why were they baptized into the faith of a resurrection, if there were none?"

We may learn from this the value of baptism to the Church. Another such instance occurs in the sixth chapter of the Epistle to the Romans: the heresy of Antinomianism had crept in; "Let us sin," said some, "that grace may abound." In refutation of this, St. Paul appeals to baptism. Here he refutes a heresy concerning the resurrection by another appeal to baptism. Some will say, "If baptism be but a form or an instrument, having not in itself any mysterious power, of what purpose is baptism?" Brethren, I reply, of much, every way; and if it were only for this, it would be much, that so long as it remains in the Christian Church, there remains a ground of appeal against heresy.

The second argument is in the thirtieth verse: "Why stand we in jeopardy every hour?" If the future life were no Christian doctrine, then the whole apostolic life, nay, the whole Christian life, were a monstrous and senseless folly. For St. Paul's life was one great living death; he was ever on the brink of martyrdom. Figuratively, speaking popularly, "after the manner of men," he had fought as with wild beasts at Ephesus. Grant an immortality, and all this has a meaning; deny it, and it was in him a gratuitous folly. A life of martyrdom proves, at all events, that men are in earnest, though they may not be true. The value of such a testimony to immortality must be further proved, by considering whether the grounds were such that men could judge of them unmistakably. St. Paul devotes the beginning of this chapter to the proof of the reality of the fact. Afterwards, by a *reductio ad absurdum*, he argues that if Christ be not risen, the whole question of right and wrong is decided in favor of wrong. St. Paul does not say, "We are mistaken," but he says, "We are found liars."

Now in what does the absurdity of this consist? The Apostles must have been either good or bad men. If good, that they should have told this lie is incredible, for Christianity is to make men not false, but better, more holy, more humble, and more pure. If bad men, why did they sacrifice themselves for the cause of goodness? In suffering and in death, they witnessed to the truth which they taught; and it is a moral monstrosity that good men should die for what they believed to be a lie. It is a gross absurdity that men should bear indignity, woe, and pain, if they did not believe that there would be an eternal life for which all this was a preparation. For if souls be immortal, then Christianity has been an inestimable blessing: spirits have begun a sanctification here which will progress for ever: but if souls be not immortal, then it is quite a question whether Christianity has blessed the world or not. We personally may think it has, but if we reject the immortality of man, there is much to be said on the other side. A recent writer has argued very plausibly that Christianity has done nothing. And if immortality be untrue, then we may almost agree with him when we remember the persecutions, the prison, and the torture chamber, the religious wars and tyrannies which have been inflicted and carried on in the name of Christ; when we remember that even in this nineteenth century cannibalism and the torture of prisoners are still prevailing. Again, are we quite sure that Christian America, with her slavery, is a great advance on pagan Rome? or Christian England either, with her religious hatreds, and her religious pride? If the Kingdom of God comes only with observation, I am not certain that we can show cause why that life of sublime devotion of St. Paul's was not a noble existence wasted.

And again, if the soul be not immortal, Christian life, not merely apostolic devotedness, is "a grand impertinence." "Let us eat and drink, for to-morrow we die," was the motto and epitaph of Sardanapalus; and if this life be All, we defy you to disprove the wisdom of such reasoning. How many of the myriads of the human race would do right, for the *sake* of right, if they were only to live fifty years, and then die for evermore? Go to the sensualist, and tell him that a noble life is better than a base one, even for that time, and he will answer: "I like pleasure better than virtue: you can do as you please; for me, I will wisely enjoy my time. It is merely a matter of taste. By taking away my hope of a resurrection you have dwarfed good and evil, and shortened their consequences. If I am only to live sixty or seventy years, there is no eternal right or wrong. By destroying the thought of immortality, I have lost the sense of the infinitude of evil, and the eternal nature of good."

Besides, with our hopes of immortality gone, the

value of Humanity ceases, and people become not worth living for. We have not got a motive strong enough to keep us from sin. Christianity is to redeem from evil: it loses its power, if the idea of immortal life be taken away. Go, then, to the sensualist, and tell him that, though the theory of a Life to come be a dream, yet that here the pleasure of doing right is a sublimer existence than that of self-indulgence. He will answer you, "Yes, but my appetites are strong, and it will cost me much to master them. The struggle will be with pain; and, at last, only a few years will be left. The victory is uncertain, and the present enjoyment is sure, and there is the banquet of life before me, and the wine sparkling in the cup, and passion rising in its might · why should I refrain?"

Do you think you can arrest that with some fine sentiment about nobler and baser being? Why, you have made him out base already. He dies, you tell him, like a dog; why should he live like an angel? *You* have the angelic tendency, and prefer the higher life. Well, live according to your nature: but *he* has the baser craving, and prefers the brute life. Why should he not live it? Ye who deny the resurrection to immortality, answer me that!

No, my brethren; the instincts of the animal will be more than a match for all the transcendental reasonings of the philosopher. If there be in us only that which is born of the flesh, only the mortal Adam, and not the immortal Christ, if to-morrow we die, then the conclusion cannot be put aside — "Let us eat and drink, for the Present is our All."

LECTURE XXX.

1 CORINTHIANS, XV. 35-45. — "But some man will say, How are the dead raised up? and with what body do they come? — Thou fool, that which thou sowest is not quickened except it die: — And that which thou sowest, thou sowest not that body that shall be, but bare grain, it may chance of wheat, or of some other grain: — But God giveth it a body as it hath pleased him, and to every seed his own body. — All flesh is not the same flesh: but there is one kind of flesh of men, another flesh of beasts, another of fishes, and another of birds. — There are also celestial bodies, and bodies terrestrial: but the glory of the celestial is one, and the glory of the terrestrial is another. — There is one glory of the sun, and another glory of the moon, and another glory of the stars: for one star differeth from another star in glory. — So also the resurrection of the dead. It is sown in corruption; it is raised in incorruption: — It is sown in dishonor; it is raised in glory: it is sown in weakness; it is raised in power — It is sown a natural body; it is raised a spiritual body. There is a natural body, and there is a spiritual body. — And so it is written, The first man Adam was made a living soul; the last Adam was made a quickening spirit."

WE have already divided this chapter into three sections. In the first and second sections we spoke of the proofs of the Resurrection; and these we found to be twofold — the *reductio ad absurdum*, which demonstrated it by showing the monstrous admissions a denier of the Resurrection was compelled to make; and the historical facts of Christ's resurrection.

In the third, we arrived at the truth that His resurrection involved in it ours, and we replied to the questions Why and When. We asked, Why does it imply our resurrection? and the answer given was, that in us there exists a twofold nature — the animal or Adamic, containing in it no germ of immortality; and the Divine or Christ-like, the spirit which we receive from the Eternal Word, and by right of which we are heirs of the Immortal Life. "For as in Adam all die, even so in Christ shall all be made alive." We asked, When shall this resurrection finally take place? and the reply given was, Not till the period which is called the Second

Advent. St. Paul, leaving the question of Immortality untouched, pronounces that Resurrection cannot be till the end of all things. For all is moving on to a mighty consummation, and the blessing of an individual part can only be with the blessing of the whole.

To-day we shall be engaged on the fourth section — the credibility of a resurrection. St. Paul, in this portion of the chapter, replies to the question of possibility, "How are the dead raised?" And this he answers by arguments from analogy. As the seed dies before it can be quickened, as there is one glory of the sun and another glory of the moon, as the imperfect precedes the perfect, as our natural life is earlier than our spiritual — so is the resurrection of the dead.

First, then, as to the nature of the argument from analogy. Analogy is probability from a parallel case. We assume that the same law which operates in the one case will in another, if there be a resemblance between the relations of the two things compared. Thus, when in reply to the disciples, who did not comprehend the necessity of His death, Christ said, "Except a corn of wheat fall into the ground and die, it abideth alone: but if it die, it bringeth forth much fruit," He was reasoning from analogy. For as in nature life comes through death, so also is it in the world of spirit. The Law of Sacrifice, which accounts for the one fact, will also explain the other. Thus, when St. Paul shows that the life of the seed is continued after apparent death in a higher form, and argues, that in like manner the human spirit may be reunited to form, he reasons from analogy. He assumes that there is a probability of the same law operating in one case as operated in the other.

But we must remember how far this argument is valid, and what is its legitimate force. It does not amount to proof; it only shows that the thing in question is credible. It does not demonstrate that a resurrection *must* be, it only shows that it *may* be. For it does not follow that because the Law of Sacrifice is found in the harvest, therefore it shall be found in the redemption of the world, and that Christ's death must redeem; but it does follow that this doctrine of Atonement is not incredible, for it is found to be in harmony with the analogies of nature. The conceivableness of the Atonement follows from the analogies drawn from nature's laws working in the wheat; but the *proof* of the Atonement is the word of Christ Himself.

It does not follow that, because after death the life in a corn of wheat appears again, therefore the life in the human soul will be continued; but it does follow that the resurrection is quite intelligible and conceivable, and the objector who says it is impossible is silenced.

Now, it is in this way that St. Paul concludes his masterly argument. He proves the resurrection from the historical fact, and by the absurdity which follows from denial of it; and then he shows that, so proved, it is only parallel to a thousand daily facts, by the analogies which he draws from the dying and upspringing corn, and from the diverse glories of the sun, and moon, and stars. Let us distinguish, therefore, between the relative value of these arguments. We live, it is true, in a world filled with wondrous transformations, which suggest to us the likelihood of our immortality. The caterpillar passes into the butterfly, the snowdrop dies to rise again, Spring leaps to life from the arms of Winter, and the world rejoices in its resurrection. God gives us all this merciful assistance to our faith. But it is not on these grounds that our belief rests. These are not our proofs; they are only corroborations and illustrations, for it does not follow with certainty that the body of man shall be restored because the chrysalis, an apparent corpse, still lives. No: we fetch our proofs from the Word of God, and the nature of the human soul: and we fetch our probabilities and illustrations from the suggestive world of types which lies all around us.

We pass on now, in the second place, to consider the credibility of the Resurrection; that is, how, according to right reason, we can believe it possible, and that it is not irrational to believe it. Now there are two difficulties advanced: Firstly, in the question, "How are the dead raised?" and in that which is a mere sneer, "With what body do they come?"

The question, How are the dead raised, may be a philosophical one. Let us understand it plainly. We are told that the entire human body undergoes a process of change every certain number of years, so that at the end of that time there is not a single particle which is the same as at first; and then there comes this question, How shall the dead be raised? with which of these bodies do they come? And again, we know that the human body is dissolved in various ways, sometimes in fire; and then comes the question, How are all these scattered portions to reunite? do we really mean that the sound of the Archangel's trumpet shall bring them all together again? And then those who are wise in such matters tell us, that there is not a single portion of the globe which has not, some time or other, been organic form. The other question is not a philosophical one, but merely a sneer, With what body do they come? It is as if the objector had said, "Let there be nothing vague: tell us all about it — you who assert you are inspired."

Now to these objections the Apostle Paul replies by analogy, and so far shows the credibility of the Resurrection. He discerns in this world three principles: First, that life, even in its lowest form, has the power of assimilating to itself atoms; — he takes the corn of wheat, which, after being apparently destroyed, rises again, appropriating, as it grows, all that has affinity with itself, such as air and moisture: that body with which it is raised may be called its own body, and yet it is a new body. It is raised anew, with stem, and leaves, and fruit, and yet all the while we know that it is no new corn: it is the old life in the seed reappearing, developed in a higher form. It is a marvellous thing to see the power whereby that which we call the germ grows; how nothing can withstand it: how it creeps, climbs, and pierces even through walls, making for itself a way everywhere. Observe the force of the argument that arises from this fact, the argument of analogy. It does not *prove* the Resurrection, but it shows its *probability*.

The second analogy that St. Paul sees in nature is, the marvellous superabundance of the creative power of God. God has planted illimited and unnumbered things. "There is one glory of the sun, and another glory of the moon, and another glory of the stars," and yet there is a difference between them — "one star differeth from another star in glory." There are gradations in all these forms — bodies celestial, and bodies terrestrial — "but the glory of the celestial is one, and the glory of the terrestrial is another." Here is an answer to all objections — "With what body do they come?" Are we to believe that God has exhausted His creative power, that He has done all He could have done, and that He could make no new form? Are we to believe that the Wisdom and the Knowledge, which have never been fathomed by the wisest, are expended, and that the power of God should be insufficient to find for the glorified spirit a form fit for it? We simply reply to the objection — "With what body do they come?" — "Look at the creative power of God?"

The third principle which St. Paul refers to, is the principle of progress. The law of the universe is not Pharisaism — the law of custom stereotyped, and never to be changed. The law of God's universe is progress; and just as it was in creation — first the lower, and then the higher — so it is throughout, progressive happiness, progressive knowledge, progressive virtue. St. Paul takes one instance: "That was not first which is spiritual, but that which is natural." At first we lead a mere animal life — the life of instinct; then, as we grow older, passion succeeds; and after the era of passion our spirituality comes, if it comes at all — *after*, and not *before*. St. Paul draws a probability from this, that what our childhood was to our manhood — something imperfect followed by that which is more perfect — so will it be hereafter: our present humanity, with all its majesty, is nothing more than human infancy.

Lastly, St. Paul finds that all this coincides with the yearnings of the human heart. "When this corruptible shall have put on incorruption, and this mortal shall have put on immortality, then shall be brought to pass the saying that is written, Death is swallowed up in victory." This is the substance of two prophecies, one in Isaiah, the other in Hosea, and expresses the yearnings of the heart for immortality. And we may observe, that these yearnings are in accordance with our own. No man, in a high mood, ever felt that this life was really all. No man ever looked on life and was satisfied. No man ever looked at the world, without hoping that a time is coming when that creation, which is now groaning and travailing in bondage, shall be brought into the glorious liberty of the Son of God. No man ever looked upon our life, and felt that it was to remain always what it now is: he could not, and would not, believe that we are left here till our mortality predominates, and then that the grave is all. And this feeling, felt in a much greater and higher degree, becomes prophecy. Isaiah says, "Death shall be swallowed up in victory." We find a yearning in our own hearts after immortality, and that not in our lowest, but in our highest moods; and when we look around, instead of finding something which damps our aspirations, we find the external world corroborating them. Then how shall we account for the marvellous coincidence? Shall we believe that these two things point to nothing? Shall we believe, and shall we say, that God our Father has cheated us with a lie? Therefore St. Paul concludes his masterly and striking argument thus: "When this corruptible shall have put on incorruption, and this mortal shall have put on immortality, then shall be brought to pass the saying that is written, Death is swallowed up in victory."

Of course, if there be no Immortality and no Resurrection, it matters not whom you injure, nor what you do. If you injure him who has trusted you, of what consequence is it? In a few years all will be past and over. And if there be no Immortality and no Resurrection, it matters not what you do to yourself, whether you injure your own soul or not. But if there be a Life to come, then the evil deed you did is not ended by its commission, but it will still go on and on. The evil you have done to others will remain throughout Eternity; the evil you have done to your own soul will spread; as when you throw a stone into a pond the circles go on widening and spreading, so will that sin spread and increase over the sea of Eternity. If there be no Resurrection, then there are deeds of sacrifice which it would be no use to do; but if there be an Immortality and a Resurrection, then whatever good you do shall never be left unrewarded: the act of purity, the act of self-denial, the act of sacrifice, will ennoble you, making you holier and better. "Be not deceived; God is not mocked: for whatsoever a man soweth, that shall he also reap;" or, as at the conclusion of this chapter: "Therefore, my beloved brethren, be ye steadfast, forasmuch as ye know that your labor is not in vain in the Lord!"

LECTURE XXXI.

1 CORINTHIANS, xv 46–58. — "Howbeit that was not first which is spiritual, but that which is natural; and afterward that which is spiritual. — The first man is of the earth, earthy: the second man is the Lord from heaven. — As is the earthy, such are they also that are earthy: and as is the heavenly, such are they also that are heavenly. — And as we have borne the image of the earthy, we shall also bear the image of the heavenly. — Now this I say, brethren, that flesh and blood cannot inherit the kingdom of God; neither doth corruption inherit incorruption. — Behold, I shew you a mystery; We shall not all sleep, but we shall all be changed, — In a moment, in the twinkling of an eye, at the last trump: for the trumpet shall sound, and the dead shall be raised incorruptible, and we shall be changed. — For this corruptible must put on incorruption, and this mortal must put on immortality. — So when this corruptible shall have put on incorruption, and this mortal shall have put on immortality, then shall be brought to pass the saying that is written, Death is swallowed up in victory. — O death, where is thy sting? O grave, where is thy victory? — The sting of death is sin; and the strength of sin is the law. — But thanks be to God, which giveth us the victory through our Lord Jesus Christ. — Therefore, my beloved brethren, be ye steadfast, unmovable, always abounding in the work of the Lord, forasmuch as ye know that your labor is not in vain in the Lord."

THE fifteenth chapter of the First Epistle to the Corinthians, which has so often fallen on our ears like music in the night amidst funereal blackness, is filled with arguments, presumptive and direct, which tend to make Immortality credible: and amongst others St. Paul uses the analogy of the harvest, and argues from it the resurrection of the body: "It is sown a natural body; it is raised a spiritual body."

Now many an objector, on hearing this saying, might plausibly ask, Why this delay? why should not God create the perfect spiritual life at once? St. Paul anticipates this, and in answer applies a general law of the universe to the case before him. Such an immediate life of spiritual glory would be contrary to the Divine order in God's creation, for the Law of that order is this: "Howbeit that was not first which is spiritual, but that which is natural; and afterward that which is spiritual."

Thus we have here a general principle adduced for a special purpose, which principle is yet not confined by St. Paul to this special case, but is felt by him to be one of universal application. For it is the peculiarity of this philosophical Apostle, that he connects Christianity with God's universe. In the Atonement, in the Resurrection, he sees no strange isolated facts, but the Truths which are found everywhere in various forms. And just as a naturalist would refer any particular species to some great type, so he finds at once the place for any Christian doctrine under some great and general Law. This principle, that the natural precedes the spiritual, it will be our business to trace to-day.

We will consider first, then, The universality of this Law. And,

Secondly, The spiritual instances given of it.

I. Its universality is disclosed in the order of Creation. No ingenuity can reconcile the formal statements respecting the creation made by Moses with those made by modern science. The story of the Creation as told by Moses is one thing, as told by men of science it is another thing altogether. For the Bible is not a scientific work; it does not deal with hypotheses, nor with formal facts which are of time, and must nesessarily vary, but it declares Eternal *principles*. It is not a revelation of the truths of Geology or Astronomy, but it is a revelation of the Character of God to us. And yet the spiritual principles declared by Moses are precisely those revealed by science. The first chapter of Genesis starts with the doctrine that the heavens and the earth, that light and darkness, were all created by One and the same God. Modern science, day by day, reveals more clearly the unity of design that pervades creation. Again, in Moses' account nothing is more remarkable than the principle of gradation on which he tells us the universe arose. And this is confirmed at every step by science. To this the accumulated strata bear their witness, to this the organic remains testify continually. Not that first which is highest, but that which is lowest: First, the formless earth, then the green herb growing on the sides of the upraised mountains, then the lowest forms of animal existence, then the highest types, then man, the last and noblest. And then, perhaps, an age to come when all shall be swept away, to make room for a higher and nobler race of beings. For "that is not first which is spiritual, but that which is natural."

Again the universality of this law is seen in the progress of the Jewish nation.

We take it as an instance of this Law among nations, because the Jews were confessedly the most spiritual of mankind. So vast is the interval between them and all others, that the collected works which, in speaking of another people, would be called a national literature, are of them called an inspired Bible. The Scriptures stand separate from all other books, unapproachable in their spirituality. Marvellous, too, was the combination in them of the Asiatic veneration — of religious awe and contemplation — with the stern moral sense which belongs to the more northern nations. You will find among Hindoos a sense of the invisible as strong, and among the German family of nations an integrity as severe, but nowhere will you find the two so united as in the history of the chosen people.

And now having considered what the Jews attained to, remember what they rose from — recollect their origin. They were a nation of slaves. Originally, too, of a stock more than commonly rude, hard, and rugged, they became in Egypt and in Palestine sensual, idolatrous, and money-loving. No history surpasses in horror the cruelty of the wars of Canaan. None tells such a tale of obstinacy, of gross indulgence, of minds apparently incapable of receiving spiritual principles. You are reminded of one of those trees, whose exposed roots are seen gnarled and twisted, hard as iron, more like rock than wood, and yet whose foliage above is rich and noble: below extends the basis of the coarse and natural, above are manifested the beautiful and spiritual.

And this was not concealed from the Jews. Their prophets unvaryingly proclaimed the national character, and described them as the "most stiff-necked of people." They were taught to say at one of their feasts: "A Syrian ready to perish was my father." They were reminded, "Look to the rock from whence you were hewn, and the hole of the pit from whence you were digged." For through many progressive stages was the great work of their elevation wrought; by slow gradations did this nation of slaves rise into being a spiritual people. "That was not first which was spiritual, but that which was natural."

The universality of this law is shown again in the progress of the human race.

"The first man Adam was made a living soul, the last Adam was made a *quickening spirit*." "The first man is of the earth, earthy: the second man is the Lord from heaven." Nothing is more common than elaborate delineations of the perfect state of the first man. If we trust such descriptions, Eden was perfect heaven, and Adam was furnished with all knowledge intuitively, and adorned with every grace. But when we get away from poetry and picture-painting, we find that men have drawn largely from their imaginations without the warrant of one syllable of Scripture to corroborate the truth of the coloring. St. Paul says Adam was "of the earth, earthy;" and again, he calls him "a living soul." Now recollect what soul (ψυχὴ) meant. The adjective corresponding to this substantive is used in 1 Cor. ii. 14, and is translated *natural:* "The natural man receiveth not the things of the spirit of God." The natural man is therefore a man with a soul, the spiritual man is the man with a spirit. Adam was therefore "a living soul," that is, a natural man — a man with intelligence, perception, and a moral sense, with power to form a society and to subdue Nature to himself. He was that, and that only.

The Fall, then, was only a necessary consequence of a state of mere nature. It was a step downwards from innocence, but also it was a step onwards — a giant step in human progress. It made goodness possible; for to know the evil, and to conquer it and choose the good, is far nobler than a state which only consists in our ignorance of both. Until the step of nature has been passed, the step of spirituality cannot be made. "That was not first which was spiritual, but that which was natural.

Thus did the Race begin to share in the spiritual; and among many nations, and by means of many men, was the progress of mankind evolved; but their light was too scattered, and their isolated lives imparted little life. So the next stage in the progress of the Race was the Birth, and Life, and Death, and risen Glory of Him who was made "a quickening Spirit." Then it was that in the fulness of time He was born, who was the blossoming of our Humanity: differing from the race that had gone before, as the flower differs from the wood on which it grows: of the same nature, and yet of another, more delicate, and more ethereal. The natural man had passed, the spiritual Man was come. The spiritual Man, whose prerogative it was, not as the first Adam, to live in Eden for himself, but as the second Adam, to die on Calvary for others; not as the first Adam, to receive happiness; but as the second Adam, to confer life. It was no longer the natural man, but the quickening Spirit, that represented the race to God. The natural had risen into the spiritual. The first man was of the earth, earthy; the second man was the Lord from Heaven.

II. The Spiritual Instances of this Law.

The law which is found to be true of Nations and of the Race, is generally true of persons also; though in particulars its influence may be modified by individual peculiarities. Generally, then, this law is true of us as men.

And, first, our natural affections precede our spiritual.

There are two tables of Commandments: "Thou shalt love the Lord thy God," and "Thou shalt love thy neighbor as thyself;" and there are two orders in which they stand to each other. In the order of importance the love of God is first; in the order of time the love of man precedes, that is, we begin by loving Man, we do not *begin* by loving God. Let us trace this principle further. Love to Man also begins lower down. We do not love our neighbors first; we do not all at once embrace the Race in our affection; we ascend from a lower point. "Thou shalt love thy neighbor as thyself" — the Table given on Sinai does not say *that:* it only specifies one kind of love — the love of children to parents. There are no rules given there of friendship, of patriotism, or of universal philanthropy; for in the Fifth Commandment they all lie as the future oak-tree lies in the acorn: the root of all the other developments of love, is love and honor unto parents. That injunction laid the foundation deep and broad. For life depends greatly on the relations: "the child is father to the man." Rarely, when the mother has been all that woman should be, and the father has been true to the protecting and guiding, the tender and strong instincts of his manhood, does the child turn out unnatural. But where there has been a want of these things, where any one part of the boy's nature has remained uncultivated, there the subsequent relationships will be ill sustained. For the friend, the husband, the citizen are formed at the domestic hearth.

There is yet one step further: out of human love grows love to God. A miserable and sad mistake is often made in opposition to this fact. There are men and women of cold and palsied affections, who think of giving to God the love which has become cold to men. Settle it in your minds, God does not work so. It is quite true that Christianity makes the sublime demand on believers, "If a man hate not father and mother, wife and children, his own life also, he cannot be my disciple;" but before that was said, it had demanded that we should "love our neighbor as ourselves," that we should "honor our father and mother." And paradoxical as it may seem, you will never attain to that state of love to God, which can sacrifice the dearest affections rather than do wrong, until you have cultivated them to the highest possible degree. For it is only by being true to all the lower forms of love, that we learn at last that fidelity to the highest love, which can sacrifice them all rather than violate its sacredness.

Again, there is another mistake made by those who demand the love of God from a child. The time does come to every child, as it came to the Childhood of Christ, when the love of the earthly parent is felt to be second to the love of the Heavenly Father; but *this is not the first*, "for that is not first which is spiritual, but that which is natural." It is true, there have been cases where children have given striking proof of love to God, but these, even to a proverb, die young, because they are precocious, unnatural, forced; and God never forces character.

For a time the father represents God, — is in the place of God to the child. He is to train the affections which afterwards shall be given to God; and the brother those which shall expand hereafter for Christ. Like the trellis round which the tendrils clasp till they are fit to transplant, so are the powers of love within the child supported and strengthened as he leans upon his father, till they are mature enough to stand alone for God. And you cannot reverse this, without great peril to the child's spiritual nature. You cannot *force* love to God. By no outrageous leaps, but by slow walking, is the spiritual love reached.

Lastly: The Moral precedes the Spiritual.

Let us remember once more the definition we have given to the word "soul," — the moral and intellectual qualities belonging to the man. And then let us take the Apostle's own words, "The first man Adam was made a living soul, the last Adam was made a quickening spirit." And this is true of all, for the history of the Jewish race, of the Human race, is repeated in the history of every individual. There is a time when the

Adam is formed within us, when the Christ begins to be formed, when we feel within us the sense of "Christ in us, the hope of glory," when the "living soul," as ruler of the man, gives place to the "quickening spirit." Ever it is true that the animal, the intellectual, and the moral precede the spiritual life.

But there are two stages through which we pass: through Temptation, and through Sorrow.

1. It was through temptation that the first Adam fell from a state of nature. It was through temptation, too, that the second Adam redeemed Humanity into a state of grace. To the first Adam this world was as a garden is to a child, in which he has nothing to do but to taste and enjoy. Duty came with its infinite demands: it came into collision with the finite appetites, and he fell. The first state is simply that of untempted innocence. In the temptation of the second Adam infinite Duty consecrated certain principles of action without reference to consequences: "Man shall not live by bread alone:" "Thou shalt not tempt the Lord thy God;" "Thou shalt worship the Lord thy God, and Him only shalt thou serve." We pass into the spiritual state when we fall. It is not *better* to do right: you *must* do right. It is not merely worse for you to do wrong — the law is, Thou shalt not!

2. Through Sorrow. Note here the difference between Adam and Christ. Adam's was a state of satisfied happiness, Christ's was one of noble aspiration; His was a Divine Sorrow, there was a secret sadness in the heart of the Son of Man. There is a difference between Childhood and Age, between Christian and un-Christian motives. Out of contemplations such as these we collect a presumption of immortality.

LECTURE XXXII.

CORINTHIANS, xvi. 1-9.—"Now concerning the collection for the saints, as I have given order to the churches of Galatia, even so do ye.—Upon the first day of the week let every one of you lay by him in store, as God hath prospered him, that there be no gatherings when I come.—And when I come, whomsoever ye shall approve by your letters, them will I send to bring your liberality unto Jerusalem.—And if it be meet that I go also, they shall go with me.—Now I will come unto you, when I shall pass through Macedonia: for I do pass through Macedonia.—And it may be that I will abide, yea, and winter with you, that ye may bring me on my journey whithersoever I go.—For I will not see you now by the way; but I trust to tarry a while with you, if the Lord permit.—But I will tarry at Ephesus until Pentecost.—For a great door and effectual is opened unto me, and there are many adversaries."

THE whole of this Epistle is fragmentary in its character; it is not purely argumentative, like that to the Romans, nor was it written to meet any one cardinal error, like the Epistles to the Galatians and Hebrews; but it arose in the settlement of a multitude of questions which agitated the Corinthian Church. The way in which St. Paul, in this chapter, enters on new ground, is very characteristic of the abrupt style of the Epistle. The solemn topic of the Resurrection is closed, and now a subject of merely local interest is introduced. The Apostle gives directions, in the first four verses, respecting a certain charitable collection to be made by the Corinthians, in conjunction with other Gentile Churches, for the poor at Jerusalem and in Judæa.

We have here an illustration of one peculiar use of Scripture. The event recorded here has long since past: the interest which hung around it was merely local: the actors in it have been buried for many centuries: the temporary distress spoken of here was long since relieved: even the Apostle himself has written simply and entirely for his own time. And yet the whole account is as living, and fresh, and pregnant with instruction to us to-day, as it was to the Corinthians of that age. Reflections crowd upon us while pondering on the history. We understand something of what is meant by Inspiration. We watch the principles which are involved in the apostolic mode of meeting the dilemma, and we find that that which was written for a Church at Corinth, contains lessons for the Church of all ages. The particular occasion is past, but the principles and the truths remain.

To-day, then, we investigate two points:

I. The call for charity.
II. The principle of its exercise.

I. The call for charity.

We learn from the fifteenth chapter of the Epistle to the Romans, at the twenty-sixth verse, the occasion of this collection. It seems that the Jewish converts in Jerusalem, being excommunicated and persecuted, were in great distress, and that St. Paul summoned the Gentile converts in Achaia, Galatia, and at Rome, to alleviate their difficulties. Now observe, first, how all distinctions of race had melted away before Christianity. This was not the first time that collections had been made for Jerusalem. Josephus tells us that they had been sent by foreign Jews to keep up the Temple at Jerusalem, that is, money had been contributed by Jews for a Jewish object. But here was a Jewish object supported by Gentile subscriptions. This was a new thing in the world.

The hard lines of demarcation were fading away for ever, the veil of Christ's Humanity was torn down. He lived no longer as the Jew, He had risen as the Man, the Saviour, not of one people, but of the world, and in Him all were one. Henceforth there was neither Jew nor Greek, bond nor free, male nor female: but Christ was All.

Observe again: Galatia and Corinth were now interested in the same object. It was not merely Corinth united to Jerusalem, or Galatia to Jerusalem, but Jerusalem, Corinth, and Galatia were linked by a common object to each other. You have seen a magnet applied to a mass of iron filings, and watched the multitude of delicate points all adhering to each other, through the invisible influence which, sent throughout them all, makes each in its turn a magnet. To scattered races and divided peoples, to separate castes and ancient enmities, Christ was the Magnet which united all. His Spirit gave to all a common interest, and that is the closest bond of union. As suggested here, the different parts of Christendom were made to feel together. Benumbed and paralyzed till then, the frame of Humanity was suddenly made to throb with a common life.

Now this had been done before in a way, by other means, which were less sacred. Two hitherto have principally been employed, War and Trade. In earlier times the different tribes of the Roman Republic, even those who were opposing parties in the city, were united on the field of battle; they felt they were warring for the same cause, and they struck as one man for their altars and their homes. Later in history we find that Trade united men by mutual interest. We will not injure others, said men, because, by so doing, we shall injure ourselves. And on this principle, the great gathering of the nations last year was a pledge of union. It was a good and great effort in its way, but still it was only an appeal to self-interest.

In a far higher, nobler, and finer way Christianity unites, first, to Christ, and then, through Christ, each to the other. We are bound up each in each, not through a common hatred, not through a common interest even, but through a common love. So it was that Galatia and Corinth worked together for Jerusalem, inspired with a common sympathy, a common affection, and therefore the Galatians loved the Corinthians, and the Corinthians the Galatians.

Here, however, a remark suggests itself. This has not been realized since, in any degree adequate to the first promise of its youth. This binding together of

Corinth, Rome, and Galatia — what has there been like it in after ages? One gleam of sunshine, the prophecy of a glorious noon to come, struck upon the world, but the promise of the day was soon overclouded. So, also, there has been nothing equal to the outpouring at Pentecost; nor has a similar self-forgetfulness ever characterized the Church since, as in that day when all things were common; nor has anything like the early miracles arisen since among the messengers of Christ. It would seem as if God gave at the outset, in that large flood of Love poured upon the Church, a specimen and foretaste of that which is to be hereafter. Just as on the Transfiguration Mount we catch a glimpse of glory, not to be repeated or realized for ages, which we feel was given to sustain a travailing world through days and years of sickness and of suffering.

Remark how in God's counsels sorrow draws out good. The Jewish Christians suffered from poverty and persecution. Well: kindly feelings awoke to life at Corinth and at Rome: these were the result of the misery at Jerusalem. Pain and Sorrow are mysteries. Inexplicable often is it, in our life, why we are afflicted; but sometimes the veil is drawn aside, and we see the reason clearly. And here, to the Church of Jerusalem, was not all this rich result of beauty and spiritual goodness cheaply purchased? Remember, the sufferers at Jerusalem could not see the meaning of their sorrow. They did not know how many a Greek and Roman was weekly laying up his store: they did not know that an Apostle was writing and contriving in their behalf. They could not see how through their pain Galatia, and Corinth, and Rome were drawn by cords of love together. They saw only their own distress, they felt only their own forlornness.

Just in the same way we often suffer, and see no good result from it. But, assuredly, we are not suffering in vain; some lesson has been taught; some sympathies have been aroused; some consolation has been given. That mysterious connection which links the universe together has brought, or will bring, good to others out of our suffering. Now here is a new aspect of consolation. That is a common and trite view, though deep in its truth, which reminds us that suffering works out *for us* a weight of glory — which tells how *our* characters are perfected through suffering. There is a higher Christian light to see our pain in: it blesses *others*. My brethren, it is a high lesson to be willing to suffer for *this* cause! This is the blessedness of the Suffering of Christ; it is the Law of the Cross; it is the vicarious principle pervading Life, that voluntarily, or involuntarily, we must suffer for others. If others are benefited involuntarily by our sufferings, then we do no more than the beasts who fulfil the law of their being unconsciously, who yield up their lives unwillingly, and, therefore, are not blest by it. But if we are willing to bear our woe, because we know that good will accrue, we know not how, or why, or when, to others, then we have indeed become partakers of Christ's Spirit, and learnt a Godlike lesson. To be willing to bear, in order to teach others! — to lose, in order that others may "through us nobler live" — that is to know something of the blessedness He knew.

Again, if this distress came through persecutions, then there was a signal fulfilment of the promise. For here relationships are *representative* only; they do but shadow out realities. Our earthly relationships typify truer spiritual ones. The father after the flesh is often not the one to whom in life we look with the most filial reverence. There is a Friend who sticketh closer than a brother. And so, in firm faith, we must move through life, nothing daunting us. *On* — onwards! Though the path be dark, we shall not be left lonely — none ever have been.

II. The principle of the exercise of Charity.

We will consider this in its manner and measure: —

1. Systematic in manner: — It was to be on the first day of the week, each one was to lay by in store as God had prospered him. That is, instead of waiting for one stirring apostolic appeal, they were to make

charity the business of their lives. Week by week they were to build up a sum for St. Paul to send to Jerusalem. This contribution slowly, systematically gathered, was to be a matter of principle, and not of impulse. It is possible that one burning speech of St. Paul's might have elicited a larger sum. But St. Paul preferred the effects of steady perseverance to those of vehement emotion. For impulse is often mere luxury. I do not say that good impulses are not to be acted on, or that warm emotions are to be cooled: they are given to facilitate benevolence; yet it is quite certain that they may cost very little. To give largely, to strip off a coat to give to a shivering man, to open your purse and richly guerdon a beggar, may, after all, be nothing more than a relief from importunity, or a compact with conscience, or a compromise with laziness.

Now, on the contrary, this systematic plan of St. Paul's costs something, and teaches something. It teaches, first, the habit of a thoughtful life; it reminds us continually that there is something which is owed to God, and therefore is not our own. In this world we are recipients, the pensioners of our Father; and it is well that, by an outward system, we should train our inward spirit to the unforgetful thought of our debt to Him. It is well that we should remember this—not to wake our fear of His austerity, but to kindle our gratitude in answer to His Love.

It teaches, secondly, self-denial. It gradually lays the foundation of a life of Christian economy; not that which sacrifices one pleasure for another: for this is but mere prudence: but that which abridges pleasure, in order that we may be able to give to God.

2. The measure of liberality was, "as God hath prospered him." Observe, St. Paul establishes a *principle* here, and not a rule. He lays down no rabbinical maxim of one tenth or one fourth. He leaves the measure of each man's charity to his own conscience. Ask thyself, he says to each, "How much owest thou unto thy Lord?"

Besides, a wide margin is here left necessarily for variety of circumstances. God prospers one man in fortune; another man in time; another, in talent; and time, talents, power of government, knowledge, keen sympathy, are often better gifts than money. It is a false view which limits charity to almsgiving. "Silver and gold have I none," said St. Peter when the lame man asked an alms, "but that which I have I give unto thee;" and the man was healed. So now, often the greatest exercise of charity is where there is *nothing given*, but where the deserving are assisted to support themselves. Often the highest charity is simply to pay liberally for all things had or done for you; because to underpay workmen, and then be bountiful, is not charity. On the other hand, to *give*, when by so doing you support idleness, is most pernicious. No evil prevails so much, or is so sheltered under specious pretexts, as the support of beggars. Yet you cannot refuse to give a street-alms if your charity has no other channel: you would feel that refusal in such a case was a mere pretext to save your money. But if your wealth is wisely and systematically given, then the refusal of idle appeals does no harm to the heart.

Now, the first principle laid down by St. Paul will explain why the second is not realized. Men do not give as God hath prospered them, because they do not give systematically; that is, they who have most are not they who give most, but the reverse. It is a fact, the more we have, the less we give. Search the annals of all societies, and you will find that the large contributions are given by those whose incomes are hundreds, and not thousands. Many are the touching cases known to all clergymen, where the savings of a servant, a governess, a workman, have more than equalled the munificence of the rich. So, also, St. Paul's experience was: The grace of God, he says, was "bestowed on the churches of Macedonia; how that in a great trial of affliction the abundance of their joy and their deep poverty abounded unto the riches of their liberality. For to their power I bear record, yea, and beyond their power they were willing of themselves."

The reason of this strange difference is, that system is easier with little than with much. The man of thousands squanders. Indulgence after indulgence presents itself to him: every impulse is satisfied immediately: he denies himself nothing: he gives as freely when he is touched by a tale of woe, as he indulges when he wants indulgence. But his luxuries and his extra expenditure grow into necessities, and he then complains of his larger liabilities and establishment. Yet, withal, it would be a startling thing if well-meaning persons, who say they cannot give, were only to compute how much annually is spent in that mere waste, which the slightest self-denial would have spared.

Now let me appeal to those who really wish, in this thing, to do right. It is not my duty, from this chapter, to make a stirring appeal to your conscience, but simply to assist with advice that desire of liberality which is already existing, but which exists without expedients or plans of action. St. Paul's principle is the only safe or true one. Systematize your charity. Save, by surrendering superfluities first. Feel that there is a sacred fund, which will be made less by every unnecessary expense. Let us learn Christian Economy first. Next we shall, by God's grace, learn Christian Self-denial. For the Corinthians gave not out of their abundance, but out of their deep poverty.

LECTURE XXXIII.

1 CORINTHIANS, xvi. 10-24. — "Now if Timotheus come, see that he may be with you without fear: for he worketh the work of the Lord, as I also do. — Let no man therefore despise him; but conduct him forth in peace, that he may come unto me: for I look for him with the brethren. — As touching our brother Apollos, I greatly desired him to come unto you with the brethren: but his will was not at all to come at this time; but he will come when he shall have convenient time. — Watch ye, stand fast in the faith, quit you like men, be strong. — Let all your things be done with charity. — I beseech you, brethren, (ye know the house of Stephanas, that it is the first-fruits of Achaia, and that they have addicted themselves to the ministry of the saints.) — That ye submit yourselves unto such, and to every one that helpeth with us, and laboreth. — I am glad of the coming of Stephanas and Fortunatus and Achaicus: for that which was lacking on your part they have supplied. — For they have refreshed my spirit and yours: therefore acknowledge ye them that are such. — The churches of Asia salute you. Aquila and Priscilla salute you much in the Lord, with the church that is in their house. — All the brethren greet you. Greet ye one another with an holy kiss. — The salutation of me Paul with mine own hand. — If any man love not the Lord Jesus Christ, let him be Anathema Maran-atha. — The grace of our Lord Jesus Christ be with you. — My love be with you all in Christ Jesus. Amen."

TO-DAY we close our exposition of the First Epistle to the Corinthians by gathering together the salutations which are contained in the conclusion.

In going through this Epistle, we cannot fail to have observed that it is altogether fragmentary. This was the natural result of its character, since it was a reply to various questions arising out of the peculiar state of the Corinthian Church. But the conclusion, as we might expect, is even more fragmentary than the rest. It is simply made up of certain information respecting St. Paul's movements, certain salutations, certain personal memorials, and notices — and a brief reminder of the First Principles interspersed throughout the foregoing chapters. It will, therefore, be necessary for us in this place to connect them together as well as we can, not expecting to find any natural division to facilitate the making of a plan, or to assist the memory in combining this scattered Epistle into a whole.

First, we notice the information given us respecting the Apostle's movements. Now we find him telling the Corinthians that he hoped to visit them, and to winter with them, but not yet, for he was to stay at Ephesus until Pentecost. I only mention this, in order to call attention to the law of the Apostolic life. He remained there, he says, "for a great door and effectual is opened unto me, and there are many adversaries." So it was not pleasure, but duty, which kept him there. Ephesus was his post, and at Ephesus he would stay. Moreover, the very circumstance which to many would have been an inducement to depart, was with St. Paul a strong one to remain: there were "many adversaries," and he was there to take his part in danger. Now in order to understand the true martyr-spirit, let us compare his behavior in the nineteenth chapter of the Acts of the Apostles, at the time of the public uproar, and his own strong expression, "If after the manner of men I have fought with beasts at Ephesus," in the fifteenth chapter of this Epistle, and we shall see at once that his feeling was: There is danger — well, then, I will stay.

Secondly, we make a remark respecting salutations generally. This Epistle has many, but they are not so numerous as in that to the Romans. In both of them individuals are mentioned by name. It was no mere general assurance of attachment he gave them, but one of his personal knowledge and affection.

1. Remark that, with St. Paul, personal considerations were not lost in general philanthropy: that because he entertained regard for the churches, and for bodies of men, he did not on this account ignore the individuals composing them. It is common enough to profess great interest and zeal for Humanity, whilst there is indifference all the time about individual men. It is common enough to be zealous about a cause, about some scheme of social good, and yet to be careless re

specting individual welfare. But St. Paul's love was from Christ's own Spirit. It was love to the Church generally, and besides, it was love to Aquila and Priscilla. And, is not this, too, the nature of God's Love, who provides for the Universe, and yet spends an infinity of care on the fibre of a leaf?

2. Remark also the value of the courtesies of life. There are many minds which are indifferent to such things, and fancy themselves above them. It is a profound remark of Prescott's, that "liberty is dependent upon forms." Did not the slow, solemn change in the English constitution, and our freedom from violent subversions, arise from the almost superstitious way in which precedent has been consulted in the manner of every change. But what is of more importance to remember is, that love is dependent upon forms — courtesy of etiquette guards and protects courtesy of heart. How many hearts have been lost irrecoverably, and how many averted eyes and cold looks have been gained from what seemed perhaps but a trifling negligence of forms!

There are three persons chiefly in reference to whom these personal notices are made — Timothy, Apollos, and the household of Stephanas.

I. In the tenth verse — "If Timotheus come, see that he may be with you without fear: for he worketh the work of the Lord as I also do" — he bespeaks respect for him, official respect, and personal consideration. It is chiefly on this personal consideration that I wish to dwell. "Let him be without fear — let no man despise him." Now consider the circumstances in which Timothy was placed. He was young in years, and he was a recent convert to Christianity. He lived in a day when the Christian profession was despised and persecuted. There was much to make him "fear." He — a young teacher — was coming to a city where gifts were unduly and idolatrously reverenced, and where even the authority of one like St. Paul was liable to be treated lightly, if he did not possess the gifts and graces of Attic oratory. There must, therefore, have been much to make it likely that he would be despised. Think how, without a friend like St. Paul to throw his mantle over him, Timothy's own modesty would have silenced him, and how his young enthusiasm might have been withered by ridicule or asperity!

In this light, St. Paul's pleading is an encouragement of goodness while yet in its tender bud. From this instance we are enabled to draw a lesson for all ages. There is a danger of our paralyzing young enthusiasm by coldness, by severity, by sneers, by want of sympathy. There are few periods in life more critical than that in which sensibilities and strong feeling begin to develop themselves in young people. The question is about to be decided whether what is at present merely romantic feeling is to become generous devotion, and to end by maturing into self-denial, or whether it is to remain only a sickly sentiment, and, by reaction, degenerate into a bitter and a sneering tone. And there are, perhaps, few countries in which this danger is so great, and so much to be guarded against, as here in England. Nowhere is feeling met with so little sympathy as here — nowhere is enthusiasm so much kept down — nowhere do young persons learn so soon the fashionable tone of strongly admiring nothing — wondering at nothing — reverencing nothing — and nowhere does a young man so easily fall into the habit of laughing at his own best and purest feelings. And this was a danger which the Apostle Paul knew well, and could not overlook. He foresaw the risk of paralyzing that young and beautiful enthusiasm of Timothy by the party-spirit of Corinth, by the fear of the world's laugh, or by the recoil with which a young man, dreading to be despised, hides what is best and noblest in himself, and consequently becomes hard and commonplace. In earlier days, Apollos himself ran the same risk. He set out preaching all the truth that he knew enthusiastically. It was very poor truth, lamentably incomplete, embracing only John's baptism, that is, the doctrine which John taught. Had the Christians met him with sneers, had they said, "This young upstart does not preach the Gospel," there had been either a great teacher blighted, or else a strong mind embittered into defiance and heresy. But from this he was delivered by the love and prudence of Aquila and Priscilla, who, we read, "took him unto them, and expounded unto him the way of God more perfectly." They made allowances: they did not laugh at his imperfections, nor damp his enthusiasm: they united him with themselves: they strengthened what was weak — they lopped away what was luxuriant: they directed rightly what was energetic. Happy the man who has been true to the ideal of his youth, and has been strong enough to work out in real life the plan which pleased his childish thought! Happy he who is not ashamed of his first enthusiasm, but looks back to it with natural piety, as to the parent of what he now is! But for one of whom this is true — how many are there whom the experience of life has soured and rendered commonplace! How many, who were once touched by the sunlight of Hope, have grown cold, settled down into selfishness, or have become mere domestic men, stifled in wealth or lost in pleasure!

Above all things, therefore, let us beware of that cold, supercilious tone, which blights what is generous, and affects to disbelieve all that is disinterested and unworldly. Let us guard against the *esprit moqueur* — the Mephistopheles spirit, which loves and reverences nothing.

II. "As touching our brother Apollos, I greatly desired him to come unto you with the brethren: but his will was not at all to come at this time; but he will come when he shall have convenient time." Upon this I will make two remarks:

1. The perfect absence of all mean jealousy in St. Paul's mind. Compare this passage with his earnest rebuke of the party of Apollos in the first chapter. On reading that, it might appear natural to say, "Oh, he cannot bear a rival!" But, behold, it was zeal for

Christ, and not jealousy of Apollos. With Apollos he felt only hearty fellowship, for he greatly "desired him to come to them with the brethren." These are some of the fine touches by which we learn what that sublime Apostle was, and what the grace of God had made him. Here, again, we see another advantage of our expository course, enabling us to trace and note down many delicate touches of character that might otherwise easily be passed over.

2. Let us pause to admire the Apostle's earnest desire to make Apollos stand well with the Corinthians. A meaner spirit, feeling that Apollos was a dangerous rival, would either have left his conduct unexplained, or would have caught at, and been even glad of the suspicion resting on him; *why* did he stay away? But St. Paul would leave no misunderstanding to smoulder. He simply stated that Apollos had reasons for not coming: "but he *will* come." This is magnanimity and true delicacy of heart.

III. The house of Stephanas: "Ye know the house of Stephanas, that it is the first-fruits of Achaia, and that they have addicted themselves to the ministry of the saints." St. Paul tells them in the next verse, to "submit themselves unto such" — to respect them. See, then, what Christianity is — Equality: yes, but not levelling. God's universe is built on subordination: so is God's Church. The spirit of the world's liberty says, "Let no man lord it over you;" but the spirit of the Gospel liberty says, "Submit yourselves one to another." Observe, however, another thing: they had addicted *themselves* to the ministry. Who had called them to it? No one, except God by an inward fitness. Yet, knowing this, St. Paul says, "Submit yourselves." There are certain things to be done in this world which require peculiar instruments and peculiar qualifications. A call from God to do such a work is often shown by a willingness to do it: a readiness to stand forward and take the lead. When this is the case, and such men try to do good, they are often met with innumerable hindrances. Take as instances, Howard and Mrs. Fry, who encountered nothing but difficulties; they were thwarted in all they undertook, and hindered on every side.

Now, St. Paul says this is wrong; you ought rather to help such. Let them take the lead — follow in their wake, and do not mar the work by any petty jealousy. "Submit yourselves rather unto such, and to every one that helpeth with us and laboreth." Observe, then, it is as much an apostolic duty to obey persons who have "addicted themselves" from inward fitness, as it is to respect an outward constitutional authority.

Lastly, the Epistle concludes with the repetition of a few First Principles. As the postscript often contains the gist of a letter — the last earnest thought, the result of a strong effort at recollection in order to leave nothing important unsaid — so we may here expect to find gathered to a point some of the essential principles of Christianity as a parting request.

Accordingly, we find the Apostle, in the thirteenth verse, saying, "Watch ye, stand fast in the faith, quit you like men, be strong," — by which he enforces the duty of Manliness. In the fourteenth verse, "Let all your things be done with charity." The Apostle's incessant exhortation to Love, is again pressed upon them in the most comprehensive form. And in the twenty-second verse, "If any man love not the Lord Jesus Christ, let him be Anathema Maran-atha." By which the rule of sympathy, and that of antipathy, is pointed out. Respecting the first of these, I address young men —

If you think Christianity a feeble, soft thing, ill adapted to call out the manlier features of character, read here, "Quit you like men." Remember, too, "He that ruleth his spirit, is greater than he that taketh a city." He who conquers passion in its might is every inch a man! Say what you will, the Christian conqueror is the only one who deserves the name.

* * * * *

LECTURE XXXIV.

July 11, 1852.

2 Corinthians, i. 1 – 14. — "Paul, an apostle of Jesus Christ by the will of God, and Timothy our brother, unto the church of God which is at Corinth, with all the saints which are in all Achaia: — Grace be to you and peace from God our Father, and from the Lord Jesus Christ. — Blessed be God, even the Father of our Lord Jesus Christ, the Father of mercies, and the God of all comfort; — Who comforteth us in all our tribulation, that we may be able to comfort them which are in any trouble by the comfort, wherewith we ourselves are comforted of God. — For as the sufferings of Christ abound in us, so our consolation also aboundeth by Christ. — And whether we be afflicted, it is for your consolation and salvation, which is effectual in the enduring of the same sufferings which we also suffer: or whether we be comforted, it is for your consolation and salvation. — And our hope of you is steadfast, knowing, that as ye are partakers of the sufferings, so shall ye be also of the consolation. — For we would not, brethren, have you ignorant of our trouble which came to us in Asia, that we were pressed out of measure, above strength, insomuch that we despaired even of life: — But we had the sentence of death in ourselves, that we should not trust in ourselves, but in God which raiseth the dead: — Who delivereth us from so great a death, and doth deliver: in whom we trust that he will yet deliver us; — Ye also helping together by prayer for us, that for the gift bestowed upon us by the means of many persons, thanks may be given by many on our behalf. — For our rejoicing is this, the testimony of our conscience, that in simplicity and godly sincerity, not with fleshly wisdom, but by the grace of God, we have had our conversation in the world, and more abundantly to you-ward. — For we write none other things unto you, than what ye read or acknowledge; and I trust ye shall acknowledge even to the end; — As also ye have acknowledged us in part, that we are your rejoicing, even as ye also are ours in the day of the Lord Jesus."

The character of the Second Epistle to the Corinthians differs considerably from that of the First. In the former Epistle, a variety of separate questions are discussed; some relating to doctrine — for example, the Resurrection: others to moral conduct, as concerning the incestuous Corinthian; others respecting ceremonies; others of casuistry, as the eating of meats offered to idols; and others regarding order in the Church, as, for example, the investigation of the value of spiritual gifts. To all these St. Paul replies, by referring each particular question back to some broad principle of Christianity.

But in the second Epistle a more personal tone is observable. It seems that certain charges had been alleged against him, probably in consequence of the severe and uncompromising way in which he had blamed their divisions and their sectarian spirit; and now, instead of being blamed by one party, he found himself accused by all. They had charged him with harshness to the incestuous person, with fickleness, with arrogance in his ministry; they said he had assumed a tone of authority which ill became him, and which was not consistent with the insignificance of his personal appearance. Accordingly, we notice that a very peculiar tone pervades this Epistle. It is the language of injured, and yet most affectionate, expostulation. One by one he refutes all the charges; one by one he calmly sets them aside: and yet you cannot read the Epistle without perceiving that, with all the firm manliness of his character, he had been wounded to the very quick. But not one word of resentment falls from his pen, only once or twice sentences of affectionate bitterness, as, for example: "For what is it wherein you were inferior to other churches, except it be that I myself was not burdensome to you? forgive me this wrong."

Our exposition to-day will embrace the first fourteen verses; and these divide themselves generally into two subjects of consideration.

I. The consolations of Affliction.
II. The testimony of Conscience.

I. Now the very terms of this division show the personal tone of the Epistle. His own afflictions, his own conscience — these are the subjects. We shall see the difference we spoke of by comparing these verses with the fourth, fifth, and sixth verses of the first chapter of the First Epistle. *There* he thanks God for *their* grace, *their* gifts, the testimony of Christ in *them;* while *here* we evidently feel the heart of the Apostle himself smarting under the sense of injustice and misconception — the want of fair treatment and of sympathy. Very naturally, therefore, he turns to the consolations of Suffering, and what Suffering means. It is the great question of thoughtful spirits, not merely, How can affliction be got rid of as soon as possible? — but, rather, Why is it? what does it mean? This is the subject of the wondrous Book of Job: from this are born the first earnest questionings of religion in all hearts, and in all ages. The Apostle then represents Affliction—

1. As a school of comfort, v. 4, 5.
2. As a school of assurance, v. 10.
3. And as a school of sympathy, v. 4.

1. As a school of comfort.

Affliction and comfort — a remarkable connection of two apparent opposites, and yet how indissoluble! For heavenly comfort — heavenly, as distinguished from mere earthly gladness and earthly happiness — is inseparable from suffering. It was so in the Life of Christ; it was immediately after the temptation that angels came and ministered to Him: it was in His agony that the angel appeared from heaven strengthening Him: it was in the preparation for the Cross that the Voice was heard, "I have both glorified it, and will glorify it again;" and it was on the Cross that the depth of Human loneliness, and the exceeding bitter cry, were changed for the trustful calm of a Spirit fulfilled with His Father's love: "Father, into thy hands I commend my spirit." And as in His life, so it is in ours, these two are never separated, for the first earnest questions of personal and deep religion are ever born out of personal suffering. As if God had said: "In the sunshine thou canst not see Me; but when the sun is withdrawn the stars of heaven shall appear." As with Job: "Not in prosperity, but in the whirlwind will I answer thee; there thou shalt hear my Voice, and see my Form, and know that thy Redeemer liveth."

2. A school of assurance.

There is nothing so hard to force upon the soul as the conviction that life is a real, earnest, awful thing. Only see the butterfly-life of pleasure men and women are living day by day, hour by hour, flitting from one enjoyment to another; living, working, spending, and exhausting themselves for nothing else but the seen, and temporal, and unreal. And yet these are undying souls, with feelings and faculties which death cannot rob them of; their chance swiftly passing, and no second chance for ever! Now pain and sorrow force upon the spirit the feeling of reality.

And again: nothing is harder than to believe in God. To do just this — simply to believe in God — in the history of each individual soul, there is no page so difficult to learn as that. When you are well, when hours are pleasant and friends abundant, it is an easy thing to speculate about God, to argue about the Trinity, to discuss the Atonement, to measure the mysteries of Existence. Christian men! when sorrow comes, speculation will not do. It is like casting the lead from mere curiosity, when you have a sound, strong ship in deep water. But when she is grinding on the rocks! Oh! we sound for God when the soul is on the rocks. For God becomes a living God, a Reality, a Home, when once we feel that we are helpless and homeless in this world without Him.

3. A school of sympathy.

There are some who are Christians, but notwithstanding are rough, hard, and rude: you cannot go to them for sympathy. You cannot confide the more delicate difficulties of the soul to them. Theirs is that rude health, which knows not of infirmities: theirs is that strong sound sense, which cannot see how a doubt can enter the spirit, and make it dark; nay, cannot understand why there should be a doubt at all. They have not suffered. But tenderness is got by suffering, both physical and mental. This was Christ's own qualification for sympathy: "We have not an high priest which cannot be touched with the feeling of our infirmities, but was in all points tempted like as we are." So that, would *you* be a Barnabas? would *you* give something beyond commonplace consolation to a wounded spirit? would *you* minister to doubt, to disappointed affection, to the loneliness of life?—then "you must suffer being tempted." Now, here we have a very peculiar source of consolation in suffering. It is the same which we spoke of in the First Epistle, when the subject of the contribution for the poor of Jerusalem came before us. Their suffering had taught many lessons to the Christians of Corinth and Galatia, had linked the Gentile Churches together in a common cause, had unconsciously drawn out sympathy and self-denial, and had kindled into a living flame the apostolical energies of St. Paul. So here: the thought that the Apostle's suffering benefited others, soothed him in his afflictions; and this is quite a peculiar consolation—one, too, which is essentially Christian. Thus we see, that Christianity is the true philosophy, after all. Consider only how moralists, how the old Stoicism had groped about in the dark to solve the mystery of pain and grief; telling you it *must* be, that it is the common lot, and, therefore, to be borne; that it benefits and perfects you.

Yes, that is true enough. But Christianity says much more to you: it says, Your suffering blesses others: it teaches *you* sympathy; it gives *them* firmness, and example, and reminds them of their frailty. How high a truth! for here is the law of the Cross: "No man dieth to himself;" for his pain and loss is *for* others, and unconsciously to himself brings with it *to* others, joy and gain.

II. The testimony of conscience.

Met by these charges from his enemies, and even from his friends, the Apostle falls back on his own conscience. Let us explain what he means by the testimony of conscience. He certainly does not mean faultlessness; for he says, "Of sinners I am chief." And St. John, in a similar spirit, declares that none can boast of faultlessness: "If we say that we have no sin, we deceive ourselves." And here St. Paul is not speaking of his own personal character, but of his ministry: and, again, he is not speaking of the blamelessness of his ministry, but of its success. No: it was not faultlessness St. Paul meant by the testimony of conscience, but this—integrity, moral earnestness in his work; he had been straightforward in his ministry, and his worst enemies could be refuted, if they said that he was insincere.

1. Now this sincerity excluded, first, all subtle manœuvring, all indirect modes of teaching. The Corinthians said, he had caught them with guile. He said, he had not: there had been no concealment of views, no doctrine of reserve, no Jesuitry, nor subtlety of reasoning in all his teaching: his conscience told him that. Yet many would have thought this subtlety the best mode of dealing with the bigoted Jews, and the intricate and versatile Greek intellect. St. Paul might have said: "These views about the Sabbath will offend the Jews; these declarations of the Christ crucified will be unpleasant to the Greeks." Instead of which, in simplicity and godly sincerity, St. Paul preached the Cross. And in this, let men say what they please, the Apostle was true to the nature of men. One of the keenest of Eastern diplomatists has left it on record, that subtlety fails in India; that there manœuvring politicians have ever been those who were most easily outwitted. For none succeed like the straightforward, blunt, simple Englishman, sailor or soldier, as long as he *is* simple. Be sure that straightforwardness is more than a match at last for all the involved windings of deceit. In your daily life, do what you feel right, say what you feel true, and leave, with faith and boldness, the consequences to God. Force men to feel of you, "Yes, he has faults, but they lie on the surface; he may be impetuous, hasty, mistaken, but what he says

he thinks: there is no *arrière pensée*, no acting in his character with a view to personal interests."

2. St. Paul's sincerity excluded all teaching upon the ground of mere authority. It is commonly taught that this or that truth is to be believed, because an inspired Apostle taught it. It is often said, It is incredible, nevertheless you must believe it, because it was accredited by miracles. But the Apostle never taught on this ground. Nay, even Christ Himself, in all His ministry, did not teach any doctrine on the ground of authority. He simply said: "If I say the truth, why do ye not believe?" "They that are of the truth, hear my voice:" "Wisdom is justified of her children." In the same way spoke St. Paul. The truth he had taught commended itself to their consciences: and so, too, throughout all his instruction, he says, "If our Gospel be hid, it is hid to them that are lost." And again: "We use great plainness of speech."

This was the secret of the Apostle's wondrous power. It was because he had used no adroitness nor craft, nor any threat of authority, but stood simply on the Truth, evident, like the sunlight, to all who had eyes to see, that thousands, go where he would, "acknowledged" what he taught. There are some men who thus interpret us to ourselves, who make us more really ourselves, from whose writings and words we feel a flash which kindles all into light at once. Of the words of such men we do not say, "How can that be proved?" We say, "It is the truth of God, and needs no proof." And such is our feeling, as we read the Word of Inspiration.

LECTURE XXXV.

JULY 18, 1852.

2 CORINTHIANS, i. 15-22. — "And in this confidence I was minded to come unto you before, that ye might have a second benefit; — And to pass by you into Macedonia, and to come again out of Macedonia unto you, and of you to be brought on my way toward Judæa. — When I therefore was thus minded, did I use lightness? or the things that I purpose, do I purpose according to the flesh, that with me there should be yea yea, and nay nay? — But as God is true, our word toward you was not yea and nay. — For the Son of God, Jesus Christ, who was preached among you by us, even by me and Silvanus and Timotheus, was not yea and nay, but in him was yea. — For all the promises of God in him are yea, and in him Amen, unto the glory of God by us. — Now he which stablisheth us with you in Christ, and hath anointed us, is God; — Who hath also sealed us, and given the earnest of the Spirit in our hearts."

THE whole tone of this Epistle is apologetical — it is defensive throughout. In other Epistles, the main subject being some Christian truth or truths, it is only incidentally that we ever learn anything respecting St. Paul himself. But in this, the main subject is St. Paul and St. Paul's conduct; and yet from chapter to chapter he digresses from his own conduct to some great principle which was dearer far to him than himself. Of course, generally, the value of this Epistle is extremely great. But its special value consists in two things: —

1. It exhibits the way in which a Christian may defend himself when maligned or misrepresented. No doubt it is very true that, in the end, character will clear itself: and a popular phrase says, with some truth, that the character which cannot defend itself, is best left without defence. Yet this may be pressed too far. An uncontradicted slander is believed readily, and often for long; and, meanwhile, influence is crippled or lost. Conceive what might have ensued, had St. Paul not met the slanders against his character with denial at

once! For few persons take the trouble to sift a charge which is not denied. Now, in the exposition of this Epistle, our attention (*inter alia*) will be frequently directed to the tone and manner in which the inspired Apostle defends himself.

2. This Epistle is valuable as peculiarly forcing our attention to the fact of the humility of St. Paul. In remembering the inspiration of the Apostles, we sometimes forget that they felt, thought, and wrote as men — that the Holy Ghost spoke through them, mixing the Divine with the human — that inspiration flowed through roused human feelings and passions. Hence there is a peculiar value in an Epistle whose main character is personal.

The link of connection between the subject of last Sunday and that of to-day is to be found in the twelfth and thirteenth verses, in which the Apostle maintains the openness and straightforwardness of his ministry. He had concealed nothing, he had used no reserve or duplicity. Nor had he taught truth to them on the mere ground of authority, but *as* truth, — that which was clear and self-evident when declared; that which they received and acknowledged.

Next he comes to a particular defence against a charge of failure of promise. The charge against him was one of duplicity or double-dealing, and this both in his public teaching, and also in his personal intercourse. His defence on the first count of the charge we have already dealt with. We come to-day to the charge as respects his personal deportment towards the Corinthians. He was, they said, a man who would teach plausibly, meaning something else all the while; all was not said out boldly by him. He was a man who would make a promise for a momentary purpose, and then break it for his own private ends. The alleged proof on which the charge was founded was, that he had promised to come to Corinth, and he had not come. The Apostle's reply includes a general defence against a general charge: and a defence of the particular case of apparent insincerity. He admits the fact, — he had intended to go to Corinth: and he had not fulfilled his intention. But he denies the inference of trifling with his word; or that it was with him, "yea yea" — and then with a juggler's dexterity, "nay nay."

The broad ground on which St. Paul denies the possibility of such conduct is, that he was a spiritual Christian. He could not do so, because it would be acting according to the flesh, that is, from interest, ambition, worldly policy, or private passions. Whereas he was in Christ; and Christ was the Christian's yea, the Living Truth; and the word is but the expression of the life. Now what Christ was, the Christian is, in degree. "Christ," says St. Paul, "was true; and God has established us in Christ." Therefore, fickleness, duplicity, or deceit, is impossible to us.

Such is the Apostle's argument. Let us notice how, even in apparent trifles, St. Paul fell back on main principles: "The Gospel goes into the life: Christ is yea, therefore be ye true." So, in another place: "Lie not one to another, seeing that ye have put off the old man with his deeds." He does not teach veracity as a separate virtue, but veracity as springing out of Christianity — a part of truth; to be veracious was simply the result of a true life: the life being true, the words and sentiments must be veracious.

Let us also see why "being in Christ" makes caprice and instability impossible. Consider what caprice is — it comes from not knowing one's own mind. A fickle-minded man's inner being is like an undisciplined mob — first one voice of passion, then another is heard — of interest, of ambition, or policy. "A double-minded man," says St. James, "is unstable in all his ways;" "he that wavereth is like a wave of the sea." And we read in Genesis: "Unstable as water, thou shalt not excel." A man who is governed by self, whose desires are legion, "purposes according to the flesh," and his yea is nay as often as yea. Now, what is the Gospel of Christ? What is it to be "established in Christ" — "anointed?" It is freedom from self, from all selfish and personal wishes. It is to say, "Not as I will, but as Thou wilt:" it is to place the right uppermost, and not pleasure. It is to be delivered from those passions whose name is Legion, and to "sit at the feet of Jesus, clothed and in our right mind." Hence a blow is struck at once at the root of instability. It is as if a ship tossed about by a hundred gusts of whirlwind were to feel suddenly a strong breeze blowing from one point, and at once to right and go steadily before the wind.

A man who is free from the manifold motives of self-will moves like the sun — steady, majestic, with no variableness, neither shadow of turning. His course can be calculated. You cannot calculate the quarter from whence the wind will blow to-morrow, but you can calculate the precise moment when the sun will reach a particular point. Such is the description of a Christian. St. Paul was a Christian; therefore he *could* not be tricky, or manœuvre, or do underhand things: the Spirit of Christ was in his heart. Observe, too, that he does not assert his truth because of his Apostleship, but because of his Christianity; — for he associated the Corinthians with himself — "us with you."

But we! — we! — how does this describe us? — changeful, vacillating, many of us tempted to subterfuges, unsteadiness, even to insincerity? Well, it *is* the portrait of a Christian; and, so far as it does not describe us, we are not Christians, we have not the Spirit — so far we *need* that Spirit to redeem us from self. For it is redemption in Christ from self, and that alone, which can make us true.

Let us note two things here, by the way: —

1. Remember that the Apostle calls this truthfulness — this gift of the Spirit — "God's seal" marking His own, and an "earnest." The true are His; none else.

Let us distinguish between an "earnest" and a "pledge." A "pledge" is something different in kind, given in assurance of something else, as when Judah gave his staff and ring in pledge for a lamb which he promised should be given afterwards. But an "earnest" is part of that thing which is eventually to be given; as when the grapes were brought from Canaan, or as when a purchase is made, and part of the money is paid down at once.

Now Baptism is a pledge of Heaven — "a sign and seal." The Spirit of Truth in us is an earnest of Heaven, it is Heaven begun. Therefore, it is a foolish question to ask, Will the true, pure, loving, holy man be saved? He *is* saved; he *has* Heaven: it is in him now — an earnest of more hereafter; God has shown him the grapes of Canaan; God has given him part of the inheritance, all of which is hereafter to be his own.

2. The solemn character of the relationship between ministers and congregations, — ver. 14.

* * * * * *

LECTURE XXXVI.

July 25, 1852.

2 Corinthians, i. 23, 24. — "Moreover I call God for a record upon my soul, that to spare you I came not as yet unto Corinth. — Not for that we have dominion over your faith, but are helpers of your joy; for by faith ye stand."

1 Corinthians, ii. 1 – 5. — "But I determined this with myself, that I would not come again to you in heaviness. — For if I make you sorry, who is he then that maketh me glad, but the same which is made sorry by me? — And I wrote this same unto you, lest, when I came, I should have sorrow from them of whom I ought to rejoice; having confidence in you all, that my joy is the joy of you all. — For out of much affliction and anguish of heart I wrote unto you with many tears; not that ye should be grieved, but that ye might know the love which I have more abundantly unto you. — But if any have caused grief, he hath not grieved me, but in part: that I may not overcharge you all."

We have seen that a double charge had been alleged against St. Paul — of duplicity both as respected his ministry, and also as respected his personal character. The charge against his personal character had been based on the non-fulfilment of his promise to visit Corinth: and we found his defence was twofold: —

1. General — resting on the moral impossibility of one in Christ being wilfully untrue; and this was our subject last Sunday.

2. Special — and this is our business to-day. This part of the defence extends from the twenty-third verse of the first chapter to the fifth verse of the second.

The first reason for the non-fulfilment of his promise was one of mercy: "Moreover, I call God for a record upon my soul, that to *spare* you, I came not as yet unto Corinth." By "spare" the Apostle means — to save them from the sharp censure their lax morality would have necessitated. They had treated this great crime which had been committed amongst them as a trifle;

they had even boasted of it as a proof of their Christian liberty: and had St. Paul gone to Corinth while they were unrepentant, his apostolic duty would have required from him severe animadversion. Now it was to spare them this that he changed his intention. It was no caprice, no fickleness, it was simply tenderness to them; by which we learn two things respecting St. Paul's character.

1. He was not one of those who love to be censors of the faults of others. There are some who are ever finding fault; a certain appearance of superiority is thereby gained, for blame implies the power of scanning from a height. There are political faultfinders, who lament over the evil of the times, and demagogues who blame every power that is. There are ecclesiastical faultfinders, who can see no good anywhere in the Church, they can only expose abuses. There are social faultfinders, who are ever on the watch for error, who complain of cant and shams, and who yet provide no remedy. There are religious faultfinders, who lecture the poor, or form themselves into associations, in which they rival the inquisitors of old. Now all this was contrary to the spirit of St. Paul. Charity with him was not a fine word: it was a part of his very being: he had that love "which thinketh no evil, which rejoiceth not in iniquity, but in the truth, which beareth, believeth, hopeth all things." It pained him to inflict the censure which would give pain to others: "to spare you I came not as yet unto Corinth."

2. St. Paul was not one of those who love to rule: "Not for that we have dominion over your faith." He had nothing within him of the mere Priest.

Let us draw a difference between the priest and the minister. Both are anxious for men's salvation, but the priest wishes to save them by his own official powers and prerogatives; while the minister wishes to help them to save themselves. Now see how exactly this verse expresses the distinction between these two spirits: "Dominion over your faith:" there is the very spirit of the Priest. "Helpers of your joy:" there is the spirit of the Minister; a desire, not to be a ruler, but a helper; not that *he* shall hold men up, but that they shall "*stand.*"

This is the great quarrel between Paganism and Christianity, between Romanism and Protestantism, between the proud pretensions of mere Churchmanship and spiritual Christianity. How are men saved? Directly through Christ? or indirectly by Christ through the priest?—by personal faith? or by the miraculous instrumentality of the sacraments? What is the Christian minister? Is he one whose manipulations and meddling are necessary to make faith and moral goodness acceptable, and to impart to them a spiritual efficacy? or is he simply one whose office is to serve his brethren, by giving to them such superior knowledge as he may possess, or such superior influence as his character may command? The Apostle's decision here is plain; and it is marvellous how any can read his writings, and support the "priestly view."

But do not mistake the meaning of the word "priest;" as used by the Church of England, it is simply a corrupted form of *presbyter*. In her formularies she does not claim sacrificial or priestly powers for her officers, but only ministerial ones. Observe, therefore, it is not a question of words, but of things: Priestcraft is a spirit, a temper of mind; and does not depend upon a name. It is not because a man is called a priest, that, therefore, he is unlike St. Paul; nor because a man is named a minister, that, therefore, he is free from the priestly temper. In Rome, where all are called priests, you have had the humble, servant-like spirit of many a Fénélon. Among Dissenters, where the word "priest" is strenuously avoided, there has been many a proud, priestly spirit, domineering and overbearing. Such men are willing—nay, zealous—that others should be saved, provided it is only through them; and hence their estimate of goodness in others is a peculiar one. Those who accept their teaching, and admit their authority, they call humble, meek, Christlike. Those who dare to doubt, who seek Truth for themselves, not blindly *their* truth, they call latitudinarians, proud, heretics, presumptuous, and self-willed. Thus the priestly estimate of saintliness is always a peculiar one, since the main element of it is obedience and submission, and a blind subservience to individual teaching. Besides, these men are always persecutors: the assumption of dominion over men's faith necessarily makes them so, although in different ways. In some ages they burn, in others curse, in others they affix stigmas and names on their fellow ministers, and bid people beware of them as dangerous teachers. Now I give you a criterion: Whenever you find a man trying to believe, and to make others believe, himself to be necessary to their salvation and progress, saying, "Except ye be circumcised, except ye believe what I teach, or except I baptize you, ye cannot be saved," there you have a priest, whether he be called minister, clergyman, or layman. But whenever you find a man anxious and striving to make men independent of himself, yea, independent of all *men;* desiring to help them — not to rest on his authority, but — to stand on their own faith, not his; that they may be elevated, instructed, and educated; wishing for the blessed time to come when his services shall be unnecessary, and the prophecy be fulfilled — "They shall no more teach every man his brother, saying, Know ye the Lord; for all shall know Him from the least to the greatest," — *there* you have the Christian minister, the servant, the "helper of your joy."

The second reason St. Paul alleges for not coming to Corinth is apparently a selfish one: to spare himself pain. And he distinctly says, he had written to pain *them*, in order that *he* might have joy. Very selfish, as at first it sounds: but if we look closely into it, it only sheds a brighter and fresher light upon the exquisite unselfishness and delicacy of St. Paul's character. He desired to save himself pain, because it gave them pain. He desired joy for himself, because his joy was theirs. He will not separate himself from them for a moment: he will not be the master, and they the school: it is not *I* and *you*, but *we;* "my joy is your joy, as your grief was my grief." And so knit together are we beloved, — minister and congregation!

Here it is best to explain the fifth verse, which in our version is badly punctuated. If we read it thus, it is clear: "If any have caused grief, he hath not grieved *me*, but in part (that I may not overcharge) you all."

To resume: — It was not to pain them merely, that he wrote, but because joy, deep and permanent, was impossible without pain; as the extraction of a thorn by a tender father gives a deeper joy in love to the child. It was not to inflict sorrow, "not that ye should be grieved, but that ye might know the love which I have more abundantly unto you." Again, it was not to save himself pain merely, that he did not come, but to save them that pain which would have given him pain. Here there is a canon for the difficult duty and right, of blame. When, — to what extent, — how, — shall we discharge that difficult duty, so rarely done with gracefulness? To blame is easy enough, with some it is all of a piece with the hardness of their temperament; but to do this delicately —how shall we learn that? I answer, Love! and then say what you will; men will bear anything if love be there. If not, all blame, however just, will miss its mark; and St. Paul showed this in the fourth verse, where love lies at the root of his censure. Nothing but love can teach us how to understand such a sentence as this from a higher Heart than his — "He looked round about Him in *anger*, being *grieved* at the hardness of their hearts."

Here, too, arises an occasion for considering the close connection between ministers and congregations. Let us compare the fourteenth verse of the first chapter — "We are your rejoicing, even as ye also are ours in the day of the Lord Jesus" — with the third verse of the second chapter — "Having confidence in you all that my joy is the joy of you all" — and what a lesson of comfort shall we not learn! But no doubt much mistake is made in representing the case of ministers now as parallel to that of the Apostles, and claiming, as is sometimes done, the same reverence for their words as the Apostles claimed rightfully for themselves. Much mistake, too, is made in drawing the parallel, or expecting it in the mutual affection of ministers and people. For gifts differ, and more than all, circumstances of trial differ; and it is only when dangers are undergone together, like those of the Apostles, that the cases can be parallel. Doubtless, in the early Church, and among the persecuted Covenanters, similar instances have occurred, but rarely do they happen in prosperous times.

Yet let me call attention to one point, in which the connection is equally solemn. I waive the question of personal affection and private influence. In the public ministry of a Church, week by week, a congregation listens to one man's teaching; year by year, a solemn connection is thus formed; for so, thoughts are infused, perforce absorbed. They grow in silence, vegetate, and bear fruit in the life and practice of the congregation; and a minister may even trace his modes of thinking in his people's conversation — not as mere phrases learnt by rote, but as living seed which has germinated in them. A very solemn thing! for what is so solemn as to have that part of a man which is his most real self — his thoughts and faith — grow into others, and become part of their being! Well, that will be his rejoicing in the judgment day; for that harvest he will put in his claim. "We are your rejoicing." It was to be *theirs* that St. Paul had taught them in simplicity and godly sincerity, truly and fearlessly. It was to be *his* that spiritual thoughts and contrite feelings had been through him infused into them, and this though they partially denied it. Still, deny it as they might, they could not rob him of his harvest.

My Christian brethren, may that mutual rejoicing be yours and mine in the day of Jesus Christ!

LECTURE XXXVII.

AUGUST 1, 1852.

2 CORINTHIANS, ii. 6-11. — "Sufficient to such a man is this punishment, which was inflicted of many. — So that contrariwise ye ought rather to forgive him, and comfort him, lest perhaps such a one should be swallowed up with overmuch sorrow — Wherefore I beseech you that ye would confirm your love toward him. — For to this end also did I write, that I might know the proof of you, whether ye be obedient in all things. — To whom ye forgive anything, I forgive also: for if I forgave anything, to whom I forgave it, for your sakes forgave I it in the person of Christ; — Lest Satan should get an advantage of us; for we are not ignorant of his devices."

THE main defence of the Apostle against the charge of fickleness in the non-fulfilment of his promise was, that he had abstained from going to Corinth in order to spare them the sharp rebuke he must have administered had he gone thither. A great crime had been committed: the Church had been compromised, more especially as some of the Corinthians had defended the iniquity on the ground of Liberty, and St. Paul had stayed away after giving his advice, that not he, but they themselves, might do the work of punishment. He gave sentence — that the wicked person should be put away, but he wished them to execute the sentence. For it was a matter of greater importance to St. Paul that the Corinthians should feel rightly the necessity of punishment, than merely that the offender should be punished. It was not to vindicate *his* authority that he wrote, but that they should feel the authority of right; and the Corinthians obeyed. They excommunicated the incestuous person; for the Epistle of the Apostle stirred up their languid consciences into active exercise. Accordingly, he applauds their conduct, and recommends them now to forgive the offender whom they had punished; so that, in this section, we have St. Paul's views respecting—

I. The Christian Idea of Punishment.
II. The Christian Idea of Absolution.

I. The Christian idea of punishment includes in it, first, the Reformation of the Offender.

This is the first and most natural object of punishment; and we infer it to have been part of St. Paul's intention, because when this end had been attained, he required that punishment should cease: "Sufficient to such a man is this punishment." Now herein consists the peculiar spirit of Christianity, that whereas the ancient system of law sacrificed the individual to the society, and feeble philanthropy would sacrifice society to the individual, Christianity would save both. It respects the decencies of life and its rights: it says the injurer must suffer: but it says, too, he also is a living soul, we must consider him: we must punish, so that he shall be made not worse, but better. So it was not only the dignity of the Corinthian Church that St. Paul thought of: he thought also of the the fallen, guilty state of his spirit, who had degraded that Church. He punished him, that his spirit might be saved in the day of the Lord Jesus.

The second thing included in this idea, is the Purification of Society. Punishment was also necessary for this reason—that sin committed with impunity corrupts the body of men to which the sinner belongs. This St. Paul declares in the First Epistle: "A little leaven leaveneth the whole lump." Now the purification of society is effected partly by example, and partly by removal of the evil. The discipline by which this removal was effected was called excommunication. At *that* time, apostolic excommunication represented to the world God's system of punishment. I do not say that it does so *now*, for the Church and the World have become so mixed, Church and State so trench upon each other's functions, that we know not where the division is. But I conceive that, in early times, the Church discipline was representative of the true idea of punishment: clearly St. Paul thought it was so. He did not think of extending it beyond the Church, for his idea of the Church was that of a pure society in the world, representing what the world should be; and so he does not require this separation to be rigidly enforced with respect to worldly men. This point is dwelt on in the fifth chapter of the First Epistle, in the tenth verse, and also in the thirteenth verse of the twelfth chapter. For God judged those without, while the Church, God's representative, judged and exhibited this principle of punishment on those within.

These two — to reform, and to serve as an example, are the only views of punishment which are found in the popular notion of it. But if we think deeper on the subject, we shall find, I believe, that there is another idea in punishment, which cannot be lost sight of. It is this — that punishment is the expression of righteous indignation: God's punishment is the expression of God's indignation, man's punishment is the expression of man's indignation. In the fifth verse of this chapter, as explained once before, St. Paul evidently thought that the guilty man had grieved — that is, offended — him partly, and partly the whole Church. Accordingly, their punishment of him was an expression of their indignation against him, as is clear from the eleventh verse of the seventh chapter, in which we must mark particularly the word "revenge," and compare it with the text of Rom. xiii. 4, — "a revenger to execute wrath," — where the word is used, not in its evil meaning, but in the sense of righteous resentment expressing itself in punishment. For there is a right feeling in human nature, which we call resentment: it exists equally in the best and the worst natures; although in the worst, it becomes malice. It existed in Christ Himself, for it is not a peculiarity of *fallen* human nature, but it is an inseparable element of human nature itself. Now let us mark what follows from this: Man is the image of God: all spirits are of the same family. So there is something in God which corresponds with that which we call resentment, stripped, of course, of all emotion, selfishness, or fury.

It is for this reason that we should strongly object to explain away those words of Scripture, "the wrath of God:" "God is angry with the wicked every day:" "the wrath of God is revealed from heaven." These sayings contain a deep and awful truth. God's punishment is God's Wrath against sin; and is not merely the consequence of lifeless laws, but the expression of the feeling of a Living Spirit. It would be most perilous to do away with these words; for if the Wrath of God be only a figure, His Love must be but a figure too. Such, therefore, is the true idea of human punishment. It exists to reform the offender, to purify society, and also to express God's and man's indignation at sin.

II. The Christian Idea of Absolution.

Before we go further, it will be well to explain some terms. Forgiveness is one thing, absolution is another. Absolution is the authoritative declaration of forgiveness. For example, when Christ said to the sick of the palsy, "Son, be of good cheer; thy sins be forgiven thee," He did not at this moment forgive him: he was forgiven already, but it was then that He declared his forgiveness.

Now the case before us is a distinct, unquestionable instance of ecclesiastical absolution. You are aware that many utterly deny the possibility of such a power existing in man, beyond a mere declaration of God's promises to faith; and the assurance of forgiveness on the part of any man would be counted, by some persons, as blasphemy. At once the cry of the Pharisees would be raised — "Who can forgive sins but God only?" Now here, in the Church of Corinth, is a sin: it is an offence not only against man, but also against God, — not a crime merely against society, but a sin, and yet St. Paul says "*I* forgive." This is absolution:

Man's declaration of God's Forgiveness — man speaking in God's stead.

1. We consider, first, the use of absolution. It was to save from remorse. Absolution is here considered as a "comfort." Let us examine this more closely. There is a difference between penitence and remorse: penitence works life, remorse works death. This latter is more destructive even than self-righteousness, for it crushes, paralyzes, and kills the soul. No one, perhaps, but a minister of Christ has seen it in all its power: but some of us can tell you how the recollection of sin committed haunts men like a fiend. And so long as society lays its ban on the offender, or so long as he feels that a secret crime, if once known, would be accursed of the world, so long hope appears to him impossible. It is in vain that you speak of God's love and mercy in Christ to such a man. He will cry, "Yes: but is He merciful to ME?" Therefore, over and above the general declaration of God's mercy, there is needed, if you would comfort truly, a special, personal, human assurance to the individual.

2. This absolution was representative. It represented the forgiveness of the congregation and the forgiveness of God. St. Paul forgave the sinner "for their sakes," and "in the person," that is, in the stead, "of Christ." Thus, as the punishment of man is representative of the punishment and wrath of God, so the absolution of man is representative of the forgiveness of God. For Human nature is representative of Divine nature. And, further, the Church represents Humanity, and the Minister represents the Church. Therefore, he who pronounces absolution at a sick man's bedside is but merely, as St. Paul was, speaking in the person of Christ. You will object, perchance: If God has forgiven the sinner, a man's word cannot add to it: if He has not forgiven him, a man's word cannot alter it. Yes, that is very true; but now, in reply, consider a distinct command of Christ: "Into whatsoever house ye enter, first say, Peace be to this house. And *if* the Son of Peace be there, your peace

shall rest upon it: if not, it shall turn to you again." Now a man might have said, "What good is there in saying "peace?" If God's peace be in that family, you cannot add to it; if not, you cannot alter it. But Christ says, Give your blessing: it will not create peace, but it will make it felt: "Your peace shall rest upon it." So if a Christian minister absolves, in Christ's words we may say, "If the sin be forgiven, that absolution will perhaps convey the soothing conviction to the soul; if not, your absolution will turn to you again."

In conclusion, remember the ministerial absolution is representative: St. Paul forgave in the name of the Christian congregation. Every member, therefore, of that congregation was forgiving the sinner: it was his right to do so, and it was in his name that St. Paul spoke; nay, it was *because* each member had forgiven, that St. Paul forgave.

Absolution, therefore, is not a priestly prerogative, belonging to one set of men exclusively. It belongs to Man, and to the minister because he stands as the representative of purified Humanity. "The Son of man," — that is, Man, — "hath power on earth to forgive sins." For society has this power collectively — a most actual and fearful power. Who does not know how the unforgivingness of society in branding men and women as outcasts, makes their case hopeless. Men bind *his* sins — *her* crimes — on earth: and they remain bound! Now every man has this power individually. The most remarkable instance, perhaps, in the Old Testament, is that of Jacob and Esau. For years the thought of his deceit, and the dread of his brother, had weighed on Jacob's heart; and when Esau forgave him, it was as if he "had seen the face of God." Be sure, this power is yours also. When a parent forgives a child, the child feels that God is nearer to him. When a master accepts a pupil's repentance, the pupil goes forth joyful from the master's presence. When schoolboys receive one who has been rejected, into fellowship again, a load is taken from that boy's bosom

When we treat the guilty with tenderness, hope rises in them towards God: their hearts say, "They love us, will not God forgive and love us too?"

It is a sublime, Godlike privilege which you have. Oh! do not quarrel with Romanist or Tractarian about the dogma. Go and make it real in your own lives. Represent on earth the Divine clemency: forgive in the Person of Christ. Loose suffering outcasts from sin, and it will be loosed in Heaven.

LECTURE XXXVIII.

AUGUST 8, 1852.

2 CORINTHIANS, ii. 12-17. — "Furthermore, when I came to Troas to preach Christ's gospel, and a door was opened unto me of the Lord, — I had no rest in my spirit, because I found not Titus my brother: but taking my leave of them, I went from thence into Macedonia. — Now thanks be unto God, which always causeth us to triumph in Christ, and maketh manifest the savor of his knowledge by us in every place. — For we are unto God a sweet savor of Christ, in them that are saved, and in them that perish: — To the one we are the savor of death unto death; and to the other the savor of life unto life, And who is sufficient for these things? — For we are not as many, which corrupt the word of God: but as of sincerity, but as of God, in the sight of God speak we in Christ."

2 CORINTHIANS, iii. 1-3. — "Do we begin again to commend ourselves? or need we, as some others, epistles of commendation to you, or letters of commendation from you? — Ye are our epistle written in our hearts, known and read of all men: — Forasmuch as ye are manifestly declared to be the epistle of Christ ministered by us, written not with ink, but with the Spirit of the living God; not in tables of stone, but in fleshy tables of the heart."

OUR last discourse closed with the eleventh verse, and was employed chiefly about St. Paul's doctrine of Christian absolution. To-day our exposition begins at the twelfth verse, which is an example of one of those rapid transitions so common in the writings of the Apostle. The first thing we have to do then, is to trace the connection. Apparently there is none: we cannot at once see what the argument has to do with St. Paul going to Troas, nor what his unrest there has to do with the voyage to Macedonia. But remember, that the main subject is St. Paul's defence against the charge of caprice. He had showed why he had not gone to Corinth according to promise. It was to enable the Corinthians to do the work of excommunication themselves, lest he should take it out of their hands, and so rob them of the spiritual discipline which comes from men's own exertions. For it is by what we do, and not by what is done for us, that we become strong or good.

St. Paul gives an additional proof that it was not forgetfulness of them which had made him change his mind: this proof was his unrest at Troas. While there, one subject engrossed all his thoughts, the state of Corinth; and the question — what would be the result of the letter he had sent? At Troas he expected to meet Titus, who was bearing the reply: but not finding him there, he could not rest; he could not take full comfort even from "the door which had been opened" for success. He left his work half finished, and he hastened into Macedonia to meet Titus. His argument, therefore, is, Did this look like forgetfulness? Did this make it probable that he "had used lightness or purposed according to the flesh?" Or did it show that he was absent unwillingly, putting force on himself, like a wise parent who refuses to see his child, though his heart is all the while bleeding at what he inflicts? This is the connection between the twelfth and thirteenth verses.

The next thing we have to do is to explain the link of thought between the thirteenth and the fourteenth verses. Here there is another startling abruptness. The Apostle on mention of Macedonia breaks off into thanksgiving: "Now thanks be unto God." Here is a notable instance of the peculiar style of St. Paul. He starts from the main subject into a digression, caused by a thought which he had not expressed, and which it was not necessary to express, since it was known to his readers. What was, then, the thought at which he broke off here into an exclamation of thanksgiving? When we have found that, the connection will be clear.

It was a thought which to the Corinthians would present itself at once. Observe, he had said that he went into Macedonia. What did he find there? He found Titus with the long-looked-for letters, containing news far better than he had hoped for; that the Corinthians had done all that he asked, had been recalled to shame for wrong and to a sense of right, that they had excommunicated the criminal, and that the criminal himself was penitent. We find this is referred to in the fifth, sixth, and seventh verses of the seventh chapter of this Epistle. As soon, therefore, as St. Paul came to the word "Macedonia," memory presented to him what had greeted him there, and in his rapid way — thoughts succeeding each other like lightning, — he says, without going through the form of explaining why he says it, "Now thanks be unto God." It may be observed, that it is only by this kind of study that the Bible becomes intelligible.

Now that the difficulty of the connection has been removed, we select from the verses two subjects for consideration: —

I. The assertion in the close of the chapter: That the Christian is always a conqueror.

II. The nature of true Christian work — in the commencement of the third chapter.

I. The assertion. "Now thanks be unto God, who always causeth us to triumph in Christ." There was a moment in the Apostle's life when he half regretted what he had done. After the letter was sent, he felt the pain of what was irrevocable: he had no rest in his spirit: for a moment he "did repent" his truthfulness; for it was possible that his firmness might have cost him the Church of Corinth. They might have rebelled against his command; they might be too little advanced in the Christian life for such severity. But when the news came, then he learnt a lesson. He had spoken in sincerity and godly truthfulness, and sincerity is best. He felt that he had won; though a few hours before, his work seemed over in Corinth. Thence we can divine the truth that the Christian is a conqueror, even in defeat. His is always a triumphant career, sooner or later. This was not a lesson for St. Paul only, but it is one also for us. On earth we have nothing to do with success or with results, but only with being true *to* God, and *for* God; for it is sincerity, and not success, which is the sweet savor before God.

Now there are two branches in which this assertion is true: —

1. The defeat of the true-hearted is victory.

2. The apparent harm done by the true-hearted is victory.

1. It was quite possible that the result might have turned out otherwise: instead of penitence, there might have been hardness; instead of strengthened, there might have been only weakened influence. Such thoughts as these must have presented themselves to the Apostle: "Do not be so bold or so decided; you will very likely cripple your influence:" and these fears might have been realized; for in this world truth is not always successful. Now, it seems a most important Christian lesson to insist upon the truth, that defeat in doing right is nevertheless Victory. Every one knows the common adage, "Honesty is the best policy:" Do right, Paul, and you will not lose influence. This is true sometimes; but St. Paul would not have been a Christian unless he had felt — I may lose *all;* and yet I will do right, and be true to conscience. Let us get rid of that false notion, that we are sure to win if we are true to conscience. No! often — most often — you must serve God at a loss. Surely the Cross should teach us, that in this world doing right, and being true, is not "the best policy," as the world understands it. The lives of the Apostles, the lives of all God's best and noblest should teach us this lesson. When did you ever hear that conscience could be saved without a self-sacrifice? For the victory of the true lies not so much in winning the contest, but in spreading a Spirit. Even had St. Paul failed in his immediate object, the conversion of the Corinthians, think you that that true Epistle of his would have lost its power in the ages to come? Impossible! and that would have been his triumph. Beyond, beyond — oh! beyond the present must we look for victory!

2. The apparent harm done by the true-hearted is victory. St. Paul might have done harm; he might have produced rebellion at Corinth. Still, should he not be true? With steadiness he clearly contemplated this possibility. His truth would be to some "the savor of death unto death;" for there can be no doubt that the faithful preaching of the Gospel sometimes kills. But it is no less the Gospel — no less a sweet savor to God. Just as the vigorous breezes that are fresh life to the strong, are death to the feeble lungs, so truth — strong truth — put before the haters of truth, makes them worse. For example, the sacrifice suggested to the rich young ruler was too strong for the weakness of his spirit, and the faint desire of good which was in him was slain. And yet is this Gospel which destroys, a sweet and acceptable savor to God, even in them that perish. An awful truth! The Gospel preached in fidelity ruins human souls. A "banquet!" — oh! know ye what ye say? It is sometimes death to hear it! And yet we must not dilute it. How the Apostle rejoiced in that day that he had been uncompromising, and firm, and true! "not dealing deceitfully with the Word of God." Even had the Corinthians perished, he must have rejoiced that their blood was not on his head.

II. The nature of true Christian work.

The work of the Apostle Paul is contained in the second verse: "Ye are our Epistle written in our hearts, known and read of all men." But let us explain the meaning of this phrase and its connection. The close of the second chapter looked like boasting — it seemed like a recommendation of himself. Now, in these verses, he is replying to the possible charge. He declares that he wanted no commendation to them, no praise, no recommendatory letters; and in this he was alluding to the ἐπιστολαὶ συστατικαὶ of the early Church. A great Christian brotherhood was the Church of Christ; and if a Christian of Corinth travelled to Rome or Galatia, he received from the bishop or congregation letters of recommendation, and was at home at once among friends. Now such a letter, St. Paul says, he did not need. Nor need any boasting be his, nor praise from himself or others: his works were too well known. What, then, were St. Paul's works? What were St. Paul's Epistles? You will answer at once, These which we hold in our hands. "No!" replies the Apostle. The Epistles of St. Paul were not those which were written then on parchment, or printed since in ink, but those which were written by God as truth on human hearts: "Ye are our Epistle."

Now, first: Observe the remarkable expression of the Apostle: his *letter!* He was writing on men's hearts; and each man here is writing something; and his writing lasts for ever. Pilate uttered a deeper truth than he thought, when he said, "What I have written, I have written." For deeds are permanent and irrevocable: that which you have written on life is for ever. You cannot rub, blot, or scratch it out: there it is for ever, your Epistle to the world and to the everlasting ages, for all eternity, palpably what you are, to be "known and read of all men." This it is which makes life so all-important. Oh! then, take care *what* you write, for you can never unwrite it again.

Secondly: The best of all Epistles is that which a man writes and engraves on human spirits, "not with ink, but with the spirit of the living God; not in tables of stone, but in fleshy tables of the heart." What then? A man's "works" — what are they? That which makes him "immortal," as we say. But what is that immortality? Well, the Pyramids were cut in tables of stone, and the monuments of Assyria are more enduring than brass, and yet *they* will wear out. There *are* works which will outlast even these — written, not in rock, but in ink; noble works of the Gifted and the Pure and True. There is the Bible, and St. Paul's Epistles as part of it. But there is something which will outlast the Pyramids and the Bible: a human soul, and the work for good or evil done upon it. This is the true Christian work; it is the highest: and yet not only that which an Apostle could do, but that which all may do. And think how many *do* it! The mother, the teacher, the governess, the tutor — not ministers and Apostles only — are doing it. Men, my Brothers, your truest, your best work, almost your sole work, is in that which lasts for ever.

Thirdly: It is fitting to distinguish between the scribe, or amanuensis, and the real author of the Epistle. St. Paul's language might have seemed a ground of boasting: had he not written that which was to last? But he makes this distinction, that it was the Epistle of Christ, ministered by him. The Spirit of Christ — He was the author of the work, and St. Paul was but the amanuensis. Suppose, for example, that the poor scribe, who wrote one of these Epistles at St. Paul's dictation, had prided himself upon it, because it was written by his pen. Yet that were not so foolish, as if some poor miserable minister or teacher, rejoicing over his success, were to misdeem the work his own.

The amanuensis? — the man? No! It is the Spirit of the living God which does the work on human hearts.

LECTURE XXXIX.

1852.

2 Corinthians, iii. 4–18. — "And such trust have we through Christ to God-ward: — Not that we are sufficient of ourselves to think anything as of ourselves; but our sufficiency is of God; — Who also hath made us able ministers of the New Testament; not of the letter, but of the spirit: for the letter killeth, but the spirit giveth life. — But if the ministration of death, written and engraven in stones, was glorious, so that the children of Israel could not steadfastly behold the face of Moses for the glory of his countenance; which glory was to be done away: — How shall not the ministration of the spirit be rather glorious? — For if the ministration of condemnation be glory, much more doth the ministration of righteousness exceed in glory. — For even that which was made glorious had no glory in this respect, by reason of the glory that excelleth. — For if that which was done away was glorious, much more that which remaineth is glorious. — Seeing then that we have such hope, we use great plainness of speech: — And not as Moses, which put a vail over his face, that the children of Israel could not steadfastly look to the end of that which is abolished: — But their minds were blinded: for until this day remaineth the same vail untaken away in the reading of the Old Testament; which vail is done away in Christ. — But even unto this day, when Moses is read, the vail is upon their heart. — Nevertheless when it shall turn to the Lord, the vail shall be taken away. — Now the Lord is that Spirit: and where the Spirit of the Lord is, there is liberty. — But we all, with open face beholding as in a glass the glory of the Lord, are changed into the same image from glory to glory, even as by the Spirit of the Lord."

The third chapter of the Second Epistle to the Corinthians is one long digression, and arose out of the necessity of explaining the apparent self-sufficiency and boasting of the seventeenth verse of the second chapter; so it is not till the beginning of the fourth chapter that the subject of the second is taken up again.

The beginning of the third chapter seems but a reiteration of this boasting; for St. Paul appeals to his work in proof of his ministry. True Christian work, according to him, was something written on human souls. Men — the hearts and spirits which he had trained — these were his Epistles to the nations: so that, if the world wanted to know what St. Paul meant to say, he replied — "Look at the Corinthian Church; that is what I have to say: their lives are my writings." The first three verses, then, are only a re-statement of his vaunt. But, then, he explains: The Corinthians are our Epistle, yet not ours, but rather Christ's. Christ is the Author, I am but the scribe. Not I, but the Spirit of the living God, made them what they are: I have only been the minister.

Hence he infers that there was no vanity in his assertion, though it looked like a boast. For the trust he had was not in himself — the writer — but in Christ, the Spirit, the Author of the work: "Such trust have we through Christ to God-ward: not that we are sufficient of ourselves to think anything as of ourselves; but our sufficiency is of God: Who also hath made us able ministers of the New Testament." Then it is that from these words "able minister" he breaks off into a digression, which occupies all the chapter, and is descriptive of the Christian ministry in contradistinction to the Jewish.

Our subject now is the *principle* of the Christian ministry; that is, the exposition and application of the Word of God. There are two modes in which this is done: —

I. That of the Letter.
II. That of the Spirit.

Or — to use more modern equivalents — we distinguish between the formal ministry and the spiritual one, — between the teaching of the Old Testament and that of the New.

Let us make, however, one preliminary remark: Ours is an exposition; and therefore we take the subject broadly. Our object is rather to get a comprehensive view of the Apostle's argument, than to pursue it into every particular. Each separate sentence might be the text of a rich sermon; but, omitting detail, we will confine ourselves to the main scope of the chapter, that is, to the contrast we have spoken of above: —

I. The ministry of the Letter.

The ministry of Moses was one of the Letter; it was a formal ministry — a ministry of the Old Testament: for a formal ministry, a ministry of the letter, and a ministry of the Old Testament, have all the same meaning. It was the business of Moses to teach maxims, and not principles; rules for ceremonial, and not a spirit of life. And these things — rules, ceremonials, maxims, law — are what the Apostle calls here the "*letter*." Thus, for instance, Truth is a principle, springing out of an inward life; but Moses only gave the rule: "Thou shalt not forswear thyself." It is impossible not to see how plainly inadequate this rule is to all that truth requires; for he who scarcely avoided perjury may have kept, nevertheless, to the letter of the law! Again, love is a principle; but Moses said simply: "Thou shalt not kill, nor steal, nor injure." Again, Meekness and subduedness before God — these are of the Spirit; but Moses merely commanded fasts. And, further, Unworldliness arises from a spiritual life: but Moses only said, "Be separate, circumcise yourselves;" for, under the Jewish law, it was separation from the surrounding nations which stood in the place of Christian unworldliness.

It was in consequence of the superiority of the teaching of principles over a mere teaching of maxims, that the ministry of the letter was considered as nothing; and this for two reasons: first, because of its transitoriness, "it was to be done away with."

Let us, then, look at this in a real, practical way. We say the Law was superseded by the Gospel. But why? By an arbitrary arrangement of God? No: but on an Eternal principle. And this *is* the principle: — All formal truth is transient: no maxim is intended to last for ever. No ceremony, however glorious, however beautiful, can be eternal; so that, though *for the time* it is a Revelation, yet it cannot last, because it is less than the whole truth. Thus, when Christ came, instead of saying, "Thou shalt not forswear thyself," He said, "Let your yea be yea, and your nay, nay:" so that the same truth which Moses had given in a limited form was stated by Christ in all its fulness, and the old *form* was superseded by the *principle;* and instead of saying, "Thou shalt not say, Fool, or Raca," Christ gave the principle of Love; and instead of commanding the devotion of the seventh part of time to God, Christianity has declared "the sanctification of all time;" and instead of a command to sacrifice, that is, to give of your best, Christ says, "Give yourself a living sacrifice to God." In all these things, observe how the form was superseded: because the higher Truth had come, the Letter was "done away."

The second reason for the inferiority of the Letter was that it *killed:* partly because, being rigorous in its enactments, it condemned for any non-fulfilment. In the ninth verse, it is called a "ministration of condemnation." The Law had no mercy—it could have none; for its duties were done or not done; there were in it no *degrees* of goodness or evil: "He that despised Moses' law died without mercy." And partly it killed, because technicalities and multiplicities of observance necessarily deaden spiritual life. It was said by Burke, that "no man comprehends less of the majesty of the English constitution than the *Nisi Prius* lawyer, who is always dealing with technicalities and precedents." In the same way none were so dead to the glory of the law of God as the scribes, who were always discussing its petty minutiæ. While they were disputing about the exact manner in which a sacrifice should be slain, or the precise distance of a Sabbath day's journey, or the exact length of a phylactery, how could they comprehend the largeness of the Spirit which said, "I will have mercy, and not sacrifice?"

This surely we can understand. Obedience is a large, free, glorious feeling; Love is an expansion of the whole heart to God; Devotion is an act of the heart, in which thought is merely silent. But could anything dull the vigor of Obedience more than frittering it away in anxieties about the mode and degree of fasting? Could aught chill Love more than the question, "How often shall my brother offend, and I forgive him?" Or could anything break Devotion — an exercise of mind where heart should be all in all — more into fragments, than multiplied changes of posture, and turnings from side to side? Such were the deficiencies of the "letter," or the ministries of the Old Testament.

Now observe: No blame was attributable to Moses for teaching thus. St. Paul calls it a "glorious ministry;" and it was surrounded with outward demonstrations — with thunders and mighty signs — to prove it so. The reason is, that maxims, rules, and ceremonies have truth in them: Moses was commissioned to teach truth so far as the Israelites could bear it; not in substance, but in shadows; not principles by themselves, but principles by rules, to the end of which the Church of Israel could not as yet see. In St. Paul's symbolic expression, a veil was before the lawgiver's face; it was truth he gave, but it was veiled; its lineaments were only dimly seen. These rules were to hint and lead up to a Spirit, whose brightness would have dazzled only the Israelites into blindness then.

II. We have now to consider the Ministry of the New Testament.

1. It was a "spiritual" ministry —

The Apostles were "ministers of the spirit," and by this St. Paul means ministers of that truth which underlies all forms, whether of word or ceremony. He does not say that it was the Holy Spirit, but "the spirit," that is, the *essence* of the Law, that the Apostles were to minister. Precisely such was Christ's own description of a wise expounder of the Word, when He compares him to a householder bringing out of his treasures "things new and old," declaring old principles under new forms. The mistake men make is this: they would have for ever the same old words, the same old forms, whereas these are ever transient: intended to exist only as long as they are needful, and then to be "done away." There *are* to be new things, but there is still something in the old things which can never alter — the spirit which underlies the words, the ancient truth which creates the form it dwells in. It is in this sense that Christ is the *Spirit* of the law, for He is "the end of the law for righteousness to every one that believeth." And St. Paul's ministry to the Jews, and to the Judaists among the Gentiles, was freedom from the letter — conversion to the spirit of the law. Blinded as were their minds, veiled as were their hearts, nevertheless liberty was coming. For "when it" (the Jewish heart) "shall turn to the Lord, the vail shall be taken away: now the Lordis that Spirit." Therefore, to turn to the Lord Christ was to turn to the spirit instead of the letter of the law; and so they would become the true Israel, free, with clear vision: for "where the Spirit of the Lord is, there is liberty" — there is the "open face" which reflects the glory of Christ.

2. The Ministry of the New Testament was a "life-giving" ministry.

First, let us touch on the figurative meaning of the word "life-giving." It is like a new life to know that God wills not sacrifice and burnt-offering, but rather desires to find the spirit of one who says, "Lo! I come to do Thy will." It is new life to know that to Love God and man is the sum of existence. It is new life — it is free thought — to know that "God be merciful to me a sinner!" is a truer prayer in God's ears, than elaborate liturgies and long ceremonials of ecclesiastical ritual.

Further: Christ was the spirit of the law, and He gave, and still gives, the gift of Life. But how? St. Paul replies, in the eighteenth verse: A living character is impressed upon us: we are as the glass or mirror which reflects back a likeness, only we reflect it livingly, it does not pass away from us as the image does from the glass, but is an imparted life, which develops itself more and more within us: for Christ is not a mere example, but the Life of the world; and the Christian is not a mere copy, but a living image of the living God. He is "changed into the same image from glory to glory, even as by the Spirit of the Lord."

Now such a ministry — a ministry which endeavors to reach the life of things — the Apostle calls (1.) *an able* — that is, a powerful — ministry. Observe, he names it thus, even amidst an apparent want of success. For such teaching may leave no visible fruits. It makes no party or sect. Its minister may seem to fail, but his victory is sure; he works powerfully, deeply, gloriously. He moulds souls for the ages to come. He works for the eternal world.

(2.) St. Paul calls it a bold ministry: "We use great plainness of speech." Ours should be a ministry whose words are not compacted of baldness, but boldness; whose very life is outspokenness, and free fearlessness: — a ministry which has no concealment, no reserve; which scorns to take a *via media*, because it is safe in the eyes of the world; which shrinks from the weakness of a mere cautiousness, but which exults even in failure, if the truth has been spoken, with a joyful confidence. For a man who sees into the heart of things speaks out not timidly, nor superstitiously, but with a brow unveiled, and with a speech as free as his spirit: "The truth has made him free."

LECTURE XL.

1852.

2 CORINTHIANS, iv. 1 – 15. — "Therefore seeing we have this ministry, as we have received mercy, we faint not; — But have renounced the hidden things of dishonesty, not walking in craftiness, nor handling the word of God deceitfully; but by manifestation of the truth commending ourselves to every man's conscience in the sight of God. — But if our gospel be hid, it is hid to them that are lost : — In whom the god of this world had blinded the minds of them which believe not, lest the light of the glorious gospel of Christ, who is the image of God, should shine unto them. — For we preach not ourselves, but Christ Jesus the Lord; and ourselves your servants for Jesus' sake. — For God, who commanded the light to shine out of darkness, hath shined in our hearts, to give the light of the knowledge of the glory of God in the face of Jesus Christ. — But we have this treasure in earthen vessels, that the excellency of the power may be of God, and not of us. — We are troubled on every side, yet not distressed; we are perplexed, but not in despair; — Persecuted, but not forsaken; cast down, but not destroyed; — Always bearing about in the body the dying of the Lord Jesus, that the life also of Jesus might be made manifest in our body. — For we which live are alway delivered unto death for Jesus' sake, that the life also of Jesus might be manifest in our mortal flesh. — So then death worketh in us, but life in you. — We having the same spirit of faith, according as it is written, I believed, and therefore have I spoken; we also believe, and therefore speak; — Knowing that he which raised up the Lord Jesus shall raise up us also by Jesus, and shall present us with you. — For all things are for your sakes, that the abundant grace might through the thanksgiving of many redound to the glory of God."

THE first two verses of this chapter contain the principles of the Christian ministry: they embrace its motives — a sense of mercy and a sense of hope : they declare its straightforwardness, its scorn of craft and secrecy, its rejection of pious frauds and adroit casuistry, and they show that its influence is moral, and not official. Hence it becomes clear that its indirect was more sure than its direct influence.

Now the connection of these two verses with the third, is through the word "every." For a reply suggested itself to St. Paul's mind from some objector; "Every man's conscience has *not* acknowledged the truth of the message, nor the heavenly sincerity of the messengers." To which the Apostle answers, The exceptions do not weaken the truth of the general assertion: to every man whose heart is in a healthy state — to all but the blinded — the Gospel is God's Light; and those to whom it is not Light are themselves dark, for the obscurity is in themselves, and not in the truth. And then, having replied to this objection, St. Paul proceeds with the same subject — the Apostolic Ministry. He represents it under two main aspects: —

I. As a Ministry of Light.

II. As a reflection, in word and experience of the Life of Christ.

I. Let us glance at the fourth and sixth verses: "the *light* of the glorious Gospel:" "God, who commanded the *light* to shine out of darkness, hath shined in our hearts, to give the *light* of the knowledge of the glory of God in the face of Jesus Christ." Compare with this what St. John says in the opening chapter of his Gospel: "The *light* shineth in darkness, and the darkness comprehended it not." Nothing could be more different than the minds of St. Paul and St. John; and yet how remarkably they coincide in this thought — they both call Revelation, "Light!" According to St. John, to live in sin was to live in darkness; it was a false life — a life of lies — in which a man was untrue to his own nature. According to St. Paul, it was to live in blindness — "blinded by the god of this world." But both Apostles concur in representing Revelation as simply the unveiling of the truth: the manifestation of things as they are. This is strikingly shown in St. Paul's metaphor: "For God, who commanded the light to shine out of darkness, hath shined in our hearts, to give the light of the knowledge of the glory of God in the face of Jesus Christ." As on the darkness of the physical world, light rose at the Eternal "Be," and all things appeared as they were, not a creation, but a manifestation — and yet, in truth, a real creation (as but for light this world were as if it were not, since it is what it is in consequence of light) : so, on the moral darkness of a world in sin and ignorance, the light of revealed truth showed things as they are, and exhibited them in their true relative proportions. That revelation created, indeed, a new world, which yet was not a creation of things that had not existed before : for the Gospel did not *make* God our Father ; it revealed what He had ever been, is, and ever shall be ; it disclosed Him, not as a tyrant, but as a Father : not as a chance, or a fate ; not as a necessary *thing*, but as a Person ; and in the Life of Christ, the Love of God has become intelligible to us. The Gospel threw light on God : light unknown before, even to the holiest hearts among the Jews. " Clouds and darkness are the habitation of His seat," spoke the Old Testament : " God is Light, and in Him is no darkness at all," declared the New. For, out of Christ, our God is only a dark, dim, and dreadful mystery. There is only an awful silence, which is never broken by an articulate voice. But all is brightness in the Redeemer's life and death.

The Gospel threw light, too, upon man's own nature. Man — a dark enigma, a contradiction to himself, with god-like aspirations and animal cravings — asks his own heart in terror, " Am I a god or beast ? " And the Gospel answers : " You are a glorious temple in ruins, to be rebuilt into a habitation of God and the Spirit, your soul to be the home of the High and Holy One, your body to be the temple of the Holy Ghost." It threw light upon the grave ; for " life and immortality " were " brought to light through the Gospel." The darkness of the tomb was irradiated ; and the things of that undiscovered land shone clear and tranquil then to the eye of faith : but not until *then*, for before, immortality was but a mournful *perhaps*.

Now there are three practical deductions from this view of Truth.

1. As to ministerial conduct. Our life is to be a

manifestation of the Gospel. Observe St. Paul's argument: — We do not tamper with the Word of God. It is not concealed or darkened by us; for our very work is to spread light, to throw sunshine on every side, and in every way fearlessly to declare the truth, to dread no consequences: for no real minister of Christ can be afraid of illumination.

2. Light is given to us that we may *spread* it. "We preach . . . ourselves your servants for Jesus' sake. For God . . . hath shined in our hearts." If He has illuminated us, then we are your servants, to give you this illumination. We should be as "a city set on a hill;" as the salt which penetrates and purifies the earth: "Ye are the light of the world." This St. Paul felt vividly: St. Paul who had himself been in darkness; and shall we refuse to feel it? we, who have had ages of light, which St. Paul had not? Our more open heaven seems to shut us out from feeling this. Perhaps we, who have been, or fancy ourselves to have been, in the brightness of his revelation all our lives, scarcely appreciate the necessity which he felt so strongly of communicating it.

3. It is the evil heart which hides the truth. Light shines on *all*, that is, all who are in a natural human state, all who can feel, all who have not deadened the spiritual sense. It is not the false life which can know the truth, but the true life receives what is akin to it: for "every one that is of the truth heareth my voice."

Thus observe — what are "the evidences of Christianity." "The evidences of Christianity" are — Christianity. The evidence of the sun is its light, and not the shadow on the dial. So Christ is divine to those who are of the truth. To some persons He is not the image of God. How will you prove to such that He is? Is it by arguing about miracles and prophecy? Is it by discussion about the true reading of texts, or by requiring belief on the authority of the Church? No. It is by means of a right heart: it is by means of God's Spirit ruling in the heart. These, and these alone, will disclose Christ to a man; for "no man can say that Jesus is Lord, but by the Holy Ghost;" and again: "The natural man receiveth not the things of the Spirit of God," and for this reason — "they are *spiritually* discerned."

Again, it is the worldly heart which hides the truth. "The god of this world hath blinded the minds of them which believe not." An awful thought! "The light of the glorious Gospel" is shut out by ourselves from our lives, apart from immorality, apart even from actual sin. For worldliness is distinct from sin, and the denunciation of it is peculiar to Christianity. It does not consist in distinct acts, nor in thoughts of transgression, but it is the spirit of a whole life, which hides all that is invisible, real, and eternal, because it is devoted to the visible, the transient, and the unreal. Christ and the world cannot exist in the same heart. Men who find their all in the world — how can they, fevered by its business, excited by its pleasures, petrified by its maxims, see God in his purity, or comprehend the calm radiance of Eternity?

II. The Apostle represents the Ministry as a reflection, in word and experience, of the Life of Christ.

1. In word. Let us compare the second verse with the thirteenth. We manifest the truth, "commending ourselves to every man's conscience," because we speak in strong belief. The minister of Christ speaks in faith; that is, in a firm conviction of Divine power arising from the Resurrection — faith in the delivering or redeeming power of God. Observe the difference between this and theological knowledge. It is not a minister's wisdom, but his *conviction*, which imparts itself to others. Nothing gives life but life. Real flame alone kindles other flame: this was the power of the Apostles: "We believe, and therefore speak:" — "We *cannot* but speak the things which we have seen and heard:" — "He that saw it bare record, and his record is true: and he *knoweth* that he saith true, that ye might believe." Firm faith in what they spoke,

that was the basis of the Apostles' strength; but in us there is one thing wanting — we only *half* believe. If we really believed the truths we deliver week after week, would not our hearts be filled with such deep earnestness, that the spectacle of men and women listening unconcernedly to the Gospel would sadden all our days, and impel us to preach as if we should never preach again?

In the fifth verse, St. Paul says he preaches Christ, and not himself. Rescue this expression from all party interpretations, and the minister will understand that he is to preach, not the Christ of this sect or that man, but Christ fully — Christ our Hope, our Pattern, our Life — Christ in us, the light which is in every man subjectively; and Christ the Light which, shining objectively in His Life, and Death, and Resurrection, daily increases, as we gaze, the Light of the Christ within us.

2. The Ministry is a reflection of Christ's Life in experience. It might be a matter of surprise, that God's truth should be conveyed through such feeble instruments — men, whom the axe and the lion could destroy. Well, the Apostle acknowledges that it is so. He calls them "earthen vessels:" he knows them to be but fragile receptacles of this "treasure." But this very circumstance, instead of proving that the Gospel is not of God, proves that it is. For what was the life of these men, but the Life of Christ over again — a Life victorious in defeat? "I fill up," says St. Paul, "that which is behind of the afflictions of Christ:" "Always bearing about in the body the dying of the Lord Jesus, that the life also of Jesus might be made manifest in our body." So that, in their sufferings, the Apostles represented the death of Christ, and in their incredible escapes, His resurrection. Figuratively speaking, their escapes were as a resurrection. Compare the word *resurrection*, used in the sense of escape, in the eleventh chapter of Hebrews, at the thirty-fifth verse. One might almost say that the Apostles bore a charmed life — a mystic resemblance

to their Lord: an existence which rose, like the fabled phœnix, into fresher being from its ashes.

Christ, then, is the mystic symbol of Christian life: His death and His resurrection are repeated in His people. Only with exquisite truthfulness, and in opposition to all one-sided exaggeration, St. Paul observes, that in some Christians the death was more exhibited, in others the Resurrection: "So then death worketh in us, but life in you." For there are various types of the Divine life, as, for example, in Christ and in John the Baptist. It takes effect sometimes on the side of the Cross, sometimes on the side of the Resurrection. In different periods of the same life, in different ages of freedom or persecution — as we have known in the depressed Church of the Albigenses and the victorious Church of England — in different persons during the same age, the Cross and the Resurrection alternate, and exist together. But in all there is *progress* — the decay of evil, or the birth of good; for "though our outward man perish, yet the inward man is renewed day by day."

It was in this way that the early Church followed Christ's Life, weekly and yearly. Friday and Sunday showed to them the Crucifixion and the Resurrection. Good Friday and Easter-day filled them with sorrow and with joy. For such is the true Christian aspect of life. We are not to choose the Cross exclusively. The death and the life of Christ are to be manifested in our mortal body. We are to let things *come* as God pleases, making both joy and sorrow divine, by infusing into them the Cross and the Resurrection. We are to show Christ forth in our lives till He comes. He is the Sun: and Christian life is as the turning of the sunflower to the Sun. This was the explanation of the mystery of St. Paul's own existence in the death and resurrection of his Lord: he was living Christ over again. Christ was Human Nature personified. In His Death, St. Paul saw the frail Humanity subject to decay; in His Resurrection, the Apostle saw human life elevated into Divine existence. He "was crucified through weakness, yet He liveth by the power of God." And so St. Paul felt that every true human soul must repeat Christ's existence. He could bear to look on his own decay; it was but the passing of the human; and, meantime, there was ever going on within him the strengthening of the Divine. Thus his own contracted, isolated existence was gone: it had been absorbed into communion with a Higher life: it had been dignified by its union with the Life of lives. Just as the tidal pulsations in the estuary, a few inches only more or less, are dignified by referring them to the ocean life with which they are connected, since they repeat what the sea performed a few hours before: so St. Paul felt himself, in connection with the great sea of Humanity and with God. Pain was sacred, since Christ had also suffered. Life became grand, when viewed as a repetition of the Life of Christ. The Apostle lived, "always bearing about in the body the dying of the Lord Jesus, that the life also of Jesus might be made manifest in" his "mortal flesh."

LECTURE XLI.

1852.

2 CORINTHIANS, iv. 16 – 18. — "For which cause we faint not; but though our outward man perish, yet the inward man is renewed day by day. — For our light affliction, which is but for a moment, worketh for us a far more exceeding and eternal weight of glory; — While we look not at the things which are seen, but at the things which are not seen: for the things which are seen are temporal; but the things which are not seen are eternal."

2 CORINTHIANS, v. 1 – 3. — For we know that if our earthly house of this tabernacle were dissolved, we have a building of God, an house not made with hands, eternal in the heavens. — For in this we groan, earnestly desiring to be clothed upon with our house which is from heaven: — If so be that being clothed we shall not be found naked."

IN our last lecture we viewed the Christian ministry as one of Light, and as a reflection of the Life of Christ in word and in experience. To-day we consider —

I. The trials of the Christian ministry.
II. The consolations of the Christian ministry.

I. Its trials: — This is ground which has been gone over before. We will glance at one or two instances of the trials of modern missionaries: I recollect Weitbrecht, who recently died at Calcutta; — and well do I remember the description he gave of the difficulties encountered by the Gospel missionaries in the East. What a picture he drew of the almost unconquerable depression which was produced by the mere thought of going back to India: to struggle with the darkening effects of universal idolatry — with the secret sense of incredulity in Christian Truth, giving rise to the ever-recurring doubt — "Can the Gospel light be only for us few, while countless myriads of the human race still walk in the 'shadow of death?'" Observe, too, the peculiar class of trials to be encountered in hot climates, which intensify the passions of our human nature, and render a resistance to opportunities offered for their gratification a difficult task indeed. For the martyr spirit is not shown merely in physical suffering.

Take another instance: — The dangers and escape of the missionary Krapf in East Africa. What obstacles did he not encounter in his endeavors to effect a chain of missions from West to East of that dreary continent! now attacked by robbers in the mountains of Bura; — and then many days without food, is forced at last to drink water from a musket-barrel, and to eat gunpowder!

Remember, too, the graves of the Christian missionaries piled so soon and so rapidly on the pestilential plain of Sierra Leone: — remember Gardiner at Terra del Fuego; — Clapperton dying amid the sands of Africa — the Landers — Mungo Park; — and you will find that the missionaries and pioneers of Christianity still encounter the same trials, the same dangers, from famine, pestilence, and the sword, of which St. Paul so eloquently speaks in his Epistles.

II. Christian consolations.

1. The comprehension of the law of the Cross.

Spiritual life is ours through temporary death: for "though our outward man perish, yet our inward man is renewed day by day." Strength is ours through suffering; for "our light affliction . . . . worketh for us a far more exceeding and eternal weight of glory." Thus, the law of our Humanity is life out of decay; the type and exemplification of which is the Cross of Christ. And this is the true soother of affliction — this one steadfast thought — the glory which is being worked out thereby. For pain and death change their character according to the spirit in which they are viewed, just as the amputation of a limb is quite as painful as the shattering of it by an accident; yet in the one case the sufferer shrieks, in the other bears it heroically: because his will goes with the operation, because he feels it is right, and knows *why* it is done. Mark, however, one distinction: It is not merely the perception of the law which makes trial tolerable, but a law personified in One whom we love. The law is, "Our light affliction, which is but for a moment, worketh for us glory." Stoicism taught that: but Christianity teaches it in the *Person* of Christ. The Cross is an abstraction until clothed in flesh and blood. Go and talk like a philosopher to one in suffering: you get an acknowledgment of your effort, but you have not soothed the sufferer. But go and tell him of the law *in Christ;* tell him that *He* has borne the Cross; and there is the peculiar Christian feeling of comfort, with all its tenderness, humanity, and *personality*. The law of the Cross is the truth, the rock truth, but only in a Person. And hence comes the hymned feeling — how much more living than a philosophy! —

> "Rock of Ages, cleft for me,
> Let me hide myself in *Thee*."

So it is that in the mere word *Cross*, there is that sentiment which no other word in the English language can supply. Law of self-sacrifice? No: that is cold, not dear to us, personal, living, like the Cross.

Oh! we live — not under laws, nor philosophical abstractions, but under a Spirit: and the true expression of Christianity is "*Christ* in you, the hope of glory." Let us exemplify this from the experience of missionaries. How beautiful and touching is the remarkable gratitude of Gardiner for a few drops of water trickling down a parched boat's side! Listen, too, to what Krapf says: — "In the sanctuary of reason I find nothing but discouragement and contradiction; but in the sanctuary of God a voice comes to me and tells me — 'Fear not; death leads to life, destruction to resurrection, the demolition of all human undertakings to the erection of the kingdom of Christ.'" Observe how this is the very principle expounded last Sunday. The death and resurrection — the law of Christian life — was his strength, as of old it was St. Paul's.

2. The contemplation of things not seen.

Two characteristics are mentioned as belonging to these things. They are, "not seen," and "eternal." Now what are these things? Not merely things unseen because they are hidden by distance, so that we shall see them hereafter, and only not now; but they are things which are not seen, because they *never* can be seen. They are not things which are superior to those which are seen; because though of the same nature, the latter perish, while the former last for ever. They are not houses which do not decay, nor clothes which do not wear out; but they are things which are eternal, because they are not material. This is the essence of the distinction and contrast. The Right, the True, the Just — these are not seen, and never will be: they are eternal, but they exist now as they will be for ever. The Kingdom of God is not fixed in one place, nor known to the eye of sense; it cannot come "by observation:" neither can ye say, "Lo! here," or "Lo! there," for there is no *locality* now, nor will there be for ever, for the things which are Eternal, Immortal, Invisible. These are the things of which St. Paul says: "Finally, brethren, whatsoever things are true, whatsoever things are honest, whatsoever things are just, whatsoever things are pure, whatsoever things are lovely, whatsoever things are of good report; if there be any virtue, and if there be any praise, think on these things." It is the outward and material things that perish: it is the inward that are renewed. Pain is for time: guilt is for ever. Physical punishment is for time; but horror can never die! Distinguish well what the heavenly is: because it is not the mere element of Time that makes things base or noble. A thrill of nerve, even if it were to last for ever, would not be heavenly. A home of physical comfort, even if it were to endure like the Pyramids, would be no sublimer than one of straw and rafters. But the everlasting Heaven of God's saints is around us now. The invisible world contemplated by the martyrs is what it was, and ever will be — visible only to faith.

3. The thought of a life beyond the grave.

Take this in connection with the sixteenth verse of the fourth chapter, with this thought in our hearts: "For which cause we faint not; though our outward man perish, yet the inward man is renewed day by day." Some men there are to whom this hope is impossible. There are some who live a merely human life: and life merely as such, since it does not necessarily imply immortality, produces no inward certainty of an existence beyond the grave. There are those who lead the life of the ephemeron, in whom there is nothing immortal, spending their days like the beasts that perish — nay, less fitted for eternity than they. No deep thoughts, no acts fought out on deep abiding principles, have been theirs. They live mere accidental beings, light mortals, who dance their giddy round above the abysses, looking at the things seen, with transient tears for sorrow, and transient smiles for joy. This life is their All; and at last they have fluttered out their time, and go forth into endless night. Why not? what is there in them that is not even now perishing. But St. Paul, beset by persecution, the martyr of the Cross, daily flying for his life, in perils by land and sea, drew immortal comforts out of all his trials. Every sorrow gave him a keener sight of the things invisible. Every peril, every decay of the outward, strengthened in him that inward man "risen with Christ," which is the earnest of our immortal life. With this hope he was comforted, and with this eternal existence growing within him, he was buoyed up above the thought of weakness or of dismay. A time would come when all should be changed: this earthly house should be dissolved; but he fainted not: for he says, "We know that . . . . we have a building of God, an house not made with hands, eternal in the heavens." The hope of immortal life was his, and with that he was consoled.

That hope was not a selfish one. There are some who say that to live a high life here, in the hope of immortality hereafter, is an unworthy object; that it is more noble to do good, and to act well, and be content to perish. Strange perversion! Is the desire of food, for the *sake* of food, selfish? Is the desire of knowledge, for the *sake* of knowledge, selfish? No! they are appetites each with its appointed end: one a necessary appetite of the body, the other a noble appetite of the mind. Then, is the desire of immortal life, for the sake of "more life and fuller," selfish? No! rather it is the noblest, purest, truest appetite of the soul. It is not happiness nor reward we seek; but we seek for the perfection of the imperfect—for the deep, abounding life of those who shall see God as He is, and shall feel the strong pulsations of that existence which is Love, Purity, Truth, Goodness: to whom shall be revealed all the invisible things of the Spirit in perfection!

LECTURE XLII.

1852.

2 CORINTHIANS, v. 4-11. — "For we that are in this tabernacle do groan, being burdened: not for that we would be unclothed, but clothed upon, that mortality might be swallowed up of life. — Now he that hath wrought us for the selfsame thing is God, who also hath given unto us the earnest of the Spirit. — Therefore we are always confident, knowing that, whilst we are at home in the body, we are absent from the Lord: — (For we walk by faith, not by sight:) — We are confident, I say, and willing rather to be absent from the body, and to be present with the Lord. — Wherefore we labor, that, whether present or absent, we may be accepted of him. — For we must all appear before the judgment seat of Christ; that every one may receive the things done in his body, according to that he hath done, whether it be good or bad. — Knowing therefore the terror of the Lord, we persuade men; but we are made manifest unto God; and I trust also are made manifest in your consciences."

IN the preceding verses St. Paul has spoken of two great consolations in ministerial trial — the thought of things invisible, and the expectation of a blessed resurrection. In considering them, I tried to explain what things invisible are; and I said they were not things unseen because separated by distance, or by reason of the imperfection of our faculties, or of any interposed veil; but they were unseen, because in their nature they were incapable of being seen — such as Honor, Truth, and Love. I tried to show how the expectation of immortality is not a selfish hope, because it is not the desire of enjoyments such as we have here, but the desire of a higher inward life — "an house not made with hands, eternal in the heavens."

But here evidently a mistake might arise. Speaking thus of a spiritual heaven, it is quite possible that men might conceive of it as a disembodied state, and suppose the Apostle to represent life in a visible form as degradation. There were such persons in the old time, who thought they could not cultivate their spirit-nature without lowering that of their body. They fasted and wore sackcloth, they lay in ashes, and eschewed cleanliness as too great a luxury. Nay, they even refused to hear of a resurrection, which would restore the body to the spirit: redemption being, according to them, release from the prison of the flesh.

In opposition to such views the Apostle here says, correctively: "Not for that we would be unclothed, but clothed upon, that mortality might be swallowed up of life." That is, it is not that we are to get rid ot something, but to gain something. Not the lowering of the body, but the strengthening of the spirit — that is spirituality. For there are two extremes into which men are apt to run: they either serve the body as a master, or crush it as an enemy. Whereas St. Paul taught that the true way of mortifying the flesh is to strengthen the spirit. The mortal will disappear in the elevation of the immortal.

Here, then, we have — first: A test of spirituality. Let us observe the description given: "We that are in this tabernacle do groan, being burdened." If we stop here, myriads deserve the name of spiritual men: for who has not groaned, being burdened, in this tabernacle? Disappointment may sicken a man of living, or the power of enjoyment may fail, or satiety may arrive to the jaded senses and feelings: or, in pain and poverty a man may long for the grave; or old age may come, when "the grasshopper is a burden." For example, Job uttered maledictions on the day when he was born: "Wherefore is light given to him that is in misery, and life unto the bitter in soul; which long for death, but it cometh not; and dig for it more than for hid treasures; which rejoice exceedingly, and are glad, when they can find the grave? If, then, the mere desire to be unclothed were spirituality, that passionate imprecation of Job's was spiritual. But St. Paul's feeling was: "Not for that we would be unclothed, but clothed upon, that mortality might be swallowed up of life." With him a desire to depart and to be with

Christ implied a yearning for a higher spiritual life, and a deeper longing for more resemblance to the mind of Christ.

Secondly: The principle of Christian assurance.

First of all, there is such a thing as Christian assurance: "Therefore we are always confident:" and again, "I know whom I have believed:" and again, "We know that if our earthly house of this tabernacle were dissolved, we have a building of God, an house not made with hands, eternal in the heavens." Such was St. Paul's assurance. We may not feel it; but, my brethren, we must not lower the standard of Christian attainment to suit our narrow lives. To many of us Heaven is an awful peradventure. It is so to most men who are living in comfort, and are not suffering for Christ. But to St. Paul, ever on the brink of that world to come, his own immortality of blessedness was no peradventure. It was not a matter of doubt with him whether he was Christ's or not. Let us, then, see the grounds of this assurance.

1st. God's purpose: "He that hath wrought us for the selfsame thing is God."

2d. God's Spirit in the soul — "an earnest."

1. God's purpose. — St. Paul would not believe that God was merely weighing His frail creatures in the balance. No: they were purposed by Him for heaven; God meant their blessedness: "For God hath not appointed us to wrath, but to obtain salvation." He had redeemed them by the blood of an everlasting covenant: "If when we were enemies, we were reconciled to God by the death of His Son, much more, being reconciled, we shall be saved by His life." Our salvation does not hang on our own desires: it is in the hands of One who loves us better than we love ourselves.

2. God's Spirit in the soul — "an earnest."

Here, in another form, is the repetition of St. Paul's view, that the literal resurrection is naturally, in the order of grace, but a development of the spiritual resurrection. To repeat the simile I have previously used:

As the vital force appears in things so different as leaf, flower, and fruit, so the Divine life manifests itself first in the spiritual, and then in the literal resurrection. And just as when the flower appears, you infer the future fruit, excluding the possibility of a blight, so when spiritual goodness appears, you infer future glory. This is Christian assurance. Therefore, if God's Spirit be in you, be confident, yet humble: rejoice with trembling, but still with unshaken trust in coming blessedness.

Hence Christian life becomes now a life of faith: "We walk by faith, not by sight." There is a life called in Scripture "a life hid with Christ in God." Now it is very easy to speak glibly and fluently of that life as a common thing. I cannot bring my lips to use such language. It is a rare and wondrous life; and so, in speaking of it, I prefer to contemplate the life of St. Paul, instead of assuming the existence of ordinary men to be such as is here described. A life like his — was it not indeed hidden with his Master in the heavens? He was ever on the brink of the grave. To him the world was crucified. He had unlearned the love of this life by an intense desire of another. The Cross of Christ was all that to him seemed beautiful; so that this present existence became a kind of banishment (v. 6) — a place of sojourn, and not a home. He moved on, free from incumbrances, ever "ready to depart and to be with Christ."

The thought of such a life has in it something very awful and sublime. It is almost fearful to think of a human being really living as St. Paul did, breathing the atmosphere of heaven while yet on earth. But I remark it now for this purpose: to remind you that the words of St. Paul cannot be, except with shocking unreality, adopted by persons who are living less spiritually than he did. There is a common, but I think most dangerous habit of using Scripture language familiarly, calling one-self "the chief of sinners," talking of "spiritual joys and experiences," and of "communion with God:" of "living by faith," and of this "pilgrim life." On *many* lips these are weak and false expressions. It is like using Goliath's armor, and thinking that thereby we get a giant's strength: while so long as we are not strong, such armor would only weaken us. And so, the fact of our using Scripture does not make us more spiritual: nay, it makes us less so, if it hides from us our weakness — if, while using the language of a spiritual giant, we forget that we are dwarfs. No, my brethren: a life of faith is a grand, solitary, awful thing. *Who* amongst us is living it?

Hence, too, Christian life is a toil (v. 9): — "We labor." In the original it is a strong word — "are zealous, put forth all our efforts." For St. Paul worked, knowing the night was coming. He strove — "ever as in his great Task-master's eye." And the motives for this toil were two: —

1. To please God.
2. To be prepared for judgment.

1. To no man did life present itself so strongly in the light of a scene for work as it did to St. Paul. That spirit which characterized his Master was remarkable in him. What was the Spirit of Christ? "I must work the works of him that sent me, while it is day:" "I have a baptism to be baptized with; and how am I straitened till it be accomplished!" "My meat is to do the will of my Father which sent me, and to finish His work." And this He did completely; at the close he says, "I have finished the work which Thou gavest me to do." This spirit was also in St. Paul. But now observe, this work was with him not a dire necessity, but a blessed privilege; for he says: "And I will very gladly spend and be spent." It was not the service of the slave: it was the joyous service of the freeman: "We are confident: *wherefore* we labor, that, whether present or absent, we may be accepted of him." He was not working to win life, but because he had life; he was laboring in love to *please* God.

2. The second motive was the feeling of accountability (v. 10): "We must all appear before the judgment seat of Christ." Now this feeling of accountability

may assume either of two forms. In a free and gen erous spirit, it may be simply a sense of duty; in a slavish and cowardly spirit, it will be a sense of compulsion; and the moment the sense of duty ends, the sense of compulsion begins. So St. Paul says: "If I do this thing willingly, I have a reward: but if against my will, a dispensation of the Gospel is committed to me." That is, "If I cheerfully do it, the doing is itself reward; but if not, then it lies on me like an obligation." This is the difference between the two feelings: *I ought*, or *I must;* the Gospel, or the Law. These feelings are repeated in every man; for the Gospel and the Law are not two periods of history only, but they are two periods in universal human experience. Where the spirit of the Gospel is not, there the spirit of the Law is. Hence the Apostle says: "Knowing, therefore, the *terror* of the Lord, we persuade men."

Consider, then, the terrors of the Judgment. Remember, St. Paul does not say merely that he shall receive according to what he hath done in the body, but that he shall receive the things done — the very self-same things he did — they are to be his punishment. To illustrate the Apostle's meaning by analogy, future retribution is the same as here on earth. God's pun ishments are not arbitrary, but natural. For example, a man commits a murder. It would be an arbitrary punishment if lightning struck him, or an earthquake swallowed him up. The inhabitants of Melita, seeing the viper fasten on Paul's hand, inferred that he was a murderer. But God's punishment for hatred and murder is hardening of the heart. He that shuts Love out, shuts out God. So again, if a man seduces another weaker than himself into crime, the earth will not open as it did for Dathan and Abiram. But God has hidden in the man's own heart the avenging law: he becomes a degraded man: the serpent-tempter's curse is his — "to go on his belly, and eat dust all the days of his life." Or again, some one is plunged in passionateness, sloth, sensual life. God will not create a material flame to burn the man; the flame is spiritual, is inward — a reptile to creep and crawl, and leave its venom on his heart. He receives the things done in the body. Now, such as that is the law of future retribution: "Whatsoever a man soweth" — not something else, but "*that* shall he also reap:" "He which is filthy, let him be filthy still." Such are some of the Scripture metaphors to show the personality of future punishment.

"Knowing, therefore, the terror of the Lord," says St. Paul, "we persuade men." Striking words! Not "we terrify," not "we threaten," but "we persuade." Here was the difference between rhetorical thunders and the teaching of one who *knew* and believed the terrors of which he spoke. Oh! contrast with this the tone in which God's ministers too often threaten sinners. They paint the torments of the lost minutely and hideously, and can yet go home to the evening meal with zest unimpaired. Think you, if such a man *believed* what he said — that the mass of his brethren were going to hell — he could sleep after his own denunciation. No! when a man *knows* the terrors of the Lord, he "persuades men." Hence came the tears of Jeremiah; hence flowed the tears of Him who knew the doom of Jerusalem. Therefore, if in our tone there be anything objurgatory, denunciatory, threatening, may God give us the spirit to *persuade!* May He teach us to believe the terrors of which we speak!

Brethren, there is no *perhaps*. These are things which will be hereafter. You cannot alter the Eternal Laws. You cannot put your hand in the flame, and not be burnt. You cannot sin in the body, and escape the sin; for it goes inwards, becomes part of you, and is itself the penalty which cleaves for ever and ever to your spirit. Sow in the flesh, and you will reap corruption. Yield to passion, and it becomes your tyrant and your torment. Be sensual, self-indulgent, inindolent, worldly, hard — oh! they all have their corresponding penalties: "Whatsoever a man soweth, *that* shall he also reap."

LECTURE XLIII.

DECEMBER 5, 1852.

2 CORINTHIANS v. 12–17.—"For we commend not ourselves again unto you, but give you occasion to glory on our behalf, that ye may have somewhat to answer them which glory in appearance, and not in heart.—For whether we be beside ourselves, it is to God: or whether we be sober, it is for your cause.—For the love of Christ constraineth us; because we thus judge, that if one died for all, then were all dead:—And that he died for all, that they which live should not henceforth live unto themselves, but unto him which died for them, and rose again.—Wherefore henceforth know we no man after the flesh: yea, though we have known Christ after the flesh, yet now henceforth know we him no more.—Therefore if any man be in Christ, he is a new creature: old things are passed away; behold, all things are become new."

IN the preceding chapters and verses, St. Paul has been magnifying his ministry. It had been, he says, a ministry of the Spirit, not of the letter (iii. 6). It had been straightforward and veracious: its authority had been that of the truth;—"commending ourselves to every man's conscience in the sight of God" (iv. 2). It had been a suffering and a martyr ministry (iv. 8, 9, 10); representative, too, of Christ in word and deed (iv. 5 and 10); unworldly (v. 2, 8, 9); and persuasive (v. 11).

In all this the Apostle glorifies his own ministry and his way of performing it. It is a glorious description, truly. But when a man speaks thus of himself, we are apt to call it boasting. So, no doubt, many of the Corinthians would call it; and hence St. Paul several times anticipates such a charge, for instance, in the first verse of the third chapter, and also in the twelfth verse of the fifth. For some of the Corinthian Church might have reasoned in this manner: "You say you commend yourself to our consciences, and that we recognize the truth of what you say from an inward plainness.

Now if all this is so plain, why commend yourself? — why so anxious to set yourself right?" But the reply is: "I do not commend myself for my own sake. It is not a personal boast. It is the only possible reply to those who require a ministry with splendid external credentials, instead of the inward witness of the heart" — (v. 12).

I. The Apostle's defence of his self-approval.

II. The general principles of life with which this self-approval was connected.

I. The Apostle's defence was founded on two reasons. First: We "give you occasion to glory on our behalf, that ye may have somewhat to answer them which glory in appearance, and not in heart." Secondly: "Whether we be beside ourselves, it is to God: or whether we be sober, it is for your cause."

1. The false teachers gloried "in appearance," in outward demonstration, in dazzling credentials, such as eloquence; or they boasted of belonging to St. Peter, or prided themselves in a superabundance of spiritual gifts. On the contrary, St. Paul says that the true Apostolic credentials are those of the heart; and accordingly, the proofs he had given were — his truth, his sufferings, his persuasiveness, his simplicity, his boldness, and his life as being an image of Christ's. This corresponds with what I have before said, namely, that the Christian ministry is a succession of the prophetical, not the priestly office. There were two sorts of teachers, priests and prophets. The priest said: "Here are my credentials. I am ordained God's messenger: therefore, what I say is to be received." The prophet said: "What I say is truth; therefore, I am to be received as from God." The priest proved, first, that he was a messenger, and thence inferred his inspiration; but the prophet declared his message, and from it inferred that he was truly sent. This is clear, from the nature of the thing. Every one knew who was the priest. But the prophet rose from amongst the people, proclaiming himself to be from God.

"Where is your proof?" was the cry of all: and the answer came — "Here, in what I say." Consequently, the priest was always heard; the prophet's words were rarely believed till he was slain: and this because men glory in appearances, not in heart. Now St. Paul's credentials were those of the heart; — "by manifestation of the truth commending ourselves to every man's conscience." It was not, "First, we prove ourselves, and then our mission;" but, "First, we declare our message, and from it we deduce our apostleship." This is the Christian ministry.

2. "Whether we be beside ourselves, it is to God." Now "Whether we be beside ourselves" means, "Whether we boast of ourselves." The vehemence of self-defence might be called so in temporary excitement. The Apostle's defence might seem like that of one deranged: as once before it appeared to the heathen Procurator: "Paul, thou art beside thyself." "Well," said St. Paul, "we adopt the words 'beside ourselves.' Be it so! it is for God's cause. We boast of our qualifications for the sake of God, to whom they all belong." Or, again, "Whether we be sober" — that is, restrain ourselves — our moderation is an example of humility to you.

There are, then, cases in which it is wise for a Christian to vindicate himself against false charges; there are others, in which it is wiser to restrain himself, and to remain silent. The Apostle's defence, vehement even so far as to provoke the charge of "being beside himself," teaches us that it is sometimes false humility, and false moderation, to lie under an undenied slur on our character or our words. To give another example: Samuel vindicated himself: "Whose ox have I taken? or whose ass have I taken? or whom have I defrauded? whom have I oppressed? or of whose hand have I received any bribe to blind mine eyes therewith? and I will restore it to you." For there are charges which must be met by legal purgation, or by avowal, or by denial; and then we must not hide nor deny the gifts with which God has endued us. In such a case, to do so, is not a vain declaration of our excellence, but a graceful acknowledgment of God's mercy: as, for example, Milton's noble boast.

On the other hand, some charges are of a nature so delicate, complicated, and shadowy, that public defence leaves the matter worse than before. It is better, then, to let time and character defend you. For there are cases in which dignified silence is the Christian's only defence. So it was in our Saviour's life. Men misinterpreted his words, and blackened his reputation. How was He to answer? Was He to go into the petty charges one by one? or was He to leave time and God to defend His cause? He was "sober for" our "cause."

II. The general principles of Life with which the Apostle's self-approval was connected.

It is the peculiarity of St. Paul's mind that he never can speak of an act as an isolated thing. You always find it referred at once to some great law, or running up into some great principle. If he sees a detached law, commanding that the ox shall not be stinted of his provender, he grasps at once the principle that "the laborer is worthy of his hire." If he forbids lying, it is because "we are members one of another." Here, too, observe how high and divine motives enter into the smallest act. Even the Apostle's self-defence was in the genuine spirit of Christianity: "The love of Christ constraineth us." All was subordinate to that. Whether we are vehement, or whether we are silent, it is because His love constrains us. Remark, then, one thing in passing: it is St. Paul's Christianity: a pervading spirit, growing into a habit, and governing his very words!

Three subjects, then, we have for consideration:—

1. The main principle of Christian Life — Love.
2. The Law of redeemed Humanity.
3. The new aspect of Humanity in Christ.

1. Love, the main principle of Christian life. Herein consists Christian liberty: a Christian is freed from the

Law, and yet he does what the Law requires, and more because his obedience is not that of "the letter, but the spirit;" as St. Paul says, the Christian is *constrained* by love to act. And why? Because God has taught him that it is beautiful and right to do so, and because God has made the Love of Christ paramount in his heart to all other love. Let us make, therefore, a distinction. When we say that a Christian is free from the Law, we do not mean that he may break it, or not, as he likes. We mean that he is bound to do right by a nobler tie than "*you must.*"

Consider the Law as expressed in the first, fifth, sixth, seventh, and eighth commandments, and then examine the relations in which a Christian is placed with regard to these commandments. Hence the Apostle says: "To them that are without law" I became "as without law"—but he explains—"being not without law to God, but under the law to Christ." And again: "Being then made free from sin, ye became the servants of righteousness."

Christian liberty, then, is a loving servitude to God. Just as if a slave were made free, and then felt himself bound in gratitude to toil with tenfold vigor for a master whom he loved instead of fearing; or just as the mother is the slave to her sick child, and would do almost impossibilities, not because it is her duty, but because she loves her child;—so the whole moral law is abrogated to us as a Law, because obedience to it is ensured in the spirit.

2. The Law of redeemed Humanity: "Because we thus judge, that if one died for all, then were all dead."

"All are dead:" that I call the law of redeemed Humanity. Let us explain this expression. It is sometimes interpreted: "If one died for all, then all must have been spiritually dead." But this is not St. Paul's meaning. Those who have intelligently followed his argument thus far, will see at once that it is beside his reasoning. There are two kinds of death—one *in* sin, before Redemption; the other *to* sin, which *is* Redemption. Here it is of the death *to* sin, and not the death *in* sin, that St. Paul speaks. This is his argument: — If One died as the representative of all, then in that death all died; not that they were dead before, but dead *then*. You will recollect that this is the great thought throughout this Epistle. Every Christian is dead in Christ's death, and risen in Christ's resurrection: "In that He died, He died unto sin once: but in that He liveth, He liveth unto God. Likewise reckon ye also yourselves to be dead indeed unto sin, but alive unto God through Jesus Christ our Lord." Again, "I am crucified with Christ: nevertheless I live; yet not I, but Christ liveth in me." So here there is exactly the same train of thought: "He died for all, that they which live should not henceforth live unto themselves, but unto Him which died for them, and rose again." — (ver. 15.) This is Christ's Redemption: He died to sin *for* all, as the Representative of all. In his death we all have died. He rose again, and Life is now owed to Him. In Christ alone, then, is the true law of our Humanity intelligible.

3. The new aspect of Humanity in Christ: "a new creature," or creation.

Humanity as a whole, and individually, is spiritualized; it is viewed in Christ as a thing dead and alive again — dead to evil, but risen to righteousness. For even such is Christ, the Son of Man (v. 16): "Yea, though we have known Christ after the flesh, yet now henceforth know we Him no more." Even Christ we know now as the Son of God, rather than as the Son of Man. So by us Christ is to be known spiritually, and not with worldly ideas, such as the Apostles had of Him when He lived. He is to be recognized no more as weak, rejected, despised, battling with evil, but as the Conqueror of Evil: for the Resurrection has shown what he was: He was "declared to be the Son of God, with power, according to the spirit of holiness, by the resurrection from the dead." Remember, however, the historical order: Christ was revealed first as Man, *then* as God; so, now, it is best to begin with the simplest aspect of Him. Teach children the simple beauty of Christ's manhood, only we must not rest there: "Now, therefore, it is not Christ who was, but Christ who is; it is Christ who died, yea, rather who is risen again: who also liveth to make intercession for us." It is the same in each individual Christian. A Christian is human nature revolutionized (v. 17). Almost the deepest thing in the Jewish mind was that exclusiveness, which made the Jew at last believe that holiness consisted in national separation. In the Jew, then, Christianity caused the abjuration of prejudice. The Gentile it freed from atheism and idolatry. In both the Jew and Gentile it changed the life of flesh and self into a spiritual and self-sacrificing existence.

My brethren, there must be a crisis in your being. It may be gradual in its progress, like John the Baptist's, or sudden, like St. Paul's; but except it take place, "except a man be born again, he cannot see the Kingdom of God."

LECTURE XLIV.

June 23, 1850.

2 Corinthians, v. 14, 15.—"For the love of Christ constraineth us; because we thus judge, that if one died for all, then were all dead: and that he died for all, that they which live should not henceforth live unto themselves, but unto him which died for them, and rose again."

It may be that in reading these verses, some of us have understood them in a sense foreign to that of the Apostle. It may have seemed that the arguments ran thus:—Because Christ died upon the cross for *all*, therefore all must have been in a state of spiritual death before; and if they were asked what doctrines are to be elicited from this passage, they would reply, "the doctrine of universal depravity, and the constraining power of the gratitude due to Him who died to redeem us from it." There is, however, in the first place, this fatal objection to such an interpretation, that the death here spoken of is used in two diametrically opposite senses. In reference to Christ, death literal; in reference to all, death spiritual. Now, in the thought of St. Paul, the death of Christ was always viewed as liberation from the power of evil: "in that he died, he died unto sin once;" and again, "he that is dead is freed from sin." The literal death, then, in one clause, means *freedom* from sin; the spiritual death of the next is *slavery* to it. Wherein, then, lies the cogency of the Apostle's reasoning? How does it follow, that because Christ died to evil, all before that must have died to God? Of course that doctrine is true in itself, but it is *not* the doctrine of the text.

In the next place, the ambiguity belongs only to the English word—it is impossible to make the mistake in the original: the word which stands for *were*, is a word which does not imply a continued state, but must imply a single finished act. It cannot by any possibility imply that before the death of Christ men *were* in a state of death — it can only mean, they became dead at the moment when Christ died. If you read it thus, the meaning of the English will emerge — if one died for all, then all died; and the Apostle's argument runs thus, that if one act as the representative of all, then his act is the act of all. If the ambassador of a nation makes reparation in a nation's name, or does homage for a nation, that reparation, or that homage, is the nation's act — if *one* did it *for* all, then *all* did it. So that instead of inferring that because Christ died for all, therefore before that all were dead to God, his natural inference is that, therefore, all are now dead to sin. Once more, the conclusion of the Apostle is exactly the reverse of that which this interpretation attributes to him: he does not say that Christ died in order that men might *not* die, but exactly for this very purpose, that they *might;* and this death he represents in the next verse by an equivalent expression — the life of unselfishness: "that they which live might henceforth live not unto themselves." The "dead" of the first verse, are "they that live" of the second.

The form of thought finds its exact parallel in *Romans*, vi. 10, 11. Two points claim our attention: —

I. The vicarious sacrifice of Christ.
II. The influence of that sacrifice on man.

I. The vicariousness of the sacrifice is implied in the word "for." A vicarious act is an act done for another. When the Pope calls himself the vicar of Christ, he implies that he acts for Christ. The vicar or viceroy of a kingdom, is one who acts for the king — a vicar's act, therefore, is virtually the act of the principal whom he represents; so that if the papal doctrine were true, when the vicar of Christ *pardons*, Christ has pardoned. When the viceroy of a kingdom has published a proclamation, or signed a treaty, the sovereign himself is bound by those acts.

The truth of the expression *for all* is contained in this fact, that Christ is the representative of humanity — properly speaking, the reality of human nature. This is the truth contained in the emphatic expression, "Son of Man." What Christ did *for* humanity was done by humanity, because in the name of humanity. For a truly vicarious act does not supersede the principal's duty of performance, but rather implies and acknowledges it. Take the case from which this very word of vicar has received its origin. In the old monastic times, when the revenues of a cathedral or a cure fell to the lot of a monastery, it became the duty of that monastery to perform the religious services of the cure. But inasmuch as the monastery was a corporate body, they appointed one of their number, whom they denominated their vicar, to discharge those offices for them. His service did not supersede theirs, but was a perpetual and standing acknowledgment that they, as a whole and individually, were under the obligation to perform it. The act of Christ is the act of humanity — that which all humanity is bound to do. His righteousness does not supersede our righteousness, nor does His sacrifice supersede our sacrifice. It is the representation of human life and human sacrifice — vicarious for all, yet binding upon all.

That Christ died for all is true —

1. Because He was the victim of the sin of all. In the peculiar phraseology of St. Paul, he died unto sin. He was the victim of sin — He died by sin. It is the appalling mystery of our redemption that the Redeemer took the attitude of subjection to evil. There was scarcely a form of evil with which Christ did not come in contact, and by which he did not suffer. He was the victim of false friendship and ingratitude, the victim of bad government and injustice. He fell a sacrifice to the vices of all classes — to the selfishness of the rich, and the fickleness of the poor: intolerance, formalism, scepticism, hatred of goodness, were the foes which crushed Him.

In the proper sense of the word, He was a victim.

He did not adroitly wind through the dangerous forms of evil, meeting it with expedient silence. Face to face, and front to front, He met it, rebuked it, and defied it; and just as truly as he is a voluntary victim whose body opposing the progress of the car of Juggernaut is crushed beneath its monstrous wheels, was Christ a victim to the world's sin: because pure, He was crushed by impurity: because just, and real, and true, He waked up the rage of injustice, hypocrisy, and falsehood.

Now this was the sin of all. Here arises at once a difficulty: it seems to be most unnatural to assert that in any one sense He was the sacrifice of the sin of all. We did not betray Him — that was Judas's act — Peter denied Him — Thomas doubted — Pilate pronounced sentence — it must be a figment to say that these were our acts; we did not watch Him like the Pharisees, nor circumvent Him like the Scribes and lawyers; by what possible sophistry can we be involved in the complicity of that guilt? The savage of New Zealand who never heard of Him, the learned Egyptian and the voluptuous Assyrian who died before He came; how was it the sin of all?

The reply that is often given to this query is wonderfully unreal. It is assumed that Christ was conscious, by His Omniscience, of the sins of all mankind; that the duplicity of the child, and the crime of the assassin, and every unholy thought that has ever passed through a human bosom, were present to His mind in that awful hour as if they were His own. This is utterly unscriptural. Where is the single text from which it can be, except by force, extracted? Besides this, it is fanciful and sentimental; and again, it is dangerous, for it represents the whole atonement as a fictitious and shadowy transaction. There is a mental state in which men have felt the burden of sins which they did not commit. There have been cases in which men have been mysteriously excruciated with the thought of having committed the unpardonable sin. But to represent the mental phenomena of the Redeemer's mind as in any way resembling this — to say that His conscience was oppressed with the responsibility of sins which He had not committed — is to confound a state of sanity with the delusions of a half lucid mind, and the workings of a healthy conscience with those of one unnatural and morbid.

There is a way, however, much more appalling and much more real, in which this may be true, without resorting to any such fanciful hypothesis. Sin has a great power in this world : it gives laws like those of a sovereign, which bind us all, and to which we are all submissive. There are current maxims in Church and State, in society, in trade, in law, to which we yield obedience. For this obedience every one is responsible; for instance, in trade, and in the profession of law, every one is the servant of practices the rectitude of which his heart can only half approve — every one complains of them, yet all are involved in them. Now, when such sins reach their climax, as in the case of national bankruptcy, or an unjust acquittal, there may be some who are, in a special sense, the actors in the guilt ; but evidently, for the bankruptcy, each member of the community is responsible in that degree and so far as he himself acquiesced in the duplicities of public dealing; every careless juror, every unrighteous judge, every false witness, has done his part in the reduction of society to that state in which the monster injustice has been perpetrated. In the riot of a tumultuous assembly by night, a house may be burnt, or a murder committed ; in the eye of the law, all who are aiding and abetting there, are each in his degree responsible for that crime ; there may be difference in guilt, from the degree in which he is guilty who with his own hand perpetrated the deed, to that of him who merely joined the rabble from mischievous curiosity — degrees from that of wilful murder to that of more or less excusable homicide. The Pharisees were declared by the Saviour to be guilty of the blood of Zacharias, the blood of righteous Abel, and of all the saints and prophets who fell before He came. But how were the Pharisees guilty? They built the sepulchres of the prophets, they honored and admired them: but they were guilty in that they were the children of those that slew the prophets; children in this sense, that they inherited their *spirit*, they opposed the good in the form in which it showed itself in *their day*, just as their fathers opposed the form displayed to theirs; therefore He said that they belonged to the same confederacy of evil, and that the guilt of the blood of all who had been slain should rest on that generation. Similarly we are guilty of the death of Christ. If you have been a false friend, a sceptic, a cowardly disciple, a formalist, selfish, an opposer of goodness, an oppressor, whatever evil you have done, in that degree and so far you participate in the evil to which the Just One fell a victim — you are one of that mighty rabble which cried, "Crucify Him, Crucify Him;" for your sin He died; His blood lies at your threshold.

Again, He died for all, in that His sacrifice represents the sacrifice of all. We have heard of the doctrine of "imputed righteousness;" it is a theological expression to which meanings foolish enough are sometimes attributed, but it contains a very deep truth, which it shall be our endeavor to elicit.

Christ is the realized idea of our humanity. He is God's idea of man completed. There is every difference between the ideal and the actual — between what a man aims to be and what he is; a difference between the race as it is, and the race as it existed in God's creative idea when He pronounced it very good.

In Christ, therefore, God beholds humanity; in Christ He sees perfected every one in whom Christ's spirit exists in germ. He to whom the possible is actual, to whom what will be already *is*, sees all things *present*, gazes on the imperfect, and sees it in its perfection. Let me venture an illustration. He who has never seen the vegetable world except in Arctic regions, has but a poor idea of the majesty of vegetable life, — a microscopic red moss tinting the surface of the snow, a few stunted pines, and here and there perhaps a dwindled oak; but to the botanist, who has seen the luxuriance of vegetation in its tropical magnificence, all that wretched scene presents another aspect; to him those dwarfs are the representatives of what might be, nay, what has been, in a kindlier soil and a more genial climate; he fills up by his conception the miserable actuality presented by these shrubs, and attributes to them — imputes, that is, to them — the majesty of which the undeveloped germ exists already. Now, the difference between those trees seen in themselves, and seen in the conception of their nature's perfectness which has been previously realized, is the difference between man seen in himself and seen in Christ. We are feeble, dwarfish, stunted specimens of humanity. Our best resolves are but withered branches, our holiest deeds unripe and blighted fruit; but to the Infinite Eye, who sees in the perfect One the type and assurance of that which shall be, this dwindled humanity of ours is divine and glorious. Such are we in the sight of God the Father, as is the very Son of God Himself. This is what theologians, at least the wisest of them, meant by "imputed righteousness." I do not mean that all who have written or spoken on the subject had this conception of it, but I believe they who thought truly meant this; they did not suppose that in imputing righteousness there was a kind of figment, a self-deception in the mind of God; they did not mean that by an act of will He chose to consider that every act which Christ did was done by us; that He imputed or reckoned to us the baptism in Jordan, and the victory in the wilderness, and the agony in the garden, or that He believed, or acted as if he believed, that when Christ died, each one of us died; but He saw humanity submitted to the law of self-sacrifice: in the light of that idea He beholds us as perfect, and is satisfied. In this sense the Apostle speaks of those that are imperfect, yet "by one offering He hath perfected for ever them that are sanctified." It is true, again, that He died for us, in that we present His sacrifice as ours. The value of the death of Christ consisted in the surrender of self-will. In the fortieth Psalm, the value of every other kind of sacrifice being first denied, the words follow, "then said I, Lo, I come, to do thy will, O God." The profound idea contained, therefore, in the death of Christ, is the duty of self-surrender.

But in *us* that surrender scarcely deserves the name; even to use the word self-sacrifice covers us with a kind of shame. Then it is, that there is an almost boundless joy in acquiescing in the life and death of Christ, recognizing it as ours, and representing it to ourselves and God as what we aim at. If we cannot understand how in this sense it can be a sacrifice for us, we may partly realize it by remembering the joy of feeling how art and nature realize for us what we cannot realize for ourselves. It is recorded of one of the world's gifted painters, that he stood before the masterpiece of the great genius of his age — one which he could never hope to equal, nor even rival — and yet the infinite superiority, so far from crushing him, only elevated his feeling, for he saw realized those conceptions which had floated before him, dim and unsubstantial; in every line and touch he felt a spirit immeasurably superior, yet kindred, and is reported to have exclaimed, with dignified humility, "And I, too, am a painter!"

Or, again, we must all have felt, when certain effects in nature, combinations of form and color, have been presented to us, our own idea speaking in intelligible and yet celestial language; when, for instance, the long bars of purple, "edged with intolerable radiance," seemed to float in a sea of pale, pure green, when the whole sky seemed to reel with thunder, when the night-wind moaned. It is wonderful how the most commonplace men and women, beings who, as you would have thought, had no conception that rose beyond a commercial speculation or a fashionable entertainment, are elevated by such scenes; how the slumbering grandeur of their nature wakes and acknowledges kindred with the sky and storm. "I cannot speak," they would say, "the feelings which are in me; I have had emotions, aspirations, thoughts; I cannot put them into words. Look there! listen now to the storm! That is what I meant, only I never could say it out till now." Thus do art and nature speak for us, and thus do we adopt them as our own. This is the way in which His righteousness becomes righteousness for us. This is the way in which the heart presents to God the sacrifice of Christ; gazing on that perfect Life, we, as it were, say, "There, that is my religion — that is my righteousness — what I want to be, which I am not — that is my offering, my life as I would wish to give it, freely and not checked, entire and perfect." So the old prophets, their hearts big with unutterable thoughts, searched "what or what manner of time the spirit of Christ which was in them did signify, when it testified beforehand of the sufferings of Christ, and of the glory which should follow;" and so with us, until it passes into prayer: "My Saviour, fill up the blurred and blotted sketch which my clumsy hand has drawn of a divine life, with the fulness of Thy perfect picture. I feel the beauty which I cannot realize: — robe me in Thine unutterable purity!"

II. The influence of that Sacrifice on man is the introduction of the principle of self-sacrifice into his nature, — "then were all dead." Observe again, not He died that we might not die, but that in His death we might be dead, and that in His sacrifice we might become each a sacrifice to God. Moreover, this death is identical with life. They who, in the first sentence, are called dead, are in the second denominated "they who live." So in another place, "I am crucified with Christ, nevertheless I live;" death, therefore — that is, the sacrifice of self — is equivalent to life. Now, this rests upon a profound truth. The death of Christ was a representation of the life of God. To me this is the profoundest of all truths, that the whole of the life of God is the sacrifice of self. God is love; love is sacrifice — to give rather than to receive — the blessedness of self-giving. If the life of God were not such, it would be a falsehood to say that God is Love; for, even in our human nature, that which seeks to enjoy all instead of giving all, is known by a very different name from that of love. All the life of God is a flow of this divine, self-giving charity. Creation itself is sacrifice — the self-impartation of the divine Being. Redemption, too, is sacrifice, else it could not be love; for which reason we will not surrender one iota of the truth that the death of Christ was the sacrifice of God — the manifestation once in time of that which is the eternal law of His life.

If man, therefore, is to rise into the life of God, he must be absorbed into the spirit of that sacrifice — he must die with Christ, if he would enter into his proper life. For sin is the withdrawing into self and egotism, out of the vivifying life of God, which alone is our true life. The moment the man sins, he dies. Know we not how awfully true that sentence is, "Sin revived, and I died?" The vivid life of sin is the death of the man. Have we never felt that our true existence has absolutely in that moment disappeared, and that *we* are not?

I say, therefore, that real human life is a perpetual completion and repetition of the sacrifice of Christ — "all are dead;" the explanation of which follows, "to live not to themselves, but to Him who died for them, and rose again." This is the truth which lies at the bottom of the Romish doctrine of the mass. Rome asserts that in the mass a true and proper sacrifice is offered up for the sins of all — that the offering of Christ is for ever repeated. To this Protestantism has objected vehemently, that there is but one offering once offered — an objection in itself entirely true; yet the Romish doctrine contains a truth which it is of importance to disengage from the gross and material form with which it has been overlaid. Let us hear St. Paul, "I fill up that which is behindhand of the sufferings of Christ, in my flesh, for His body's sake, which is the Church." Was there, then, something behindhand of Christ's sufferings remaining uncompleted, of which the sufferings of Paul could be in any sense the complement? He says there was. Could the sufferings of

Paul for the Church, in any form of correct expression, be said to eke out the sufferings that were complete? In one sense it is true to say, that there is one offering once offered *for* all. But it is equally true to say, that that one offering is valueless, except so far as it is completed and repeated in the life and self-offering *of* all. This is the Christian's sacrifice. Not mechanically completed in the miserable materialism of the mass, but spiritually in the life of all in whom the Crucified lives. The sacrifice of Christ is done over again in every life which is lived, not to self, but to God.

Let one concluding observation be made — self-denial, self-sacrifice, self-surrender! Hard doctrines, and impossible! Whereupon, in silent hours, we sceptically ask, Is this possible? is it natural? Let preacher and moralist say what they will, I am not here to sacrifice myself for others. God sent me here for happiness, not misery. Now introduce one sentence of this text of which we have as yet said nothing, and the dark doctrine becomes illuminated — "the *love* of Christ constraineth us." Self-denial, for the sake of self-denial, does no good; self-sacrifice for its own sake is no religious act at all. If you give up a meal for the sake of showing power over self, or for the sake of self-discipline, it is the most miserable of all delusions. You are not more religious in doing this than before. This is mere self-culture, and self-culture being occupied for ever about self, leaves you only in that circle of self from which religion is to free you; but to give up a meal that one you love may have it, is properly a religious act — no hard and dismal duty, because made easy by affection. To bear pain for the sake of bearing it, has in it no moral quality at all, but to bear it rather than surrender truth, or in order to save another, is positive enjoyment, as well as ennobling to the soul. Did you ever receive even a blow meant for another in order to shield that other? Do you not know that there was actual pleasure in the keen pain far beyond the most rapturous thrill of nerve which could be gained from pleasure in the midst of painlessness? Is not the mystic yearning of love expressed in words most purely thus, Let me suffer for him?

This element of love is that which makes this doctrine an intelligible and blessed truth. So sacrifice alone, bare and unrelieved, is ghastly, unnatural, and dead; but self-sacrifice, illuminated by love, is warmth and life; it is the death of Christ, the life of God, the blessedness, and only proper life of man.

LECTURE XLV.

DECEMBER 12, 1852.

2 CORINTHIANS, v. 18-21. — "And all things are of God, who hath reconciled us to himself by Jesus Christ, and hath given to us the ministry of reconciliation; — To wit, that God was in Christ, reconciling the world unto himself, not imputing their trespasses unto them; and hath committed unto us the word of reconciliation. — Now then we are ambassadors for Christ, as though God did beseech you by us: we pray you in Christ's stead, be ye reconciled to God. — For he hath made him to be sin for us who knew no sin; that we might be made the righteousness of God in him."

THE last verses on which we spoke declared the Christian aspect of human nature, and the law of regenerated Humanity. The aspect of Humanity in Christ is a new creation: in Him human nature is re-created (v. 17). Consequently, every one is to be looked at now, not merely as a man, but as a brother in Christ. No man is to be known now any more after the flesh. A more striking instance of this is not to be found than the way in which Philemon was desired by St. Paul to consider Onesimus his slave. The "middle wall of partition" has been broken down for ever between Jew and Gentile, between class and class.

The law of Humanity in Christ is, that "they which live should not henceforth live unto themselves, but unto Him which died for them," (v. 15). Such is the Christian law of sacrifice: to present our bodies and souls to Christ as a living offering. It is no longer the law of nature which rules our life, no longer self-preservation, self-indulgence; but it is self-surrender towards God and towards man.

We come now to another subject, and the connection between it and the former is contained in the eighteenth verse. All this, says St. Paul, arises out of the reconciliation effected between God and man by Christ.

First, then, we will speak of Christ's work — the reconciliation of God to man.

Secondly, the work of the Christian ministry — the reconciliation of man to God.

I. God "hath reconciled us to Himself by Jesus Christ." Now reconciliation is identical with atonement. In *Romans*, v. 11, the word "atonement" occurs, but on referring to the margin you will find that it is the same word which is here translated "reconciliation." Here, therefore, you might read: "Who hath *atoned* us to Himself by Jesus Christ." We cannot repeat this too often. The "atonement" of the Bible is the reconciliation between God and man.

Now atonement or reconciliation consists of two things: — 1. The reconciliation of God to the world. 2. The reconciliation of the world to God.

1. We say that God needed a reconciliation. On the other hand, the Unitarian view is, that God requires nothing to reconcile Him to us, that he is reconciled already, that the only thing requisite is to reconcile man to God. It also declares that there is no wrath in God toward sinners, for punishment does not manifest indignation. Nothing can be more false, unphilosophical, and unscriptural. First of all, take one passage, which is decisive: "But now after that ye know God, or rather are known of God, how turn ye again to the weak and beggarly elements, whereunto ye desire again to be in bondage?" St. Paul is there describing the Christian state, and he declares that the being recognized of God is more characteristic of the Gospel state than recognizing God. "Know God:" here is man reconciled to God. "Are known of Him:" here is God reconciled to man. St. Paul holds it a more adequate representation of the Gospel to say, Ye are known of God, that is, God is reconciled to you — than to say, Ye know God, that is, ye are reconciled to God. So much for those persons who recognize the authority of Scrip-

ture, and assert at the same time that it does not speak of an Atonement which reconciles God to man.

Next, it is perilous to explain away, as a mere figure of speech, those passages which speak of God as angry with sin. God is angry with the wicked, and the first proof of this is to be drawn from our own conscience. We feel that God is angry; and if that be but figurative, then it is only figurative to say that God is pleased. There must be some deep truth in those expressions, or else we lose the personality of God.

2. The second proof comes to us from the character of Christ. He was the representative of God: of God under the limitations of Humanity. Now Christ was "*angry*." That, therefore, which God feels, corresponds with that which in pure Humanity is the emotion of anger. No other word, then, will adequately represent God's feeling, but the human word *anger*. If we explain away such words, we lose the distinction between right and wrong: we lose belief in God: for you will end in believing there is no God at all, if you begin with explaining away His feelings.

Again, it is said that God needs no reconciliation, because he is immutable. But remember that, God remaining immutable and the sinner changing, God's relation to the sinner changes. "God is Love," but love to good is hatred to evil. If you are evil, then God is your enemy. You change God by being changed yourself. You thus alter the relation: and hence St. James says, "Draw nigh to God, and He will draw nigh to you."

Now the way in which the text speaks of the reconciliation of God to us is, "Not imputing their trespasses:" for the Atonement is made when God no longer reckons the sinner guilty. Here is the mystery of the Atonement. God is reconciled to men for Christ's sake. Earnestly I insist that the Atonement is through Christ. God is reconciled to Humanity in Christ; then to us through Him: "God was in Christ." It was a Divine Humanity. To that Humanity God is reconciled: there could be no enmity between God and

Christ: "I and my Father are One." To all those in whom Christ's Spirit is, God imputes the righteousness which is as yet only seminal, germinal; a seed, not a tree; a spring, not a river; an aspiration, not an attainment; a righteousness in faith, not a righteousness in works. It is not, then, an actual righteousness, but an imputed righteousness. Hence we see what is meant by saying, "reconciled or atoned through Christ." We do not mean that each man reconciles himself as Christ did, by being righteous; but we mean that God views him favorably as partaking of that Humanity which has been once exhibited on earth, a Holy, Perfect, and Divine thing. "God was in Christ, reconciling the world unto Himself, not imputing their trespasses unto them."

But we must distinguish this from a vulgar notion of the Atonement. Some use it as meaning *appeasal*, not reconciliation: not that the All Holy One was reconciled to Humanity by seeing in it His own image, and received full satisfaction by beholding the perfect sacrifice of the Will of the Man to the Will of God; but that not having taken out the full satisfaction of punishment in one place, He was content to do it in the *other*. Justice, they say, must strike: and if He can strike the innocent, it is richer satisfaction of justice than striking the guilty. Strange justice! Unjust to let the guilty go free, but quite just to punish the innocent! So mournfully do we deface Christianity! It is singular that the Romanists have a similar perversion. There are pictures which represent the Virgin as interposing between the world and her angry Son; laying bare her maternal bosom by way of appeal, and the Son yielding that to His mother's entreaty, which He would not do for Love. What the Virgin is to the Romanist, that is Christ to some Protestants. Observe that, according to both opinions, there are two distinct Beings, one full of Wrath, the other full of Mercy. Those Romanists make Christ the Person of fury, and Mary the Person of mercy. Some Protestants represent God the Father as the wrathful Being, and Christ as the Loving One. But the principle in both views is the same.

No! this text contradicts that notion. It was not Christ appeasing his Father's wrath, but His Father descending into Humanity through Him; and so, by taking the manhood into God, reconciling the world unto Himself. "God was in Christ, reconciling the world to Himself." It was God's infinite Love which redeemed the world, and not God's fury which was appeased. God created a Divine Humanity, and so, changing the relation between man and Himself, reconciled Himself to man. And this Divine Humanity sacrificed itself *for* us. It was a vicarious sacrifice. The sacrifice of Christ was the meritorious cause of our acceptance. What was there in it which satisfied God? Was it the punishment inflicted? No! It was the free offering of Christ's Will even unto death. "Therefore, doth my Father love me, because I lay down my life for the sheep."

II. The work of the Christian ministry — the reconciliation of man to God.

Now distinguish Christ's position from ours. It was Christ's work to reconcile God to man. That is done, and done for ever; we cannot add anything to it. That is a priestly power: and it is at our peril that we claim such a power. Ours is ministerial: His alone was priestly. We cannot infuse supernatural virtue into baptismal water; we cannot transform bread and wine into heavenly aliment. We can offer no sacrifice: the concluding sacrifice is done. "By one offering He hath perfected for ever them that are sanctified." So far, then, as we represent anything besides this as *necessary*, so far do we frustrate it, and turn the Christian ministry into a sacrificial priesthood. We are doing as did the Galatians of old.

Therefore the whole work of the Christian ministry consists in declaring God as reconciled to man: and in beseeching with every variety of illustration, and every degree of earnestness, men to become reconciled to God. It is this which is *not* done. All are God's children by *right;* all are not God's children in fact. All are sons of God; but all have not the Spirit of sons, "whereby they cry, Abba, Father." All are redeemed, all are not yet sanctified.

LECTURE XLVI.

DECEMBER 19, 1852.

2 CORINTHIANS, vi. 1-10. — "We then, as workers together with him, beseech you also that ye receive not the grace of God in vain. — (For he saith, I have heard thee in a time accepted, and in the day of salvation have I succored thee: behold, now is the accepted time; behold, now is the day of salvation.) — Giving no offence in anything, that the ministry be not blamed: — But in all things approving ourselves as the ministers of God, in much patience, in afflictions, in necessities, in distresses, — In stripes, in imprisonments, in tumults, in labors, in watchings, in fastings; — By pureness, by knowledge, by long-suffering, by kindness, by the Holy Ghost, by love unfeigned, — By the word of truth, by the power of God, by the armor of righteousness on the right hand and on the left, — By honor and dishonor, by evil report and good report: as deceivers, and yet true; — As unknown, and yet well known; as dying, and, behold, we live; as chastened, and not killed; — As sorrowful, yet alway rejoicing; as poor, yet making many rich; as having nothing, and yet possessing all things."

THE last chapter closed with the subject of Reconciliation. It declared that the atonement between God and man consisted of two parts: God atoned to man by the work of Christ; man atoned to God by the work of the Christian ministry. For the work of the Christian minister presupposes the work of Christ; and his message is, "God is reconciled to you, be ye reconciled to God." In this sixth chapter, St. Paul proceeds with this ministry of reconciliation. We will consider —

I. His appeal.
II. The grounds of that appeal.

I. St. Paul's appeal was, "that ye receive not the grace of God in vain." *The grace of God.* Grace is favor, and the particular grace here spoken of is the reconciliation of God in Christ (vs. 14-19). That

Christ died for all, and that God is reconciled to all — this is the state of Grace. Now the word *grace* being exclusively a Scriptural one, is often misunderstood, and seems mysterious: it is supposed to be a mystical something infused into the soul. But grace is only God's favor; and a state of grace is the state in which all men are, who have received the message of salvation, which declares God's goodwill towards them. So speaks St. Paul in the Epistle to the Romans. The Corinthians had received this grace; they were baptized into the name of God the Father, and Christ the Son. They were told that God was their Father and their Friend. Now we shall understand what St. Paul meant by beseeching them not to receive that grace in vain. It was a question once discussed with great theological vehemence, whether men who had once been recipients of grace could fall from it finally and irrevocably. Some replied warmly that they can, while others, with equal pertinacity, affirmed that it was impossible. Part of the cause of this disagreement may be taken away by agreeing on the meaning of the word *grace*. By grace some meant the Spirit of God, and they held, that the soul which has once become one with God, is His for ever. Undoubtedly this has the sanction of Scripture in various forms of expression. For example, "Fear not, little flock; for it is your Father's good pleasure to give you the kingdom:" "I give unto them eternal life; and they shall never perish, neither shall any man pluck them out of my hand." Again: "No man is able to pluck them out of my Father's hand:" "While I was with them in the world, I kept them in thy name: those that thou gavest me I have kept, and none of them is lost, but the son of perdition:" "Whom he did predestinate, them he also called; and whom he called, them he also justified: and whom he justified, them he also glorified." We cannot read these passages, without perceiving that there is an inner circle of men in the Kingdom of Grace, in whom God's Spirit dwells, who are one with God, in whom His Holy Ghost is a well of water springing up into everlasting Life,—"the general assembly and church of the first-born, which are written in heaven."

On the other hand, by *grace* some meant that state in which all Christians are, as redeemed from the world by Christ's blood, called to be saints, and to whom the high privileges of God's Church are revealed. Now it is unquestionable, that not all who are recipients of that grace, and redeemed into that mercy, will be saved. This first verse itself implies that they may receive the grace of God in vain. So says Christ: "Every branch in me that beareth not fruit, is hewn down and cast into the fire." Remember, too, the parable of the fig-tree in the vineyard, which was unfruitful, and was sentenced. Again, such exhortations as "Quench not the Spirit," imply that He may be quenched. And such warnings as these, "It is impossible for those who were once enlightened, and have tasted of the heavenly gift, and were made partakers of the Holy Ghost, if they shall fall away, to renew them again unto repentance." And again, "He that despised Moses' law died without mercy. Of how much sorer punishment, suppose ye, shall he be thought worthy, who hath trodden under foot the Son of God?"—prove that this grace received, may yet be received in vain. These are very awful passages, and they prove at least, that if there be those in whom the Love of God is a perennial fountain of spiritual strength, yet there are also those to whom all the promises have been made in unfeigned sincerity, who have professed religion with warmth—nay, who in Christ's name have done many wonderful works—and yet to whom He shall declare at the last, "I never knew you." So near may we approach to the Kingdom of God, and yet come short of attaining it!

II. The grounds of the Apostle's appeal:—

1. The thought that the time of grace is limited. St. Paul quotes from Isaiah:—"I have heard thee in a time accepted, and in the day of salvation have I

succored thee." Observe the principle on which this prophecy is quoted. Prophecy records the principle of God's dealings. Now here was a precedent, declaring the limitation of the time during which grace is open; and St. Paul applying it, says, "*Now:*" just such a a limited moment as there was in Isaiah's day, the same is now. Let us dwell upon this thought—that there is a day of grace: for example, the respite before the Flood: "My spirit shall not always strive with man: yet his days shall be an hundred and twenty years." There was, then, a space allowed for repentance. Again, to Nineveh was given a respite of forty days. A year's grace was allotted to the fig-tree in the parable. Jerusalem, too, had such a day: "If thou hadst known, even thou, at least in this thy day, the things which belong unto thy peace:" but then her day of grace was past; her day of blindness had come. Now that which is declared of the world before the Flood, of Nineveh, of the fig-tree, of Jerusalem, is the history of each separate soul. Every man has his day of grace: what in vulgar English we should call his "chance." There comes to each man a crisis in his destiny, when evil influences have been removed, or some strong impression made – after an illness, or an escape, or in some season of solitary thoughtfulness or disappointment. It were an awful thing to watch such a spirit, if we knew that he is on the trial now, by which his everlasting destiny is to be decided! It were more awful still to see a man who has passed the time of grace, and reached the time of blindness: and to know that the light is quenched for ever; that he will go on as before, and live many years, and play his part in life; but that the Spirit of God will come back to that soul no more for ever!

2. The second ground on which St. Paul urged his appeal, was the earnest affectionateness of his own ministry. He appealed on the ground of the work of Christ, and on the ground of the work of those who were co-operators with Christ: "We, then, as workers together with Him, beseech you"—(v. 1). This

appeal is followed up by an account of his conduct as a fellow-worker: "Giving no offence in anything, that the ministry be not blamed" — (vi. 3, 4), which again is succeeded by that glorious and touching description of ministerial devotedness, which no Christian can read without humiliation. It was the unexaggerated picture of a human life actually lived out in this selfish world of ours! Upon this I make two observations: —

First: The true return for ministerial devotedness is a life given to God. St. Paul details the circumstances of his own rare ministry, and he asks, in return, not the affection of the Corinthians, nor their admiration, but this: that they "receive not the grace of God in vain:" and again (v. 13), "Now for a recompense in the same . . . . be ye also enlarged." To all human hearts affection is dear, and respect and veneration precious. But none of these things is true *payment.* Hence St. Paul says: "Therefore, my brethren, dearly beloved and longed for, my *joy and crown*, so stand fast in the Lord." And again he says: "As also ye have acknowledged us in part, that we are your rejoicing, even as ye also are ours in the day of the Lord Jesus." And St. John, in his Second Epistle, writes: "I rejoiced greatly that I found of thy children walking in truth;" and again, in his Third Epistle, he says to Gaius: "I have no greater joy than to hear that my children walk in truth." This, I do not say is, but ought to be, the spirit of every minister of Christ: to feel that nothing can reward him for such efforts as he may have been permitted to make — nothing, except the grace of God received, and life moulded in accordance with it. No deference, no love, no enthusiasm manifested for him, can make up for this. Far beyond all evil or good report, his eye ought to be fixed on one thing — God's truth, and the reception of it.

Secondly: The true apostolical succession. Much has been said and written to prove the ministers of the Church to be lineally descended from the Apostles; and, further, to prove that none but they are commissioned to preach God's word, to administer God's sacraments, or to convey the grace of Christ. We do not dispute this: we rather admit and assert it. For purposes of order, the Church requires a lineal succession; that is, authority delegated by those who have authority. But this is a poor line of succession — to take the outward descent as all, and to consider the inward as nothing. It is the same mistake that the Jews made in tracing their descent from Abraham's person, and forgetting their spiritual descent from Abraham's Father. Now the grounds of apostleship alleged here are all spiritual; *none* are external. Again, in the twelfth chapter of this Epistle, St. Paul says: "Truly the signs of an apostle were wrought among you in all patience, in signs, and wonders, and mighty deeds." Thus St. Paul does not graft his right of appeal on any proud, priestly assumption, but on an inward likeness to Christ. Therefore, the true apostolical succession, is, and must be, a spiritual one. The power of God is not conveyed by physical contact, but by the reception of a Spirit. He is a true minister who is one from sharing in the spirit of an Apostle, not from the ordination and descent from an Apostle. True, there is a succession. The mind of Christ, as set forth in his Apostles, acts on other minds, whether by ideas or character, and produces likeness to itself. Love begets love; faith generates faith; lofty lives nourish the germs of exalted life in others. There is a spiritual birth. John was the successor of the spirit of Elias. Luther was the offspring of the mind of Paul. We are children of Abraham, if we share in the faith of Abraham; we are the successors of the Apostles, if we have a spirit similar to theirs.

LECTURE XLVII

DECEMBER 26, 1852.

2 CORINTHIANS, vi. 11–18. — "O ye Corinthians, our mouth is open unto you, our heart is enlarged. — Ye are not straitened in us, but ye are straitened in your own bowels. — Now for a recompense in the same, (I speak as unto my children,) be ye also enlarged. — Be ye not unequally yoked together with unbelievers: for what fellow ship hath righteousness with unrighteousness? and what communion hath light with darkness? — And what concord hath Christ with Belial? or what part hath he that believeth with an infidel? — And what agreement hath the temple of God with idols? for ye are the temple of the living God; as God hath said, I will dwell in them, and walk in them; and I will be their God, and they shall be my people. — Wherefore come out from among them, and be ye separate, saith the Lord, and touch not the unclean thing; and I will receive you, — And will be a Father unto you, and ye shall be my sons and daughters, saith the Lord Almighty."

IN our last lecture we saw that St. Paul, after explaining the grace of God to a world reconciled in Christ, had besought the Corinthians not to receive that grace in vain. For a passage in Isaiah assured them that it might be in vain: it announced the awful truth that there is such a thing as a day of grace, and that that day is limited. Accordingly, as an ambassador first, and then as a fellow-worker with God, in which capacity he enumerates his sufferings and labors, St. Paul entreats them not to receive that grace in vain. In the close of this chapter, he expresses more definitely his meaning. For a general entreaty to become a Christian is vague. Sanctification is made up of many particulars. To use the grace of God is a duty composed of various branches. Two of these are chiefly dwelt on here. The duty of separation from the world, and of purification from evil.

To-day we shall only consider the former.

I. The exuberance of apostolic affection.
II. The recompense desired.

I. The Apostle's affection overflows in an exuberant apostrophe: "O ye Corinthians, our mouth is open unto you, our heart is enlarged" (v. 11). His love was deep, and this flow of eloquence arose out of the expansion of his heart. But, in explaining this, we take the second clause first, as the former is the result of the latter.

First: "Our heart is enlarged." Now what makes this remark wonderful in the Apostle's mouth is, that St. Paul had received a multitude of provocations from the Corinthians. They had denied the truthfulness of his ministry, charged him with interested motives, sneered at his manner, and held up to scorn the meanness of his appearance. In the face of this his heart expands! — partly with compassion. Their insults and haughty tone only impressed him with a sense of their need, with the feeling of their wandering ignorance. They were his "children." How could he resent even unmerited reproach from them, bound as they were to him by so dear a tie? He had suffered for them: He pardoned them, for they did it ignorantly. His spirit sought for them the only excuse it could. Thus spoke before him One who loved even more than he: for the same thought occurs in the dying words of Christ: "Father, forgive them, for they know not what they do." How worthy a successor of his Master's spirit! How generous! What a well-spring of Love, inexhaustible in its freshness as in its life! And this is the true test of *gracious* charity. Does the heart expand or narrow as life goes on? If it narrows, if mis conception or opposition wither love, be sure that that love had no root. If love is slain by injury, or even enmity, was it love in its truest sense? "If ye love them which love you, what reward have ye? do not even the publicans the same?" And this love is given to all, partly from looking on all as immortal souls in Christ. The everlasting principle within makes all the difference. For it is not the mere instinct of lovingness which makes the Christian : — to love the soul in Christ, *imputing* righteousness to it as God does, knowing the powers it has in it to produce good — feeling what it should be, and what it may become, and loving it as Christ loved it — this is the Christian charity. Hold fast to love. If men wound your heart, let them not sour or embitter it; let them not shut up or narrow it; let them only expand it more and more, and be able always to say with St. Paul, " My heart is enlarged."

Secondly. St. Paul's eloquence: " Our mouth is open unto you." He might have shut his lips, and in dignified pride refused to plead his own cause. But instead, he speaks his thoughts aloud — freely, not cautiously; and, like Luther in after times, lays his whole heart open to view. This he does in words which, even though a translation, and that translation from a language which was not the Apostle's own, stirs the soul within us. " Out of the abundance of the heart the mouth speaketh." Be sure that a man who speaks so, has nothing to conceal. St. Paul had no after-thought, no reservation in his life or on his lips: he was a genuine man, true in the innermost recesses of his spirit.

II. The recompense desired.

He asked for the enlargement of their heart towards him: which was to be shown in separation from the world. This is always a difficult subject, yet it is the only true recompense of ministerial work. Now, in explaining any passage of Scripture, two things have to be done: first, to put ourselves in possession of the circumstances under which the words were spoken, to endeavor to realize the society, persons, feelings and customs of the body of men, and of the time, to whom and in which the passage was addressed; secondly, to discern in what point and principles the passage corresponds with our circumstances. For otherwise we misinterpret Scripture, misled by words and superficial resemblances. This is what Christ meant in His description of the wise Scribe, who "brings out of his treasures things new and old." For the great office of the expounder is to adapt old principles to new circumstances, and to read the present through the past.

First, then, let us comprehend the words and the circumstances to which they applied. We take the passage, "Be ye not unequally yoked together with unbelievers." Here the metaphor is drawn from two. ill-matched animals dragging the same vehicle or plough: two animals of different sizes or tempers, who pull either different ways, or with different degrees of speed. The plain import, then, of the figurative expression is — Separate from the unbelievers, avoid close intimacy with them. "Come out from among them, and be ye separate, saith the Lord, and touch not the unclean thing."

Next, let us consider the circumstances. Bear in mind what we learnt in the First Epistle: — one of the great parties at Corinth was the party of "liberty." They knew the freeness of Christ's Gospel; they understood that the distinction of days was done away with, that there was no difference between clean and unclean meats, that flesh offered to idols was not polluted. They comprehended that all the Jewish ceremonial holiness was but typical, and that the separateness of "touch not, taste not, handle not," was done away with. Now the danger which these persons incurred was, that, breaking down every barrier, they left nothing between themselves and evil. They prided themselves on their liberty, they went to idol feasts, they treated Saturday like Monday, they mixed freely with the world. Apparently, they were not even afraid to marry with the heathen; and in this daring admixture, and unrestrained indulgence in *all* things permitted, they ran the risk of gradually imbibing the spirit and temper of the world of evil with which they mingled. Accordingly, "Be ye not unequally yoked," meant, "Beware of sharing in the vices and corruption of the heathen."

Secondly, let us consider how to apply this injunction to our own times. Clearly the *letter* of the command is inapplicable. for in two points, at least, the parallel does not hold. First, heathen feasts do not exist among us. In the days of the Apostle they were connected with abominable profligacy. And again, there is no sharp and marked distinction now, as there was then, between those who are, and those who are not, on the side of Christ. At that time baptism severed mankind into two great bodies, the world and the Church. But now, all being baptized, the command, "Be ye not unequally yoked with unbelievers," cannot mean the same thing as it did then. Therefore, only the *spirit* of the injunction can be applied to us. We may discern this from considering the grounds and reasons of the prohibition. Independent of the impossibility of agreement in the deepest sympathies, independent of there being no identity of tastes, no identity of antipathies, there were two strong grounds for this command.

1. The first ground was Immorality: "What fellowship hath righteousness with unrighteousness?" In England we are an inconsistent people. A rigid barrier exists between class and class, and is almost never broken, except in two instances: wealth and talent break it down. Let a man amass enormous wealth, and he will find at his board the noblest in the land. It matters not that he became rich in some questionable way, that shrewd suspicions are entertained of foul practices and unfair means: no one asks about that. Again, talent of a certain class — that talent which amuses — breaks down the rigid line of demarcation. The accomplished man or woman who, though notoriously profligate, can wile away an evening, is tolerated — nay, courted — even in the Christian drawing-room. Now, understand me, I do not say that the breaking down of conventional barriers is undesirable. If goodness did it — if a man, low in birth, were admired because of his virtues — oh! it would be well for this land of ours! But where wealth and talent, irrespective of goodness, alone possess the key to unlock our English exclusiveness, there plainly the apostolic injunction holds, because the reason of it holds: "What fellow-

ship hath righteousness with unrighteousness? Separate, then, cut yourself adrift from the profligate man of wealth, from the immoral man of talent. If you must have dealing with them, let it be only in the way of business; but no intimacy, no friendship with them should be yours.

2. The second ground was Irreligion: "What part hath he that believeth with an infidel?" There is much danger, however, in applying this law. It is perilous work when men begin to decide who are believers and who are not, if they decide by party badges. A man worships in a certain congregation, is taught by a certain minister, does not subscribe to certain societies; whereupon by that which arrogates to itself the title of the "religious world," he is at once pronounced an unbeliever, and not a Christian. This spirit besets our age, it is rife in this town, and demands the earnest protest of lip and life from every true man. For nothing more surely eats out the heart of religion, which is love, than this spirit of religious exclusiveness, and of judging others. Nothing more surely brings out the natural, innate popery of the heart. Better, far better than this, is it to risk the charge, falsely brought, which Christ endured, of being worldly, "a friend of publicans and sinners." Nevertheless, there is an irreligion which "he who runs may read." For the atheist is not merely he who professes unbelief, but, strictly speaking, every one who lives without God in the world. And the heretic is not merely he who has mistaken some Christian doctrine, but rather he who causes divisions among the brethren. And the idolater is not merely he who worships images, but he who gives his heart to something which is less than God; for a man's god is that which has his whole soul and worship, that which he obeys and reverences as his highest. Now there are innumerable doubtful cases where charity is bound to hope for the best; but there is also abundance of plain cases: for where a man's god is money, or position in society, or rank, there the rule holds, "Come ye apart."

This, then, is the spirit of the passage:—A law holds wherever the reason of it holds. Wherever union in the highest cannot be, wherever *idem velle, atque idem nolle*, is impossible, there friendship and intimate partnership must not be tried. One word, however, as to the mode of this separation. It is not to be attained by an affectation of outward separateness. The spirit of vanity and worldly pride is not avoided by the outward plainness of Quakerism. Beneath the Quaker's sober, unworldly garb, there *may* be the canker of the love of gain; and beneath the guise of peace, there may be the combative spirit, which is worse than War. Nor can you get rid of worldliness by placing a ban on particular places of entertainment, and particular societies. The world is a spirit rather than a form; and just as it is true that wherever two or three are met together in His name, God is in the midst of them, so if your heart is at one with His Spirit, you *may*, in the midst of worldly amusements—yet not without great danger, for you will have multiplied temptations—keep yourself unspotted from the World.

LECTURE XLVIII.

JANUARY 2, 1853.

2 CORINTHIANS, vii. 1. — "Having therefore these promises, dearly beloved, let us cleanse ourselves from all filthiness of the flesh and spirit, perfecting holiness in the fear of God."

THE recompense which St. Paul asked in return for his exuberant affection towards the Corinthians, was defined in our last lecture in two particulars: 1. Separation from the world. 2. Separation from all uncleanness. These were to be his reward; it was these the Apostle longed for. It was not affection for himself that he desired, but devotion to God. We took the first part last Sunday, — unworldliness, or separation from the world. To-day we will consider the second part of the recompense he asked, — Personal Purification.

First, then, as to the ground of the request: "Having these promises." Now these promises are: the In-dwelling of God; His free reception of us; His Fatherhood and our sonship: and they are contained in the sixteenth, seventeenth, and eighteenth verses of the sixth chapter. But, first, observe the Gospel principle of action: it is not, Separate yourself from all uncleanness in order that you may *get* a *right* of sonship; but, *Because* ye are sons of God, therefore be pure. It is not, Work in order to be saved; but, Because you *are* saved, therefore work *out* your salvation. It is not, Labor that you may be accepted; but, Labor, because you are accepted in the Beloved. Christian action advances from the right of the sonship, to the fact of sonship, and not *vice versâ*. In other words: Ye are the sons of God: here are God's promises; therefore become what you are reckoned to be: let the righteousness which is *imputed* to you become righteousness *in* you. "Ye are the temple of God:" therefore cleanse yourself. God is your Father, therefore be pure. Thus we see that St. Paul first lays down Christian privileges, and then demands Christian action; and in this the mode of the Law is reversed. The Law says: "This do, and thou shalt live." The Gospel says: "This do, because thou *art* redeemed." We are to work, not in order to win life, but because life is already given. Only so far as we teach this principle, do we teach Christ's Gospel: it is salvation by grace, salvation by free grace, salvation by sovereign grace; it is God's favor freely given, without money and without price; not for worth, or goodness, or merit of ours. So speaks St. Paul: "After that the kindness and love of God our Saviour toward man appeared, not by works of righteousness which we have done, but according to His mercy He saved us."

We all know the power and force of this kind of appeal. You know there are some things a soldier will not do, *because* he is a soldier: he is in uniform, and he cannot disgrace his corps. There are some things of which a man of high birth and lineage is incapable: a long line of ancestry is a guarantee for his conduct: he has a character to sustain. Precisely on this ground is the Gospel appeal made to us. Ye are priests and kings to God: will you forget your office, and fall from your kingship? Shall an heir of glory disgrace his heavenly lineage? Ye are God's temple, in which He dwells: will you pollute *that?* Observe on what strong grounds we stand when we appeal to men as having been baptized. St. Paul spoke to all the Corinthians as being the temple of God. Now, if baptism were a magical ceremony, or if it were a conditional blessing, so that a baptized child were only God's child hypothetically, how could I appeal to this congregation? But since I am certain and sure, that every man whom I address is God's child, that his baptism declared a fact which already existed, and that he is a recipient of God's loving influences, I, as Christ's minister, can and must say: "Having, therefore, these promises, dearly beloved, let us cleanse ourselves from all filthiness of the flesh and spirit, perfecting holiness in the fear of God." I can say to every one of you: "Ye are the temple of God, therefore keep God's dwelling pure."

Secondly, let us consider the request itself. St. Paul demanded their holiness, that is, their separation from impurity; for holiness, or sanctification meant, in the Jewish language, separation. In Jewish literalness, it meant separation from external defilement. But the thing implied by this typical separation was that inward holiness of which St. Paul here speaks. We must keep ourselves apart, then, not only from sensual, but also from spiritual defilement. The Jewish law required only the purification of the flesh; the Gospel, which is the inner spirit of the Law, demands the purification of the spirit. The distinction is made in the Epistle to the Hebrews: "For if the blood of bulls and of goats, and the ashes of an heifer sprinkling the unclean, sanctifieth to the purifying of the flesh: How much more shall the blood of Christ, who through the eternal Spirit offered himself without spot to God, purge your conscience from dead works to serve the living God?" Concerning the former, I will say but little now. There is a contamination which passes through the avenue of the senses, and sinks into the spirit. Who shall dislodge it thence? "Hear," said Christ, "and understand: Not that which goeth into the mouth defileth a man; but that which cometh out of the mouth, this defileth a man." "For out of the heart proceed evil thoughts." The heart — the heart — there is the evil! The imagination, which was given to spiritualize the senses, is often turned into a means of sensualizing the spirit. Beware of reverie, and indulgence in forbidden images, unless you would introduce into your bosom a serpent, which will creep, and crawl, and leave the venom of its windings in your heart.

And now what is the remedy for this? How shall we avoid evil thoughts? First: By the fear of God — "Our God is a consuming fire." Compare with this: "For the word of God is quick, and powerful, and sharper than any two-edged sword, piercing even to the dividing asunder of soul and spirit, and of the joints and marrow, and is a discerner of the thoughts and intents of the heart." An awful thought! a Living God, infinitely pure, is conscious of your contaminated thoughts! So the only true courage sometimes comes from fear. We cannot do without awe: there is no depth of character without it. Tender motives are not enough to restrain from sin; yet awe is not enough. Love and Hope will keep us strong against passion, as they kept our Saviour strong in suffering, "who for the joy that was set before Him endured the cross, despising the shame."

Secondly: By the promises of God. Think of what you are — a child of God, an heir of Heaven. Realize the grandeur of saintliness, and you will shrink from degrading your soul and debasing your spirit. It is in reading saintly lives, that we are ashamed of grovelling desires. To come down, however, from these sublime motives to simple rules, I say, first of all, then, cultivate all generous and high feelings. A base appetite may be expelled by a nobler passion; the invasion of a country has sometimes waked men from low sensuality, has roused them to deeds of self-sacrifice, and left no access for the baser passions. An honorable affection can quench low and indiscriminate vice. "This I say, then, Walk in the spirit, and ye shall not fulfil the lusts of the flesh." I say, secondly, Seek exercise and occupation. If a man finds himself haunted by evil desires and unholy images, which will generally be at periodical hours, let him commit to memory passages of Scripture, or passages from the best writers in verse or prose. Let him store his mind with these, as safeguards to repeat, when he lies awake in some restless night, or when despairing imaginations, or gloomy, suicidal thoughts, beset him. Let these be to him the sword, turning everywhere to keep the way of the Garden of Life from the intrusion of profaner footsteps.

Lastly: Observe the entireness of this severance from evil — "*perfecting* holiness." Perfection means, then, entireness, in opposition to one-sidedness. This is plain from many passages of Scripture. Thus: "Be ye therefore perfect, even as your Father, which is in heaven, is perfect." Again, it is not "Love them which love you," but "Love your enemies." Again: "This also we wish, even your perfection:" "Not as though I had already attained," says St. Paul, "either were already perfect:" and here he says, "perfecting holiness." This expression seems to be suggested by the terms *flesh* and *spirit;* for the purification of the flesh alone would not be perfect, but superficial, holiness. Christian sanctification, therefore, is an entire and whole thing; it is nothing less than presenting the whole man a sacrifice to Christ. "I pray God your whole spirit and soul and body be preserved blameless." For we should greatly mistake, if we supposed the Apostle meant here only one class of sins, when he speaks of purifying ourselves from "all filthiness in flesh and spirit:" for what are they which in Christ's catalogue defile the man? They are thefts, blasphemies, evil witness, murders, as well as what we especially call sins of uncleanness.

LECTURE XLIX.

JANUARY 26, 1853.

2 CORINTHIANS, vii. 2–8. — "Receive us; we have wronged no man, we have corrupted no man, we have defrauded no man. — I speak not this to condemn you: for I have said before, that ye are in our hearts to die and live with you. — Great is my boldness of speech toward you, great is my glorying of you: I am filled with comfort, I am exceeding joyful in all our tribulation. — For when we were come into Macedonia, our flesh had no rest, but we were troubled on every side; without were fightings, within were fears. — Nevertheless God, that comforteth those that are cast down, comforted us by the coming of Titus; — And not by his coming only, but by the consolation wherewith he was comforted in you, when he told us your earnest desire, your mourning, your fervent mind toward me; so that I rejoiced the more. — For though I made you sorry with a letter, I do not repent, though I did repent: for I perceive that the same epistle hath made you sorry, though it were but for a season."

THE remainder of this chapter, which we began last Sunday, is almost entirely personal, having reference to the relations existing between St. Paul and the Corinthian Church. In the sixth chapter he had spoken of his expressed affection towards them, and asked for a return. That return is contained in the words, "Be ye reconciled to God." We found that the reconciliation itself consisted of two particulars — separation from the world, and separation from all impurity. Subordinate to this is a request for the only personal acknowledgment and recompense they could make for his affection: "Receive us," said St. Paul: "let there be an affectionate understanding between us." Our subject to-day, therefore, chiefly bears on St. Paul's personal character, — his feelings and ministerial conduct.

I. The ground on which he urged this request.
II. The grounds on which he hoped it.

I. He urged it on the ground that he deserved it. It was a simple matter of justice. "We have wronged no man, we have corrupted no man, we have defrauded no man." Recollect the charges alleged against him: venality; preaching the Gospel for gain; and the accusation of the false teachers, who said, "He has overreached you — taken you in." Now the Apostle meets these charges simply by an assertion of his innocence, but an assertion which appealed at the same time to their own witness. No one who read those words could doubt whether he was guilty, for there is a certain tone in innocence not easily mistaken. There are some voices that *ring* true. This reminds us of Samuel's purgation of himself when laying down his judgeship. A worthy close! Two precedents are these, most worthy of thought, both for ministerial and secular life. Only consider how great in Samuel's case, and in St. Paul's, was the influence of integrity! There is nothing from which it so much behoves a public servant — especially one in a sacred office — to be perfectly free, as from the very suspicion of interested motives. If he cannot say openly, and to his own heart, "I have not been bribed either by the hope of favor or popularity, or by the dread of offending; neither personal fear, nor personal hope, has ever shaped one sentence, or modified one tone, or kept back one truth," he may rest assured his work cannot stand. Honesty, uprightness, integrity of character, are sometimes called mere moral virtues: and religious people are too often deficient in these points: but the bright honor of the Apostle Paul was never stained. He could say, "I have wronged no man." There is, however, one touch of graceful delicacy in the *way* he made this assertion of his innocence, which must not be passed over, if we would rightly appreciate the character of St. Paul. A coarser and ruder man would have cared for nothing but the proof of his own integrity. Now St. Paul perceived that the broad assertion of this might give pain. It might cover with confusion those who had suspected him. It might seem to them as if this were spoken *at them* in indirect reproach. It might even wound those who had not suspected him, as if his protest were a bitter reflection upon them. Therefore, he adds, "I speak not this to condemn you;" that is, "I am not defending myself against you, but to you. I am not reproaching you for past injustice: I only say these things to assure you of my undiminished love."

There was one thing in the character of St. Paul, which often escapes observation. Carlyle calls him "an unkempt Apostle Paul;" and some say of him, "He was a man rude, brave, true, unpolished." We all know his integrity, his truth, his daring, his incorruptible honesty. But besides these, there was a refined and delicate courtesy, which was for ever taking off the edge of his sharpest rebukes, and sensitively anticipating every pain his words might give: so that to have been rebuked by him would have been less painful than to be praised by most other men. Remember the exquisite courtesy with which his request to Philemon is put. Remember the delicate exception in his answer to Agrippa: "I would to God that not only thou, but also all that hear me this day, were both almost, and altogether such as I am, except these bonds." Remember, too, how he pours love over one of his strongest condemnations in Philippians: "For many walk, of whom I have told you often, and now *tell you even weeping*, that they are the enemies of the cross of Christ." This is something of the tender tact, the Christian art, which marks the character of this Apostle. Observe, it is only Love which can give that. It was not *high* breeding; it was rather *good* breeding. High breeding gracefully insists on its own rights; good breeding gracefully remembers the rights of others. We have all seen that dignified courtesy which belongs to high birth, which never offends as long as it is not personally harmed. But we know that that will not last: provocation makes it as bitter and as vulgar as the breeding of the most uncultured mechanic. Far — far above this, is the polish which the highest Christianity gives to the heart. It is not "gentility," but gentleness. It is the wisdom from above, which is first pure, then *gentle*.

There is a rough, rude, straightforward honesty which is just and upright, which can say these words as St. Paul did: "I have wronged no man." Perforce we respect such integrity. But Christianity requires something more: not gold only, but gold thrice refined; not a building of precious stones only, but of exquisite polish also; for there is a rough way, and a gentle way, of being true. Do not think that Christian polish weakens character, as polish thins the diamond. The polish of the world not only saps strength of character, but makes it even unnatural. Look at St. Paul, with all that grace of a feeling almost feminine in its sensitiveness — was there ever anything in human character more daringly impassioned, more full of noble energy and childlike impulsiveness! That is what the grace of Christ can do.

II. The grounds for the Apostle's hope of a good understanding with the Corinthians. To put it in one word: he rested it on his candor; he hoped it, because he had been true with them in all his dealings: "Great is my boldness" — that is, freedom — "of speech toward you." But let us explain. When we were going through the First Epistle, we found that a scandalous crime had been committed by a Corinthian Christian; it was the crime of incest. Now consider the difficulty in which St. Paul was placed. If he rebuked the Corinthians, he would probably destroy his own interest, and irreparably offend them. If he left the crime unnoticed, he might seem to connive at it, or gloss it over. Besides this, the subject was a delicate one to enter upon: it touched family honor and family feelings. Might it not be wise to leave the wound unprobed? Moreover, we all know how hard it is to deal harshly with the sins of those we love, of those to whom we are indebted, or who are indebted to us.

Any of these considerations might have made a less straightforward man silent. But St. Paul did not hesi tate: he wrote off at once that First Epistle, which goes into the matter fully, with no false delicacy—calling wrong, wrong, and laying upon those who permitted it, and honored it, their full share of blame. Scarcely, however, had the Apostle written the Epistle, and irrevocably sent it, than misgivings began to cross his mind, as we see in the eighth verse, where he says, "I did repent." To some persons this would be perplexing. They cannot understand how an inspired Apostle could regret what he had done: if it were by Inspiration, what room could there be for misgivings? And if he regretted an act done under God's guidance, just as any common man might regret a foolish act, how could the Apostle be inspired? But this, which might perplex some, exhibits the very beauty and naturalness of the whole narrative. God's inspiration does not take a man and make a passive machine of him, as a musician might use a flute, breathing through it what tones he pleases, while the flute itself is unconscious, unresisting, and un-coöperating. When God inspires, His Spirit mixes with the spirit of man, in the form of thought, not without struggles and misgivings of the human element. Otherwise it would not be human: it would not be inspiration *of* the man, but simply a Divine echo *through* the man. Very beautiful is this account of the inspired letter of St. Paul to the Corinthians; so real, so human, so natural!

These misgivings lasted a considerable time. In the twelfth verse of the second chapter, we learn that at Troas they had not subsided. He went there on his way to Macedonia, in order the soonor to meet Titus, with the reply from the Corinthians; and in this chapter we learn that these doubts had even gathered strength: "For, when we were come into Macedonia, our flesh had no rest, but we were troubled on every side; without were fightings, within were fears." Here I make a remark by the way: It is by passages such as these alone, that we can appreciate and understand the real trials of apostles and missionaries. Here was a journey from Asia to Corinth, through various places.

Now the obvious trials of such a course all could comprehend. Perils by sea; perils from the Jews; perils from governors; perils of travel; hardships and privations: these were the trifles which tried a spirit like St. Paul's. For it is not hardships that are the wearing work of life. It is anxiety of heart and mind; it is the fretting, carking cares of deep solicitude: one sorrow, one deep, corroding anxiety, will wear deeper furrows in a cheek and brow, than ten campaigns can do. One day's suspense will exhaust more, and leave the cheek paler, than a week's fasting. Thus it is a low estimate of the depth of apostolic trial to say, that physical suffering was its chief element. And if this be true, how much more degrading is it so to treat of the Sufferings of Christ, of whom the Prophet said: "He shall see of the travail of His *soul*, and be satisfied." We degrade His Life and Death by pictures of His physical suffering and His bodily agony on the Cross. For it was not the nails that pierced His hands which wrung from Him the exceeding bitter cry, but the iron that had entered into His soul.

To return from this digression. In Macedonia St. Paul met Titus, bearing a letter from the Corinthians, by which it appeared that his rebuke had done its work. Instead of alienating, it had roused them to earnestness: they had purged themselves of complicity in the guilt, by the punishment and excommunication of the offender. This was the Apostle's comfort; and on this ground he built his sanguine hope that the Corinthians would receive him, and that there would be no more misunderstanding — v. 7. Now let us see the personal application — the principles derivable from these facts.

First, I infer the value of explanations. Had St. Paul left the matter unsettled, or only half settled, there never could have been a hearty understanding between him and Corinth. There would have been for ever a sense of a something reserved; there would have been a wound, which never had been probed. Whenever, then, there is a misunderstanding between man and man, or harsh words reported to one as said by the other, the true remedy is a direct and open request for explanation. In the world's idea, this means satisfaction in the sense of revenge; in the Christian sense it means examination in order to do mutual justice. The rule for this is laid down by Christ: "Moreover, if thy brother shall trespass against thee, go and tell him his fault between thee and him alone: if he shall hear thee, thou hast gained thy brother." It is the neglect of this rule of frankness that pepetuates misunderstandings. Suspicions lie hid, and burn, and wrankle; and sentences, and half sentences, are reported by persons who do not *mean* to make mischief, but who effectually do so. Words are distorted and misconstrued, and two upright men, between whom one frank, open conversation would set all right, are separated for ever.

Secondly, I infer the blessing, not merely the duty, of entire truthfulness. The affectionate relations between St. Paul and the Corinthians, though interrupted, were restored again, because he had been true. Candor and straightforwardness were the bond of attachment. Henceforward, however their friendship might be tried, however his love might be maligned, they would feel sure of him, and he would never fear an explanation. A firm foundation had been laid for an abiding relation between the Apostle and his Church. Learn, then, never to smooth away, through fear of results, the difficulties of love or friendship by concealment, or a subtle suppression of facts or feelings. Reprove, explain, submit with all gentleness, and yet with all truth and openness. The deadliest poison you can instil into the wine of life is a fearful reserve, which creates suspicion, or a lie, which will canker and kill your own love, and through that your friend's. The great blessings of this life are Friendship and Affection. Be sure that the only irreparable blight of both is falseness.

LECTURE L.

June 30, 1850.

2 Corinthians, vii. 9, 10. — "Now I rejoice, not that ye were made sorry, but that ye sorrowed to repentance: for ye were made sorry after a godly manner, that ye might receive damage by us in nothing. — For godly sorrow worketh repentance to salvation not to be repented of: but the sorrow of the world worketh death."

That which is chiefly insisted on in these verses, is the distinction between sorrow and repentance. To grieve over sin is one thing, to repent of it is another.

The Apostle rejoiced, not that the Corinthians sorrowed, but that they sorrowed unto repentance. Sorrow has two results; it may end in spiritual life, or in spiritual death; and, in themselves, one of these is as natural as the other. Sorrow may produce two kinds of reformation — a transient, or a permanent one — an alteration in habits, which, originating in emotion, will last so long as that emotion continues, and then, after a few fruitless efforts, be given up, — a repentance which will be repented of; or, again, a permanent change, which will be reversed by no after thought — a repentance not to be repented of. Sorrow is, in itself, therefore, a thing neither good nor bad: its value depends on the spirit of the person on whom it falls. Fire will inflame straw, soften iron, or harden clay: its effects are determined by the object with which it comes in contact. Warmth develops the energies of life, or helps the progress of decay. It is a great power in the hot-house, a great power also in the coffin; it expands the leaf, matures the fruit, adds precocious vigor to vegetable life: and warmth, too, develops, with tenfold rapidity, the weltering process of dissolution. So, too, with sorrow. There are spirits in which it develops the seminal principle of life; there are others, in which it prematurely hastens the consummation of irreparable decay. Our subject, therefore, is the twofold power of sorrow: —

I. The fatal power of the sorrow of the world.
II. The life-giving power of the sorrow that is after God.

I. The simplest way in which the sorrow of the world works death, is seen in the effect of mere regret for worldly loss. There are certain advantages with which we come into the world. Youth, health, friends, and sometimes property. So long as these are continued, we are happy; and because happy, fancy ourselves very grateful to God. We bask in the sunshine of His gifts, and this pleasant sensation of sunning ourselves in life, we call religion; that state in which we all are before sorrow comes, to test the temper of the metal of which our souls are made, when the spirits are unbroken and the heart buoyant, when a fresh morning is to a young heart what it is to the skylark. The exuberant burst of joy seems a spontaneous hymn to the Father of all blessing, like the matin carol of the bird; but this is not religion: it is the instinctive utterance of happy feeling, having as little of moral character in it, in the happy human being, as in the happy bird. Nay more — the religion, which is only sunned into being by happiness, is a suspicious thing: having been warmed by joy, it will become cold when joy is over; and then, when these blessings are removed, we count ourselves hardly treated, as if we had been defrauded of a right; rebellious, hard feelings come; then it is you see people become bitter, spiteful, discontented. At every step in the solemn path of life, something must be mourned which will come back no more; the temper that was so smooth becomes rugged and uneven; the benevolence that expanded upon all, narrows into an ever dwindling selfishness — we are alone; and then that death-like loneliness deepens as life goes on. The course of man is downwards, and he moves with slow and ever more solitary steps, down to the dark silence — the silence of the grave. This is the death of heart; the sorrow of the world has worked death.

Again, there is a sorrow of the world, when sin is grieved for in a worldly spirit. There are two views of sin: in one it is looked upon as wrong; in the other, as producing loss; loss, for example, of character. In such cases, if character could be preserved before the world, grief would not come: but the paroxysms of misery fall upon our proud spirit, when our guilt is made public. The most distinct instance we have of this is in the life of Saul. In the midst of his apparent grief, the thing still uppermost was, that he had forfeited his kingly character: almost the only longing was, that Samuel should honor him before his people. And hence it comes to pass, that often remorse and anguish only begin with exposure. Suicide takes place, not when the act of wrong is done, but when the guilt is known; and hence, too, many a one becomes hardened, who would otherwise have remained tolerably happy; in consequence of which we blame the exposure, not the guilt; we say, if it had hushed up, all would have been well; that the servant who robbed his master, was ruined by taking away his character; and that if the sin had been passed over, repentance might have taken place, and he might have remained a respectable member of society. Do not think so. It is quite true that remorse was produced by exposure, and that the remorse was fatal; the sorrow which worked death arose from that exposure, and so far exposure may be called the cause: had it never taken place, respectability, and comparative peace, might have continued; but outward respectability is not change of heart.

It is well known that the corpse has been preserved for centuries in the iceberg, or in antiseptic peat; and that when atmospheric air was introduced to the exposed surface it crumbled into dust. Exposure worked dissolution, but it only manifested the death which was already there; so with sorrow: it is not the living heart which drops to pieces, or crumbles into dust, when it is revealed. Exposure did not work death in the Corinthian sinner, but life.

There is another form of grief for sin, which the Apostle would not have rejoiced to see; it is when the hot tears come from pride. No two tones of feeling, apparently similar, are more unlike than that in which Saul exclaimed, "I have played the fool exceedingly," and that in which the Publican cried out, "God be merciful to me a sinner." The charge of folly brought against oneself, only proves that we feel bitterly for having lost our own self-respect. It is a humiliation to have forfeited the idea which a man had formed of his own character — to find that the very excellence on which he prided himself, is the one in which he has failed. If there were a virtue for which Saul was conspicuous, it was generosity; yet it was exactly in this point of generosity in which he discovered himself to have failed, when he was overtaken on the mountain, and his life spared by the very man whom he was hunting to the death, with feelings of the meanest jealousy. Yet there was no real repentance there; there was none of that in which a man is sick of state and pomp. Saul could still rejoice in regal splendor, go about complaining of himself to the Ziphites, as if he was the most ill-treated and friendless of mankind; he was still jealous of his reputation, and anxious to be well thought of. Quite different is the tone in which the Publican, who felt himself a sinner, asked for mercy. He heard the contumelious expression of the Pharisee, "this Publican," with no resentment; he meekly bore it as a matter naturally to be taken for granted — "he did not so much as lift up his eyes to heaven;" he was as a worm which turns in agony, but not revenge, upon the foot which treads it into the dust.

Now this sorrow of Saul's, too, works death: no merit can restore self-respect; when once a man has found himself out, he cannot be deceived again. The heart is as a stone: a speck of canker corrodes and spreads within. What on this earth remains, but endless sorrow, for him who has ceased to respect himself, and has no God to turn to?

II. The divine power of sorrow.

1. It works repentance. By repentance is meant, in Scripture, change of life, alteration of habits, renewal of heart. This is the aim and meaning of all sorrow. The consequences of sin are meant to wean from sin. The penalty annexed to it is, in the first instance, corrective, not penal. Fire burns the child, to teach it one of the truths of this universe — the property of fire to burn. The first time it cuts its hand with a sharp knife, it has gained a lesson which it never will forget. Now, in the case of pain, this experience is seldom, if ever, in vain. There is little chance of a child forgetting that fire will burn, and that sharp steel will cut; but the moral lessons contained in the penalties annexed to wrong-doing are just as truly intended, though they are by no means so unerring in enforcing their application. The fever in the veins and the headache which succeed intoxication, are meant to warn against excess. On the first occasion they are simply corrective; in every succeeding one they assume more and more a penal character, in proportion as the conscience carries with them the sense of ill desert.

Sorrow, then, has done its work, when it deters from evil; in other words, when it works repentance. In the sorrow of the world, the obliquity of the heart towards evil is not cured; it seems as if nothing cured it; heart-ache and trials come in vain; the history of life at last, is what it was at first. The man is found erring, where he erred before. The same course, begun with the certainty of the same desperate end which has taken place so often before.

They have reaped the whirlwind, but they will again sow the wind. Hence, I believe, that life-giving sorrow is less remorse for that which is irreparable, than anxiety to save that which remains. The sorrow that ends in death hangs in funereal weeds over the sepulchres of the past. Yet the present does not become more wise. Not one resolution is made more firm, nor one habit more holy. Grief is all. Whereas sorrow avails *only* when the past is converted into experience, and from failure lessons are learned which never are to be forgotten.

2. Permanence of alteration; for, after all, a steady reformation is a more decisive test of the value of mourning than depth of grief.

The susceptibility of emotion varies with individuals. Some men feel intensely, others suffer less keenly; but this is constitutional, belonging to nervous temperament, rather than moral character. *This* is the characteristic of the divine sorrow, that it is a repentance "not repented of;" no transient, short-lived resolutions, but sustained resolve.

And the beautiful law is, that in proportion as the repentance increases the grief diminishes. "I rejoice," says Paul, that "I made you sorry, though it were *but for a time.*" Grief for a time, repentance for ever. And few things more signally prove the wisdom of this Apostle, than his way of dealing with this grief of the Corinthian. He tried no artificial means of intensifying it — did not urge the duty of dwelling upon it, magnifying it, nor even of gauging and examining it. So soon as grief had done its work, the Apostle was anxious to dry useless tears — he even feared "lest haply such an one should be swallowed up with overmuch sorrow." "A true penitent," says Mr. Newman, "never forgives himself." O false estimate of the gospel of Christ, and of the heart of man! A proud remorse does not forgive itself the forfeiture of its own dignity; but it is the very beauty of the penitence which is according to God, that at last the sinner, realizing God's forgiveness, does learn to forgive himself. For what other purpose did St. Paul command the Church of Corinth to give ecclesiastical absolution, but in order to afford a symbol and assurance of the Divine pardon, in which the guilty man's grief should not be overwhelming, but that he should become reconciled to himself? What is meant by the Publican's going *down to his house* justified, but that he felt at peace with himself and God?

3. It is sorrow with God — here called "godly sorrow:" in the margin, "sorrowing according to God."

God sees sin not in its consequences, but in itself; a thing infinitely evil, even if the consequences were happiness to the guilty instead of misery. So sorrow according to God, is to see sin as God sees it. The grief of Peter was as bitter as that of Judas. He went out and wept bitterly; how bitterly none can tell but they who have learned to look on sin as God does. But in Peter's grief there was an element of hope; and that sprung precisely from this — that he saw God in it all. Despair of self did not lead to despair of God.

This is the great, peculiar feature of this sorrow; God is there, accordingly self is less prominent. It is not a microscopic self-examination, nor a mourning in which self is ever uppermost; *my* character gone; the greatness of *my* sin; the forfeiture of *my* salvation. The thought of God absorbs all that. I believe the feeling of true penitence would express itself in such words as these: — There *is* a righteousness, though I have not attained it. There is a purity and a love, and a beauty, though my life exhibits little of it. In that I can rejoice. Of that I can feel the surpassing loveliness. My doings? They are worthless, I cannot endure to think of them. I am not thinking of them. I have something else to think of. There, there; in that Life I see it. And so the Christian — gazing not on what he is, but on what he desires to be — dares in penitence to say, That righteousness is mine: dares, even when the recollection of his sin is most vivid and most poignant, to say with Peter, thinking less of himself than of God, and sorrowing as it were with God — "Lord, Thou knowest all things, Thou knowest that I love Thee."

LECTURE LI.

1853.

2 CORINTHIANS, vii. 11–16. — "For behold this selfsame thing, that ye sorrowed after a godly sort, what carefulness it wrought in you, yea, what clearing of yourselves, yea, what indignation, yea, what fear, yea, what vehement desire, yea, what zeal, yea, what revenge! In all things ye have approved yourselves to be clear in this matter. — Wherefore, though I wrote unto you, I did it not for his cause that had done the wrong, nor for his cause that suffered wrong, but that our care for you in the sight of God might appear unto you. — Therefore we were comforted in your comfort: yea, and exceedingly the more joyed we for the joy of Titus, because his spirit was refreshed by you all. — For if I have boasted anything to him of you, I am not ashamed; but as we spake all things to you in truth, even so our boasting, which I made before Titus, is found a truth. — And his inward affection is more abundant toward you, whilst he remembereth the obedience of you all, how with fear and trembling ye received him. — I rejoice therefore that I have confidence in you in all things."

TO-DAY we touch upon the last of those notices respecting St. Paul's treatment of the incestuous Corinthian, which have so repeatedly interwoven themselves with the argument of the First and Second Epistles. The general subject has successively brought before us the nature of human punishment, as not being merely reformatory, nor exemplary, nor for safety's sake, but also as being declarative of the indignation of society, and through society, of the indignation of God against sin. Again, it has taught us to consider excommunication and absolution, and what these ecclesiastical words express; and also to consider the power of binding and loosing lodged in Humanity — an actual and awful power, often used with fearful injustice and evil results: as when a person, cut off for ever from return, is driven to despair, "swallowed up with overmuch sorrow." Now these are real powers, dispute as men may about the ecclesiastical meaning to be given to them.

Every one daily, and often unconsciously, exercises them: and to do this rightly is no easy task: for it is difficult to punish wisely, and it is equally difficult to forgive wisely. It is rare even that we rebuke in a true and prudent spirit. Hence, the whole history of St. Paul's dealing with this offender is one of exceeding value, being so full of wisdom, firmness, justice, and exquisite tenderness. Most truly it is an inexhaustible subject!

The portion of it which we shall consider to-day, is the Christian manner of rebuke. We take two points:—

I. The spirit of apostolical rebuke.
II. The apostolical doctrine of repentance.

I. The spirit of apostolical rebuke.

First: It was marked by unflinching severity: "I do not repent; ... for I perceive that the same epistle hath made you sorry, though it were but for a season. Now I rejoice, not that ye were made sorry, but that ye sorrowed to repentance: for ye were made sorry after a godly manner, that ye might receive damage by us in nothing." St. Paul rejoiced then, in the pain he had inflicted: his censure had not been weak: severely, truthfully he had rebuked. Let us inquire the reason of this joy. St. Paul rejoiced because the pain was transitory, while the good was permanent; because the sorrow was for a time, but the blessing for ever; because the suffering was in this world, but the salvation for eternity: for the sinner had been delivered to "Satan for the destruction of the flesh, that the spirit may be saved in the day of the Lord Jesus." The criminal had undergone public shame and public humiliation; his had been private grief, and many searchings of heart; and all this had not only taught him a lesson, which never could be forgotten, and strengthened him by terrible discipline against future weakness, but also had set up for the Corinthians a higher standard, and vindicated the purity of Christian life and the dignity of the Christian Church. This was the pain, and these were its results. Seeing these results, St. Paul steadily contemplated the necessary suffering.

Let us now infer from this a great truth — the misfortune of non-detection. They who have done wrong congratulate themselves upon not being found out. Boys sin by disobedience; men commit crimes against society: and their natural impulse is to hush all up, and if what they have done is undiscovered, to consider it a happy escape. Now the worst misfortune that can happen is to sin, and to escape detection; shame and sorrow do God's work, as nothing else can do it. We can readily conceive that, if this shame and scandal had been hushed up, then the offender would have thought it a fortunate escape, and sinned again. A sin undetected is the soil out of which fresh sin will grow. Somehow, like a bullet wound, the extraneous evil *must* come out in the face of day, be *found* out, or else be acknowledged by confession. I do not say it should be disclosed publicly. It suffices if a few — or even one person only — have known it, and then condemned and absolved the offender.

Let me ask, then, who here is congratulating himself, is whispering to his own heart, My sin is not known, I shall not be disgraced, nor punished? Think you, that because undetected, you will escape with impunity? No — never! Your sin is there rankling in your heart: your wound is not probed, but only healed over falsely; and it will break out in the future, more corrupted, and more painful than before.

Secondly: The Apostle's rebuke was marked by the desire of doing good. It is a thing common enough to be severe. We are severe enough on one another, both in our view of public punishment and in our condemnation of one another's faults. But the question is, What is at the bottom of this zeal? It is no rare thing to find men who can be severe in rebuke: but the thing which is uppermost is evidently themselves — their own fidelity, courage, and truthfulness. They tell you of your faults, but you feel it is not your reformation, but their own vain-glory they are trying to secure. Now St. Paul was not thinking of himself, but of the Corinthians. This is manifest from several verses in this chapter. Take the ninth verse: "That ye might receive damage by us in nothing;" or the eleventh: "In all things ye have approved yourselves to be clear in this matter;" or the sixteenth: "I rejoice, therefore, that I have confidence in you in all things." The Apostle was not delivering his own soul, but he was trying to save their souls.

Let us, therefore, examine ourselves. We blame, and find fault, and pass judgment upon our neighbor freely; we boldly condemn public men. Why is this? Is it to show to ourselves, and others, how good we are — how we cannot abide sin? or is it to do good? It is often a duty to express disapprobation strongly and severely, to discountenance vice most earnestly; but then we do it not in St. Paul's spirit, unless it is done for the sake of amelioration.

Thirdly: The Apostle's rebuke was marked by a spirit of justice. We refer to the twelfth verse: "Wherefore, though I wrote unto you, I did it not for his cause that had done the wrong, nor for his cause that suffered wrong, but that our care for you in the sight of God might appear unto you." That is, his interference was not partisanship. There was in it no taking of a side, no espousing the cause of the injured, nor *mere* bitterness against the criminal: but a holy, godly zeal, full of indignation, but not of vindictiveness. In one word, it was Justice. Now this is exactly what some of the best amongst us find most difficult — those especially of us who possess quick, sensitive, right, and generous feelings. We can be charitable, we can be indignant, we can forgive; but we are not just. Especially is this the case with women: the natural sensitiveness and quick nature of their feelings, particularly in their conceptions of right and wrong, hinder them from looking at things calmly enough to judge correctly Again: this justice is most difficult when religious interests are involved: as, for example, in the quarre between the Roman Catholic and the Protestant, who judges fairly? To be just is not easy: for many qualities go to make up justice. It is founded on forbearance, self-control, patience to examine both sides, and freedom from personal passion.

Fourthly: St. Paul's rebuke was marked by joyful sympathy in the restoration of the erring. Very beautiful is the union of the hearts of Paul and Titus in joy over the recovered—joy as of the angels in heaven over "one sinner that repenteth."

II. The apostolic doctrine of repentance.

St. Paul rejoiced because the Corinthians sorrowed: but in doing so, he carefully distinguished the kind of sorrow which he rejoiced to have caused. In order to follow him, we must see what different kinds of sorrow there are.

1. The sorrow of the world, which is not desirable, because it is *of* the world. There is an anxiety about loss, about the consequences of mis-doing, about a ruined reputation, about a narrowed sphere of action. Now sin brings all these things; but to sorrow for them is not to sorrow before God. To sorrow for such things is only a worldly grief, because it is only about worldly things. Observe, therefore, that pain, simply as pain, does no good; that sorrow, merely as sorrow, has in it no magical efficacy: shame may harden into effrontery, punishment may rouse into defiance. Again, pain self-inflicted does no good. It is a great error when men, perceiving that God's natural penalties and hardships strengthen and purify the spirit, think to attain to a similar good by forcing such penalties and hardships upon themselves.

It is true that fire, borne for the sake of Truth, is martyrdom; but the hand burnt in ascetic severity does not give the crown of martyrdom, nor even inspire the martyr's feeling. Fastings, such as St. Paul bore from inability to get food, give spiritual strength; but fastings endured for mere exercise, often do no more than produce feverishness of temper. This holds good, likewise, of bereavement. The loss of those dear to us — relations and friends — when it is borne as coming from God, has the effect of strengthening and purifying the character. But to bring sorrow wilfully upon ourselves, can be of no avail towards improvement. The difference between these two things lies in this, that when God inflicts the blow, He gives the strength: but when you give it to yourself, God does not promise aid. Be sure this world has enough of the Cross in it: you need not go out of your way to seek it. Be sure there will always be enough of humiliation and shame, and solitariness for each man to bear if he be living the Christ-life. They need not be self-inflicted.

2. The sorrow of this world is not desirable, because it "works death;" and this it does in two ways, literally and figuratively. And first, literally. We do not need instances to show that there is nothing like wearing sorrow to shorten life. Death from a broken heart is not uncommon; and when this is not the case, how often have we seen that the days of existence are abridged, the hair grows gray, all the fresh springs of being are dried up, and all the vigor and force of brain and life decay! When the terror of sorrow came on Nabal, his heart became as a stone, and died within him, and in ten days all was over. When the evil tidings came from the host of Israel, the heart of the wife of Phinehas broke beneath her grief, and in a few hours death followed her bereavement.

Figuratively, too, the sorrow of this world "works death:" for grief, unalloyed with hope, kills the soul, and man becomes powerless in a protracted sorrow, where hope in God is not. The mind will not work; it feels no vigor; there is no desire to succeed, no impulse to undertake, for the spirit of enterprise and the eagerness in action are over and gone for ever. The zest of existence is no more: "the wine of life is drawn." Hours, days, and years drag on in feeling's sickly mood; and the only things which pass not away are melancholy and uselessness, now become "the habit of the soul."

Once more: The sorrow of this world "works death" spiritually. Grief works death. It is a fearful thing to see how some men are made worse by trial. It is terrible to watch sorrow as it sours the temper, and works out into malevolence and misanthropy. Opposition makes them proud and defiant. Blow after blow falls on them, and they bear all in the hardness of a sullen silence.

Such a man was Saul, the first king of Israel, whose earlier career was so bright and glorious; to whom all that lay before and around him, seemed only to augur happiness. These all gradually darkened, and a something was at work at the heart of his life. Defeat and misfortune gradually soured his temper, and made him bitter and cruel. The fits of moody grief became more frequent, and then came, quickly, sin on sin, and woe on woe. Jealousy passed into disobedience, and insanity into suicide. The sorrow of the world had "worked death."

The second kind of sorrow we mentioned is godly sorrow, and we will consider: first, its marks; secondly, its results.

1. Its marks.—First: Over these we shall run rapidly. Moral earnestness, which is here, in the eleventh verse, called "carefulness." My brethren, the one difficulty in life is to be in earnest. All this world, in the gala day, seems but a passing, unreal show. We dance, light-hearted, along the ways of existence, and nothing tells us that the earth is hollow to our tread. But soon some deep grief comes, and shocks us into reality; the solid earth rocks beneath our feet: the awfulness of life meets us face to face in the desert. Then the value of things is seen; then it is that godly sorrow produces carefulness; then it is that, like Jacob, we cry, "How awful is this place! how solemn is this life! This is none other but the house of God, and this is the gate of heaven!" Then it is that, with moral earnestness, we set forth — walking circumspectly, weighing, with a watchful and sober eye, all the acts and thoughts which make up life.

Next, this godly sorrow "worketh fear:" not an unworthy terror, but the opposite of that light recklessness which lives only from day to day. Again, it worketh "vehement desire," that is, affection; for true sorrow — sorrow to God — softens, not hardens the soul. It opens sympathies, for it teaches what others suffer; it gives a deeper power of sympathy and consolation, for only through suffering can you win the godlike ability of feeling for other's pain. It expands affection, for your sorrow makes you accordant with the "still sad music" of humanity. A true sorrow is that "deep grief which humanizes the soul;" often out of it comes that late remorse of love, which leads us to arise and go to our Father, and say, "I have sinned against Heaven and in Thy sight."

Again, "clearing of themselves," that is, anxiety about character. Some one has said, that "to justify one's deeds unto oneself is the last infirmity of evil;" he means, that when we cease to do that, then evil is strong: for as long as a man excuses himself, there is hope. He has, at least, a standard of right and wrong still left. Now there is a recklessness of grief for sin, out of which a man wakes when he begins to feel hope, and tries to wipe off the past, when, in St. Paul's words, a godly sorrow urges him to *clear* himself.

Lastly, it is a sorrow which produces "revenge." We interpret this as indignation against wrong in others and in ourselves. Nowhere is this more remarkable than in David's Psalms; and though these are personal, yet still the feeling which gave them birth is a deep and true one, without which all goodness is but feebleness.

These, together, make up repentance unto salvation.

Finally, the results: 1. "Not to be repented of." 2. "Sorrow's memory is sorrow still." No! not *that* sorrow. No man ever mourned over the time spent in tears for sin. No man ever looked back upon that healing period of his life as time lost. No man ever regretted things given up or pleasures sacrificed for

God's sake. No man on his dying bed ever felt a pang for the suffering sin had brought on him, if it had led him in all humbleness to Christ. No man ever regretted the agony of conquest, when he felt the weight upon his heart to be less through sorrow even by a single sin. But how many a man on his death-bed has felt the recollection of guilty pleasures as the serpent's fang and venom in his soul!

LECTURE LII.

1853.

2 Corinthians, viii. 1-12. — "Moreover, brethren, we do you to wit of the grace of God bestowed on the churches of Macedonia; — How that in a great trial of affliction the abundance of their joy and their deep poverty abounded unto the riches of their liberality. — For to their power, I bear record, yea, and beyond their power they were willing of themselves; — Praying us with much entreaty that we would receive the gift, and take upon us the fellowship of the ministering to the saints. — And this they did, not as we hoped, but first gave their own selves to the Lord, and unto us by the will of God. — Insomuch that we desired Titus, that as he had begun, so he would also finish in you the same grace also. — Therefore, as ye abound in everything, in faith, and utterance, and knowledge, and in all diligence, and in your love to us, see that ye abound in this grace also. — I speak not by commandment, but by occasion of the forwardness of others, and to prove the sincerity of your love. — For ye know the grace of our Lord Jesus Christ, that, though he was rich, yet for your sakes he became poor, that ye through his poverty might be rich. — And herein I give my advice: for this is expedient for you, who have begun before, not only to do, but also to be forward a year ago. — Now therefore perform the doing of it; that as there was a readiness to will, so there may be a performance also out of that which ye have. — For if there be first a willing mind, it is accepted according to that a man hath, and not according to that he hath not."

In the last chapter of the First Epistle mention was made of a contribution which the Corinthians were systematically to store up for the poor brethren at Jerusalem. To-day we enter on a fresh treatment of the same topic, and on a subject different from those we have lately been engaged with. This contribution St. Paul collected in his journeys from the Christian Churches. In this chapter he records the largeness of the sum which had been given him by the Churches of Macedonia, and urges the Church of Corinth to emulate their example.

We consider two points: —

I. Nature of Christian liberality.
II. Motives urged on the Corinthians.

I. Nature of Christian liberality as exemplified in that of the Churches of Macedonia. First, it was a grace bestowed from God: — "Moreover, brethren, we do you to wit of the grace of God bestowed on the churches of Macedonia" (v. 1). And again: "Insomuch that we desired Titus, that as he had begun, so he would also finish in you the same grace also" (v. 6).

Now there are many reasons besides this mentioned by St. Paul, which make liberality desirable. For example, there is utility. By liberality hospitals are supported, missions are established, social disorders are partially healed. But St. Paul does not take the utilitarian ground; though in its way it is a true one. Again, he does not take another ground advanced by some; — that liberality is merely for the advantage of the persons relieved: "For I mean not that other men be eased, and ye burdened" (v. 13): as if the benefit of the poor were the main end; as if God cared for the poor, and not for the rich; as if to get from those who have, and bestow on those who have not, were the object of inciting to liberality. St. Paul distinctly denies this. He takes the higher ground: it is a grace of God. He contemplates the benefit to the soul of the giver. Charity is useful, but also *lovely:* not a mere engine in our nature to work for social purposes, but that which is likest God in the soul.

Secondly: Christian liberality was the work of a willing mind: For if there be first a willing mind, it is accepted according to that a man hath, and not according to that he hath not" (v. 12). Plainly, it is not the value of the contribution, but the love of the contributor, which makes it precious. The offering is sanctified, or made unholy in God's sight, by the spirit in which it is given. The most striking passage in which this truth is illustrated is that of the widow's mite. Tried by the gauge of the treasurer of a charity, it was next to nothing. Tried by the test of Charity, it was more than that of all. Her coins, worthless in the eyes of the rich Pharisee, were in the eyes of Christ transformed by her love into the gold of the Eternal City.

Yet St. Paul does not say that a willing mind is all. He makes a wise addition: "Now therefore perform the *doing* of it." Because, true though it is that willingness is accepted where the means are not, yet where the means *are*, willingness is only tested by performance. Good feelings, good sentiments, charitable intentions, are only condensed in sacrifice. Test yourself by action: test your feelings and your fine liberal words by self-denial. Do not let life evaporate in slothful sympathies. You wish you were rich: and fancy that then you would make the poor happy, and spend your life in blessing? Now — now is the time — now or never. Habituate your heart to acts of giving. Habituate your spirit to the thought, that in all lives something is owed to God. Neglect this now, and you will not practise it more when rich. Charity is a habit of the soul, therefore now is the time. Let it be said, "He hath done what he *could*."

Thirdly: The outpouring of poverty (v. 2). As it was in the time of the Apostle, so it is now. It was the poor widow who gave all. It was out of their deep poverty that the Macedonians were rich in liberality. There is something awful in those expressions of Scripture which speak of riches as shutting up the soul. "It is easier," said Christ, "for a camel to go through the eye of a needle, than for a rich man to enter into the kingdom of God:" "Not many mighty, not many noble are called," writes St. Paul. Again: "Woe unto you that are rich! for ye have received your consolation." Now we do not expect these sayings to be believed: they are explained away. No man *fears* riches. Yet it is a fact, generally, that a man's liberality does not increase in proportion as he grows rich. It is exactly the reverse. He extends his desires; luxuries become necessaries. He must move in another sphere, keep more servants, and take a larger house. And so, in the end, his liberality becomes proportionately less than what it was before. Let any one who has experienced an advance of wealth compare his expenditure when he had but a few annual pounds, with his expenditure after he became rich. Let any one compare the sums given in charity by those of moderate income with the sums given by the wealthy. Here, in England, the rich give their hundreds, the poor their thousands. There are many things to account for this fact. The rich have large liabilities to meet: or they possess large establishments which must be kept up. There is a growing sense of money's value, when each sovereign stands for so much time. Still, whatever may be the mitigating circumstances, the fact remains. And the inferences from it are two: —

1. Let this circumstance be a set-off against poverty and privations. God has made charity easier to you who are not the rich of this world, and saved you from many a sore temptation. It is written, "Better is a dinner of herbs where *love* is, than a stalled ox and hatred therewith."

2. Let this fact weaken the thirst for riches, which is the great longing of our day: "The wealthiest man among us is the best." Doubtless riches are a good; but remember that the Bible, if it be true, is full of warnings respecting them. Think alone of this one: "They that *will* be rich fall into temptation and a snare."

Fourthly: It is a peculiarity in Christian liberality that it is exhibited to strangers. In the case before us, the charity was displayed in behalf of the poor at Jerusalem, and was a contribution sent from Gentiles to Jews. Love of Christ, then, had bridged over that gulf of ancient hatred. The Spirit of Christ had been given in these words: "If ye love them which love you, what reward have ye? do not even the publicans the same? And if ye salute your brethren only, what do ye more than others?" "But I say unto you, Love your enemies, do good to them that hate you." The power of these words, ratified by a Life, had spread through the ancient Church, and Gentile, and Jew were united to each other by a common love.

Now, I say, there is nothing but Christianity which can do this. Without Christ, there must be dissension between race and race, family and family, man and man. Think of the old rancors of the heathen world. This spirit of dissension was the great question of ancient ages, and was the origin of their wars. In times before the Dorian was matched against the Ionian, the Samaritan hated the Jew; and the Jew shrank from the pollution of the Samaritan, and looked on the Gentile as an outcast; until He came, who "is our Peace, who hath made both one, and hath broken down the middle wall of partition."

But, it is said, philanthropy does this. Philanthropy! It is a dream without Christ. Why should I love the negro or the foreigner? You can give no reason except an opinion. Why should I not be as exclusive as I please, and shrink from other nations, and keep up national hatreds, when even the analogy of nature is on my side, and I see the other inhabitants of this planet waging war on one another, bird with bird, beast with beast? Well, in reply to that, Christianity reveals in Christ the truth which lies below our human nature — GOD. We are one in Christ — one Family. Human blessedness is impossible except through union one with another. But union is impossible except in GOD.

This was the truth taught by the shew-bread piled upon the altar. Each loaf was offered for, and represented a tribe: and the whole twelve, with different characteristics and various interests, were yet one in God, and therefore one with each other. And this truth was realized in Christ, in whom all the tribes of the world and all the opposing elements of society meet and mingle. We have an altar whereof they have no right to eat that serve the tabernacle.

These are the main characteristics of Christian liberality. But observe, this liberality is not necessarily the giving of money. Almsgiving is recommended in the Bible, but it is not necessarily the true form now in our altered state of things. For indiscriminate almsgiving is injurious both to the giver and the receiver: to the giver, as it encourages indolence; to the receiver, as it prevents independence and exertion. Again, remember there may be true liberality, when a man gives nothing to religious societies. Suppose he spends his money in employing labor wisely, suppose he gives good wages, suppose he invests capital in enterprises which call out the highest qualities — then such a man, although directly giving nothing, indirectly gives much, and is charitable in the true sense of the word.

II. Motives to Christian liberality.

1. Christian completeness (v. 7). The Corinthians were orthodox; they had strong convictions of the liberty of Christianity. Gifts of eloquence abounded in the Church; they were deeply grounded in truth: they were active in thought and active in work — nay more, they had much zeal and love for their teachers; and yet, without this liberality, their Christianity would have been most incomplete: "As ye abound in everything, in faith, and utterance, and knowledge, and in all diligence, and in your love to us, see that ye abound in this grace also." The same idea is fully worked out in the thirteenth chapter of the First Epistle. Moreover, this verse exhibits the true conception of Christianity: It is not a set of views, nor is it faith, nor devotional feeling: but it is *completeness* of Humanity. We are to grow up in the knowledge of Christ, till we *all* come in the unity of the faith and of the knowledge of the Son of God to perfect *men* — to the "measure of the stature and fulness of Christ. Again, St. Paul says: "This also we wish, even your perfection:" and to the Thessalonians: "I pray God your whole spirit, and soul, and body be preserved blameless." And Christ places this high standard before His disciples as their aim: "Be ye therefore perfect, even as your Father which is in Heaven is perfect." For it is the work of Christ to take the whole man, and present him a living sacrifice to God.

2. Another motive of Christian liberality is emula-

tion. Compare verses one to eight of this chapter, and also the eleventh chapter of *Romans*, at the eleventh verse. Observe here the truth of Scripture. Ordinary, feeble philanthropy would say, "Emulation is dangerous." Cowper calls it parent of envy, hatred, jealousy, and pride. Yet there is such a feeling as emulation in our nature, and the Bible says it has a meaning; nay, is not wrong, but in its place a true and right affection of Humanity. So St. Paul here took advantage of this feeling. The Macedonian Church had raised the standard of Christian liberality high, and the Corinthians are stimulated not to fall below that standard.

But had the Apostle said, "Be not beaten by those Macedonians" — had he called natural prejudices into play — a Corinthian to yield to a Macedonian! then all the evil passions of our nature had been stimulated. In giving largely the Corinthians would have learned to hate the Macedonians; and to give more for the sake of triumphing over them, Instead of this, St. Paul exhibits the Macedonians as worthy of admiration, and exhorts the Corinthians to enter the lists in honorable rivalry. Herein, I believe, lies the difference: Emulation, meaning a desire to outstrip individuals, is a perverted feeling; emulation, meaning a desire to reach and pass a standard, is a true feeling — the parent of all progress and of all excellence. Hence set before you high models. Try to live with the most generous, and to observe their deeds. Unquestionably, good men set the *standard* of life.

3. The last motive alleged is the example of Christ (ver. 9). Here we must observe, first, that Christ is the reference for everything. To Christ's Life and Christ's Spirit St. Paul refers all questions, both practical and speculative, for a solution. For all our mysterious human life refers itself back to Him. Christ's Life is the measure of the world. Observe, again, it is in spirit, and not in letter, that Christ is our example. The Corinthians were asked to give money for a special object; and Christ is brought forward as their example. But Christ did not give money, He gave Himself. His

riches were perfect happiness; His poverty was humiliation; and He humbled Himself, that we, through His poverty, might be made rich. He gave Himself to bless the world. This, then, is the example; and it is the spirit of that example which the Corinthians are urged to imitate.

It was *giving*, it was Love that was the essence of the Sacrifice. The form was a secondary thing. It was Life in His case, it was money in theirs; the one thing needful was a love like His, which was the desire to give, and to bless.

LECTURE LIII.

1853.

2 CORINTHIANS, viii. 13-15. — "For I mean not that other men be eased, and ye burdened; — But by an equality, that now at this time your abundance may be a supply for their want, that their abundance also may be a supply for your want: that there may be equality: — As it is written, He that had gathered much had nothing over; and he that had gathered little had no lack."

THE eighth chapter of the Second Epistle to the Corinthians, the latter part of which we enter on to-day, concerns a contribution collected by St. Paul from the Gentile Christians for the Jewish Christians at Jerusalem. Part of this we have already expounded, namely, as regards the nature of Christian liberality, and the motives on which St. Paul urged it. But there still remain several points which we had not time to consider in the last lecture, and which are, nevertheless, only a continuation of the same subject.

Christian charity, we saw, was a "grace" of God, not merely useful, but also beautiful. We found it a thing whose true value is measured not by the amount given, but by the willingness of heart of the giver. We learnt also that it springs up in the soil of poverty, rather than in that of wealth.

We considered, further, two motives on which St. Paul urges it: — 1. Christian completeness. 2. Christian emulation. To-day we take two points more:

I. The spirit in which he urged Christian liberality.
II. The additional motives which he brought to bear.

I. The Apostle spoke strongly; not in the way of coercion, but of counsel and persuasion. In the eighth verse he says, "I speak not by commandment;" and again, in the tenth, "And herein I give my advice." Both expressions, taken together, mean simply: "I do not order this, I only advise it."

Now here is a peculiarity which belongs to the teaching of the Apostles. They never spoke as dictators, but only as counsellors. St. Peter says: "Neither as being lords over God's heritage." And St. Paul marks still more strongly the difference between the dictatorial authority of the priest, and the gentle helpfulness of the minister: "Not for that we have dominion over your faith, but are helpers of your joy." The Church of Rome practises a different system. There are two offices in that Church, director and confessor. It is the duty of the confessor to deal with guilt, to administer punishment and absolution; and it is the duty of the director to deal with action, to solve cases of difficulty, to prescribe duties, and to arrange the course of life. Rome has reduced this to a system, and a mighty system it is. For when the confessor and director have done their work, the man is wholly, Will and Conscience, bound over to the obedience of the Church. This is the righteousness at which Rome aims, to abrogate the individual will and conscience, and substitute the will and conscience of the Church. But, remember, I select Rome simply because Rome has reduced it to a *system*. Do not think it is confined to Rome; it belongs to human nature. There is not a minister or priest who is not exposed to the temptation which allures men to this practice, to try to be a confessor and director to his people, to guide their conscience, to rule their wills, and to direct their charities.

But obesrve how entirely alien this was from St. Paul's spirit. He of all men, the Apostle of liberty, *could* not have desired to bind men even to himself in subjection. He hated slavery: most of all, the slavery of mind and conscience; nay, he consoled the slave, because he was free in heart to Christ (1 Cor. vii, 21, 22).

According to the Apostle, then, a Christian was one who, perceiving principles, in the free spirit of Jesus Christ, applied these principles for himself. As examples of this, remember the spirit in which he excommunicated (1 Cor. v. 12, 13) and absolved(2 Cor. ii. 10):

and remark, in both these cases — where the priestly power would have been put forward, if anywhere — the entire absence of all aim at personal influence or authority. St. Paul would not even *command* Philemon to receive his slave (*Philemon*, 8, 9, 13, 14). And in the case before us he would not *order* the Corinthians to give, even to a charity which he reckoned an important one. He would never have been pleased to have had the naming of all their charities, and the marking out of all their acts. He wanted them to be men, and not dumb, driven cattle. That pliable, docile, slavish mind, which the priest loves and praises, the Apostle Paul would neither have praised nor loved.

II. Observe the spirit in which St. Paul appeals to the example of Christ (ver. 9). He urges the Corinthians to be liberal by the pattern of Christ. He places Him before them for imitation: but observe in what spirit he does it: —

1. Remark the tendency in the mind of St. Paul to refer everything back to Christ. Even when you least expect it; when there seems no similarity, he finds a precedent for every duty in some sentence or some act of Christ. For example, when the Apostle delivered his last charge to the weeping Church of Ephesus, he urged on them the duty of supporting the weak by loving labor, and enforced it thus: "I have showed you all things. How that so laboring ye ought to support the weak, and to remember the words of the Lord Jesus, how He said, It is more blessed to give than to receive." So in the case before us he is urging on the Church of Corinth to contribute money; and at once he recurs back to the example of Christ: "Ye know the grace of our Lord Jesus Christ, that, though He was rich, yet for our sakes He became poor, that ye through His poverty might be rich."

To a Christian mind Christ is all; the measure of all things: the standard and the reference. All things centre in Him. The life and death of Christ got by heart, not by rote, must be the rule for every act.

2. Remark, again, that St. Paul finds the parallel of Christian liberality, not in the literal acts, but in the Spirit of Christ. The liberality asked from the Corinthians, was the giving of money; the liberality of Christ, was the giving of Himself. Literally, there was no resemblance; but the spirit of both acts was the same: sacrifice was the law of both. In the act of giving money out of penury, the eagle eye of St. Paul discerns the same root principle — the spirit of the Cross — which was the essence of the Redeemer's sacrifice.

This is the true use of the Life of Christ; it is the *spirit* of that Life to which we should attain. It is not by saying Christ's words, or by doing Christ's acts, but it is by breathing His spirit, that we become like Him. For "if any man have not the spirit of Christ, he is none of His."

Let us observe the feeling with which St. Paul regarded Jesus, as we find it expressed in the ninth verse of this chapter. We cannot but remark how incompatible it is with the Socinian view of Christ's person. The doctrine taught by Socinianism was, that Christ was a mere man. The early followers of this creed held this doctrine on the authority of Scripture. They said, that the Apostles never taught that he was more than man; and they explained away all the passages in which the Apostles seemed to hint at the reverse. But here is a passage which defies misconstruction: "Though He *was* rich, yet for your sakes He became poor." When was Christ rich? Here on earth, never: He whose cradle was a manger, and for whom the rich provided a grave! There can be but one interpretation of the text. Christ was rich in that glory which He had with His Father before the world.

There can be no mistake about what St. Paul thought. We hold this passage to be decisive as to St. Paul's feeling. Nor can you say that this belief in Christ's Divinity was a dogma separable from St. Paul's Christianity; this belief *was* his Christianity. For the difference between what he was from the hour when he saw his Master in the sky, and what he had previously been, was exactly measured by the difference between the feeling with which he regarded Jesus, when he considered Him as an impostor to be crushed, and the feeling in which he devoted all the energies of his glorious nature to Him as his Lord and his God, whom to serve he felt was alone blessedness.

3. Again, in St. Paul's spirit of entreaty, we remark the desire of reciprocity (ver. 13, 14, 15). It might have been supposed that because St. Paul was a Jew, he was therefore anxious for his Jewish brethren; and that in urging the Corinthians to give liberally, even out of their poverty, he forgot the unfairness of the request, and was satisfied so long as only the Jews were relieved — it mattered not at whose expense. But, in answer to such a supposed reproach, the Apostle says, "I mean not that other men be eased, and ye burdened" — but I desire an *equality*, I ask that the rich may equalize his possessions with the poor. This is *now* a remarkable expression, because it is the watchword of Socialists. They cry out for equality in circumstances; and the Apostle says, "Let there be equality of circumstances." It is worth while to think of this.

The principle laid down is, that the abundance of the rich is intended for the supply of the poor; and the illustration of the principle is drawn from a miracle in the wilderness: "As it is written, He that had gathered much had nothing over: and he that had gathered little had no lack." Here, then, in the wilderness, by a miraculous arrangement, if any one through greediness gathered more manna than enough, it bred worms, and became offensive; and if through weakness, or deep sorrow, or pain, any were prevented from collecting enough, still what they had collected was found to be sufficient.

In this miracle, St. Paul perceives a great universal principle of human life. God has given to every man a certain capacity and a certain power of enjoyment. Beyond that he cannot find delight. Whatsoever he heaps or hoards beyond that, is not enjoyment, but disquiet. For example: If a man monopolizes to himself rest which should be shared by others, the result is unrest — the weariness of one on whom time hangs heavily. Again, if a man piles up wealth, all beyond a certain point becomes disquiet. Thus thought St. James: "Your gold and silver is cankered." You cannot escape the stringency of that law; he that gathereth much, hath nothing over. How strangely true is that old miracle! How well life teaches us that whatever is beyond enough breeds worms, and becomes offensive!

We can now understand why the Apostle desired equality, and what that equality was which he desired. Equality with him meant reciprocation — the feeling of a true and loving brotherhood; which makes each man feel, "My superabundance is not mine; it is another's: not to be taken by force, or wrung from me by law, but to be *given* freely by the law of love.

Observe, then, how Christianity would soon solve all questions. Take as instances: What are the rights of the poor? What are the duties of the rich? After how much does possession become superabundance? When has a man gathered too much? You cannot answer these questions by any science. Socialism cannot do it. Revolutions will try to do it, but they will only take from the rich and give to the poor; so that the poor become rich, and the rich poor, and we have inequality back again. But give us the Spirit of Christ. Let us all become Christians. Let us love as Christ loved. Give us the spirit of sacrifice which the early Church had, when no man said that ought of the things he possessed was his own; then each man's own heart will decide what is meant by gathering too much, and what is meant by Christian equality.

We shall answer all such questions when we comprehend the principle of this appeal: "Ye know the grace of our Lord Jesus Christ, that, though He was rich, yet for your sakes He became poor, that ye through His poverty might be rich."

LECTURE LIV.

MARCH, 1853.

2 CORINTHIANS, viii. 16-24. — "But thanks be to God, which put the same earnest care into the heart of Titus for you. — For indeed he accepted the exhortation; but being more forward, of his own accord he went unto you. — And we have sent with him the brother, whose praise is in the gospel throughout all the churches; — And not that only, but who was also chosen of the churches to travel with us with this grace, which is administered by us to the glory of the same Lord, and declaration of your ready mind: — Avoiding this, that no man should blame us in this abundance which is administered by us: — Providing for honest things, not only in the sight of the Lord, but also in the sight of men. — And we have sent with them our brother, whom we have oftentimes proved diligent in many things, but now much more diligent, upon the great confidence which I have in you. — Whether any do inquire of Titus, he is my partner and fellow-helper concerning you: or our brethren be inquired of, they are the messengers of the churches, and the glory of Christ. — Wherefore show ye to them, and before the churches, the proof of your love, and of our boasting on your behalf."

2 CORINTHIANS, ix. 1-15. — "For as touching the ministering to the saints, it is superfluous for me to write to you: — For I know the forwardness of your mind, for which I boast of you to them of Macedonia, that Achaia was ready a year ago; and your zeal hath provoked very many. — Yet have I sent the brethren, lest our boasting of you should be in vain in this behalf; that, as I said, ye may be ready: — Lest haply if they of Macedonia come with me, and find you unprepared, we (that we say not, ye) should be ashamed in this same confident boasting. — Therefore I thought it necessary to exhort the brethren, that they would go before unto you, and make up beforehand your bounty, whereof ye had notice before, that the same might be ready, as a matter of bounty, and not as of covetousness. — But this I say, He which soweth sparingly shall reap also sparingly; and he which soweth bountifully shall reap also bountifully. — Every man according as he purposeth in his heart, so let him give; not grudgingly, or of necessity: for God loveth a cheerful giver. — And God is able to make all grace abound toward you; that ye, always having all sufficiency in all things, may abound to every good work: — (As it is written, He hath dispersed abroad; he hath given to the poor: his righteousness remaineth for ever. — Now he that ministereth seed to the sower both minister bread for your food, and multiply your seed sown, and increase the fruits of your righteousness;) — Being enriched in everything to all bountifulness, which causeth through us thanksgiving to God. — For the

administration of this service not only supplieth the want of the saints, but is abundant also by many thanksgivings unto God ;—Whiles by the experiment of this ministration they glorify God for your professed subjection unto the gospel of Christ, and for your liberal distribution unto them, and unto all men ; — And by their prayer for you, which long after you for the exceeding grace of God in you. — Thanks be unto God for his unspeakable gift."

THE ninth chapter continues the subject of the collection for the poor Christians in Jerusalem, and with it we shall expound the close of the eighth chapter, which we left unfinished in our last lecture.

We take three points for consideration : —

I. The mode of collecting the contribution.
II. The measure of the amount.
III. The measure of the reward.

I. Mode of collection. St. Paul intrusted this task to three messengers : — to Titus, who was himself eager to go ; to a Christian brother whom the churches had selected as their almoner ; and to another, whose zeal had been tested frequently by St. Paul himself.

The reasons for sending these messengers are given in an apologetic explanation. The first was, to give the Corinthians time, in order that the appeal might not come at an inconvenient moment : "I have sent the brethren," writes St. Paul, "lest our boasting of you should be in vain on this behalf ; that, as I said, ye may be ready." Observe the tender wisdom of this proceeding. Every one knows how different is the feeling with which we give when charity is beforehand, from that with which we give when charitable collections come side by side with debts and taxes. The charity which finds us unprepared, is a call as hateful as that of any creditor whom it is hard to pay. St. Paul knew this well — he knew that if the Corinthians were taken unawares, their feelings would be exasperated towards him with shame, and also towards the saints at Jerusalem, to whom they were constrained to give. Therefore, he gave timely notice.

Again, he had sent to tell them of the coming of these messengers, in order to preserve their reputation for charity. For, if the Corinthians were not ready, their inability to pay would be exhibited before the Macedonian church, and before the messengers; and from this St. Paul wished to save them.

Observe here two points: — First, the just value which the Apostle set on Christian reputation. For the inability of the Corinthians to meet the demands made on them, would be like insolvency in mercantile phrase, and would damage their character. We all know how insolvency damages the *man*, how he feels humbled by it in his own sight, and "ashamed" before men. Such a man dare not look the collector or the creditor in the face; or, if he dare, it is through effrontery contracted by a habit which is hardened against shame: or, there are mean subterfuges which accustom the mind to the deceit it once hated: or, if there be none of these, or the man be too true or haughty to bend to such things, there are other sights and thoughts which tear a proud heart to pieces. In any way the man is injured by insolvency.

Secondly: Observe the delicacy of the mode in which the hint is given: "We (that we say not, ye) may not be ashamed." St. Paul makes it a matter of personal anxiety, as if the shame and fault of non-payment would be his. In this, there was no subtle policy; there was no attempt to get at their purses by their weak side. St. Paul was above such means. It was natural, instinctive, real delicacy; and yet it was the surest way of obtaining what he wished, and that which the deepest knowledge of the human heart would have counselled. For thereby he appealed not to their selfish, but to their most unselfish feelings: he appealed to their gratitude, their generosity, to everything which was noble or high within them. The Corinthians would feel — We can bear the shame of delinquency ourselves, but we cannot bear that Paul should be disgraced. This is a great principle — one of the deepest you can have for life and action. Appeal to the high est motives, appeal whether they be there or no, for you make them where you do not find them. Arnold trusted his boys, avowing that he believed what they affirmed, and all attempt at deceiving him ceased forthwith. When Christ appealed to the love in the heart of the sinful woman, that love broke forth pure again. She loved, and He trusted that affection, and the lost one was saved. Let men say what they will of human nature's evil, a generous, real, *unaffected* confidence never fails to elicit the Divine spark.

Thirdly: It was in order to preserve his own reputation that St. Paul shielded himself from censure by consulting appearances; for if so large a sum had been intrusted to him alone, an opening would have been left for the suspicion of appropriating a portion to himself. Therefore, in the twentieth and twenty-first verses, he especially "avoids" this imputation by saying "that no man should blame us in this abundance which is administered by us: providing for honest things, not only in the sight of the Lord, but also in the sight of men." In this is to be observed St. Paul's wisdom, not only as a man of the world, but as a man of God. He knew that he lived in a censorious age, that he was as a city set on a hill, that the world would scan his every act and his every word, and attribute all conceivable and even inconceivable evil to what he did in all honor.

Now, it was just because of St. Paul's honor and innocence that he was likely to have omitted this prudence. Just because the bare conception of malversation of the funds was impossible to him, we might have expected him to forget that the world would not think it equally impossible. For to the pure all things are pure, to the honest and the innocent suspicion seems impossible. It was just because St. Paul felt no evil himself, that he might have thoughlessly placed himself in an equivocal position.

It is to such — men guileless of heart, innocent of even the thought of dishonesty, children in the way of the world — that Christ says, "Be ye wise as serpents."

Consider how defenceless St. Paul would have been had the accusation been made! Who was to *prove* that the charge of peculation was false? The defence would rest on St. Paul alone. Moreover, though he were to be acquitted as free from guilt, a charge refuted is not as if a charge had never been made. The man once accused goes forth into society never the same as before; he keeps his position, he practises his profession, his friends know him to be true and honest; but, for years after, the oblivious world, remembering only the accusation, and forgetting the fulness of the refutation, asks, "But were there not some suspicious circumstances?"

It is difficult to be for ever cautious, to be always thinking about appearances: it may be carried too far — to a servility for the opinions of men: but in all cases like this of St. Paul, a wise prudence is necessary. Experience teaches this by bitter lessons as life goes on. No innocence will shield, no honor, nor integrity bright as the sun itself, will keep off altogether the biting breath of calumny. Charity *thinketh* no evil, but charity is rare; and to the world the honor of an Apostle Paul is not above suspicion. Therefore it is that he says: "Let not your good be evil spoken of." Therefore it is that he, avoiding the possibility of this, sent messengers to collect the money, "providing for things honest in the sight of all men."

II. The measure of the amount. The Apostle did not name a sum to the Corinthians: he would not be lord over their desires, or their reluctance; but he gave them a measure according to which he exhorted them to contribute.

First, then, he counselled them to be liberal; "As a matter of bounty and not as of covetousness." Secondly, he asked them to give deliberately: "Every man according as he purposeth in his heart." Thirdly, the Apostle exhorted the Corinthians to bestow cheerfully: "Not grudgingly, or of necessity: for God loveth a cheerful giver."

It was one aim of St. Paul, in sending beforehand to the Corinthians, that they might be able to give largely, not stintingly or avariciously. Here we may observe that the Apostle did not speak, as we often preach — in an impassioned manner, in order to get a large collection of money, — trying by rhetoric and popular arts, by appeals to feeling and to personal influence, to gain his end. No: he left the amount to themselves. Yet he plainly told them that a *large* contribution was what God asked. Remember that the solemnity of this appeal has no parallel now; it was almost a solitary appeal. But now — now, when charities abound, to speak with the same vehemence on every occasion, to invoke the name of God, as if to withhold from this and that charity were guilt, is to misapply St. Paul's precedent. In the multitudinous charities for which you are solicited, remember one thing only — give liberally *somewhere*, in God's name, and to God's cause. But the cases must depend on yourselves, and should be conscientiously adopted.

The second measure of the amount was that it should be *deliberate:* "Every man according as he purposeth in his heart."

Let us distinguish this deliberate charity from giving through mere impulse. Christian charity is a calm, wise thing; nay, sometimes, it will appear to a superficial observer, a very hard thing — for it has courage to *refuse.* A Christian man will not give to everything; — he will not give because it is the fashion; he will not give because an appeal is very impassioned, or because it touches his sensibilities. He gives as he "*purposeth* in his heart." Here I remark again, that often the truest charity is not giving but employing. To give indiscriminately now often ruins by producing improvidence. In the days of the Apostle, things were different. The Jew who became a Christian lost all employment. Remember, too, with respect to charitable collections, that charity should be deliberate. Men often come determined beforehand to give according to the eloquence of the appeal, not according to a calm resolve, and from a sense of a debt of love to God which rejoices in giving. I do not say that a man is never to give more than he meant, when touched by the speaker; because, generally, men mean to give too little. But I say that it is an unhealthy state of things, when a congregation leave their charity dependent on their ministerial sympathies. Let men take their responsibilities upon themselves. It is not a clergyman's business to think for his congregation, but to help them to judge for themselves. Hence, let Christian men dare to refuse as well as dare to give. A congregational collection should not be obtained by that mere force of eloquence which excites the sensibilities, and awakens a sudden and shortlived impulse of giving, but it should rather be to them an opportunity to be complied with "as every man purposeth in his heart."

III. The measure of the reward. — The measure of all spiritual rewards is exactly proportioned to the acts done. The law of the spiritual harvest is twofold: — 1. A proportion in reference to quantity. 2. A proportion in reference to kind.

1. In reference to quantity: "He which soweth sparingly, shall reap also sparingly." Hence may be inferred the principle of degrees of glory hereafter. In the Parable of the Talents, each multiplier of his money received a reward exactly in proportion to the amount he had gained; and each, of course, was rewarded differently. Again: "He that receiveth a *prophet* in the name of a prophet," — that is, because he was a prophet, — "shall receive a *prophet's* reward; and he that receiveth a *righteous* man in the name of a righteous man, shall receive a *righteous* man's reward." "They that be wise shall shine as the brightness of the firmament" — that is their reward; "and they that turn many to righteousness, as the stars for ever and ever" — a reward different from the former. The right hand and left of Christ in His kingdom are given only to those who drink of His cup, and are baptized with His baptism. Thus there is a peculiar and appropriate re-

ward for every act; only remember, that the reward is not given for the merit of the act, but follows on it as inevitably in the spiritual kingdom, as wheat springs from its grain, and barley from its grain, in the natural world. Because this law of reward exists, we are given encouragements to labor: "Let us not be weary in well doing, for in due season we shall reap, if we faint not." Again: "Therefore, my beloved brethren, be ye steadfast, unmovable, always abounding in the work of the Lord, forasmuch as ye know that your labor is not in vain in the Lord."

2. In reference to kind. The reward of an act of charity is kindred with the act itself. But St. Paul lays down the broad law: "Whatsoever a man soweth, *that* shall he also reap." He reaps, therefore, not something else, but that very thing which he sows. So in the world of nature, a harvest of wheat comes not from sown barley, nor do oak forests arise from beech mast, but each springs from its own kind; the "herb yielding seed after his kind, and the tree yielding fruit, whose seed was in itself, after his kind." Thus also is it in the spiritual world. He that soweth to the flesh shall not reap of the spirit, nor shall he who soweth to the spirit reap of the flesh.

Now here often a strange fallacy arises. Men sow their carnal things — give their money, for example — to God; and because they have *apparently* sown carnal things to God, they expect to reap the same. For instance, in pagan times, fishermen or farmers sacrificed their respective properties, and expected a double fishery or harvest in return. The same pagan principle has come down to us. Some persons give to a Jews' Conversion Society, or to a Church Missionary Society, and confidently hope for a blessing on their worldly affairs as a result. They are liberal to the poor, "lending to the Lord," in order that He may repay them with success in business, or an advance in trade.

The fallacy lies in this: the thing sown was *not* money, but spirit. It only *seemed* money, it was in reality the feeling with which it was given which was sown. For example, the poor widow gave two mites, but God took account of *sacrifice*. The sinful woman gave an alabaster box of ointment, valued by a miserable economist at three hundred pence. God valued it as so much love. Both these sowed not what they gave, but spiritual seed: one love, the other sacrifice. Now God is not going to pay these things in coin of this earth: He will not recompense Sacrifice with success in business, nor Love with a legacy or a windfall. He will repay them with spiritual coin *in kind*.

In the particular instance now before us, what are the rewards of liberality which St. Paul promises to the Corinthians? They are, first: The Love of God (ver. 7). Secondly: A spirit abounding to every good work (ver. 8). Thirdly: Thanksgiving on their behalf (ver. 11, 12, 13). A noble harvest! but *all* spiritual. Comprehend the meaning of it well. Give, and you will not get back again. Do not expect your money to be returned, like that of Joseph's brethren, in their sacks' mouths. When you give to God, sacrifice, and know that what you give *is* sacrificed, and is not to be got again, even in this world; for if you give, expecting it back again, there is no sacrifice: charity is no speculation in the spiritual funds, no wise investment, to be repaid with interest, either in time or eternity!

No! the rewards are these: Do right, and God's recompense to you will be the power of doing more right. Give, and God's reward to you will be the spirit of giving more: a blessed spirit, for it is the Spirit of God himself, whose Life is the blessedness of giving. Love, and God will pay you with the capacity of more love; for love is Heaven — love is God within you.

LECTURE LV.

MARCH 20, 1853.

2 CORINTHIANS, x. 1–18.—"Now I Paul myself beseech you by the meekness and gentleness of Christ, who in presence am base among you, but being absent am bold toward you:—But I beseech you, that I may not be bold when I am present with that confidence, wherewith I think to be bold against some, which think of us as if we walked according to the flesh.—For though we walk in the flesh, we do not war after the flesh:—(For the weapons of our warfare are not carnal, but mighty through God to the pulling down of strongholds;)—Casting down imaginations, and every high thing that exalteth itself against the knowledge of God, and bringing into captivity every thought to the obedience of Christ;—And having in a readiness to revenge all disobedience, when your obedience is fulfilled.—Do ye look on things after the outward appearance? If any man trust to himself that he is Christ's, let him of himself think this again, that, as he is Christ's, even so are we Christ's.—For though I should boast somewhat more of our authority, which the Lord hath given us for edification, and not for your destruction, I should not be ashamed:—That I may not seem as if I would terrify you by letters.—For his letters, say they, are weighty and powerful; but his bodily presence is weak, and his speech contemptible.—Let such an one think this, that, such as we are in word by letters when we are absent, such will we be also in deed when we are present.—For we dare not make ourselves of the number, or compare ourselves with some that commend themselves: but they measuring themselves by themselves, and comparing themselves among themselves, are not wise.—But we will not boast of things without our measure, but according to the measure of the rule which God hath distributed to us, a measure to reach even unto you.—For we stretch not ourselves beyond our measure, as though we reached not unto you: for we are come as far as to you also in preaching the gospel of Christ:—Not boasting of things without our measure, that is, of other men's labors; but having hope, when your faith is increased, that we shall be enlarged by you according to our rule abundantly,—To preach the Gospel in the regions beyond you, and not to boast in another man's line of things made ready to our hand.—But he that glorieth, let him glory in the Lord.—For not he that commendeth himself is approved, but whom the Lord commendeth."

THE Second Epistle has till now been addressed to those in Corinth who felt either love or admiration for St. Paul, certainly to those who owned his authority.

But with the tenth chapter there begins a new division of the Epistle. Henceforth we have St. Paul's reply to his enemies at Corinth, and his vindication is partly official and partly personal. They denied his apostolic authority and mission, declared that he had not been appointed by Christ, and endeavored to destroy his personal influence in the Church by sneers at his bodily weakness, his inconsistency, and his faithlessness to his promise of coming to Corinth, which they imputed to a fear of his own weakness of character. Powerful enough in letter-writing, said they, but when he comes, his presence, his speech, are weak and contemptible. To these charges St. Paul answers in the remaining chapter. We will consider two subjects: —

I. The impugners of his authority.
II. His vindication.

I. The impugners of his authority. It is necessary to distinguish these into two classes, the deceivers and and the deceived; else we could not understand the difference of tone, sometimes meek, and sometimes stern, which pervades the Apostle's vindication. For example, compare the second verse of this chapter with the first, and you must remark the different shades of feeling under which each was written. This change of tone he himself acknowledges in the fifth chapter of this Epistle: "For whether we be beside ourselves, it is to God; or whether we be sober, it is for your cause." His enemies had been embittered against him by the deference paid to him by the rest of the Church. Hence they tried to make him suspected. They charged him with insincerity (2 Cor. i. 12, 13, 18, 19). They said he was ever promising to come, and never meaning it; and that he was only powerful in writing (2 Cor. x. 10). They accused him of mercenary motives, of a lack of apostolic gifts, and of not preaching the Gospel. They charged him with artifices. His Christian prudence and charity were regarded as means whereby he allured and deceived his followers. We must also bear in mind that it was a party spirit with which the Apostle had to deal: "Now this I say, that every one of you saith, I am of Paul; and I of Apollos; and I of Cephas; and I of Christ." (1 Cor. i. 12).

Now, we are informed in this chapter, that of all these parties his chief difficulty lay with that party which called itself Christ's. This was not the school inclined to ritual, which followed St. Peter, nor the Pauline party, which set its face against all Jewish practices, and drove liberty into license; nor yet that which had perhaps a disposition to rationalize, and followed Apollos, who, having been brought up at Alexandria, had most probably spent his youth in the study of literature and philosophy. But it was a party who, throwing off all authority, even though it was apostolic, declared that they received Christ alone as their Head, and that He alone should directly communicate truth to them.

First, then, let us observe, that though these persons called themselves Christ's, they are nevertheless blamed in the same list with others. And yet what could seem to be more right than for men to say, "We will bear no name but Christ's; we throw ourselves on Christ's own words — on the Bible; we throw aside all intellectual philosophy: we will have no servitude to ritualism?" Nevertheless, these persons were just as bigoted and as blameable as the others. They were not wrong in calling themselves Christ's; but they were wrong in naming themselves so distinctively. It is plain that by assuming this name, they implied that they had a right to it more than others had. They did not mean to say only, "We are Christ's," but also, "You are *not* Christ's." God was not, in their phraseology, *our* Father, but rather the Father of our *party*; the Father of us only who are the elect. In their mouths that Name became no longer comprehensive, but exclusive. Thus St. Paul blamed all who, instead of rejoicing that they were Christians, prided themselves on being a particular kind of Christians. The great doctrine of one Baptism taught the feeling of Christian brotherhood. All were

Christ's: all belonged to Him: no one sect was his exclusively, or dared to claim Him as their Head more than another.

This is a feeling which is as much to be avoided now as it was in the time of the Apostle. We split ourselves into sects, each of which asserts its own peculiar Christianity. This sectarianism falsifies the very *principle* of our religion, and therefore falsifies its forms. It falsifies the Lord's Prayer. It substitutes for *our* Father, the Father of me, of *my* church or party. It falsifies the creed: "I believe in Jesus Christ *our* Lord." It falsifies both the sacraments. No matter how large, or true, or beautiful the name by which we call ourselves, we are for ever tending to the sectarian spirit when we assume some appellation which cuts others off from participation with us: when we call ourselves, for example, Bible Christians, Evangelicals, Churchmen — as if no one but ourselves deserved the name.

Secondly, let us observe, that however Christian this expression may sound, "We will take Christ for our teacher, and not His Apostles or His Church," the spirit which prompts it is wrong. This Christ-party amongst the Corinthians depreciated the Church, in order to exalt the Lord of the Church; but they did so wrongly, and at the peril of their religious life. For God's order is the historical; and these men separated themselves from God's order when they claimed an arbitrary distinction for themselves, and rejected the teaching of St. Paul and the Apostles, to whom the development of the meaning of Christ's doctrine had been intrusted. For the phase of truth presented by St. Paul was just as necessary as that prominently taught by Christ. Not that Christ did not teach all truth, but that the hidden meaning of His teaching was developed still further by the inspired Apostles.

We cannot, at this time, cut ourselves off from the teaching of eighteen centuries, and say, "We will have none but Christ to reign over us;" nor can we proclaim, "Not the Church, but the Lord of the Church." We cannot do without the different shades and phases of knowledge which God's various instruments, in accordance with their various characters and endowments, have delivered to us. For God's system is mediatorial, that is, truth to men communicated through men.

See, then, how, as in Corinth, the very attempt to separate from parties may lead to a sectarian spirit, unless we can learn to see good in all, and Christ in all. And should we, as this Christ-party did, desert human instrumentality, we sink into self-will: we cut ourselves from the Church of God, and fall under the popery of our own infallibility.

What dangers on every side! God shield us! For these present days are like those of which we are speaking. The same tendencies are appearing again: some are disposed to unduly value law and ritual, some aspire to a freedom from all law, some incline to *literary* religion, and some, like the Christ-party here spoken of, to pietism and subjective Christianity. Hence it is that the thoughtful study of these Epistles to the Corinthians is so valuable in our time, when nothing will avert the dangers which threaten us but the principles which St. Paul drew from the teaching of Christ, and has laid down here for the admonition of His Church at Corinth.

II. His vindication. St. Paul vindicated his authority, because it was founded on the power of *meekness*, and it was a spiritual power in respect of that meekness. The weapons of his warfare were not carnal: "Though we walk in the flesh," he says, "we do not war after the flesh," — that is, We do not use a worldly soldier's weapons, — we contend, not with force, but with meekness of wisdom and with the persuasiveness of truth. This was one of the root principles of St. Paul's ministry: If he reproved, it was done in the spirit of meekness (Gal. vi. 1); or if he defended his own authority, it was still with the same spirit (2 Cor. x. 1). Again, when the time of his departure was at hand, and he would leave his last instructions to his son Timothy, he closes his summary of the character of ministerial work by showing the need of meekness: "The servant of the Lord must not strive, but be gentle unto all men, apt to teach, patient, in meekness instructing those that oppose themselves."

Here again, according to his custom, the Apostle refers to the example of Christ. He besought the Corinthians "by the meekness and gentleness of Christ." He vindicated his authority, because he had been meek, as Christ was meek: for not by menace, nor by force, did He conquer, but by the might of gentleness and the power of meekness: "Who, when He was reviled, reviled not again; when He suffered, He threatened not." On that foundation St. Paul built; it was that example which he imitated in his moments of trial, when he was reproved and censured. He confessed his own "baseness of appearance:" when others had low thoughts of him, he had low ones of himself.

Thus it happened, that one of the Apostle's "mightiest weapons" was the meekness and lowliness of heart which he drew from the Life of Christ. So it ever is. Humility, after all, is the best defence. It disarms and conquers by the majesty of submission. To be humble and loving — that is true life. Do not let insult harden you, nor cruelty rob you of tenderness. If men wound your heart, let them not embitter it; and then yours will be the victory of the Cross. You will conquer as Christ conquered, and bless as He blessed. But remember, fine *words* about gentleness, self-sacrifice, meekness, are worth very little. Talking of the nobleness of humility and self-surrender, is not believing in them. Would you believe in the Cross and its victory? then live in its spirit — act upon it.

Again, St. Paul rested his authority not on carnal weapons, but on the spiritual power of truth. Consider the strongholds which the Apostle had to pull down and subdue. There were the sophistries of the educated, and the ignorant prejudices of the multitude. There were the old habits which clung to the Christianized heathen. There was the pride of intellect in the arrogant Greek philosophers, and the pride of the flesh in the Jewish love of signs. There was — most difficult of all — the pride of ignorance. All these strongholds were to be conquered: every thought was to be brought "into captivity to the obedience of Christ."

For this work St. Paul's sole weapon was Truth. The ground on which he taught was not authority: but "by manifestation of the truth" he commended himself to "every man's conscience." His power rested on no carnal weapon, on no craft or personal influence; but it rested on the strong foundation of the truth he taught. He felt that truth must prevail. So neither by force did St. Paul's authority stand, nor on his inspired Apostleship, but simply by the power of persuasive truth. The truth he spoke would, at last, vindicate his teaching and his life; and he calmly trusted himself to God and time. A grand, silent lesson for us now! when the noises of a hundred controversies stun the Church: when we are trying to force our own tenets on our neighbors, and denounce those who differ from us, foolishly thinking within ourselves that the wrath of man will work the righteousness of God.

Rather, Christian men, let us teach as Christ and His Apostles taught. *Force* no one to God; menace no one into religion: but convince all by the might of truth. Should any of you have to bear attacks on your character, or life, or doctrine, defend yourself with meekness: and if defence should but make matters worse — and when accusations are vague, as is the case but too often — why, then, commit yourself fully to truth. Outpray — outpreach — outlive the calumny!

LECTURE LVI.

1853.

2 CORINTHIANS, xii. 1–21. — "It is not expedient for me doubtless to glory. I will come to visions and revelations of the Lord. — I knew a man in Christ about fourteen years ago, (whether in the body, I cannot tell; or whether out of the body, I cannot tell: God knoweth;) such an one caught up to the third heaven. — And I knew such a man, (whether in the body, or out of the body, I cannot tell: God knoweth;) — How that he was caught up into paradise, and heard unspeakable words, which it is not lawful for a man to utter. — Of such an one will I glory: yet of myself I will not glory, but in mine infirmities.—For though I would desire to glory, I shall not be a fool; for I will say the truth: but now I forbear, lest any man should think of me above that which he seeth me to be, or that he heareth of me. — And lest I should be exalted above measure through the abundance of the revelations, there was given to me a thorn in the flesh, a messenger of Satan to buffet me, lest I should be exalted above measure. — For this thing I besought the Lord thrice, that it might depart from me. — And he said unto me, My grace is sufficient for thee: for my strength is made perfect in weakness. Most gladly therefore will I rather glory in my infirmities, that the power of Christ may rest upon me. — Therefore I take pleasure in infirmities, in reproaches, in necessities, in persecutions, in distresses for Christ's sake: for when I am weak, then am I strong. — I am become a fool in glorying; ye have compelled me: for I ought to have been commended of you: for in nothing am I behind the very chiefest apostles, though I be nothing. — Truly the signs of an apostle were wrought among you in all patience, in signs, and wonders, and mighty deeds. — For what is it wherein you were inferior to other churches, except it be that I myself was not burdensome to you? forgive me this wrong. — Behold, the third time I am ready to come to you; and I will not be burdensome to you: for I seek not yours, but you: for the children ought not to lay up for the parents, but the parents for the children. — And I will very gladly spend and be spent for you: though the more abundantly I love you, the less I be loved. — But be it so, I did not burden you: nevertheless, being crafty, I caught you with guile. — Did I make a gain of you by any of them whom I sent unto you? — I desired Titus, and with him I sent a brother. Did Titus make a gain of you? walked we not in the same spirit? walked we not in the same steps? — Again, think ye that we excuse ourselves unto you? we speak before God in Christ: but we do all things, dearly beloved, for your edifying. — For I fear, lest, when I come I shall

not find you such as I would, and that I shall be found unto you such as ye would not: lest there be debates, envyings, wraths, strifes, backbitings, whisperings, swellings, tumults: — And lest, when I come again, my God will humble me among you, and that I shall bewail many which have sinned already, and have not repented of the uncleanness and fornication and lasciviousness which they have committed."

THE Apostle Paul, in the preceding chapter, had adduced evidence of the greatness of his sufferings in his witness to the truths he had received from Christ. The extent of his labors was proved by his sufferings, and both were, in a manner, an indirect proof of his apostleship. In the passage we consider to-day — a passage of acknowledged difficulty — he advances a direct proof of his apostolic mission. Let us, however, before proceeding, understand the general structure of the passage. The point in question all along has been St. Paul's authority. The Corinthians doubted it, and in these verses, in proof of it, he alleges certain spiritual communications of a preternatural kind, which had been made to him. To these he adds, in the twelfth verse, certain peculiar trials; all of which together made up his notion of apostolic experience. A man divinely gifted, and divinely tried — that was an Apostle. But it is remarkable, that he reckons the trials as a greater proof of apostleship than the marvellous experiences (ver. 9).

There is but one difficulty to clog this outset. It would seem that St. Paul, in reference to the revelations, is not speaking of himself, but of another man (ver. 1 – 5); more especially in the fifth verse: "Of such an one will I glory: yet of myself I will not glory, but in mine infirmities." Nevertheless, the fact of St. Paul's identity with the person he speaks of is beyond a doubt. All difficulty is set at rest by the sixth and seventh verses, where he allows that the man so favored is himself.

It remains only to ask how St. Paul came to speak of himself under the personality of another. For this I suggest two reasons: — 1. Natural diffidence. For the more refined and courteous a man is, the more he will avoid, in conversation, a direct mention of himself; and, in like manner, as civilization advances, the disinclination to write even of self in the first person, is shown by the use of the terms "the author," and "we;" men almost unconsciously acting in that spirit of delicacy, which forbids too open an obtrusion of oneself upon the public.

That this delicacy was felt by St. Paul is evident from what he says in the fourth chapter of the First Epistle, in the sixth verse, and from the whole of that chapter, where he speaks of "laborers," "ministers," and of the Apostles generally, though all the while the particular person meant is himself. From this twelfth chapter and from the eleventh, it is evident all along that he has been forced to speak of self only by a kind of compulsion. Fact after fact of his own experiences is, as it were, wrung out, as if he had not intended to tell it. For there is something painful to a modest mind in the direct use of the personal pronoun "I," over which an humble spirit, like the Apostle's, throws a veil.

2. The second reason I suggest for this suppression of the first person is, that St. Paul chose to recognize this higher experience as not entirely yet his true self. He speaks of a divided experience of two selves, two Pauls: one Paul in the third heaven, enjoying the beatific vision: another yet on earth, struggling, tempted, tried, and buffeted by Satan. The former he chose rather to regard as the Paul that was to be. He dwelt on the latter as the actual Paul coming down to the prose of life to find his real self, lest he should be tempted to forget or mistake himself in the midst of the heavenly revelations.

Such a double nature is in us all. In all there is an Adam and a Christ — an ideal and a real. Numberless instances will occur to us in the daily experience of life; the fact is shown, for example, in the strange discrepancy so often seen between the writings of the poet or the sermons of the preacher, and their actual lives. And yet in this there is no necessary hypocrisy, for the one represents the man's *aspiration*, the other his attain ment. In that very sentence, however, there may be a danger; for is it not dangerous to be satisfied with mere aspirations and fine sayings? The Apostle felt it was; and, therefore, he chose to take the lowest — the actual self — and call that Paul, treating the highest as, for the time, another man. Hence in the fifth verse he says: "Of such an one will I glory: yet of *myself I will not* glory, but in mine infirmities." Were the crawling caterpillar to feel within himself the wings that are to be, and be haunted with instinctive forebodings of the time when he shall hover above flowers and meadows, and expatiate in heavenly air, — yet the wisdom of that caterpillar would be to remember his present business on the leaf, to feed on green herbs, and weave his web, lest, losing himself in dreams, he should never become a winged insect at all. In the same manner, it is our wisdom, lest we become all earthy, to remember that our visions shall be realized, but also it is our wisdom, lest we become mere dreamers, or spiritually "puffed up," to remember that the aspiring man within us is not yet our true self, but, as it were, another man — the "Christ within us, the hope of glory."

Our subject to-day, then, is "spiritual ecstasy."

I. The time when this vision took place — "Fourteen years ago." The date is vague, "*about* fourteen years ago," and is irreconcilable with any exact point in our confused chronology of the life of St. Paul. But some have supposed that this vision was identical with that recorded (*Acts*, ix.) at his conversion; but it is evidently different: —

First: Because the words in that transaction were not "unlawful to utter." They are three times recorded in the Acts, with no reserve or reticence at all.

Secondly: Because there was no doubt as to St. Paul's own locality in that vision. He has twice recorded his own experience of it in terms clear and unmistakeable. His spirit did not even seem to him to be caught up. He saw, external to him above, a light, and heard a voice, himself all the while consciously living upon earth: nay, more, so far from being exalted, he was stricken to the ground. Here, however, the difficulty to the Apostle's mind is, not respecting the nature of the revelation, but how and where he was himself situated: "Whether in the body, or out of the body, I cannot tell." He was not psychologist enough for that.

Thirdly: The vision which met him on the road to Damascus was of an humbling character: "Saul, Saul, why persecutest thou me?" In that sorrow-giving question there was no ground for spiritual pride. On the other hand, in *this* case, the vision was connected with a tendency to pride and vain-glory. For, lest he should be puffed up "beyond measure," a messenger of Satan came to buffet him.

So, evidently, the first appearance was at the outset of his Christian life; the other, in the fulness of his Christian experience, when, through deep sufferings and loss for Christ's sake, prophecies of rest and glory hereafter came to his soul to sustain and comfort him. And thus, in one of those moments of high hope, he breaks forth: "Our light affliction, which is but for a moment worketh for us a far more exceeding and eternal weight of glory."

II. This very circumstance, however, that it was *not* the vision which occurred to him near Damascus, reveals something more to us. By our proof to the contrary, we have reaped not a negative gain, but a positive one. If the vision here spoken of had been that at his conversion, it would have been alone in his experience. There could come afterwards no other like it. But if it was not, then the ecstasy mentioned in this chapter did not stand alone in St. Paul's experience. It was not the first, — no, nor the last. He had known of many such, for he speaks of the "abundance of the revelations" given to him (ver. 7). This marks out the man. Indeed, to comprehend the visions, we must comprehend the man. For God gives visions at his own will, and yet according to certain laws, He does not inspire every one. He does not reveal His mysteries to men of selfish, or hard, or phlegmatic temperaments. But when He gives preternatural communications, then He prepares beforehand by a peculiar spiritual sensitiveness. Just as, physically, certain sensitivenesses to sound and color qualify men to become gifted musicians and painters, — so, spiritually, certain strong original susceptibilities mark out the man who will be the recipient of strange gifts, and see strange sights of God, and experience deep feelings, immeasurable by the ordinary standard.

Such a man was St. Paul — a very wondrous nature — the Jewish nature in all its strength. We all know that the Jewish temperament peculiarly fitted men to be the organs of a Revelation. Its fervor, its moral sense, its veneration, its indomitable will, all adapted the highest sons of the nation for receiving hidden truths, and communicating them to others. Now all this was, in its fulness, in St. Paul. A heart, a brain, and a soul of fire: all his life a suppressed volcano; — his acts "living things with hands and feet;" his words, "half battles." A man, consequently, of terrible inward conflicts: his soul a battle-field for heaven and hell. Read, for example, the seventh chapter of the Epistle to the Romans, describing his struggle under the law. You will find there no dull metaphysics about the "bondage of the will," or the difference between conscience and will. It is all intensely personal. St. Paul himself descends into the argument, as if the experience he describes were present then! "O wretched man that I *am!* who shall deliver *me* from the body of this death?" So, too, in the sixteenth chapter of the Acts. He had no abstract perception of Macedonia's need of the Gospel. To his soul a *man* of Macedonia presents himself in the night, crying, "Come over, and help us." Again, we find in the eighteenth chapter of the Acts, that while the Apostle was at Corinth, beset with trials, surrounded by the Jews thirsting for his blood, a message came in a vision, and the Lord spoke to him, telling him to fear not. Now, I believe, such a voice has spoken to us all, only we explained it away as the result of our own reasoning. St. Paul's life was with God; his very dreams were of God. A Being stood beside him by day and night. He saw a form which others did not see, and heard a voice which others could not hear.

Again, compare the twenty-seventh chapter of the Acts, twenty-third verse; where we are told that when he was a prisoner, tossed for many nights upon the tempestuous sea, he yet saw the angel of that God, "Whose he was, and Whom he served." Remember his noble faith, his unshaken conviction, that all would be as the vision and the voice of God had told him.

Ever you see him on the brink of that other world. Even his trials and conflicts were those of a high order. Most of us are battling with some mean appetite or gross passion. St. Paul's battles were not those of the flesh and appetites, but of spirit struggling with spirit. I infer this partly from his own special gift of chastity, and partly from the case which he selects in the seventh of Romans, which is "covetousness"—an evil desire, but still one of the spirit.

Now to such men, the other world is revealed as a reality which it cannot appear to others. Those things in heaven and earth which philosophy does not dream of, these men see. But, doubtless, such things are seen under certain conditions. For example, many of St. Paul's visions were when he was "*fasting*," at times when the body is not predominant in our humanity. For "fulness of bread" and abundance of idleness are not the conditions in which we can see the things of God. Again, most of these revelations were made to him in the midst of *trial*. In the prison at Philippi, during the shipwreck, while "the thorn was in his flesh," then it was that the vision of unutterable things was granted to him, and the vision of God in His clearness came.

This was the experience of Christ Himself. God does not lavish His choicest gifts, but reserves them. Thus, at Christ's baptism, before beginning His work, the Voice from Heaven was heard. It was in the Temptation that the angels ministered to Him. On the Transfiguration Mount the glory shone, when Moses and Elias spake to Him of His death, which He should accomplish at Jerusalem. In perplexity which of two things to say, the Thunder Voice replied, "I have both glorified it, and will glorify it again." In the Agony, there came an angel strengthening Him.

Hence we learn, that Inspiration is, first, not the result of will or effort, but is truly and properly from God. Yet that, secondly, it is dependent on certain conditions, granted to certain states, and to a certain character. Thirdly, that its sphere is not in things of sense, but in moral and spiritual truth. And, fourthly, that it is not elaborated by induction from experience, but is the result of intuition. Yet, though inspiration is granted in its *fulness* only to *rare*, choice spirits like St. Paul, we must remember that in *degree* it belongs to all Christian experience. There have been moments, surely, in our experience, when the vision of God was clear. They were not, I will venture to say, moments of fulness, or success, or triumph. In some season of desertion, you havé, in solitary longing, seen the skyladder as Jacob saw it of old, and felt Heaven open even to *you;* or in childish purity — for "Heaven lies around us in our infancy" — heard a voice as Samuel did; or, in some struggle with conscience and inclination, heard from Heaven the words, "Why persecutest thou *Me?*" or, in feebleness of health, when the weight of the bodily frame was taken off, whether it were in delirium or vision, you could not say but Faith brightened her eagle eye, and saw far into the tranquil things of Death; or, in prayer, you have been conscious of more than earth present in the silence, and a Hand in yours, and a Voice that you could hear, and almost the Eternal breath upon your brow.

III. Lastly, this spiritual ecstasy is unutterable: unutterable, however, in two degrees: —

1. "Unspeakable" (ver. 4). This it is, simply because the things of the Spirit are untranslateable into the language of the intellect. Feelings, convictions, emotions — love, duty, aspiration, devotion — in what sentences will you express to another what you feel and mean by these?

Conceive, then, a translation to Heaven, and a return from thence. How would the man describe the things seen and heard? In the fourth chapter of Revelation the attempt is made, but it instantly takes the form of symbols and figures. A throne is there, and One is there like a jasper and a sardine stone: a rainbow like an emerald encircles all. Seven Spirit Lamps are burning: the lightnings, and thunderings, and voices, are heard, and the sea of glass shines like crystal. Thus did the writer, in high symbolic language, attempt, inadequately, to shadow forth the glory which his spirit realized, but which his sense saw not. For Heaven is not scenery, nor anything appreciable by ear or eye: Heaven is God *felt*.

Hence, when at Pentecost, the rushing wind filled men with the afflatus of the Holy Ghost, and they tried to utter in articulate words what they felt, is it not perfectly intelligible why, to the unsympathetic bystanders, they seemed like men "filled with new wine?"

Again, this ecstasy was unutterable, because "*not lawful* for a man to utter." Christian modesty forbids. There are bridal moments of the soul: and not easily forgiven are those who would utter the secrets of its high intercourse with its Lord. There is a certain spiritual indelicacy in persons who cannot perceive that not everything which is a matter of experience and knowledge is, therefore, a subject for conversation. There are some things in this world too low to be spoken of, and some things too high. You cannot discuss such subjects without vulgarizing them.

Thus, when Elijah and Elisha went together from Gilgal to Jordan, the sons of the prophets came to Elisha with that confidential gossip which is common in those who think to understand mysteries by talking of them: "Knowest thou," they asked, "that the Lord will take away thy master to-day?" Remember Elisha's dignfied reply: "Yea, I know it: hold ye your peace."

God dwells in the thick darkness. Silence knows more of Him than speech. His Name is Secret: therefore beware how you profane His stillnesses. To each of His servants He giveth "a white stone, and in the stone a new name written, which no man knoweth saving he that receiveth it."

THE END.

www.ingramcontent.com/pod-product-compliance
Lightning Source LLC
LaVergne TN
LVHW021139110826
845150LV00005B/1067

9781425548902